Students: A Gendered History

Carol Dyhouse

 Routledge
Taylor & Francis Group

LONDON AND NEW YORK

First published 2006
by Routledge
2 Park Square, Milton Park, Abingdon, OX14 4RN

Simultaneously published in the USA and Canada
by Routledge
270 Madison Avenue, New York, NY 10016

Routledge is an imprint of the Taylor & Francis Group

© 2006 Carol Dyhouse

Typeset in Garamond Book by
Keystroke, Jacaranda Lodge, Wolverhampton
Printed and bound in Great Britain by
MPG Books Ltd, Bodmin

British Library Cataloguing in Publication Data
A catalogue record for this book is available from the British Library

Library of Congress Cataloging in Publication Data
Dyhouse, Carol, 1948–
 Students : a gendered history / Carol Dyhouse.
  p. cm. — (Women's and gender history)
 Includes bibliographical references and index.
1. Education, Higher—Great Britain—History—20th century.
2. Women—Education (Higher)—Great Britain—History—20th century.
I. Title. II. Series.
 LA636.8.D94 2005
 378.1′98′0941—dc22   2005017434

ISBN 0–415–35818–3 (pbk)
ISBN 0–415–35817–5 (hbk)

Contents

List of figures and tables   vii

Introduction   ix

PART I

Access and ambitions   **1**

1 Going to university in England between the wars: access,
  funding and social class   3

2 Men and women in higher education in the 1930s: family
  expectations, gendered outcomes   34

3 Driving ambitions: women in pursuit of a medical education,
  1890–1939   60

4 Wasted investments and blocked ambitions? Women
  graduates in the postwar world   79

5 Gaining places: the rising proportion of women students in
  universities after 1970   97

PART II

Coeducation and culture   **119**

6 Siege mentalities   121

CONTENTS

7 Women students and the London medical schools,
1914–1939: the anatomy of a masculine culture   137

8 'Apostates' and 'Uncle Toms': challenges to separatism in
the women's college   155

9 Troubled identities: gender, status and culture in the mixed
college since 1945   172

10 The student rag   186

Conclusion   204

Notes   210
Select bibliography: works used in the text   256
Index   264

৯

Figures and tables

Figures

2.1 Subject choice by social class for (a) men and (b) women   53
4.1 Numbers of women marrying, England and Wales   93
5.1 Proportion of students in UK universities who were female,
     1919–2000   99
5.2 Numbers in initial teacher training, UK, 1955–2000   116

Tables

1.1 Numbers of full-time students, England only, 1901, 1937/8   4
1.2 Numbers of questionnaires distributed to and completed by
     graduates   9
1.3 Social class of origin of respondents in each university   10
1.4 Students beginning their schooling in public elementary
     schools, percentages   11
1.5 Source of external funds for university studies   17
1.6 Social class of origin and external funding type   29
2.1 Numbers taking each subject, men and women   36
5.1 Student numbers in the 'new universities' of the 1960s,
     men and women   102

ಶ⁑

Introduction

Universities, with debates over access, funding, student fees, maintenance and debt, are almost constantly in the news. There have been seismic changes in the scale and structure of higher education over the last century, and at the same time student experience has changed dramatically since 1945. The experience of 'going to university' has become much more common, an experience confined to less than 2 per cent of 18-year-olds before the Second World War, but shared by something like a third of young people today. It is well known that the present government wants to see half of all 18- to 30-year-olds experiencing some form of higher education. There were around 50,000 students in some thirty universities/ university colleges in Britain in 1939; by the end of the century the number of higher education institutions (HEIs) had risen to 166 and more than 1.5 million students were studying at the undergraduate level. The number of first-year students in publicly funded HEIs as a whole in the UK exceeded one million for the first time in the academic year 2003/4.[1]

Some of the most dramatic aspects of social change in higher educa-tion over the last hundred years have been associated with gender. A 'typical' university student at the beginning of the century was a full-time undergraduate male. The part-time female student is arguably more representative of higher education today. On the eve of the Second World War women constituted less than a quarter of the university student population, a level of participation which remained fairly stable until the late 1960s when it began to rise, slowly at first but steadily gathering momentum. By the end of the 1960s, the proportion of female students had only just climbed back to the level reached in the 1920s, before the Depression of the interwar years, and there is some justification for identifying a turning point in the early 1970s, after which the growth in female participation has been continuous. Women overtook men as a proportion of UK undergraduates in 1996/7 and their share of higher education has continued to increase at a rate higher than that for men. The Higher Education Statistics Agency (HESA) reported that in 2003/4 nearly 60 per cent of first-year places in higher education went to women. The Higher Education Funding Council for England (HEFCE) study of *Young Participation in Higher Education*, in 2005, emphasized that by 2000, a young woman was 18 per cent more likely to enter higher education than her male peer.[2]

These major quantitative changes in women's participation in higher education have both reflected and served to drive tremendous changes in institutions and also in the social relations between men and women more broadly conceived. At the beginning of the century the 'elite' institutions of higher education – Oxford, Cambridge and the medical schools – were indisputably patriarchal in structure, and the idea of women being granted equality of access to these institutions, let alone being eligible for senior or powerful positions within their portals, was barely imaginable. Women could not graduate in Oxford before 1920; in Cambridge they had to wait until 1948 before they were allowed degrees. Today, the proportions of men and women students in 'Oxbridge' are roughly equal, more women than men embark upon a training in medical schools, and whilst prospects of promotion to senior positions are still more difficult for women, particularly in 'elite' universities, no-one would suggest that they are negligible.

Reflecting on the history of concern for equality of opportunity in higher education in the 1990s, A.H. Halsey suggested that a longstanding critique of the university for failing to make use of the talents of working-class children had more recently widened to include a concern with gender and with ethnicity: 'Class, gender and ethnicity are now the three giants in the path of aspirations towards equity in the distribution of opportunity . . . '[3] But a concern with women's access to university education was in no sense 'new': the issue had been prominent in the campaigns of feminists since Victorian times. What *had* changed, arguably since the Robbins Report in the early 1960s, was the nature of social expectation that girls had as much claim to a higher education as boys. The taken-for-grantedness of this claim, once limited to the radical agenda of feminists, had spread to large sections of the general public.

The story of women's entry into higher education, once a historical narrative of intrepid pioneers facing near-insurmountable odds, can undoubtedly be constructed as a success story, 'a battle won', although history is rarely simple or one-dimensional, and 'victories' may look less complete as circumstances change. (It could be argued, for instance, that women's prominence in universities has increased at a time when the status of these institutions themselves is under threat.) Nonetheless, it is interesting to observe how the 'success story' of women's access to higher education has often been obscured by competing narratives focusing on the obduracy of social class, or more recently, on boys' 'underachievement'.[4]

The social history of higher education is not a well-developed area of research and enquiry in the UK and accounts focusing upon institutional change rarely explore changing patterns of student aspiration, expectation and experience. In an earlier study (*No Distinction of Sex? Women in British universities 1870–1939*, 1995), I set out to give a reasonably comprehensive account of women teachers and students in universities other than Oxford and Cambridge before the Second World War in Britain. This new volume includes more detailed studies of Oxford and Cambridge, particularly in relation to the admission of women students into formerly male colleges; it also contains studies of gender in medical education. The book does not claim to be comprehensive in any way, but aims to bring together and to build upon research carried out since the publication of the previous text, in the form of closely related studies all of which explore aspects of gender and the history of universities over the last century.

Whilst the title of this book indicates a concern with the gendered nature of student experience, the text gives primacy to women's experiences. This reverses the emphasis found in many works on the history of education which focus primarily on the male. Given that women students are now a majority in higher education, I am not sure that my approach calls for apology. As a feminist historian, my research has primarily focused on women, although I have become increasingly aware of the need for work with a wider focus: one cannot fully understand the experience of women without paying attention to masculine experiences and to the construction of masculine identities. In this way, the first two chapters attempt to compare and contrast the experience of men and women students. Chapter 7 is subtitled 'the anatomy of a masculine culture' because it is impossible to understand the problems faced by women bent on securing a medical education in the first half of the last century without appreciating the ways in which the medical schools offered a curriculum intimately related to the construction of a particular form of masculine professional identity. The sections of the book exploring the advent of coeducation and the mixed college similarly highlight the threat that women students were seen to represent to 'traditional' institutions and to masculine student identity, as well as the reluctance of some women to abandon the protected space of the separate women's college. The final chapter focuses on the ways in which changing relationships between men and women students were reflected in the history of the university rag, an important feature of student social life. However, I am all too well aware that more work needs to be done on the history of masculine student identities and cultural life. Paul Deslandes' study of masculinity in turn of the century Oxford and

Cambridge, *Oxbridge Men: British masculinity and the undergraduate experience, 1850–1920*, suggests that this will be a rich field for research.

The volume is divided into two main sections.

Part I, 'Access and ambitions', focuses upon what students and their families wanted and expected from higher education. Did men and women go to university for the same reasons? What kinds of family support did students depend upon for what was often an expensive investment in the future of daughters and sons? What kinds of ambition impelled women to study medicine in the early twentieth century, at a time when university medical schools were intensely patriarchal institutions? The teaching profession absorbed a majority of women graduates for much of the last century: were women happy with this situation and when did this change? The last chapter in this section, 'Gaining places . . .', represents an attempt to explain the dramatic rise in women's take-up of university education in the final decades of the last century.

The chapters in Part II, 'Coeducation and culture', share a focus on gendered identities, institutional culture and student life. They explore aspects of the demise of single-sex institutions in higher education over the last century, and some of the conflicts engendered by 'coeducation'. The final chapter turns to the history of 'the student rag' and what this tells us about the relationships between men and women, university authorities, students and society more generally over the past century.

The research on which the book is based was made possible by a series of grants, and I would like to acknowledge my indebtedness to the Spencer Foundation, the Wellcome Trust and the Economic and Social Research Council. A generous grant from the Spencer Foundation between 1993 and 1995 enabled me to carry out the detailed work on the history of women students and staff in British universities before 1939 which was reflected in *No Distinction of Sex?*, and it allowed me to get started on the questionnaire-based study of women who graduated from English universities before the Second World War. ESRC funding for a project on 'The value of a university education as perceived by students and their families before the war' (R000-23-7596) made it possible for me to extend this study to include a comparable number of male graduates. I am grateful to the Wellcome Trust for the award of a Research Leave Fellowship in 1996/7, to investigate women's medical education between the wars. Detailed work on the move towards coeducation in colleges in Oxford, Cambridge and London was underpinned by a small grant from the Spencer Foundation in 2000. Most recently, an ESRC award for a project entitled 'Gaining places: stagnation and growth in the proportion of women in universities' (RES 000-22-0139) in 2003/4 provided the opportunity to investigate long-term trends in gender participation in higher education in the UK. None of these bodies bear any responsibility for the views expressed in this volume, which remain my own.

Some of the chapters in this book draw upon material that has appeared in somewhat different form elsewhere. I am grateful to the editor and publishers of the *Journal of Social History* for permission to reproduce material which was originally published in my article 'Family patterns of social mobility through higher education in England in the 1930s' (Summer, 2001). My thanks to Taylor and Francis <http://www.tandf. co.uk/journals> for permission to draw upon material from three articles previously published in *History of Education*: 'Going to university in England between the wars: access and funding' (vol. 31, no. 1, 2002); 'Signing the pledge? Women's investment in university education and teacher training before 1939' (vol. 26, no. 2, 1997), and '"Apostates" and "Uncle Toms": accusations of betrayal in the history of the mixed college in the 1960s' (vol. 31, no. 3, 2002). My thanks to Blackwell Publishing for allowing me to use material from my article, 'Women students and the London medical schools, 1914–1939: the anatomy of a masculine culture', which originally appeared in *Gender and History*, vol. 10, no. 1, April 1998, and to Triangle Journals Ltd, publishers of *Women's History Review*, for permission to reproduce sections of material that first appeared in 'Driving ambitions: women in pursuit of a medical education, 1890–1939' (vol. 7, no. 3, 1998) and 'Troubled identities: gender and status in the history of the mixed college in English universities since 1945' (vol. 12, no. 2, 2003). It has not proved possible to trace the copyright holder of the poem 'Selling the pass' which was published anonymously in the *Oxford Times* on 3 July 1964, and which is reproduced in the appendix to Chapter 6. I hope that the author (almost certainly male) will forgive me.

Lastly, I want to extend thanks to a large number of people who have supported and encouraged my work over the last few years. I owe an immense amount to the archivists and librarians in universities and colleges all over the country who have welcomed my visits and supplied me with documentary material. Alumni and development officers were equally important in facilitating contact with elderly male and female graduates. At the University of Sussex, Richard Whatmore (as Head of the History Department) supplied sturdy encouragement, deftly removing many obstacles to the writing of this book. Claire Langhamer, Ian Gazeley and (until leaving Sussex) Alex Shepard (occupying offices near to my own) sustained and diverted with warmth, wit and corridor conversation. Thanks to Richard Aldrich, Joyce Goodman, Roy Lowe, Sheldon Rothblatt, Pat Thane and Ruth Watts. The final manuscript of this book benefited considerably from the comments and suggestions of an anonymous reader, to whom I am grateful. Sadly, two long-term mentors, Harold Perkin and Brian Simon, died whilst I was carrying out this research. Both supplied inspiration and encouragement over many years, and I remember them here with gratitude and great affection. I am grateful to June Purvis and Jenny Shaw for support and friendship over many years, and to colleagues and friends at Sussex and elsewhere for ideas and companionship. My daughters, Alex and Eugénie, are a fount of inspiration, tolerance and humour. Nick von Tunzelmann, as ever, has been unstinting in his support.

Part I

Access and ambitions

Chapter One

≈

Going to university in England between the wars
Access, funding and social class

The socialist politician Jennie Lee is probably best remembered for her vision of expanding popular access to university education in Britain through the establishment of the Open University in the 1960s. Writing as a young woman, some twenty years before this event, she reflected on her own educational experiences and entry into political life in a volume of autobiography entitled *This Great Journey*.[1] She noted that she had often been asked how it had been possible for her, as the daughter of a coal-miner, to go to university (she had studied at the University of Edinburgh between 1922 and 1926). This had been possible, she explained, through a combination of public support and private (i.e. parental) self-sacrifice. Fife Educational Authority provided schooling up to university entrance, and then presented her with a maintenance allowance of £45 per annum whilst at university. The Carnegie Trust took care of half of her class fees. She lived in a rented room rather than a women's hostel, a much more economical option at the time. Her parents struggled to help. There is a moving account of how her mother, normally cautious and risk averse, defied her father's strict opposition to gambling in any form by putting a shilling each way on the Derby one year 'with a view to assisting Providence'.[2] Clothes suitable for college had to be obtained on credit: equally against the grain. Patricia Hollis, Jennie Lee's recent biographer, describes how on Saturdays, when Jennie's father was free from work, he would cycle the twenty miles from the family home to Edinburgh, bringing home-cooked food supplies and freshly laundered clothes, and taking back clothes to be washed or mended.[3]

Scottish universities have long prided themselves on their 'democratic' tradition, and on having been able to offer access to talented youngsters from impecunious homes. Fees might be considered to have been less of a deterrent after the Carnegie bequest in 1901/2, which guaranteed the fees for students of Scottish birth attending universities in Scotland.[4] By 1938 the 'age participation ratio' (i.e. the proportion of the age group attending university) in Scotland was 3.1 per cent, as compared with only 1.5 per cent in England and Wales.[5] Although there were differences in the recruitment pattern between institutions – Glasgow, for instance, seems to have drawn from a wider social base than did Edinburgh – R.D. Anderson has suggested that the Scottish 'democratic myth' did indeed have substance, in that 'perhaps twenty per cent of Scottish university students could properly be described as "working class"',[6] whilst another 20 per cent or so were the children of 'intermediate' or lower middle-class homes, the sons and daughters of shopkeepers, clerks and so forth. It is probably safe to conclude that at least 40 per cent of the students in Scottish universities between the wars came from families beneath the strata of the economically secure professional and managerial classes.

Although age participation rates remained low by international standards, the number of students in English universities rose significantly between 1900 and 1935. Oxford and Cambridge doubled their intake during these years, whilst the number of full-time students in the other nine universities with charters and five university colleges which existed by 1939 more than trebled (Table 1.1).[7] Contemporaries were conspicuously divided in their judgement about whether this expansion was 'a good thing' or not. Some suggested that the country was producing too many graduates in the hostile labour market of the later 1930s, expressing concern about whether this would breed discontent amongst the 'overqualified'.[8] The problem of graduate unemployment was widely discussed as a European phenomenon.[9] Since a smaller proportion of the population in England (as compared with Scotland, Wales, Germany or North America) enjoyed the benefits of a university education, English observers were not above

Table 1.1 Numbers of full-time students, England only, 1901, 1937/8

		All English universities		Oxford & Cambridge		Other English universities	
		Total	% M/F	Total	% M/F	Total	%
1901	Men	11,755	84.9	5,367	90.9	6,388	80.4
	Women	2,090	15.1	535	9.1	1,555	19.6
	Total	13,845		5,902		7,943	
1937/8	Men	28,409	78.1	9,380	87.0	19,029	74.3
	Women	7,969	21.9	1,398	13.0	6,571	25.7
	Total	36,378		10,778		25,600	

Source: UGC figures, 1929/30, 1937/8.

congratulating themselves on this very limited access to higher education, which they saw as keeping the problem of graduate unemployment within bounds.[10]

On the other side were those who kept up a chorus of protest against the 'waste' of talent, drawing attention to the insuperable social, educational and economic difficulties faced by highly intelligent children from working-class homes who had little chance of continuing their education beyond the elementary school. In *Social Progress and Educational Waste* (published in 1926), Kenneth Lindsay had estimated that less than 1 per cent of those attending the public elementary schools went on to university.[11]

Students: social background

Controversy of this kind, and the somewhat patchy evidence available, have made it much more difficult to generalize about the social background of those studying in English as compared with Scottish universities before 1939. In 1938, Lancelot Hogben's *Political Arithmetic* included an essay by David Glass and J.L. Gray on 'Opportunity in the older universities', which submitted that 'there were no grounds for complacency towards the rate at which the older universities are opening their doors to students of the poorer classes.'[12] They were referring here to Oxford and Cambridge. Studies of Oxbridge make it clear that these institutions catered for a social elite: students from working-class homes, and women, were very much outnumbered by those who might be seen as having regarded college life as something in the nature of a 'finishing school for young gentlemen'.[13] But if Oxford and Cambridge can in the main be seen as having functioned to confirm privilege rather than to offer opportunities for social mobility on any scale, can the same be said of England's 'other' universities? Alongside the three-fold increase in full-time student numbers between 1900 and 1937/8 shown in Table 1.1, many contemporary observers saw the university population as having been 'democratized'. Doreen Whiteley, whose report on funding and social access to higher education was published in 1933, concluded that by that time going to university could certainly no longer be regarded as 'the privilege of the well-to-do'.[14]

Richard Hoggart, whose background was far from 'well-to-do', 'went up' to his local University of Leeds in 1936. In the first volume of his autobiography, published just over half a century later, he attempted a social portrait of the student body in Leeds during the 1930s.[15] There had been around 1700 students (two women to every seven men), the great majority of them (1300) being local. The students, he recalled, fell into 'three easily identifiable, locally drawn groups'. The first group were unambiguously middle-class, the sons of millowners studying textiles in order to take over

5

family businesses, or 'the gilded youth of West Yorks coming in from the hills each day in two-seater sports coupés', many of whom were studying medicine. The middle group were less well-off but had parents who could either shoulder fees 'or find charities which would pay' – the children of parsons, teachers and the like. The third group were 'the really local and the poorest', lower-middle and working-class students on scholarships or (more importantly) Board of Education grants for intending teachers. These were the 'RSTs' or Recognised Students in Training, who were committed to following their degrees with one year's teacher training and a certain number of years' schoolteaching: if they chose not to honour this commitment, they were in danger of being asked to repay their grants. Students in this third group (in which Hoggart numbered himself) had to be economical in their habits, they dressed cheaply and commuted to the university daily by bus or by tram.

Hoggart's picture is not dissimilar to that drawn by 'Bruce Truscot' in *Redbrick University* (1943), where the opportunities and lifestyle of the Oxbridge undergraduate are compared with the experience of 'Bill Jones' of Redbrick:

> Poor Bill Jones! No Hall and Chapel and oak-sporting for him; no invitations to breakfast at the Master's Lodgings; no hilarious bump suppers or moonlight strolls in romantic quadrangles; no all-night sittings with a congenial group round his own – his very own – fireplace. No: Bill goes off five mornings a week to Redbrick University exactly as he went to Back Street Council School and Drabtown Municipal School for Boys – and he goes on his bicycle, to save the twopenny tramfare.[16]

Truscot's description goes on in this vein, highlighting the shortcomings of provincial university buildings and facilities ('dirty, sordid' staircases, 'grimy' classrooms, etc.) and the depressing prospect facing 'Bill Jones' of an evening spent at home in a crowded living room helping sisters with homework and listening to 'Dad's politics' and 'Mum's grievances' when his mind should be thrilling to new worlds.[17] It is difficult to know how to interpret this kind of tone and stereotyping, which sounds uncomfortably patronizing today. Even Truscot probably felt that he had been rather carried away by his own rhetoric, adding (rather lamely) a footnote to the effect that 'not all Redbrick undergraduates come from these particular varieties of Drabtown school and home'. Many, he conceded came from *good* schools (though seldom the best) and comfortable homes. Nonetheless, he stoutly maintained that the *average* student's background was aptly portrayed by his description.[18]

This chapter will introduce material to clarify our understanding of the social background of those who studied in English universities before

1939 and explore the ways in which they financed their studies. It will be suggested that, leaving aside Oxbridge, the social composition of the student body was not dissimilar to that in Scotland. Notwithstanding the differences in the age participation ratio mentioned above, the many differences in educational history and provision between these two countries, and differences in social structure, it would appear that the *proportions* of lower middle-class and working-class students in universities on both sides of the border were much the same.

In the attempt to assess the social significance of the expansion of university education in the early part of the twentieth century, this and the following chapter draw partly on archival material, but principally on surveying the experience of around 1,200 men and women who studied in universities (other than Oxbridge) before the Second World War.

In 1995 I carried out a survey of the social background, educational careers and life histories of a sample of women who graduated from six English universities or university colleges before 1939. Around 800 four-page questionnaires were distributed to groups of women who had studied at the Universities of Manchester, Bristol and Reading; at University College London, and at Royal Holloway and Bedford Colleges (now amalgamated) of the University of London. This choice of institutions reflected a desire to select different kinds of institution (older and newer foundations, institutions in different parts of the country, mixed as well as single-sex colleges), but equally depended upon the interest and co-operation of Alumni and Development Officers with access to lists of current addresses of former students (Data Protection Legislation bars any simple issuing of lists of addresses, and in each case the questionnaires had to be mailed by the institutions concerned). The rate of response was excellent, with over five-eighths (63.5 per cent) of the questionnaires being returned (see Table 1.2).[19] Many of the women wrote long letters, or sent pieces of autobiographical writing; even more took the trouble to answer my questions (several of which were open-ended) in elaborate detail.

The response to this inquiry proved a rich source of data, affording detailed information about why these women had chosen to go to university, the attitudes of their parents, and the ways in which they had financed their studies. The evidence suggested interesting questions (and potentially some answers) relating to the issue of how different social groups had looked upon higher education as an investment; albeit an often costly investment requiring considerable financial sacrifice on the part of parents living through the Depression. However, I soon realized that it would not be possible to understand the picture fully without collecting similar data for male graduates. My study of women had been made possible by a grant from the Spencer Foundation. In 1998 I was fortunate to receive funding from the Economic and Social Research Council, which allowed me to conduct a similar study focusing upon male graduates.

Collecting similar data from male graduates posed certain problems. Women have a longer life expectancy than men, many male graduates tragically lost their lives in the 1939–45 war, and a gap of three years between contacting the female and the male graduates in the research had a significant impact. Women represented only about one-quarter of the student population in the 1930s, but even so, to achieve my goal of collecting a similar number of completed questionnaires from each sex I had to extend the number of universities from six to eight for the sample of male graduates. In the end I distributed 1085 questionnaires to male graduates from the Universities of Manchester, Bristol, Reading, Liverpool and Leeds, from University College London and King's College, London, and from the former University College of Nottingham. The rate of response (over 53 per cent) was lower than that of the women but still very high, and once again, people were extraordinarily generous, both in their replies and in sending me or directing me to a mass of further information (autobiographies, entries in *Who's Who*, correspondence, newspaper articles, etc.). A fuller breakdown of the numbers of questionnaires circulated to men and women graduates of the separate institutions, together with those completed and returned, is given in Table 1.2.

Categorization in terms of social class is a process that is always beset with difficulties. In order to arrive at some kind of social profile of the graduates in my sample I decided to classify according to father's occupation into seven groups, following in the main the scheme devised by John Hall and D. Caradog Jones in 1950, on the ground that this reflected contemporary views of social structure.[20] The categories were (1) Professional and High Administrative, (2) Managerial and Executive, (3) Higher Non-Manual, (4) Lower Non-Manual, (5) Skilled Manual, (6) Semi-Skilled Manual, and (7) Unskilled Manual. Where there were problems in grading occupations broadly designated, such as 'farmer' or 'engineer', I drew upon other information supplied by respondents which gave indications of social position, such as the kind of school attended or details of family finance. Only a small minority of respondents had mothers in regular occupation outside the home, but in cases where they did, particularly when mothers were widows or in the handful of cases where mothers worked in higher-status occupations than fathers, this information was taken into account.

The results of this analysis of social class origins are given in Table 1.3, which shows percentages for men and women separately, giving percentages in each university by social class, and also percentages in each social class by university.

There is an interesting pattern of variation between institutions, in that the colleges of the University of London seem to have attracted a higher proportion of students from social classes 1 and 2 than did the 'redbricks'. Even allowing for the small numbers of men in the sample who studied at the University College of Nottingham, we can see that contemporary

Table 1.2 Numbers of questionnaires distributed to and completed by graduates

1 Women

	Nos. distributed	Nos. completed	Response rate %
Bristol	123	88	71.5
Manchester	225	136	60.4
Reading	108	63	58.3
Royal Holloway & Bedford[1]	230	145[2]	63.0
University College London	108	72	66.7
Total	794	504	63.5

1   Numbers distributed cannot be separated because of confidentiality.
2   Royal Holloway 58; Bedford 87.
Note: Some late returns from King's College and Bristol (in which women replied to the men's questionnaire) were not counted in these responses.

2 Men

	Nos. distributed	Nos. completed	Response rate %
Bristol	97	59	60.8
King's College London	133	74	55.6
Leeds	164	96	58.5
Liverpool	195	95	48.7
Manchester	260	120	46.2
Nottingham	42	22	52.4
Reading	44	18	40.9
University College London	150	93	62.0
Total	1085	577	53.2

observations of Nottingham as having drawn a higher proportion of its student body from lower down the social scale than most other university level institutions are well borne out.[21] The social profile is broadly similar for men and women, although there was a slightly higher proportion of women from social classes 1 and 2, and a slightly higher proportion of men from the Semi-Skilled Manual group (class 6). Contemporary observers often suggested that the women students in the 'civic' or 'modern' universities came from slightly higher social class backgrounds than the men.[22] It should be remembered that a much higher proportion of men went to Oxford or Cambridge than did women: as seen in Table 1.1, in the late 1930s, one in three of the men attending a university in England went to Oxbridge, whereas the proportion for women was barely one in six. This may account in part for the difference. There is also the consideration that many sons from social classes 1 and 2 may not have contemplated a university education at all, but have gone straight into family businesses.[23]

Table 1.3 Social class of origin of respondents in each university

1 **Men**: Percentages in each social class of origin, by university

Univ.	%PHA	%MEx	%HNM	%LNM	%SKM	%SSM	%UM	%ng	Total
BR	14	24	17	19	10	12	2	4	59
KC	24	20	23	12	7	4	0	9	74
LS	13	32	22	10	7	11	1	3	96
LP	22	22	21	14	11	2	1	7	95
MC	13	28	17	18	11	9	1	4	120
NT	0	14	36	14	14	14	9	0	22
RD	11	22	22	22	11	6	0	6	18
UC	30	26	23	2	14	3	0	2	93
Total	18.2	25.1	21.0	12.7	10.2	7.1	1.0	4.7	577

2 **Women**: Percentages in each social class of origin, by university

Univ.	%PHA	%MEx	%HNM	%LNM	%SKM	%SSM	%UM	%ng	Total
BD	29	37	15	3	11	1	0	3	87
BR	17	34	17	7	11	5	3	6	88
MC	16	26	28	5	12	7	1	5	136
RD	16	48	14	11	8	2	2	0	63
RH	16	38	26	3	17	0	0	0	58
UC	38	24	13	6	15	3	0	3	72
Total	21.4	33.1	19.6	5.8	12.3	3.4	1.0	3.4	504

Key:

Universities		*Social classes*	
BD	Bedford College	PHA	Professional, Higher Administrative
BR	Bristol	MEx	Managerial, Executive
KC	King's College London	HNM	Higher Non-Manual
LS	Leeds	LNM	Lower Non-Manual
LP	Liverpool	SKM	Skilled Manual
MC	Manchester	SSM	Semi-Skilled Manual
NT	Nottingham	UM	Unskilled Manual
RD	Reading	ng	not given
RH	Royal Holloway College		
UC	University College London		

The aggregates in Table 1.3 suggest that just over half (54 per cent) of the women and around 43 per cent of the men in my sample were from family backgrounds which we can clearly designate as middle-class. Leaving aside a small proportion of 'not givens', the rest, i.e. 52 per cent of the men and 42 per cent of the women, were from lower middle- or working-class homes. In representations of the social character of the student population at this time, obviously much will depend on whether one sees class 3, the group of students classified as having come from 'Higher Non-Manual' family backgrounds, as having had more in common with the middle or instead the working class. I would suggest that the nature of the occupations represented in class 3, including commercial travellers, railway and post office clerks, small shopkeepers and the like, justifies their being grouped with the working-class rather than the securely middle-class families in this picture. This would certainly accord with the self-perceptions of those from this kind of background in my sample, who sometimes described themselves unequivocally as 'working-class'. One of my respondents, who had graduated from Liverpool in 1938, penned a note on the back of his questionnaire. 'What I hope', he wrote, 'is that you will be able to undermine the myth that only the rich and the "posh" got to a university in the 1930s! This is far from the truth' (this man's father had been a department supervisor in a factory).

The information on patterns of schooling provided by this research (and from elsewhere) broadly supports this picture. Whiteley, in 1933, estimated that around 36 per cent of the students admitted to English universities in 1929/30 (excluding Oxford, Cambridge and London) had been scholars at public elementary schools (she gave 10.8 per cent as the comparable proportion for Oxbridge and 15.6 per cent for the University of London).[24] A report published by the University Grants Committee in 1939 calculated that the proportion of ex-elementary school scholars entering English universities for the first time in 1937/8 (again excluding Oxford, Cambridge and London) was 45.5 per cent.[25] My own information on patterns of schooling is far from complete, since many respondents gave details about secondary schools only, but it indicates that at least 47 per cent of the men in the sample, and at least 33 per cent of the women, began their careers in public elementary schools (Table 1.4).

Table 1.4 Students beginning their schooling in public elementary schools, percentages

University/College	Men	Women
Bedford College	–	25
Bristol	56	38
King's College London	45	–
Leeds	52	–
Liverpool	35	–
Manchester	55	38
Nottingham	68	–
Reading	50	29
Royal Holloway College	–	38
University College London	32	20
All	*47*	*33*

Note: 'not given' results are excluded.

The cost of a university education

Despite the financial obstacles confronting those from less advantaged backgrounds, a sizeable number thus managed nevertheless to make their way through university, in an era before mandatory grants were available. How was this possible? How much did it cost to go to university? In 1916 a Board of Education Committee suggested that the cost of residence and instruction at 'one of the modern universities' could be estimated at an average of £90 per annum (at prewar figures).[26] In the mid to late 1930s, university tuition fees averaged around £40 p.a. (higher for science subjects, lower for arts). The cost of residence in a university hall or hostel varied considerably, from around £40 to £75 p.a. Fees for residence in London might be higher still. In 1933 Doreen Whiteley estimated that around £130 p.a. would cover the expenses of a student in arts or science (medicine was more expensive) at a provincial university, allowing £40 for tuition, £75 for residence and £25 for travelling, pocket money, laundry and books. This was considerably less than the cost of studying at a college in Oxford or Cambridge, which she estimated at from £160 to 240 p.a. for a woman, and from £200 to 275 p.a. for a man.[27] To give a sense of what these figures mean, C.L. Mowat estimated that in the mid-1930s around three-quarters of all families in Britain could be described as 'working-class', with an income of £4 a week or less (£208 p.a.).[28]

However it should be noted that a very large proportion of those studying at a provincial university in the 1930s 'got by' on considerably less than the £130 p.a. figure cited above by attending their local university and living at home. According to figures which were published by the University Grants Committee just before the war, around half of those studying in the English universities (excluding Oxford and Cambridge) lived at home. In Great Britain as a whole, 42.7 per cent of female undergraduates chose to live at and study from home.[29] Altogether, 33 per cent of my own sample followed this pattern, although the percentage varied between institutions. All of the students at Royal Holloway were resident in college, whereas of the Manchester contingent, over half (55.9 per cent) of the women continued to live at home. The pattern of residence differed between men and women in that a higher proportion of men than women (33 per cent, compared with 18 per cent) lived in lodgings. University authorities acting *in loco parentis* often insisted on women students living in halls or hostels if they could not live at home. The UGC figures show more than a third (36 per cent) of the women students in English universities living in halls or hostels, as compared with only 14 per cent of the men. The remainder, 53 per cent of the men, and 46 per cent of the women, lived at home. Amongst the respondents in my survey, 43 per cent of the women and 63 per cent of the men recorded that they had lived at home whilst studying.

Daughters were more likely to be expected to contribute to household duties than sons, and a few women mentioned that they had turned down opportunities to study away from home because they felt it necessary to help their families. Gender-specific expectations were also reflected in the testimony of a man who remembered that, even when studying away from home, he was able to 'economize' on expenditure by parcelling his laundry up and sending it home: his mother would post back clean linen at the end of the week.

Financial support

How much did my respondents remember about the factors that shaped the decisions they made about university entrance and choice of course, and the ways in which they financed their studies? Memory turned out not, on the whole, to be a problem. Most gave careful answers to questions about their reasons for going to university, and particularly on the issue of finance. Very few admitted to having no memory of these issues and, significantly, those who confessed to ignorance about cost were almost without exception from wealthier backgrounds than the majority.

This last group was likely to include those who had chosen medicine as a career. Coralie Rendle-Short, for instance, who studied medicine in Bristol in the mid-1930s, was the daughter of a Professor of Surgery at the same university and she commented that: 'I never heard costs or finance mentioned! I presume that my father paid everything.' Elizabeth Topley, who studied medicine at University College London in the later 1930s and whose father was Professor of Bacteriology at the London School of Hygiene, similarly indicated that she had 'no recollection, no knowledge' of how the cost of her education had been met. A medical education was much more expensive than other forms of university training. Ruth Colyer, who studied at University College around the same time as Elizabeth Topley, recalled that her education was paid for entirely by her father (a dental surgeon), 'who told me in 1934 it would cost him £2000'. Sources of financial support outside the family, for those who wanted to study medicine, were very few and far between, and my sample includes a significant number of women who told me that they would dearly loved to have studied medicine, but that their families simply could not have afforded it.

The vivid recall of financial detail by the majority of my respondents reflects the importance of the issue at the time and the ingenuity which often went into the piecing together of scholarships, and the finding of ways and means. The winning of particular scholarships, of course, was likely to be remembered with pride. The son of a mechanical engineer[30] who studied the same subject at Manchester in the mid 1930s wrote as follows:

In the spring of 1934 I took the Manchester University Entrance Scholarship Examinations, and was lucky enough to be awarded a Beckwith Engineering Entrance Scholarship, valued at £60 p.a. for three years. I was also awarded a Cheshire County Scholarship, valued at £25 p.a. for three years, and at the end of my first year was given an Ashbury Scholarship of £35 p.a. for two years. After graduating in 1937 I was given a University Grant which enabled me to remain at Manchester for a further year; I was then awarded an MSc degree in 1938.

My 'income' up to graduation was £(60×3) plus £(25×3) plus £(35×2) which comes to £325. The approximate cost of an Honours Degree in Engineering was £188.7, the cost breakdown being – tuition fees £143.3, examination fees £8, laboratory deposits £14, textbooks £15, and graduation fee £8.4. Up to graduation, therefore, the excess of my income over cost was £325–£188.3, which equals £136.3.

During my four years at university I lived at home, and travelled up to Manchester each day, as did more than half the students in my year. My surplus of £136 up to graduation went a long way towards keeping me fed and clothed, and left a little over for tennis club fees!

This man was clearly fortunate. Others remembered having had more of a struggle. The son of an unemployed sheet-metal worker, whose mother was reduced to taking in laundry to keep the family together, recorded that:

I sat for and won a studentship from University College Nottingham which covered tuition fees but nothing else. My local authority was a very poor one, with only two grammar schools . . . I was the only student in my school to sit the Higher School Certificate in my year (which I passed at credit level in each subject), and to apply for a grant, but I was refused. As a consequence I had to inform UCN that I was unable to take up their offer, and I started 'Pupil Teaching' in the village school of a neighbouring village.

U. C. Nottingham responded by offering to grant me a further £25 p.a. if the local authority would do likewise. After considerable negotiating and pleading by my Mother on my behalf, the local authority finally agreed to loan me £25 p.a., interest free.

Finally a distant family relative (a spinster lady) agreed to *loan* me £2 per month, interest free. On the strength of this minimum amount of funding . . . I entered UCN some six weeks after the start of the Autumn Term.

The same careful piecing together of scholarships, grants and loans was also necessary for girls from modest circumstances who sought the kind of education which might provide a passport to a securer future, most probably in secondary schoolteaching.[31] The following are fairly representative.

> I won a Wiltshire Major Scholarship, of which 14 were awarded in the County in 1929, on the result of my entry in the Bristol Higher Certificate Examinations. It was worth £120 p.a. for a period of three years. Tuition fees were approx. £30 p.a., and residential fees £60. The remainder – £30 – had to cover all my other expenses. My mother helped me to buy material to make my own clothes.[32]

> I obtained a grant from the Board of Education. (Yes, I was committed to teaching.) This depended on a recommendation from my school and required the names of three referees. I think the grant covered the University fees and £34 towards living expenses at a Hall of Residence. My parents made up the rest of the Hall fees – £30, and Union membership, £3 annually.[33]

Lillian Kay was a student at Bedford; she was awarded her BSc in Mathematics in 1936. Her father was a retired blacksmith who had previously worked on the railway. At the time she was studying the family were living on 15s. 9d. per week:

> (10 shillings Old Age pension, 5s. 9d. pension for 50+ years on the railway!) and bed and breakfast visitors in the summer, there was no question of money from home, tho' they would willingly keep me in holidays. As father had worked for the railway, I did get the concession of 1/4-fare tickets.

Hardly surprisingly, Miss Kay could recall issues of finance in considerable detail:

> The Kent Education Committee awarded me the maximum – £40 loan and £40 grant per annum. The fees at Bedford were £40 per annum. With another girl, I lived in digs in Southfields – we shared the bedroom, had breakfast, and evening meal, for £1 a week each. The three terms were ten weeks, so that accounted for £30. I then had £10/annum left, for essentials, such as books, stationery, travel . . . and luxuries such as midday meals (usually afforded), clothes, toothpaste . . . (rarely if ever afforded).
> For my training year at Cambridge I managed to borrow an extra £20, so I owed altogether £180. This took 5 years to repay, at £3 a month. My salary was £18/month. I took my parents with me to my first post, gave mother £10 (£5/month for an excellent rented house, £5 for

food etc.), paid Kent Education Committee £3, a little put aside for income tax. I had £1 a week left over for myself: absolute luxury. The first month I treated myself to a pink satin petticoat.

John Tearle obtained a place at Imperial College, London, but could not afford to take it up, because of his father's unemployment. Instead, he made superhuman (but successful) attempts to piece together scholarships which would enable him to study at his local university college. He obtained a college scholarship of £25, a Hayward scholarship (£25), a further £25 from the Nottingham Co-operative Society, and a charitable scholarship of £10 intended for 'the poor of the City of Nottingham'. His sister, a gifted mathematician, was urged by her teachers to try for Oxbridge. The family discussed this, but it was effectively out of the question financially. There were grants available for teacher training, and Anne opted for this path in order to allow other siblings their chance. 'I wanted to teach, anyway', she told me.[34]

Financial support for university studies therefore came from a variety of sources. The main sources of support for the men and women in my sample are shown in Table 1.5. The most important sources of support were local authority scholarships (for men and women) and grants from the Board of Education made to students who declared their intention of becoming teachers (especially for women), though again the picture is one of diversity.

G.S.M. Ellis had pointed out in a report for the Sir Richard Stapley Educational Trust in 1924 that, at the turn of the century, 'practically no path existed by which girls of working class parentage could reach the University.'[35] It had been much harder for girls than boys to secure the financial support necessary for a university education. The Board of Education's Consultative Committee on Scholarships for Higher Education in 1916 had expressed the opinion that it was in any case undesirable for girls to be competing for the same entrance scholarships as boys, or in the same examinations. This was partly because they subscribed to turn-of-the-century ideas about sex differences in physiological and intellectual capacity:

Examinations for girls at school leaving age occasion a greater physiological strain than in the case of boys; it is undesirable to subject adolescent girls to the extra strain of competing with boys. Secondly, though the psychology of examinations has been little explored, it may be taken as probable that an examination which is suitable for boys is not necessarily as suitable for girls, and that either sex has certain lines of work which it is specially qualified to follow. Girls should have their own examinations for these scholarships, on lines devised for girls.[36]

Table 1.5 Source of external funds for university studies

1 Men: Percentages in each university obtaining each type of funding

Univ.	SS	LA	BofE	SchSch	CollSch	Loan	Other	Pledge	Total*
BR	0	31	39	7	12	14	25	41	*59*
KC	7	35	11	5	16	4	23	12	*74*
LS	2	31	17	9	22	8	26	16	*96*
LP	4	26	14	9	11	8	19	14	*95*
MC	3	34	20	10	18	3	25	20	*120*
NT	0	27	18	0	50	27	32	32	*22*
RD	6	28	44	28	6	17	28	44	*18*
UC	3	29	9	9	17	9	19	9	*93*
Total	3	31	18	9	17	8	23	19	*577*

2 Women: Percentages in each university obtaining each type of funding

Univ.	SS	LA	BofE	SchSch	CollSch	Loan	Other	Pledge	Total*
BD	10	29	23	13	10	8	13	25	*87*
BR	3	31	42	8	1	5	8	43	*88*
MC	6	33	38	10	8	11	13	40	*136*
RD	8	27	29	6	6	10	6	25	*63*
RH	14	34	16	19	36	9	17	19	*58*
UC	6	19	8	1	11	8	11	11	*72*
Total	7	29	28	10	11	9	12	30	*504*

* Numbers in italics.
Notes
NB: Totals do not add to 100% because of family sources, multiple external sources, etc.
For the key to universities, see Table 1.3.
Key to funding types: SS = State Scholarship; LA = Local Authority grant; BofE = Board of Education grant; SchSch = School scholarship; CollSch = College scholarship; Pledge = Pledge to teach.

The Committee had strongly recommended that more scholarships should be made available to, and reserved for, girls.

The availability of scholarships had improved by the 1930s. In this light, Doreen Whiteley's report for the Trust in 1933 adopted a markedly more optimistic tone.[37] Although there were still grounds for concern (such as the tendency of local authorities to replace grants to poorer students by loans, and a continuing lack of scholarships for girls), she emphasized that over half of university entrants benefited from some form of financial assistance aside from family support. The path however remained a narrow one. In what follows I shall examine the main forms of support which were available to young men and women who set their sights on a university education before the Second World War.

State Scholarships

The most prestigious awards were the State Scholarships, hotly competed for. Originally 200 in number, they were first introduced by the Board of Education in 1920, partly in response to the Report of the Consultative Committee mentioned above. They were suspended as a result of economy measures in 1922 but reintroduced in 1924.[38] Though the number was increased to 300 per year in 1930, Whiteley estimated the proportion of successful candidates as less than one in fourteen in 1931.[39] There was a good deal of controversy about how these should be divided between boys and girls. At first, they were divided equally, half being reserved for the boys, half for the girls. However, pressure mounted from headmasters who argued that since the boys performed better than the girls in School Certificate examinations, they should be entitled to a greater share of the scholarships. The headmistresses countered with the objection that boys had many more sources of funding available to them than girls. When the number of State Scholarships was increased from 200 to 300 in 1930, it was decided to allocate 188 to boys, leaving 112 for the girls.[40] The Board argued that, as future teachers, girls had other sources of funding open to them. But the matter remained contentious throughout the 1930s. State Scholarships tended to go to those students whose sights were set on Oxbridge. A Report published in the National Union of Teachers' Higher Education Bulletin, in 1925, pointed out that of the 198 awards made in 1924, 94 went to students going to Oxford and Cambridge.[41]

The slightly higher proportion of women over men holding State Scholarships in my sample thus reflects the fact that fewer women than men went to Oxford or Cambridge. These awards were highly prized because of their competitive nature and the status they conferred on the recipient, but also because a State Scholarship left a woman (in theory, at least) free to decide for herself on the nature of her future career. There was no pledge, or commitment to teach after graduation: Edith Smith, for instance, who graduated in French from Bedford in 1938, and whose father was a chauffeur/mechanic, recalled that she had been delighted to be awarded a State Scholarship which left her 'free to choose any career'. Her family

> could not have afforded to pay anything. I had been offered a Board of Education grant, dependent on a 'pledge' to teach, but I was able to avoid this obligation when I accepted the State Scholarship.

Local Authority funding

The two reports on the system of Local Authority awards in the interwar period compiled by Ellis in 1925 and Whiteley in 1933 both emphasized that there was little consistency in policy and practice between authorities in various parts of the country. The value of awards varied considerably, as did application of a 'means test' in relation to parental income. Local Authority awards were a crucial source of funding for university students generally: in 1911/12 their annual value was estimated at £56,893, the average value of an award being around £43–£44.[42] The system of awards was extremely patchy, since local authorities differed widely in their practices: some (around one-third of them in 1911/12) making no awards to university scholars at all. Girls were almost everywhere at a disadvantage. In 1911/12, of the 464 university scholarships made by LEAs in England, 373 went to boys and only 91 to girls.[43]

Whiteley felt that some progress had been made by 1933 and that local authorities were moving towards equity for girls, but pointed out that the percentage of women in the student population in Britain as a whole had actually diminished between 1924/5 (30.7 per cent) and 1930/1 (27.2 per cent), attributing this in part to the difficulty of girls obtaining scholarships, and in part to family attitudes rating girls' education as less important than their brothers in a time of economic recession.[44] Just under a third (29 per cent of the women, 31 per cent of the men) of my sample recorded that they had received scholarships or awards from their local authorities. The amounts varied widely, from around £40 p.a. as a common figure, up to £100 p.a. Respondents were well aware of the vagaries and variations: certain local authorities had a reputation for being generous, others the converse. Mrs Battye, who went from Hastings High School to study mathematics at Royal Holloway, was one of the less fortunate, recalling that:

> The local authority gave a £50 scholarship each year to a student going on to university education. As there were two of us with the same needs and qualifications we had £25 each – one third per term. My family paid the rest – with difficulty.

A man whose family lived in Dewsbury remembered that he had obtained the highest marks in his school (Batley Grammar) for Higher School Certificate, but that the grant of £65 p.a. which he had received from Dewsbury education authority had been conspicuously less than that of some of his classmates who had lived in the West Riding. Two of his friends had been able to go to Cambridge on the strength of the West Riding's generosity, whilst he himself had had to settle for living at home and studying at Leeds.

Despite such issues, Local Authority awards, Municipal and Major County Scholarships were an important source of finance. However, my evidence strongly confirms the lack of consistency in this system of awards across the country as a whole. Some local authorities made awards which could be held in addition to state or other scholarships, others did not. Some authorities do seem to have made their awards conditional upon a commitment to teach after graduation, sometimes in the employment of the same authority. Others, particularly in the context of the recession, moved towards a system of offering repayable loans instead of grants, a practice noted and deplored by Whiteley in her study of 1933. Mrs Wilmot, who studied history at Bedford and whose father was a cabinet-maker and carpenter, remembered, for instance, that

> I was awarded a State Scholarship and a Local Authority grant for my degree course at Bedford: my parents supported me during vacations; my scholarship was enough to pay for term-time accommodation and books. When I went on to Teacher Training the LEA (Leicester) stopped the grant and offered a loan. I was not required to 'pledge' to work for them but at the time History graduates were thick upon the ground and I could not get a Grammar School position – I am sure that the LEA quickly found me a place in an 'Intermediate' school so that they would be sure to get their loan repaid!

Scholarships awarded by schools, universities and other charitable bodies

There was some possibility of support in the form of scholarships awarded by schools and individual universities, as well as those from guilds, private charities and other public bodies. Ellis had drawn attention to the fact that in the early twentieth century girls were far less well catered for than boys. There were fewer endowed schools for girls, schools which might be in a position to offer scholarships to leavers. Although some girls' schools (notably the Girls' Public Day School Trust foundations) had established a close connection with the universities, they had done so 'without any perceptible assistance from public funds'.[45] The universities themselves offered far fewer scholarships and bursaries to girls than were available to boys.

Lists of grant-awarding bodies were compiled and published by Doreen Whiteley and also by Edith Morley (for the Fabian Society's Women's Group).[46] Boys were eligible for many more of these awards than were girls. Kitchener Scholarships (for the sons of officers or ex-servicemen), and support from religious bodies for those studying theology or divinity, were not available to girls. The relative importance of these other categories of support for the graduates in my sample can be seen in Table 1.5. Although there was little difference between the proportions of men and women benefiting from school scholarships, the awards going to the women were often very small; the older endowed boys' secondary schools were richer than most girls' schools and were able to offer more generous support to ex-pupils. There were more college scholarships for boys, and these were more commonly linked to the study of scientific and technical subjects.

The profile of girls receiving some kind of college award in my study is skewed by the inclusion of ex-students from Royal Holloway, which was particularly well endowed by its founder Sir Thomas Holloway and his family. A number of women in my sample were recipients of Founder's, Entrance and Driver awards. Altogether 36.2 per cent of the women who studied at Royal Holloway College received college scholarships of some kind (as compared with 10.8 per cent of the sample as a whole). Indeed, some of the women who studied there told me that they had been persuaded to turn down offers from other institutions precisely because they had been offered scholarships from Royal Holloway. The availability of these awards sometimes attracted women who might have preferred (all other things being equal) to have studied elsewhere. Mrs Ethelwyn Higman (née Tanner), for instance, had been encouraged by her teachers at school to set her sights on Westfield College:

> I found out that the work needed was very similar for Royal Holloway, so I entered for both. Westfield offered me an Exhibition of £10 and RHC offered a Scholarship of £60 so of course I took it.

A woman who won an entrance scholarship to Royal Holloway to study botany in the early 1930s also had a scholarship from her independent girls' boarding school:

> this was, however, halved after my first year because another girl showed equal achievement and promise and, moreover, I had by then won a Driver Scholarship at RHC, but hardly of the same value. My father was somewhat shattered.

University College Nottingham was fortunate in being in a position to offer scholarships to intelligent young people from needy backgrounds on the strength of endowments from W.H. Revis and Jesse Boot, and at least half of my respondents from Nottingham had benefited from college scholarships or awards.

Amongst the women who studied in Manchester, one had benefited from the Lydia Kemp Bequest, another had held a 'Manchester 1918' Scholarship. The latter had been made available by supporters of women's education who had sponsored a campaign in Manchester, in 1918, to raise funds to provide a more adequate supply of university scholarships for girls.[47] Mrs Joyce Reid (née Smalley) who was awarded a first-class degree in French from Manchester in 1939, had been attracted to Manchester from Kent. Her father was a market gardener, and her mother ran a small green-grocery business, selling the produce. Mrs Reid recorded that she had

> won three scholarships to Manchester: William Hulme Bursary; Alice Faye Exhibition; Ashburne Hall Scholarship. These – and a loan of £80 from the Kent Education Committee – covered my university expenses. My family supported me during vacations.

Mrs Margaret Harris (née Davies), studied geography at Bedford College in the early 1930s. She chose

> not to accept a grant because of the required commitment to teaching for five years. As a pupil of the North London Collegiate School I was awarded the 'Sophie Bryant Leaving Exhibition', [and there was also] a small inheritance from an uncle.

Many of these scholarships tended to operate 'regressively' rather than 'progressively', serving to benefit those from the 'better' secondary schools; not least, one suspects, because the teachers in those schools were better informed and placed to direct their pupils' attention to the possibilities of applying for support.

Board of Education Scholarships for students intending to teach

Following the foundation of the 'day training departments' in universities in the 1890s (the predecessors of modern university departments of education), the universities' involvement in teacher education in Britain had grown rapidly.[48] In 1890 the government had drawn up regulations for the administration of grant aid to these institutions. Students would receive their general education in the ordinary classes of the university, whilst their professional training would be the responsibility of the day training departments. Academic and professional work was originally combined in a two-year course of training, although students could remain for a third year if they wished (and could afford) to study for a degree. Many universities and university colleges had responded immediately to what was seen as an opportunity to expand student intake. Day training departments or colleges were established in 1890 in Manchester, Newcastle, Nottingham, Birmingham, Cardiff and at King's College, London. Similar institutions were set up in Sheffield, Cambridge, Liverpool and Leeds in the following year. Oxford, Bristol and Aberystwyth followed in 1892, Bangor in 1894, and Reading and Southampton in 1899. Experience soon showed the 'concurrent' model of academic and professional study combined in a two-year course to be onerous and unsatisfactory, and after 1911, a three-year academic course, followed by one year of teacher training, became the preferred pattern.[49]

It is clear that the numbers of students entering universities across the country rose sharply as a consequence of these developments. After 1910, the Board of Education's scheme for training secondary teachers allowed students who pledged their intention to teach to be eligible for grant support over four years, covering tuition fees and providing an allowance for maintenance. In 1955 the historian W.H.G. Armytage contended that

> it is not too much to say that the civic universities in their struggling years, and the university colleges all along, owed the very existence of their arts faculties and in many cases their pure science faculties to the presence of a larger body of intending teachers whose attendance at degree courses was almost guaranteed by the State.[50]

Large numbers of these intending teachers were female, and it is clear that the rising number of women entering universities across the country before 1914 was a direct consequence of these training provisions. The Board of Education's Annual Report for 1923/4 observed that for girls and women, a university education was 'a new thing', when looking at

> the growth of the last forty years. New careers, formerly closed to them altogether, have been opened, but . . . the better prospects of the teaching profession and its severer demands have developed the habit of graduating before entry upon it. Probably a large proportion of the girls proceeding to Universities go to the Training Departments which feed both the Elementary and the Secondary branches of the profession.[51]

The Board's estimates of expenditure for 1923/4 show that 4017 students received university training grants in those years.[52] Of these, 1977, or nearly 50 per cent, were women. The maintenance grants that the women received were smaller than those awarded to their male counterparts. From 1911 onwards the subsidy that the Board allowed for a male student living in recognized accommodation was £35 per annum; women received £10 less.[53]

Board of Education Scholarships for teacher training were a very significant source of funding for women attending university before the Second World War. In all 148, or 29.5 per cent of my sample of women graduates, indicated that they had received support from the Board of Education or from local authorities on condition that they signed a pledge, or undertook some kind of commitment to teach for a definite period (ranging from two to five years) after graduation. Many of these women 'pledged' themselves at the beginning of their course of study, enrolling as students of the Training Departments in Manchester or Bristol with Board of Education support for the full four-year period (three years of study for a degree, followed by a training year). A few of the older women in my sample had followed the earlier 'concurrent' form of training. There were many variations of the pattern. Some women recorded that their parents paid for the first one or two years of degree work, and that they subsequently committed themselves to teacher training in order to take advantage of the grant support available. Another common pattern was to accept training awards for a one-year teaching diploma to be taken immediately after graduation.

Board of Education Scholarships were also important in enabling men from poorer backgrounds to reach university. At least fifty of the men in my sample indicated that this had been the case for them, though many had been less than wholehearted about teaching, and some freely confessed that they had dreaded the prospect. One man who had wanted to study medicine at Cambridge, but failed to get the Kitchener Scholarship which would have made this possible, accepted a Board of Education grant which would enable him to study botany at Bristol University instead. Another, a graduate in English from Bristol (the son of a semi-skilled workman) recorded:

> My desire on leaving school was for Ordination. My Headmaster said 'Teach first'. It has to be remembered that in those days the only way to get a grant-aided place at University was to go as an intending teacher. The primary aim of Grammar Schools was . . . to get as many pupils as possible to University. So many students, including me, became Board of Education protégés without having any burning desire to teach.

Some parents made financial sacrifices in order to avoid restricting the choice of careers for their daughters or sons in this way. But not all parents could, or would, pay. Lily Roberts, whose father was an electrical engineer, graduated in Modern History from Reading in 1930. She had had no choice other than to accept a grant from the Board of Education:

> . . . and for it had to sign a commitment to teach for five years. I had another grant – can't remember where from and I borrowed the rest of the cost from teachers and friends. My parents paid nothing. My father wouldn't and my mother couldn't.

The system of recruiting teachers by making awards for university education conditional upon a 'pledge' to teach had its critics from the outset. As early as 1914 Professor Edith Morley argued that young people were being 'bound too early by a contract they (found) it hard to break', and that the teaching profession was ill served by being staffed by reluctant recruits. Morley drew attention to the need for more generous provision of grants: 'There should be other paths from elementary and secondary school to the University than that which leads to the teacher's platform.'[54] By the 1930s, voices were raised claiming that the teaching profession was 'overstocked', and competition for posts in secondary schools was intense. Many of my respondents described the difficulties that they had experienced in securing teaching posts, and what Brian Simon, as President of the National Union of Students in 1939/40, described as 'a modern system of indentured labour' seemed increasingly indefensible.[55] Nonetheless, the Board of Education awards widened access to universities in England considerably before 1939.

Memories of signing a pledge or commitment to teach varied. It was sometimes a very formal commitment. Kathleen Uzzell, who studied English at Bristol, graduating in 1933, received a grant for teacher training, part of which had to be paid back when she started teaching. She remembers that:

> We were told we were expected to teach for at least five years. When we were first at University we were called into a room where we were told we had to swear an oath to teach for five years, but it was pointed out that it was a 'moral not a legal' oath. . . . The promise to teach for five years meant a promise not to marry as there were no married female teachers except war widows.

However, another woman, who received local authority and Board of Education support for her degree in Chemistry at University College London in the later 1930s, records that in her case:

> No pledge was made before the award of the B. of E. grant, but at the end of the course we were asked to sign a statement acknowledging that our course had been provided by public money, and our resulting obligation.

The Board of Education's Regulations for the Training of Teachers give the full text of the recommended 'Form of Undertaking to be executed by Students' who received financial assistance from the Board to follow a course of training 'provided by a University or by a Local Educational authority or by some other corporation possessing a common seal'. The highly legalistic language of this 'indenture', with its requirements of witnesses, seals and signatures, cannot but have left those students who signed it with the strongest impression of the seriousness of their commitment.[56] The 1918 version of this indenture required male students to pledge themselves to teach 'in an Approved School' for seven years within 'a period of obligation' of ten years after the completion of training. The provision for the repayment of grants in the case of failing to meet these obligations were stipulated in detail. It would appear that this fairly elaborate schedule of commitment was later abandoned in favour of a much more simple 'form of declaration of intent', whereby the student promised that she or he availed her or himself of grant aid 'in order to qualify myself for the said profession and for no other purpose'. Examples of this simplified form of declaration were given in the Board's Regulations from 1920.[57] Percy Yates, who graduated from Manchester in French in 1935, remembered signing a pledge to teach for three years after training, but added that the Professor of Education had assured the students that 'it was "a matter of honour"', and that the document had no legal value, 'since we were all "minors" at the time of signing'. However, W.A.C. Stewart has suggested that the formal commitment or pledge remained in force at least until 1950.[58] Most of my respondents indicate that the commitment to teach was seen as binding, at least until the years immediately preceding the Second World War, when a shortage of teaching posts was evident across the country.

Understandings of the situation (and practices) also seem to have varied considerably, and several of my respondents suggested that rulings were relaxed or abandoned in the build-up to wartime. However, a number of those in the sample who had accepted grants for teacher training but who subsequently decided against entering the teaching profession were required to repay their grants, and this had clearly caused heart-searching and hardship.

Many of those who signed 'the pledge' did so without any qualms: they wanted to teach, and teaching, in a Grammar School at least, appeared to be one of the most sensible options for an intelligent girl who would need to earn her own living, or for young people of both sexes who dreamt of security and a pension. Marjorie Quilleash, who graduated from Manchester in Latin in 1936, explained that:

> I am Manx and the Isle of Man has its own independent Education Authority. There were in the 1930s three University Scholarships annually for the 'top' 3 candidates and there were no grants. My best hope of University depended on being accepted for teacher training with tuition fees paid, and as teaching was my aim, I willingly agreed to the 'pledge'. I received a loan of £40 p.a. for Hall of Residence charges to be repaid at the same rate. Family had to finance travel, books, pocket money etc.

But there were many others in my sample who were less enthusiastic about teaching and who explained that they had had little choice. Joan Cooper, whose father was a commercial traveller, graduated with an Arts degree from Manchester in 1935. She had always wanted to be a social worker, and even as a schoolgirl she had taken to working at the Ancoats Settlement in Manchester during the evenings and at weekends. Joan Cooper eventually went on to build a highly distinguished career in social work and public service. But there was an interlude: the only way she had been able to get to university had been to sign the pledge that would secure a grant from the Board of Education. Teaching held few attractions for her, but between 1935 and 1941 she had to 'mark time' in the profession in order to honour her obligation to the Board.

There were some young people who could not face 'doing time'. Mrs Goldie (née Carruthers) had received help from the Board of Education to complete her BSc (she had studied at Royal Holloway) in 1936. She explained that:

> When I decided that teaching was 'not for me' I started paying back the Board of Education Grant. However, when my father married again (in 1942) a small legacy belonging to my mother was divided between us (my father, brother, sister and myself) and I was able to clear the debt.

Mabel Hall (BSc, Bristol, 1933) had received a Board of Education grant which committed her to teaching, but

> as I took a job in the Civil Service after a year's traumatic teaching (in a private school which went bankrupt after a term and a half) and receiving no payment, then supply teaching in very unsatisfactory circumstances, I had to repay most of this.

Loans

Where grants were unavailable, and parents were unwilling or could not afford to finance their son's or daughter's education there was sometimes recourse to loans, from other family members or elsewhere. Mrs Marjorie Southgate's father was headmaster of 'a council school' in Shropshire. Her mother had been a teacher before marriage. During Marjorie's final year at Manchester her sister was also a student, and finance was tight. Marjorie borrowed £40 from her father for this last year and paid him back during her first year of teaching. Parents were understandably reluctant to see their offspring saddled with debt so early in their lives but sometimes there seemed no alternative. Peggy Marshall was the daughter of a master builder in Bournemouth, and graduated in mathematics from Bedford in 1939. She wrote that there had been

> No grants available – Bournemouth gave one Scholarship to a girl, two to boys – I didn't get one, nor any other help. No pledge by then. I borrowed from a London agency for the first year, much to my Father's horror and had to take a £100 Life Insurance to cover it and had to pay it back when I began teaching – salary £250 per year with £150 deducted for residence.

Whiteley was critical of the idea of local authorities offering student loans on the grounds that these authorities were ignoring their 'duties of providing equal opportunities to all classes of able students, accepting the less costly and less glorious role of moneylender'.[59] Those most needy of loans, she argued, were the most necessitous, and she found it 'strange logic that the more heavily handicapped student should be required to refund the additional help he needs'. Barbara Castle, who went up to St Hugh's in Oxford in 1929, recorded in her autobiography that she had very nearly missed out on the experience. With two siblings already in higher education, her father 'said desperately that he just had not the wherewithal to keep me at university'. Barbara's mother, 'outraged at this threat to her youngest child, put on her tigress act', storming in to Bradford Town Hall to make a case to the director of education. This initiative resulted in a scholarship of £50 plus a loan for the same amount: a huge relief at the time, although Barbara emphasized that having graduated in the depressed 1930s, the loan proved 'a millstone round my neck for many years'.[60] Table 1.6 (linking father's occupation and funding source) shows that – as Whiteley pointed out – the incidence of loans fell most heavily on students from less well-off backgrounds.

When compared with loans, as Table 1.6 shows, both local authority awards and Board of Education scholarships operated fairly progressively amongst my sample, and allowed many who would not otherwise have been able to afford it the opportunity of a higher education.

Family finance

Nevertheless it is clear that most students, even those from the least affluent homes, were to some degree dependent on family finance, even if only to the extent of being fed and accommodated during vacations. The decision to study at a local university, close enough to allow daily commuting from the parental home, was of course common. Around 39 per cent of the men in my sample and 41 per cent of the women recorded that their families bore 'all or most' of the cost of their going to university, at least

Table 1.6 Social class of origin and external funding type

1 **Men**: Percentages in each social class obtaining each type of funding

Class	SS	LA	BofE	SchSch	CollSch	Loan	Other	Pledge	Total*
PHA	0	8	3	2	15	3	14	3	105
MEx	3	19	8	9	17	3	19	9	145
HNM	3	30	20	7	17	8	24	20	121
LNM	4	29	29	1	4	11	26	27	73
SKM	5	51	29	14	19	14	39	32	59
SSM	5	56	41	7	27	15	32	41	41
UM	0	50	50	0	17	33	33	50	6
ng	4	48	4	7	11	4	22	4	27
Total	3	28	17	6	16	7	23	17	577

2 **Women**: Percentages in each social class obtaining each type of *funding*

Class	SS	LA	BofE	SchSch	CollSch	Loan	Other	Pledge	Total*
PHA	4	10	12	6	7	1	7	12	108
MEx	5	29	28	13	13	5	13	26	167
HNM	10	33	36	8	11	9	10	37	99
LNM	17	41	41	14	7	17	7	45	29
SKM	8	44	37	6	15	18	18	45	62
SSM	12	59	29	18	12	24	24	59	17
UM	20	60	20	0	0	20	0	40	5
ng	12	24	24	6	6	18	12	18	17
Total	7	31	28	9	11	9	12	30	504

* Numbers.
Notes
NB: Totals do not add to 100% because of family sources, multiple external sources, etc.
ng = not given (indicators such as father's occupation inadequate to judge the class of origin).
For the key to social classes, see Table 1.3; for the key to funding types, see Table 1.5.

another third of each sex indicating that their families had borne 'some or part' of the expense. This is in line with contemporary estimates such as that by Whiteley in 1933, which suggested that over half of university entrants at that time were benefiting from some kind of scholarship, bursary or support from public funds.[61] In some cases fathers paid up willingly, encouraging their daughters to make the most of opportunities that they had not always enjoyed themselves. Mrs Crowther graduated from Manchester in 1932. She records that her family paid for her degree course. Her father, who was a District Superintendent with the London-North Eastern Railway, 'would not allow me to apply for a Major Scholarship as we could manage, and so many couldn't, without help'. She did, however, receive a Board of Education grant for her postgraduate teaching certificate at Hull University College in 1933, for which she had to sign a commitment to teaching: 'I can't remember for how long.'

But even when students lived away from their parental homes in term time, their families were often obliged to support them during vacations. Only a very small number of my respondents indicated that they had been able to secure paid work during vacations – indeed, most of them responded to my question about vacation employment with incredulity, reminding me in no uncertain terms about the lack of paid work available during the Depression and pointing out that it would have been socially unacceptable for them to have taken jobs even if there had been any available. Thus quite aside from the 'opportunity' costs, to parents of modest means, of foregoing a son's or daughter's potential earnings whilst they were in higher education, a goodly proportion of the cost of a university education fell on families.

Stories of parental sacrifice were a recurring theme in the questionnaires. There was much scrimping and borrowing. The son of a cloth-overlooker in a cotton mill who graduated from Manchester in 1935 recorded that, aside from his tuition fees which were paid by the local authority, his parents met all of the cost of his university education. His mother had not been earning, and his father's wage at the time had been under £3 per week. 'How they managed I do not know,' he wrote, 'they sacrificed so much for me.' The son of an accounts clerk who graduated from King's College London in the early 1930s remembered that his tuition fees alone had accounted for around one-third of his father's annual income. Both of these men had been only children. Larger families of course added to the burden of education, even amongst the more middle-class families. The son of a clerical executive working in the London County Council Public Health Department remembered that his father had had quite a struggle to support three children through to graduation on a salary of £500 p.a. – even though the LCC had given help with fees. Those from larger families often reported that younger siblings had had to wait for older siblings to graduate, in order not to put too much strain on the family budget at any one time.

The son of a driller on Merseyside remembered his widowed father's anxiety when a headmaster suggested that the boy should go to college. 'It was with great misgivings, and much worry about the cost of it all that he allowed me to go to university.' There were many similar stories. There can be little doubt that the extraordinary amount of detail about costs recalled by many of my respondents stemmed from vivid memories of difficulty and feelings of obligation from that time.

Mothers were particularly important in making it possible for young people from working-class backgrounds to go to university. Many of my respondents emphasized their debt to their mothers. 'I have appreciated the opportunity to fill in this questionnaire', wrote one man, because 'it provides me with a chance to pay tribute to my widowed mother who toiled away as a school cook in order to make it all possible.' Only a small

minority of the graduates indicated that their mothers had been in employment at the time when they went to college, but the range of ways in which
mothers contrived to provide economic as well as moral support was quite
extraordinary. Some took in lodgers or laundry, others did dressmaking,
kept corner shops, or ran small businesses selling cakes, sandwiches, and
in one case, ice-cream made in her backyard. One mother became a cook
in the hall of residence in which her son lived at university. Widows had
to be particularly resourceful if they were determined, as many of them
were, to give their sons 'a good start in life'. The widowed mother of a
man who graduated from Bristol supplemented her small pension by
working as a domestic servant so that her son could complete his studies.
Another mother became a publican when her husband (who had been a
pharmacist) died, so that her son could qualify as a doctor. No historian
can possibly deny that the odds were massively stacked against the like-
lihood of children from the working class acquiring a secondary education
before 1939, let alone proceeding to any university.[62] But feats of self-
sacrifice on the part of some parents, determined that their children should
have a better life, sometimes made this possible.

Many respondents emphasized this experience of family sacrifice and
struggle. Mrs Daisy Ball (née Jones), whose father owned a small metalcraft
works, graduated in General Arts from Manchester in 1937. She had never
wanted to teach, but was attracted by the idea of becoming a Hospital
Almoner. Her family decided to pay for her education, but 'with some sacrifice'. Dr Barbara Dick (née Jessell), who studied medicine at Manchester
in the 1930s, records that her father, a doctor, had three children at university at the same time at one point: 'It was quite a struggle, as he would
tell us.'

I began this research expecting to find a pattern of middle-class
daughters (at least) encountering parental (and most probably paternal)
reluctance to their university aspirations, stemming from a conviction that
a degree would be 'wasted' on a daughter destined for marriage. Indeed,
Doreen Whiteley's explanation of the fall off in the numbers of women
going to university between 1924/5 and 1930/1 was that, in addition to
the paucity of scholarships available to girls, they 'were expected to stand
aside in order to allow their brothers to proceed to a further education',
especially during times of hardship.[63] There is of course an important sense
in which my sample is unrepresentative, in that it only selects the women
who made it to university, and it cannot hope to represent the experience
of the numbers who 'got away'.

There were certainly cases where fathers were quite unsympathetic to
daughters' ambitions and disinclined to offer financial support. Mary
Corbin, who followed up her BSc in zoology from Bristol with a PhD in
marine biology, and who gave her father's occupation as 'landowner',
recorded that her 'parents were opposed to my attendance at university

throughout my career: science was not considered a suitable subject for a young lady.' Nonetheless, only about a dozen of my 500 women recorded that their fathers had opposed the idea of their going on to further study, and rather more indicated that their fathers had suggested or even insisted upon it. It was evident that even in many of the better-off families, daughters were subject to economic imperatives: they might be expected to, or needed to earn. Dr Celia Westropp (who graduated from Oxford but as a medical student did her clinical training at King's College Hospital, London)[64] was the daughter of a banker. Her father willingly shouldered the cost of her medical education, but as she pointed out, she had five siblings, and:

> All six of us had to have a training to earn a living, odd in those days, but my father had a widowed mother and unmarried sister to support.

Mrs Marjorie Gibson (née Morrell) recorded that her father's side of the family considered educating girls a waste of money. Her mother's family thought differently, and it was her mother who paid for all of Marjorie's college education, using her share of her own parents' inheritance. Very few of the mothers of the women in my sample would have had such means available to them. Professor Dorothy Blair (née Greene), who graduated from Royal Holloway in 1935, recalled that (like Marjorie Morrell's mother) her mother had been much more keen to foster independence in her daughters than Dorothy's father, but Mrs Greene would not have had the resources to pay for Dorothy's education. A total of 434 (87.5 per cent or seven-eighths) of my 504 women gave their mother's occupation as 'house-wife', 'mother' or 'none' at the time at which they entered college.

What emerges very strongly from my evidence is an impression of the sheer chanciness of the circumstances that allowed many of the men and women in my sample to embark on a university education. Stories of having inherited a small legacy from a distant relative, or having been offered a loan from a spinster aunt, were comparatively common. A farmer's daughter who graduated from Bedford in the later 1930s, mentioned that, when it came to the cost of her higher education:

> All my aunts helped – I lived with two aunts in Hendon for my first two years (my father's sisters); and for my third year my mother's three sisters paid for the expensive residence in college.

All her aunts were well educated. Her father's sisters had been schooled at the North London Collegiate ('the elder under Frances Mary Buss'), and her mother's sisters at a pioneering educational establishment in Scotland.

The networks of family obligation spread wide, and uncles, grandparents and godparents and other relations frequently gave support. Brothers sometimes paid for sisters when fathers died. Older sisters in teaching posts often contributed to the costs of their brothers' education. The son of an unemployed railway signalman thought he had no hope of studying medicine at university, but 'My teachers and my sister, newly trained to teach, made it possible; everyone in my family rallied round,' he recalled. A man who studied dyeing and colour chemistry at Leeds University courtesy of a Clothworker's scholarship from his school in Gloucestershire recorded that his parents had very limited means (his father worked as a chauffeur). Help with maintenance came from his grandmother who worked as a laundress; she sent him ten shillings or whatever she could afford in an envelope, each week.

A handful of respondents mentioned receiving some financial support from their teachers. One man, whose father was a carpenter, had no grant, and could envisage no way of continuing his studies. A teacher from his Midlands grammar school went to see the boy's parents with the offer of meeting all the expenses of four years of study at Bristol University. This he did: his protégé secured a BSc in maths and physics and a teacher's certificate; sixty years later he told me that he had always referred to his teacher as 'St George'. Another example of fortuity came from James Horrocks, who retired as a consultant pathologist, and who had qualified in medicine from Manchester in 1939. In 1926, ten years before he embarked upon his university course, he had won a national 'scholarship competition' organized by a newspaper, the *Daily Despatch*. The young James won the boys' (8–10 years) scholarship of £100, and

> My old Council School got a 'wireless set' capable of receiving the schools transmission on Station 2ZY. It cost a staggering £10, and got a civic reception at the school.

Mr Horrocks' parents decided not to take the award immediately; ten years later, their son at Manchester University, the newspaper paid them exactly £100.

Jennie Lee's story of how she secured a university education in Scotland in the 1920s would have sounded very familiar to many of the graduates who shared their histories with me.

Chapter Two

ช

Men and women in higher education in the 1930s

Family expectations, gendered outcomes

Having explored the ways in which men and women struggled to get to university in Chapter 1, I turn now to what going to university succeeded in doing for them. We have seen how funding, especially but not only for women students, could be tied by 'the pledge' to teacher training. In this chapter, I shall look at the expectations of the students and those who supported them – particularly their families – regarding outcomes. Drawing upon evidence furnished by the questionnaire survey described in the previous chapter, I want to consider the extent of social mobility made possible by attending 'provincial' English universities between the wars.

Insofar as there has been a consensus of opinion in more recent years about the social significance of university expansion in England before 1939, it can probably best be summarized by reference to the work of sociologists, particularly Jean Floud, David Glass and A.H. Halsey, and historians such as Michael Sanderson and R.D. Anderson.[1] It is usually argued that, although the numbers of students from working-class backgrounds going to university increased during this period, they did so less dramatically than did the numbers of those from the middle class. Hence proportionally, the greatest increments of educational and social opportunity afforded by university expansion must be seen as having gone to the 'service class'.[2] Oxford and Cambridge, of course, retained many of the characteristics of what Harold Perkin has described as 'optional finishing schools for young gentlemen' well after 1939.[3] But both Perkin and Sanderson have suggested that the 'other' English universities offered greater opportunities for social mobility.[4] Anderson's carefully nuanced discussions of this subject have greatly illuminated our awareness of the social differences between Scottish, Welsh and English institutions, as well as exploring the relationship between higher education and social elites in

Britain.[5] Even so, Anderson has admitted that, 'Generalisation about the social role of the English provincial universities is hampered by the absence of systematic information about their students' backgrounds', although with some exceptions, 'the sources usually describe them as essentially middle class'.[6] The evidence presented in the previous chapter suggests a rather different picture, but the issue of social mobility remains to be explored. There is also the question of whether men and women benefited equally from opportunities for mobility through higher education.

It is well known that patterns of employment in Britain after 1945 show female workers concentrated in low-paid, unskilled, part-time or temporary jobs. Commenting on this in a recent social history, Martin Pugh observed that:

> It is particularly noticeable that in the higher professions, women's position improved from 5 per cent in 1921 to only 9 per cent by 1966. This was a reflection of their failure to significantly expand their access to higher education. Amongst university graduates, for example, women comprised 27 per cent in the 1920s, but remained stuck at around this level through to the late 1950s when a slight rise took place.[7]

The proportion of women in the undergraduate population as a whole did in fact 'peak' at the end of the 1920s: thereafter it declined slightly, and remained at around 23–24 per cent until the 1960s, reaching 28 per cent – no higher than the 1920s – in 1968.[8] The proportion thereafter rose in sustained fashion, as discussed in Chapter 5 of this book.

R.D. Anderson has reminded us that universities were 'far from being the chief distributors of elite jobs and status' in British society even in the 1950s.[9] Nevertheless, university education was clearly linked with the development of 'professional' careers. Women had, of course, been pushing for entry into the professions since the beginnings of Victorian feminism. To understand why they 'failed to expand their access to higher education', and why the progress they made in entering professional occupations was so slow, requires careful study of a wide range of social factors. Amongst these we would need to consider the expectations of women themselves, and of their families, the hostility of male professionals keen to protect occupational territory and status, particularly in times of recession, and social norms and attitudes shaping the division of labour in the family, particularly insofar as these fostered opposition to the idea of married women's work. Some of these wide-ranging issues are taken up in this chapter, and will be explored further in Chapter 4.

Vocational aspirations and university choice for men

The questionnaires described in Chapter 1 yielded a huge amount of detail about why people had chosen to go to university, and I shall not attempt anything approaching a full summary here. The answers given to questions about goals and aspirations reveal patterns of difference around social class and gender, and class and gender equally played their part in shaping subject choice. To begin with, there was a marked difference between the sexes in the extent to which those going to university recalled having had specific vocational goals. Some 391 (68 per cent) of the men had had clear vocational ambitions when beginning study, and a further 78 indicated less specific vocational goals, making 81 per cent in all (interestingly, this comes close to Brian Simon's estimate that around 88 per cent of those entering 'the modern universities' between the wars had decided upon their occupations before entry[10]). Only 38 per cent of the women in my study indicated that they had had clear vocational goals, although this proportion rises to 51 per cent if we include general vocational aspirations.

Where men indicated specific vocational aspirations these were likely to be in medicine (157 men, 28 women), engineering (67 men, 1 woman), theology (19 men, 0 women), law (21 men, 1 woman) or science (133 men, 96 women). Science is a difficult category because its more applied variants, such as dyeing and colour chemistry or leather technology (both specialisms at Leeds), were effectively male preserves. Women tended to do biology, botany or zoology (I have chosen not to count 'domestic science' as science). A breakdown of the subjects studied by those in my sample is given in Table 2.1.

The costs of studying medicine and engineering were high, and it is not surprising to find that amongst the men, 66 per cent of those who elected for medicine and 52 per cent of those who took engineering sciences had backgrounds in social classes 1 and 2. There was a tendency for sons to

Table 2.1 Key

Key:			
Universities		*Subjects*	
BD	Bedford College	AR	Arts (General and Fine)
BR	Bristol	HU	Humanities (esp. Languages)
KC	King's College London	TH	Theology
LS	Leeds	LA	Law
LP	Liverpool	SS	Social Sciences[1]
MC	Manchester	MA	Mathematics[2]
NT	Nottingham	NS	Natural Sciences
RD	Reading	ES	Engineering Sciences
RH	Royal Holloway College	MD	Medicine
UC	University College London	AG	Agriculture
		DS	Domestic Science

Table 2.1 Numbers taking each subject, men and women

1 Men

Univ.	AR	HU	TH	LA	SS	MA	NS	ES	MD	AG	Arts	Sci	Total
BR	2	3	2	2	11	4	10	9	16	0	20	39	59
KC	0	3	13	4	7	5	10	11	21	0	27	47	74
LS	0	10	2	1	4	3	35	12	29	0	17	79	96
LP	6	12	0	6	8	6	11	14	25	7	32	63	95
MC	5	18	2	4	14	7	33	12	25	0	43	77	120
NT	0	2	0	0	1	4	12	2	0	1	3	19	22
RD	1	3	0	0	0	0	7	0	0	7	4	14	18
UC	4	13	0	4	3	6	15	7	41	0	24	69	93
Total	18	64	19	21	48	35	133	67	157	15	170	407	577

2 Women

Univ.	AR	HU	TH	LA	SS	MA	NS	ES	MD	AG	DS	Arts	Sci	Total
BD	2	22	0	0	23	16	24	0	0	0	0	47	40	87
BR	1	34	0	0	18	4	20	0	7	0	4	53	35	88
MC	21	50	0	1	21	11	23	0	9	0	0	93	43	136
RD	3	13	0	0	13	2	8	0	0	18	6*	29	34	63
RH	7	18	0	0	8	17	8	0	0	0	0	33	25	58
UC	5	27	0	0	9	5	13	1	12	0	0	41	31	72
Total	39	164	0	1	92	55	96	1	28	18	10	296	208	504

* Diploma students.
Note: Science (*Sci*) excludes Domestic Science.
1 includes History and Geography unless offered in humanities or sciences combinations.
2 includes Maths with Physics.

follow fathers in these occupations, indeed it was not uncommon for middle-class fathers to take an active or even directive role in charting their sons' careers for them. Christine Heward, in her study of boys at Ellesmere School between 1929 and 1950, found that middle-class fathers 'managed' and directed their sons' education through public school with an eye to their careers, and my evidence would support this.[11] Several of the male respondents from middle-class backgrounds indicated that 'their' choice of subject and university had in fact been their father's. In more than one case this had unfortunate results: a graduate from Leeds confessed that he had gone to university to study engineering because his father 'wished it, for prospect reasons': he had never been comfortable in his career. A graduate from Reading, the son of a factory manager in Sheffield, recorded that his studies in horticulture had been governed by his father's plan of 'setting him up' with his own nursery. In an age of rather less than formal entry procedures, it was not uncommon for fathers to 'have a word' with professors at the local university about their sons' prospects, particularly in medicine and engineering. Fathers in social classes 1 and 2 held the purse strings: one graduate from Leeds recorded that his father (a wool merchant) had shouldered the cost of nine years of university education for him, whilst he qualified first in dentistry, and subsequently to practise medicine. One man, who as a youth nurtured a strong desire to study medicine, found his father strongly opposed: he had offered his son £5000 on condition he abandoned his medical ambitions and went into the family business instead (the son held out, and his father 'came round' and paid up for medicine).

It was certainly common for middle-class fathers to discuss professional opportunities and the state of the job market with their sons. A graduate from Bristol remembered that he had decided against following his passion for chemistry at university because his father, an analytical chemist himself, had argued that he 'had seen far too many science graduates applying as lab boys, unable to find suitable employment', His father suggested he do dentistry instead, because there was less overcrowding in that profession. Similarly the son of an engineer who wanted to follow in his father's footsteps took paternal advice about poor employment prospects in the early 1930s and was encouraged to opt for medicine instead (he recorded somewhat ruefully that the demand for engineering graduates was to rise steadily a few years later). Some young men from middle-class homes were more independent about their choices, but they were secure in the knowledge that their fathers would support them, especially if they were 'realistic' in their goals.

In the lower reaches of the middle class, where there was much more dependence on grants and scholarships, as Hoggart observed of his 'middle group' at Leeds,[12] there were fewer reports of such specific paternal direction. Many men recalled their parents' cherished ambitions for their sons to gain a foothold in some 'professional' occupation with security of employment and an adequate wage. E.L. Haste, the son of a textile designer and 'middle manager' in a Bradford mill, financed his studies in civil engineering at Leeds with a local scholarship, and both a grant and a loan from Bradford Corporation. He lived at home throughout his course, involving a daily journey of ten miles each way. Mr Haste recalled his decision-making process thus:

> Thinking about my future career it seemed to me that I needed a profession. That meant something like medicine, law, engineering or accountancy. Medicine took too long, accountancy would be unexciting, law too expensive, but engineering fitted nicely.

This focus on the advantages of professional employment is very much in evidence when one looks at the explanations given for going to university by men who came from homes lower down the social scale. Here, sons were not unlikely to inherit fathers' ambitions, which had been cut short by financial exigency. James Lightbown, who went on to a distinguished career in analytical chemistry, working particularly on antibiotics, recorded that his father, who had run a small retail pharmacy, had once cherished an ambition to do work in the Laboratory of the Government Chemist. However, at the time when Dr Lightbown began his studies in pharmacy at the University of Manchester in the mid 1930s, he recalls that his major preoccupation was that of finding a job with a pension.

Families who suffered in the Depression of the 1930s were often desperately keen to enable their sons to obtain the qualifications for secure employment, and many men recorded this as their major goal in continuing study. It was not uncommon for respondents to heavily underscore the words 'secure job with a pension' in their answers to my question about why they went to university. The answers given to this question included the following:

> I saw education as the key to the professions . . . and thus as a means of escape from the threat of manual or clerical drudgery (Dr C. Hentschel, father an intermittently employed engraver; modern languages UCL).

> I thought H.E. would offer the chance to move from a working class milieu to a professional career (Mr A. Hall, father a commercial traveller; engineering KCL).

> Any youngster in the East End of London during the 20s and 30s knew that the way out of the ghetto came through education. This would

lead to a professional career rather than a commercial one . . . (widowed mother kept a sweet shop; medicine UCL).

. . . courses leading to professional qualifications were eagerly sought . . . it was a fact of life in those hard times that people without qualifications worked in dirty blue overalls, doing the unpleasant jobs for a pittance. They were the first to be laid off when times were harder (father a foreman patternmaker and foundry manager; engineering Manchester).

My working class family were consciously aiming to 'better themselves', socially, educationally and economically. I followed the tradition (Dr J. Weston, father a postal sorting office supervisor, mother head-teacher of a small village church school; physics Nottingham).

Many respondents emphasized that higher education had represented the possibility of *escape*: from the looming threat of unemployment, from poverty, from small village communities, from the prospect of working 'on the land or the railway', 'from a miserable Pennine valley and a black future'. 'I continued with higher education to avoid going on the dole', wrote the son of a post office morse operator who began studying German at Liverpool in 1935: 'Unemployment hung before us like a black cloud . . . my parents were almost fanatical about education . . . [I] was in a sense forced along the road to university.'

This respondent indicated somewhat unusually (for the men in my sample) that he had had no clear idea about planning a career when going to university. A grant from the City of Liverpool financed his first year of study. At that point he obtained a grant from the Board of Education for which he had to commit himself to five years' teaching after graduation. It is clear from the sample as a whole that the sons of families lower down the social scale who were dependent upon these Board of Education scholarships were in the main those who were least clear about their vocational goals. The 'pledge' to teach was often made out of strategic compliance, since there appeared no other way of obtaining financial support for study. In Chapter 1 we encountered the son of a semi-skilled workman who concluded that: 'many students, including me, became Board of Education protégés, without any burning desire to teach.' This man, who taught for a few years and then became a clergyman, spoke for many of the men in my sample, a sizeable number of whom 'got out' of teaching as soon as they could. A number did so gratefully with the outbreak of war. But where other sources of financial support were available, the men's calculations about how their studies would improve career prospects were often very carefully thought through. Mr White, whose father managed a local coal-stocking and machine tool business, opted for mining and metallurgy at

Leeds. He had wanted to read medicine but family funds could not stretch to this, nor to veterinary science, his second choice. He chose mining at Leeds 'because of its wonderful reputation for graduate employment'. Another, similarly, whose father was a chauffeur in the rural South of England, went north to Leeds because 'Professor Rowe, in the Dyeing and Colour Chemistry Department, had a reputation for always placing his graduates in very good jobs in industry.'

Vocational aspirations and university choice for women

As was pointed out above, the women in my sample were much less likely to record having had specific vocational ambitions in going to university. Of those who did, a small number aimed at medicine, most of the others recording that their aim was to teach in a grammar school. This raises a number of questions. The research of Janet Howarth and Mark Curthoys on women students at Oxford and Cambridge before 1914 led them to suggest the possibility of a 'dual market' for women in higher education, a market which encompassed those who sought a degree as a passport to earning a living (most commonly in teaching, since other openings for women were few at the time), but also a group of middle-class women seeking knowledge and culture for its own sake, without any real intention of entering the labour market.[13] There was a sense in which this latter group enjoyed more freedom in their choice of subject and curriculum than their male peers, who had to think about their earning potential.[14] However, my own evidence would suggest that any such women were very much in the minority amongst those who attended non-Oxbridge universities between the wars. This is because most of my female respondents emphasized that their somewhat hazy career aspirations had gone hand-in-hand with a sense of pressing urgency about the *need* to earn a living, and a marked frustration about the lack of openings they remembered being able to envisage as young women.

The twenty-eight women who qualified in medicine in my group were (even more conspicuously than the male medics) from middle- and upper middle-class backgrounds. Again, it was common for such women to follow fathers or other family members who had studied medicine. Unlike the men from affluent homes, some of these women used the language of 'escape' that we have observed as characteristic of men from homes lower down the social scale. Here, however, it was the conventions of middle-class femininity, rather than the poverty of working-class life, that were seen as constricting. One female medical graduate from Bristol, for example, judged that her degree had transformed her life because 'it got me out of a humdrum background of looks and clothes and the importance of wearing hats and gloves and using the right fork'.

A few women gave explicitly feminist reasons for going to university. These included the (smallish) number of those whose mothers were themselves graduates, as well as some girls who had been inspired by teachers conscious of the legacy of the pioneers of girls' education in Victorian times. Mary Howarth (whose father had been a vicar), who graduated from Reading in 1933, noted that her headmistress had known both Miss Beale and Miss Buss, and that she had insisted that 'it was essential for women to obtain degrees so that they could influence policies in a society which was largely male dominated in the late 1920s'. Rosie Bentham, the daughter of the managing director of an engineering firm in Manchester, went to UCL to read geography with 'strong support' from her family who believed that women should be educated 'for the opportunity of independence as opposed to marriage' (she herself never married). 'My mother was a suffragette manquée', wrote Joan Venn (BSc), 'and she wished me very much to go to Bedford – the oldest women's college.'

Women from families lower down the social scale gave reasons for going to university which were in essence very similar to those given by men from similar backgrounds. Even though their career aspirations were less focused, the economic imperative of escaping from unemployment, rural communities and lowly prospects in the labour market preponderated. Going to university (Manchester) 'set me free from the everyday grind of my parents' life,' wrote one woman, whose father had been a weaver, whilst her mother did part-time cleaning to help with the family wage. Mrs Reid, whose father was a market gardener and whose mother ran a small greengrocery business, pieced together several scholarships to enable her to go from Kent to study French in Manchester. 'I had no idea what higher education could offer me,' she wrote, 'and no career plans – apart from a determination not to go "into service".'

Women frequently recorded that they 'had always wanted to teach'; others had the choice pushed upon them. 'From the time I could speak I was told I wanted to be a teacher,' wrote Ella Day (BSc Manchester). 'To my parents, poor and working class, it was the only way to lift us into a better life.' 'I could not have gone to university without teacher training grants,' pointed out another Manchester woman graduate, 'so there was no choice of profession.' Nellie Goldie (whose father was a grocer's assistant) studied mathematics at Royal Holloway: 'It was assumed that I would teach,' she remembered, 'but I dreaded the idea. I did *not know* what other career was open to a mathematics enthusiast at that time.' 'Career planned by receiving Board of Education grant, without much enthusiasm on my part', wrote another Royal Holloway woman. A long list of women confessed having had early ambitions to be something other than a teacher: a diplomat, a solicitor, a research chemist, business manager, veterinary surgeon, etc. Annie Parris (then Poulter) recorded that, when she was 16 years old, her father had told her that 'now women had the vote, we could take any career we wished.' 'Little did he know!' she added ruefully. Her father (a senior accountant with a shipping company) had 'insisted' she get a degree, and Miss Poulter went to Reading to read agriculture. She graduated with a first in agricultural botany in 1929, then 'discovered that there were no jobs in agriculture for any of the women graduates.'

Patterns of family support for mobility: women

Parents sometimes elected to shoulder the cost of a degree course in order to prevent their daughter from having to 'pledge' herself to teaching. Mrs Joyce Hinton (née Boothroyd), who graduated from Bristol in 1939, was encouraged to go to university by both parents (father an electrician, mother a former teacher). Her sister had already preceded her to Bristol on a Board of Education grant, but Joyce had known from an early age that she did not want to teach. She wanted to be a secretary to a politician, or to go into industry. As a general background for these ambitions, she was attracted to the BA in Commercial Subjects. Her parents agreed to pay her tuition fees: they could not afford residential fees, so it was agreed that she should continue to live at home.

Given that opportunities for women in professional work other than teaching were still very limited in the 1930s, it was something of an act of faith for middle-class fathers to invest in their daughters' education with confidence that this would 'pay off'. Many fathers nevertheless chose to make the investment, though the intention was sometimes frustrated. A woman whose father was secretary and general manager of a small company told me that, although she herself thought she would probably end up teaching history in a secondary school, her father had discouraged her from applying for a Board of Education grant and decided to pay for her years at Bristol himself, because he wanted to leave her free for other kinds of work if she could find an alternative to schoolteaching (she ended up teaching because nothing else presented itself). Similarly, Dora Crouch, whose father ran a jewellery business, recorded that her family had paid up for her education at Bedford:

> (I think at some sacrifice) because they did not want me to 'pledge' to teach as they thought other opportunities might open up.

Miss Crouch ended up as a schoolteacher, too.

As noted in Chapter 1 and also above, there were instances in my responses of fathers being unsympathetic to the higher education of their daughters, though the number of cases reported was much smaller than one might have anticipated (but note again the 'bias' in my sample, since only those who did go to university were approached). Only two of the women graduates, however, suggested that their mothers had opposed the idea of their going to university. The story in the main was one of strong motherly support and backing. A woman who qualified in medicine at Bristol just before the war emphasized that 'all the menfolk in my family [were] totally behind the higher education of their womenfolk', but at the same time she paid tribute to the strong encouragement she had received from her mother in going to university, adding that:

> My mother's mother, born in Carmarthenshire in the 1850s, was left a widow in 1886 with two daughters and three sons. She devoted her energies to ensuring a career to the two sisters, and left the sons to find their own way in the world. According to my own mother, this splendid lady said 'boys will always survive, girls won't unless they have an education and a career'. Both became teachers, and carried on preaching the gospel of education for girls. I believe I owe this grandmother a very great deal.

It is interesting that a much greater proportion of the women in my sample (72 per cent, as compared with only 46 per cent of men) mentioned strong parental encouragement to go on to further study after leaving school. This may reflect the fact that higher education was less of a common choice for girls than for boys, who took parental support more for granted. The authors of some recent studies of social mobility have suggested that mothers may have a stronger influence on daughters' educational ambitions and career aspirations than fathers, who have correspondingly more influence on their sons.[15] As R.L. Miller and B.C. Hayes have pointed out, this idea of the influence of the same-sex parent on children's occupational aspirations would be congruent with role modelling or socialization theory.[16] As was indicated above, few of the graduates in my sample had mothers who were in regular employment outside the home at the time when they went to university, and there is little indication that many of these mothers had financial resources of their own. Mrs Gibson (née Morrell), who studied English at Royal Holloway just before the war, was the daughter of an engineer. She recorded that when her mother (a housewife) inherited some money from her own parents she immediately earmarked this to pay for her daughter's university tuition.

In those cases where middle-class fathers were sceptical about the value of sending daughters to university, mothers might intervene. Marjorie Morrell remembered that her mother had had to persuade her father that a girl had as much right to a full education as a boy ('The suffragettes, and Ibsen's plays, were often discussed in my mother's family . . . '). But even where mothers had had little education themselves, their support for their daughters was strongly evident. Lillian Kay, whose mother (aged 62 at the time that Lillian went to Bedford) 'had never heard of universities', recalled that her mother had been enthusiastic about her daughter attaining qualifications in the hope that she 'would not have to work as hard as she had done'.

Patterns of family support for mobility: men

Maternal support and feats of sacrifice in the interests of bettering a son's prospects were a recurrent theme in the experience of the male graduates. The range of ways in which mothers managed to provide material as well as moral support was wide. As detailed in Chapter 1, there were examples of mothers who iced cakes, kept chickens and took in laundry and lodgers to help with finance. One male graduate recorded that his mother made ice-cream in her backyard, and set up a small business selling tea and sandwiches to the village policemen in order to eke out resources. Some mothers who had left teaching on marriage were often in the comparatively fortunate position of being able to return to work in order to boost income temporarily: A man who studied engineering at King's remembered that his mother had worked as a supply teacher in order to be able to send him £2 10s. per week in her weekly letter whilst he was at college. Widows – whether middle- or working-class – often had to be particularly resourceful. A male graduate from Leeds described how his widowed mother had rented a house near the university in order to provide a base for her four sons to study for professional careers. Another widow moved in as house-keeper to her unmarried sister (who did research in dairying in Shinfield), who in turn paid for her nephew's education at Reading University (the nephew became a distinguished professor of geology). Mr A. Vines (BSc botany, Bristol) recorded that his mother's pension as a war widow had been just under £2 per week. She had taken on domestic work (for around £1 per week) to help support him in full-time education. Dr W. Parker, who graduated from Manchester in 1936, explained how, when his father (a pharmacist) had died whilst he was a student, his 'ambition to qualify in medicine had crashed'. His mother responded, 'if you are game, I am – I will take a pub to qualify you', and so she did.

This picture, reinforced in many other accounts, of mothers pulling out all stops to support their sons, particularly, raises interesting questions about women's role in facilitating social mobility through education in this period. Although the evidence from this research supports the picture drawn by Christine Heward's work on the role of middle-class fathers and their sons, it suggests that for young men from families lower down the social scale it was mothers rather than fathers who often played a decisive role.[17] There were several cases where fathers had wanted their boys to take up jobs on leaving school and were reportedly very anxious and uneasy about the cost of sending their sons to college. Professor G.H.

Arthur, who graduated from Liverpool in veterinary science in 1939, remembered that his father, a farmer, was less than happy about his son's ambitions because he felt insecure about financing five years at college at a time of severe depression in farming. It had been his mother who encouraged his plans. Another, who read English at Manchester, was the son of a greengrocer's assistant and a former domestic servant: he emphasized that it had been his mother's determination that at least one of her children 'should have a fair chance in life'. Edgar Scholey (BSc Leeds, 1936), whose father was a teacher, remembered that it had been his mother who had borrowed the money to send him to university. Ken Millins, whose father worked as a toll clerk for the Grand Union Canal, went to the University of Reading with maternal encouragement and support. His father had been keener that he should take up the opportunity of a traineeship with Price Waterhouse, though 'he was not obstructive in any way'. It is not difficult to appreciate why many working-class (and indeed lower middle-class) fathers were anxious about cost: as noted in Chapter 1, the son of an accounts clerk who graduated from King's in the early 1930s pointed out that tuition fees alone absorbed a third of his father's annual income.

A graduate in medicine (Leeds, 1939) was the son of a wholesale fruit merchant. His mother (who had never worked outside the home) 'was very ambitious for her children'. In her view 'doctors, schoolmasters, bank managers and parsons were all respected members of the community' and she was determined that her son should join them. Similarly, the son of a builder and former seamstress recalled that, although both of his parents had supported his decision to read physics at Leeds, it was his mother who was particularly determined to 'give me a stable career, which no-one could touch' (this son went on to become a distinguished physicist). John Copley's father was a music teacher. Both of his parents were ambitious for their son's education (he graduated from Leeds with a first class degree in English in 1938). However it was his mother's outlook which had shaped 'family policy': an (uncertificated) teacher herself before marriage, Alice Copley's view of the world was structured by a sharp division between those who were 'qualified' and those who were not.[18] This was the ultimate class distinction, and there was no doubt in her mind about which side of the fence her son would end up on.

There were numerous stories of this kind. I am well aware of the dangers of sentimentalizing the role of working-class mothers and of feminist critiques of the representations of self-sacrificing but all-powerful mothers which feature in so many (male) working-class autobiographies and life histories of the period.[19] However, my observations are in accordance with those accounts of mothers' role and agency in educational matters found in surveys nearer to the time, such as that of Jackson and Marsden.[20] I would submit that mothers often played an important part in mediating between two class-based forms of masculinity between the wars. As more traditional, work-based forms of masculinity tied up with apprenticeship, skill and regular wages were increasingly under threat and undermined by economic depression, the prospect of acquiring 'qualifications' through a longer period of study and material dependency on the family looked like a more sensible investment. Working-class fathers might find themselves less well placed to act as role models for their sons, and it was here that their wives' motherly aspirations for their boys, not to mention these women's diplomacy and resourcefulness in negotiating agreement about expenditure on higher education, often came into focus.

In a very large number of cases, the decision to support a daughter or a son through college was ultimately a family decision, and one which – as seen in Chapter 1 – was discussed between parents, children, and sometimes grandparents, uncles, aunts and wider kin. In a period in which unemployment and its attendant hardships put families under considerable strain, networks of economic dependence on extended families often came into play. Dr John Tearle (who studied physics at Nottingham, and whose success in piecing together scholarships etc. has been related in Chapter 1) remembered very well the complex process of decision-making which had gone on in his family during the Depression. His father, an aerial ropeway engineer, had been unemployed through most of the period 1929–34. His mother had been an uncertificated schoolteacher in her youth, although she had been obliged to resign on marriage. There were five clever children in the family.

> We fell upon hard times in the late 1920s, when my sisters and I were all at the only grammar school in the city of Nottingham . . . Contracts for work in our father's field dried up, and it is not surprising that he thought that education beyond 14 was a luxury we could not afford, but our mother refused to give up and went back to work as a supply teacher. Father found occasional work beneath his capabilities, and life on the dole and National Assistance was degrading for him; and being dependent on a wife at work was alien to the culture of the times.
>
> It is impossible for anyone who has not lived through those years to appreciate how bleak the Depression was for the unemployed. But we knew that the only way out of poverty was to take our education as far as we could. My elder sister and I were usually at or near the top of our forms, and didn't need any spur to succeed.

Careers for women graduates

Careers advice, where available for women graduates, could be brutally inadequate. One woman remembered that:

> In 1936 a careers adviser was appointed at Bedford. Having still no idea what to do on finishing my degree, I consulted her. She asked me what I wanted to do. I said I did not know. She said, 'If you don't know, I'm sure I don't.' End of interview. I started on a secretarial course, but abandoned it.

Mrs Hubner, who graduated from Royal Holloway College in History in 1934, recalled that:

> I cannot remember any really worthy incentive I had to go to University. My father had a Cambridge Degree and my elder brother an Oxford Degree and I was obsessed with the idea of putting the magic letters BA after my name. There seemed to be little a female could do in the Thirties except teach, and I did not want to do that.

Mrs Hubner adds that there was a 'glut of female labour when I left College', so she

> took a 6 month secretarial course in London from where I got a secretarial job in a rather seedy London office of a Patent Medicine Firm.

In his well-known study of *The Universities and British Industry, 1850–1970*, Michael Sanderson commented on 'the flavour of the insecurity, poverty, fly-by-night quality of life of women graduates who tried to break out of the well-worn path to teaching in the 1920s'.[21] My evidence suggests that the predicament of women graduates in the 1930s was much the same. Very few of my sample, even among the 38 per cent who took degrees in the sciences (other than medicine), could find jobs outside teaching.[22]

Mrs Prescott Clark (née Norreys Coleman) had proceeded from Cheltenham Ladies' College to Bedford, where she read physics. She had wanted to be a doctor or an engineer, but her father (a medical practitioner himself) had disapproved, so she had 'compromised' with physics. The 'cooling out' process continued after graduation: 'It was nearly impossible to get a job in physics other than teaching when I graduated. I was a *woman*.' Zoë Coleman applied for a post at Woolwich Arsenal in 1937. She was turned down, on the grounds that she was about to be married, in the same year. Another found that it was difficult to get into agricultural research, even with her first class degree in Botany. When she *did* secure a post (via 'a certain amount of nepotism'), she soon lost it on account of her engagement to a colleague:

> So I spent much time and shoe-leather exploring any possible job (including quality control in a *sardine* factory), none of which came to anything . . .

She then tried to resign herself to 'cleaning and polishing her little flat' until the war came, when she signed on at the local Labour Exchange and was given a job addressing ration books.

Of course jobs were in short supply everywhere in the late 1930s. One of my respondents, asked to give details of her first appointment after graduation, wrote: 'Jobs! You must be joking. In *London*?' A significant proportion of the women in my sample who had indicated that they had been relieved to be awarded state or other scholarships which (in theory) allowed them to by-pass any commitment to teaching found themselves reduced to considering posts in schools simply because there seemed no other option. But teaching jobs, equally, were thin on the ground. A shortage of posts in relation to the numbers applying had been evident since the early 1930s, and in 1932 the Annual Report of the Board of Education announced that in consultation with the Teacher Training Departments in universities, the Board had decided on a 10 per cent reduction in the number of teachers-in-training. This was to take effect in two stages, with a 6 per cent drop in 1933 to be followed by a further reduction of 4 per cent in 1934.[23]

The women in my survey who had sought teaching posts in the late 1930s often recalled that this had been a dispiriting task, and that they had had to make seemingly endless applications before securing a job. One woman, who graduated from Manchester in 1937 and secured her teaching diploma one year later, remembered that she had been the first of her cohort of 172 fellow students to get a teaching post, and that this was the fiftieth post she had applied for: 'Teaching posts were very scarce and some of my fellow students never got one – especially women.' Another Manchester graduate, who qualified in 1939, recalled that she 'sent over 100 applications' before securing a temporary teaching post. Yet another, who qualified from Manchester in 1937, testified to having had to make about sixty applications before being appointed to her first post in January of the year after completing her Teacher's Diploma.

Graduate women who envisaged teaching as their career set their sights, in the main, on a high school or grammar school. One of those just mentioned notes that she 'never applied for an elementary school – big difference in salary and status from grammar school, I suppose.' But many female graduates had to lower their expectations in this respect, even earlier in the 1930s. Lily Roberts, who graduated from Reading in 1930, explained that her first post had been:

> Teaching at Grimethorpe in an elementary school – 60 girls at 11+, 7 months after leaving University – couldn't get in to a secondary school – they would only take a History teacher with an Oxford or Cambridge degree – stayed 3 months – it was awful!

Another who graduated from Manchester in 1937 had hoped to teach in a grammar school but couldn't find an opening:

> My first post was a teacher of all subjects at a Church School in a rather poor neighbourhood where the girls left school at 14 years. I was teacher of the top class (ages 12–14) of mixed ability. At the start of the school year there were 53 in the class, but the numbers went down at Christmas and Easter as the girls reached their 14th birthday. There were two quiet, clever girls in the class who were a considerable help to me. They had both passed scholarships to Grammar School, but their parents had refused to let them go.

A sad reflection, indeed, on the fate of numerous intelligent girls of the period. The outbreak of war helped many of the women in my study to secure jobs vacated by men, both in teaching and elsewhere. Evidence recounted in Chapter 1 above suggests that the 'pledge' tended to be waived or overlooked by many authorities just before and during the war. Several women felt that they had 'escaped' from teaching on account of the war, although it didn't always work in this way. A graduate in history from Royal Holloway in 1939 observed that, in her case, 'Registration meant directed to teaching, the last thing I had intended to do!'

In fact around 68 per cent (341) of the women graduates in my sample found themselves teaching for part if not all of their careers. There was, after all, very little choice. The proportions varied slightly between the universities and colleges represented in the study. More than three-quarters (78.7 per cent) of the women who studied at Manchester University went into teaching at some point. The figure was lowest among the women who had been students at University College London (45 per cent). This was partly because UCL trained for librarianship and medicine, but also because of the more 'cosmopolitan' character of its student population. Several of the women who studied at UCL were the daughters of professional, middle-class men who were living and working abroad. A comparatively low proportion of Reading's women graduates in my sample (58 per cent) went into teaching: again, Reading offered routes, albeit limited, into other occupations for a few women who had chosen to study agriculture, horticulture or dairying.

Teaching, then, be it a vocation, the only realistic option or a last resort, remained the fate of the majority of women graduates in this period. The grants-in-aid of training which were made available by the Board of Education and local authorities were both an escape route and a cul-de-sac for girls from modest or poor homes who wanted to study at university. These grants undoubtedly provided opportunities for many, few of whom would have questioned the advantages – in terms of personal, social and intellectual development – that they had derived from a higher education. The great majority of the women who returned their questionnaires to me looked back on the years in which they had studied for their degrees as a time of stimulus, happiness and fulfilment. Conspicuously fewer expressed the same kind of sentiments about the 'training' element in their courses, or the Diploma in Education year, some of the women commenting that they had found this unhelpful, or even a waste of time.

Nevertheless, entering teaching as a graduate was seen as infinitely preferable to the training college route, both before and after the war. A degree lent cachet, and none of the men or women in my sample recorded any personal preference for teaching in an elementary school. One or two of my respondents mentioned that they had refused to consider training colleges because these were associated with a narrow, illiberal regime. Social class played an important part here, but so too did intellectual aspiration. The stigma which some attached to training colleges persisted after the war. Education departments might retain a low status within the universities, but as W.H.G. Armytage emphasized in his remark quoted in Chapter 1, the English civic universities had come to depend upon the supply of students financed by teacher training grants before the 1950s.[24]

Somewhat ironically, amongst my sample of women graduates were several who congratulated themselves on having 'got out of' teaching during the war. Some of them married, and stayed at home. By the 1950s and 1960s their children had grown up, and they found themselves contemplating a return to paid employment of some kind. The country needed teachers again. The (by then) Ministry of Education had set up a Working Party on the Supply of Women Teachers, which had reported in 1949,[25] emphasizing the need to take immediate steps to persuade more girl school-leavers to consider teaching as a career if an acute shortage of schoolteachers was to be averted. Schools fixed their hopes on married women returners. Mrs Garner (BSc, Royal Holloway, 1935) had previously worked as an analytical chemist. In the early 1960s:

Due to an acute shortage of science teachers in Malvern where we were living, I was sucked back into teaching, subjects such as Physics requiring massive updating.

A BSc graduate from Royal Holloway (1937) similarly began a second career as a science teacher. So even more of my sample of women graduates ended up in teaching after all.

Careers for male graduates

We have seen that a much larger proportion of men than of women went to university with focused vocational goals. This was reflected in their subject choice, which at the same time bore a clear relation to social background, as Figure 2.1 demonstrates.

Men were much more likely to study medicine than women, but the possibilities of their doing so were far greater if they came from families in social classes 1 and 2. Around 157 of the male graduates in my sample elected for medical subjects (including physiology, pharmacy and dentistry), as compared with 28 of the women. Around 90 of these 157 men ended their careers as hospital consultants, or in academic medicine, another 50 as general practitioners or as medical practitioners in the armed forces. The various branches of engineering attracted a large proportion (67) of male students, but only one intrepid woman. These subjects had a strong vocational application, of course, and sizeable numbers of men went into civil and aviation engineering, working for companies such as Metropolitan Vickers and Rolls Royce. The difference between the proportions of men and women opting for natural sciences was not so marked (133 men, 96 women). But the career paths of these graduates varied dramatically according to gender, with something like 85 of the men opting for work in industry (particularly for ICI), and industrial research in chemicals, pharmaceuticals and the gas, oil and electrical industries.[26] It is difficult to be precise about numbers or proportions because of career changes and developments over the life cycle, but it would be reasonable to suggest that something over 350 (60 per cent) of the male graduates went into subject-related occupations in medicine, engineering, natural and industrial science, broadly defined. There were 19 male graduates in theology (no women, at this time); rather more than this number became clergymen, since a number of male graduates entered the church later in their careers. Around 40 of the male graduates entered the civil service or ended up in administrative careers. Around 15 chose architecture or town planning, another 20 entered the legal profession.

Men from families lower down the social scale were more likely to opt for humanities/arts-based subjects than were men from more affluent homes: this probably reflected the fact that the former group, more dependent on Board of Education and state funding, exercised a 'freer' choice of subjects than those influenced by fathers with a clear views on labour market outcomes. It would be fair to say that those male graduates

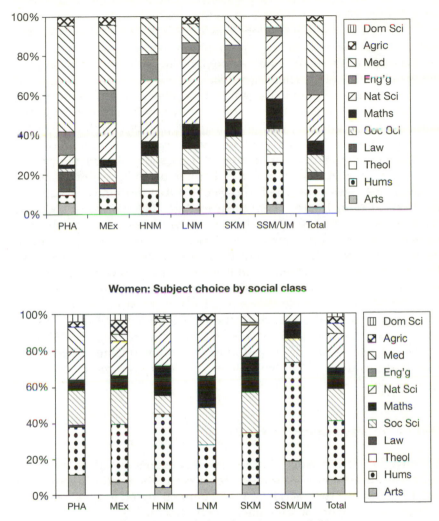

Figure 2.1 Subject choice by social class for (a) men and (b) women

in my sample who recorded that they had found some difficulty in securing employment after graduation came largely from this group, mainly
because, like the women graduates, they had found themselves frustrated
by the shortage of secondary school teaching posts in the late 1930s.
Around 120 (21 per cent) of the male graduates indicated that they had
had experience of schoolteaching at some point in their careers: less than
one-third of the proportion for women. What is particularly striking is just
how few of the men ended their careers in the position of classroom

teaching – only around 35 were in this position, and several of these were deputy headmasters. The great majority of men who embarked upon schoolteaching ended their careers as headmasters, in higher education, or in educational administration. This generation of graduates made a notable contribution to the expansion of universities in the postwar years. A total of 35 of the men in my sample became university professors, as compared with 7 of the female graduates.

For the male graduates in the study, the overall picture was one of substantial career advantage. Many recognized that their university education had played a major role in shaping their opportunities in life, recording that their degrees had furnished an indispensable foundation for their occupations and careers, or an essential passport to professional life. The son of an engraver ('intermittently unemployed'), who had studied modern languages at UCL and who went on to a distinguished career in the British Council, remembered that for him, as for many of his peers, higher education had appeared the 'key to the professions . . . a means of escape from the threat of manual or clerical drudgery'. In his retirement, he reflected that he had been much more successful, in financial terms, than his non-graduate siblings, and that without a university education his own career would have been unthinkable. Many expressed views of this kind. An impressive proportion of the men in the study achieved some form of personal and public distinction. I counted 3 MBEs, 8 CBEs and 8 OBEs in the sample, five men were knighted, and two became Fellows of the Royal Society – these were just what were notified to me. Eleven of the men sent me entries from *Who's Who*, although even more could have done so had they wished it.

Did university education pay?

To what extent did family investment in higher education 'pay'? The benefits of a university education are of course notoriously difficult to isolate and to measure, and here I shall confine myself to some fairly preliminary assessments of 'outcomes'. A whole range of factors came into play in influencing the course of the careers followed by the graduates in this sample. Some of the men suggested that their experiences of National Service during wartime were probably as important as their university training in shaping their careers, and others observed that although their degrees had secured them an entrée into certain jobs and professions, any subsequent 'successes' called for more complex explanation.

One fairly crude estimation of social mobility can be arrived at by comparing social class of origin with that of destination. We have seen that only 43 per cent of the men in my sample were from social backgrounds unambiguously classified as social classes 1 and 2. In comparison, all these male graduates, whatever their origins, ended up in jobs that would clearly locate them in these top two classes. There was only one case where I entertained some doubt about this, that of a man who had trained as a teacher but who had never managed to secure a post in a grammar school. After a spell in elementary schools he had turned to supply teaching, but had then given up and set himself up in a small laundrette which he ran until retirement at 70 years of age.

There were numerous stories of quite dramatic upward social mobility, a subject upon which many of the men in my sample chose to reflect. Dr Tearle, whose description of the hardships endured by his family in Nottingham between the wars was quoted above, mused upon the fact that, by the time that his own children reached university age, his income was such that their entitlement to grants was limited to the £50 minimum which then applied. Another man, who read physics at UCL, vividly described the poverty of his family background in the 1930s (his father, a chauffeur mechanic, had suffered a physical breakdown through overwork and anxiety, and his mother had been a seamstress who 'had turned to hairdressing'). After a very successful career in the Patent Office he reflected poignantly on the contrast between his own material circumstances in old age (he pointed out to me that as a pensioner, he was still subject to higher-rate income tax) and that of his parents. This was no isolated example by any means: many male graduates from poor and modest backgrounds undoubtedly became wealthy men, and it would be fairly safe to conclude that almost all of the men in my sample were enjoying reasonable comfort in their retirement. One indication of this was the frequency with which they emphasized the pleasure of being able to contribute to the cost of their grandchildren's careers at university.

The picture was far less clear for the women graduates, 67 per cent of whom married. Unmarried women who remained in employment were mainly in teaching, and a substantial proportion of this group remained in classroom teaching until retirement. We have seen that this was rare amongst the men: most of the men who had originally started out as class-room teachers either became headmasters, or they left schoolteaching after the war, sometimes for lectureships in higher or further education, or for posts in educational administration. In sharp contrast to the men, a number of the unmarried women graduates who had stayed in school-teaching confessed to some anxiety about their economic circumstances. One particularly moving account came from a woman who was currently living as a spinster in her late 80s in a nursing home. She had spent much of her life supporting a widowed, invalid mother, and was anxious about whether her pension would 'hold out' to cover her cost of living in a home for very much longer. Again, this was no isolated example. As graduate teachers, who had mainly (although not wholly) been employed for a large part of their careers in grammar schools, I decided to categorize single women teachers in social classes 1 and 2. Graduate teachers retained a higher social status than non-graduates, a distinction which had been particularly marked in the 1930s but persisted after the war and through the extensions of secondary education which followed the Butler Education Act. However, there is no doubt that the economic position and earning capacity of the graduate women teachers in my sample remained conspicuously below that of the men.

Where women married, there is the question of whether and to what extent their social class position should be seen as deriving from that of their husbands. The fact that women's employment histories after marriage were commonly intermittent, chequered and part-time, makes for problems. Where they were widowed early (far from uncommon in my sample, not least on account of the war), or where marriages broke up (relatively uncommon in my group), women clearly experienced dramatic changes in their social and economic position. Hardly surprisingly, those women in my sample who fell into these two groups were amongst those who were most likely to have reported that their graduate status had represented 'a lifeline'.

The question of whether a university education was 'wasted' on a woman was much debated in the 1950s, a subject which we will return to in Chapter 4. Research carried out by Judith Hubback, originally published as a Political and Economic Planning study, *Graduate Wives*, in 1954, and subsequently as a book, *Wives Who Went to College* (1957), purported to show that it wasn't.[27] These publications generated a lively and voluminous correspondence in the press at the time, much of which centred around Hubback's emphasis that the popular stereotype of the woman graduate as a bluestockinged spinster was no longer pertinent in an age when three-quarters of graduate women were likely to marry. Her finding that just over half of her sample of 1,165 married women graduates were at the time involved in full-time or part-time employment tended to get lost in the welter of jocular remarks about marriageability and horn-rimmed spectacles, much relished by the popular press of the day.[28]

Hubback's sample comprised graduate women of different age groups, whereas my own, focused on graduates mainly in their 80s, was made up of women looking back on their full life histories of family and career. Nevertheless, some of the findings are strikingly similar. The fact that two-thirds rather than three-quarters of the women in my group married probably reflects the inclusion of Royal Holloway in my sample, since (like Hubback) I found that 36 per cent of women graduates indicated that they met their marriage partners at university, and women who studied at this all-female, rather isolated college in Egham during the period had manifestly fewer chances of socializing with the opposite sex than did women in more coeducational settings (only 60 per cent of the Royal Holloway women married, and none of these met their spouse at university). A not insignificant number of women (and some of the men) judged that one of the benefits of going to university was that it had widened their choice of marriage partner. It is hard to escape surmising that for many of the women (unlike the men) this offered more opportunities for upward social mobility than those otherwise available through educational achievement in a gendered labour market.[29]

Although it is extremely difficult to summarize the information about women's employment histories that the questionnaires yielded, around 51 per cent of the women graduates appear to have stayed in paid employment more or less continuously until retirement. Prominent amongst this group were, of course, the 33 per cent of women who never married, many of those who married but remained childless, many of the women doctors, and some of the teachers. Around 36 per cent of the sample 'took time off' for childrearing, returning to employment later on a full- or part-time basis. Around 12 per cent seem to have given up paid employment permanently either on marrying, or after the birth of a first child. Less than 1 per cent of the sample indicated that they had never taken up paid employment after graduation. My questions about work elicited long and detailed answers from women, and they were commonly troubled, defensive or somewhat polemical in tone. They ranged from the explicitly feminist (like the graduate from Royal Holloway who remembered the joy of securing a job as a book reviewer, 'I was more than just a housewife and Mum. I was a real person') to its assertive antithesis ('I did *not* work ever again, thank God. Too busy looking after my family and enjoying doing so. Consider this a woman's most privileged job'). The quality of this evidence richly illustrates the controversial status of married women's work after the war and well into the second half of the twentieth century, a theme which will be returned to in Chapter 4. Very few of the graduate women, even among those who remained single and in paid work throughout their lives, replied to my questions about employment as did a large proportion of the men, namely by simply attaching CVs.

All in all, the attempt to classify women according to social class proved frustratingly difficult. If one assumes that women who remained married could be classified largely according to their husbands' occupations then almost all of this group would realistically fall into social classes 1 and 2. Ranking according to the women's occupations, where married women were involved in full- or part-time employment, would produce a very different picture, and such a picture would never come into clear focus because of the chequered quality of women's working lives, and particularly their tendency to take jobs at very different levels of status and remuneration at different points of their life-cycle. However, widowhood and old age could and did entail a dramatic downward turn in social circumstances for the women who had married: there were many stories from women who had had to take secretarial and clerical-administrative jobs well below the level for which their graduate status might be thought to have qualified them when their husbands had died. When husbands died young, and wives were left with small children to support, the situation was particularly difficult. The general pattern amongst those in my sample who had fallen into this category had been to attempt to return to teaching, falling back upon kinship networks (particularly their own mothers) for help with childcare. The complaint that few of the jobs which were available to women paid sufficient for childcare or household assistance was near universal.

It would be difficult to escape the conclusion that graduate status came nowhere as near to providing the clear economic and social advantages for women that it did for men. The majority of the women in this study indicated that they had gone to university for economic reasons: they had wanted to improve their earning capacity, and they wanted better jobs. That their vocational ambitions tended to be less specific than their male counterparts probably reflected an all-too-realistic perception of the lack of openings for women outside teaching at the time.

Questions about the ways in which and the extent to which education confers earning power have long intrigued economists. In *The Inequality of Pay* (1977), (Sir) Henry Phelps Brown emphasized that certain forms of training, such as in medicine, were a necessary condition for entry into certain occupations and could therefore be regarded as an investment (as in human capital theory).[30] However by no means all forms of higher education could be regarded as falling into this category: they might be necessary but not sufficient conditions of incremental earning capacity, and hence they might be seen, he suggested, as 'a road and not a bus'. For many of the middle-class men in this study who read medicine, science and engineering, their education was a bus. For men from families lower down the social scale it was sometimes a bus to schoolteaching, but they were soon on the road to higher things. The few women who did medicine managed to squeeze themselves on to a bus, although there was much more room on those that led to the school gates – often the end of the line. For the rest of the women, graduating from a university can probably best be seen as starting out on a long, slow road to an uncertain destination.

However, social mobility has to be seen as an inter-generational as well as a lifetime process. There is no reason for supposing that graduate mothers were any the less ambitious for their children's success than their own mothers had been for theirs. Indeed, amongst the women graduates, one of the most commonly perceived benefits of higher education was that they felt able to support and encourage the education of their own children. This idea of 'cultural capital' bequeathed to the next generation lies at the root of perceptions of the demand for higher education as spreading like a 'virus' or 'infection' in society, or as 'snowballing' through successive generations of the population.[31] One woman who graduated from Bristol before the war reflected that, 'More than anything, I feel that our degrees set the tone for the education of our children', and concluded that 'if our success is to be measured by theirs, then we did reasonably well.' There was a large amount of agreement between many of the men and women in the sample that going to university had been an immensely rich experience, and one which had opened new worlds for them, many of the men making similar observations about the ways in which their own education had impacted upon the life chances of their children and their grandchildren.

Chapter Three

 махайку

Driving ambitions

Women in pursuit of a medical education, 1890–1939

> It became tiresome to be asked by comparative strangers what made me decide to study medicine. To have enlightened them would have been to tell my life-history, my ideals and ambitions.[1]

Isabel Hutton's memoirs, *Memories of a Doctor in War and Peace*, were published in 1960. She began by recalling how many people whom she barely knew had inquired about why she had decided to become 'a lady doctor', a decision which had marked her from the beginning as something 'rare and strange'. Her somewhat flippant, stock reply to this question had often been an honest one, 'To earn my living', which frequently shocked her inquirers, who 'seemed to want to hear something more revealing, romantic or highfalutin'.[2]

The previous chapter has shown how the young women in my sample had less focused career plans than their male peers when seeking to become students at provincial universities between the wars. Most hoped that their time at university would set them on the road to gainful employment, but they found it difficult to be precise about particular jobs. Whatever their feelings about schoolteaching as a career, most women graduates ended up teaching, not least because a 'pledge' to teach had offered a source of funding where parental resources and other forms of support were limited, but also because there were few alternative forms of 'graduate' work for women.

One group, at least, however stood out from this general pattern. We have seen how women medical students often came from better-off financial backgrounds: it was not uncommon for them to have grown up in families where fathers or uncles practised medicine (this was the case for over a third of the women doctors in my sample). In this chapter I will go slightly further back in time to explore the kind of ambition that was necessary, even in such favourable circumstances, if women were to succeed in launching themselves on a medical career. I use the word 'driving' to express both the degree of ambition and also the reserves of self-discipline and self-control exhibited by many of the first generations of medical women. I will suggest later in this chapter that it is not too fanciful to suggest that *driving*, and an interest in cars, might function as a metaphor for these very qualities of ambition and control in the lives of women doctors in the early decades of the last century.

Isabel Hutton (née Emslie) qualified just before the First World War when there were only around 1,000 women on the Medical Register in Britain. Their numbers had grown steadily since women first began to qualify in the late nineteenth century: in 1891 there had been twenty-five women on the Register. The 1914–18 war encouraged many more to qualify and the numbers rose sharply, to 2,100 by 1921. By 1939/40 the figure stood at about 6,300.[3] Status and salaries varied widely amongst this group of women, as with their male colleagues: those in hospital appointments might be earning as little as £50 p.a., whereas a highly paid elite in private and consulting practice could command as much as £1,000 p.a.[4] Women were disadvantaged, in comparison with men, in all manner of ways and in all branches of the profession; but in comparison with other women workers, even in the professions more narrowly defined, their position ranked high. Feminists saw women doctors as key exponents of women's claims and capacities in the workplace and in the public sphere. It is hardly surprising that contemporaries showed interest in exploring the sources of their goals, motivations and career ambitions.

The story of women's struggle first to enter, and subsequently to gain equal opportunities with men in the medical profession in Great Britain since the 1860s and 1870s had never been a tale of steady progress. Narratives of the earlier part of this struggle frequently employed metaphors of mountain climbing or of the battlefield: one of the earliest of these narratives, written by E. Moberly Bell in 1953, was entitled *Storming the Citadel*.[5] The last three chapters of Moberly Bell's book attempted something of a balance sheet of losses and gains for medical women after the First World War. During the 1920s a number of voices were raised prophesying 'the permanent extinction of women doctors'. The market was held to be overstocked, and the opportunities for employment poor. 'Not unnaturally', according to Moberly Bell, the older London hospitals which had admitted women students for clinical instruction during the war reconsidered this policy, and decided to revert to one of only admitting men.[6] In the 1930s, the problems facing women students seeking their clinical education in London became acute. At the same time, it had to be conceded that women doctors faced continuing discrimination in obtaining post-graduate appointments and training, and many informal barriers to their employment (particularly if married) remained. Nonetheless, Moberly Bell concluded, particularly in the light of the recommendations of the Goodenough Report of 1944, which came down firmly on the side of coeducational provision in medical education (suggesting that the payment of Exchequer Grants to schools should be dependent upon their admitting students of both sexes), 'the battle is won'. The writers of the Goodenough Report had paid tribute to the pioneering and important work of the London School of Medicine for Women in establishing the claims of women in the profession, and hence it could be proclaimed that 'at the moment of victory the keys of the citadel were handed over with generosity'.[7]

This account begs a large number of questions.[8] The archives of the London (Royal Free Hospital) School of Medicine contain a valuable series of scrapbooks dating from the late nineteenth century and preserving a mass of newspaper clippings and other articles relating to all aspects of the history of women in medicine over the last hundred years or so. Even a cursory glance through these will show that this history has been punctuated by a whole series of proclamations about battles having been won, which all too frequently turned out to be rather hollow or illusory victories. Not unrepresentative, for instance, was the claim of the *Daily Telegraph* in October 1916, which declared that 'the crusade' to establish women in medicine had grown, 'gathered force, and finally secured its conquests'.[9] A spate of newspaper headlines a few years later, asking whether women doctors were a failure and commenting on 'the sex war in medicine', foster scepticism.[10] Heated controversy over the 'quotas' of women admitted to medical schools after the Second World War and over the question of whether an expensive medical training was 'wasted' on women who were likely to marry and leave the profession continued through the 1960s and beyond.

Several accounts have focused on the institutional obstacles which women had to face in their struggle to obtain medical qualification in the late Victorian years.[11] There has been much less work on the educational and life experiences of women doctors in the first half of the present century. This was a period characterized by constant change in the structure of the medical profession as a whole: some of these changes are themselves only beginning to attract the attention of historians.[12] Our ideas about 'the professions' and concepts of 'professionalism' have been closely bound up with assumptions about social class and gender, and writers such as Ann Witz and Mary Ann Elston have established the necessity of moving the historical sociology of the professions 'on to less androcentric terrain'.[13] We have accounts which have celebrated the achievements of women doctors in the two world wars,[14] but much less understanding, for instance, of the growth in opposition to the admission of women students in many of the London medical schools between the wars, which will be discussed in Chapter 7 below. Here I want to explore some of the 'driving forces' for women who sought such an education.

There is no shortage of source material. What follows is based on the reading of autobiographical accounts, biographies and my own question-naires and interviews with elderly women doctors. I have also made use of obituaries, and archival collections from the London (Royal Free Hospital) School of Medicine for Women (LSMW) and the Medical Women's Federation (MWF). All these sources raise their particular problems of methodology and interpretation, but their careful reading can illuminate precisely those issues of representation, gender and professional identity which are interesting to the historian.[15]

Women who chose medicine chose something unconventional and out of the ordinary. Many of the first generation of women who sought a medical education were inspired by a sense of 'woman's mission' to other women.[16] Dr Mary Murdoch told a cohort of new students at the LSMW in 1904 that she dreamt of a future in which it would be seen as 'one of the barbarisms of a past age that a medical man should ever have attended a woman'.[17] In this respect it might be argued that some of the pioneers had sought to expand notions of women's work rather than to challenge the idea of separate spheres. Articles on medicine as a profession for women in respectably feminine journals such as the *Lady*, the *Lady's Pictorial*, or *Beauty's Queens* tended to emphasize the femininity of 'Lady Doctors' with photographs of female practitioners wearing fashionable dress and in elegant profile.[18] Much space was devoted to detailing the womanly prettiness and cosy decor of the students' common room at the LSMW.[19] Some of this may be seen as a kind of impression management, an attempt to cosmeticize or render more palatable the essentially shocking impact of knowing that women had worked on human anatomy in the dissecting room. Students found piquancy in the contrast between the external impression of respectable femininity contrived for public appear-ances and their awareness of the real nature of some of their work. In an article published in the *Ludgate* in 1897, Arabella Kenealy mused on 'the drawing room prettiness' of the LSMW, so reassuring to visitors, but confessed:

> We always enjoyed a sort of grim and secret satisfaction, remembering that these shocked conventional persons had sat for an hour on the identical spot where a leaden table, or a tank of anatomical 'horrors' had been and would be again tomorrow. Because they thought that the flowers and baize and our best frocks 'so very nice and womanly, you know', and a 'female medical college not the least bit shocking', with the exception perhaps of 'those horrid little wretches in bottles upstairs'.[20]

However demure the appearance, the idea of young women studying medicine produced a *frisson* or even struck chill into many a bourgeois heart, and there was no getting away from the fact that many contemporaries, in Kenealy's experience, found the students 'odd', and 'inquired our ages and whether we had been baptized'.[21]

Carolyn Heilbrun has written insightfully about the forms and prescriptions of nineteenth-century women's life histories, noting that conventional narratives were characterized by safety and closure, traditionally ending with marriage.[22] It was difficult for women to find 'a tone of voice in which to speak with authority',[23] and to confess to any desire for power and control over their own lives. Women who sought to study medicine certainly had to admit to a desire for knowledge, and for power and control over their lives, and in doing so they were bound to find themselves in protest against what Nancy Miller has termed 'the available fiction of female becoming'.[24] These women had to invent new plots and new narratives in which the quest for learning and meaningful work would assume a central role; they had to get into the driving seat.

Given the obstacles that had to be faced, the fact that women doctors often told their stories in terms of having received a calling or having been possessed by a mission is scarcely surprising. To have felt possessed by forces outside one's control was probably easier than owning up to one's own, 'unfeminine' ambition. Ida Mann entitled her autobiography *The Chase*, confessing to a sense of always having responded to such, whether to her familiar spirit, or to 'a veiled and mysterious It (or Id)', adding 'I do not know whether it chases me or I pursue it.'[25]

Gladys Wauchope, fond of hunting in her youth, tells her readers:

> One night the thought flashed upon me: 'I could do this medical work.' It was as though a call came, and I answered: 'Here I am, send me.' Since then I have been like a horse ridden in blinkers, and seeing only straight in front.[26]

These and many similar accounts share the features of a literary genre, that of the quest or the folk-fairy tale. The accounts generally feature a time in youth when the heroine finds herself beset with doubts, aimlessness and indecision. There follows a key moment of revelation, an awareness of a call, or a crucial turning point when the decision is made to take up medicine. The narrative then moves on to describe a series of trials, checks, hurdles and difficulties which the heroine overcomes with persistence and fortitude. She is sustained in her quest by helpers, fairy godmothers and the interpretation of omens or possession of a talisman with magical or mystic powers.[27]

We know that the life of a middle-class 'daughter at home' could generate a strong sense of frustration in intelligent girls, and the personal histories of women doctors show many examples of this.[28] Mary Murdoch's biographer presents her subject as having been liberated from her aimlessness by her mother's death, which forced her to consider ways of earning her own living. Before this happened she had used her time for music, fishing and dancing, but 'her spirit was chafing at the limitations of her home life and at the small amusements of the country town' and she later regarded these as 'wasted years'.[29] Octavia Wilberforce occupied her early years in rose-growing, housekeeping and golf, bickering with her mother and trying to encapsulate her feelings about 'the uselessness of my life' in verse.[30] Gladys Wauchope's life had centred on fox-hunting. Her only formal tasks, she tells us, 'were to feed the five dogs, to do the flowers, and to entertain our guests'.[31] Frances Kenyon 'put up her hair' in 1912 and 'came out' at the Oswestry Ball. She found herself in a state where she was

> unsure of myself, unsure of everything. I was drifting along in a kind of half-life, more and more withdrawn and introverted.[32]

Frances had had vague ideas about becoming a nurse, but 'did nothing to prepare myself for it . . . I seemed to have no will, and no interest. I just escaped through music . . . '[33]

Ida Mann's experience was rather different from that of Murdoch, Wilberforce, Wauchope and Kenyon in that, although she had grown up in a middle-class family, her father had not been rich enough to contemplate keeping her as 'a daughter at home'. He had sent her to Clarke's Business College with a view to her working as a clerk in the Civil Service. Ida found her boring, routine work in the Post Office Savings Bank intolerable and feared that she would go insane: 'I once saw a young woman go mad at her desk. She was removed and never seen again.' She tells us that she would lock herself in the lavatory and howl and weep and bite her wrists in 'bursts of soundless screaming'.[34]

All these writers go on to decide a turning point, or a key moment of revelation when their destinies clarified. For Octavia Wilberforce this moment came in a solitary reverie in a beechwood:

> Now the time had come when I felt compelled to decide my future: was I born to be a bond slave to family life forever? . . . I left the beechwood with an iron determination not to be lazy or cowardly but to carve out my own career and study Medicine, however hard it might be.[35]

For Ida Mann a visit to the London Hospital in Whitechapel proved auspicious. She went with a party of girls from the office who had made a collection in aid of hospital funds, and found herself fascinated, and wanting more knowledge.[36] A prosaic enough experience, one might think, but the form and the language employed in describing and assessing the experience is that of Revelation and mystical Conversion. 'Suddenly everything changed', and Ida found herself 'reborn'.[37] She describes having had a dream in which she found herself in a dark room, with a longing to die, and was confronted by two doors. One led to death, the other led out to bright sunshine and a blue sky. She took the second door, and awoke. After the visit to Whitechapel 'my yearning for the life of a medical student became almost a physical pain'.

> I had no vision of myself as a ministering angel, or even as a practising doctor. I saw only the endless enchanted avenue of ever-expanding knowledge down which one sped, rejoicing, to the ultimate reaches of speculation and discovery. I went to bed early and fell at once into a terrifying trance in which I saw what lay before me, inescapable and foreordained.[38]

The account is nothing if not dramatic. Ida tells us that she 'sweated with terror' but found 'unutterable delight' in the idea of a mystical surrender: she had chosen the sunlit door.

> Had I not written in childhood, 'I may not stoop to tend the sacred hearth flame, for I must climb alone to light a star.'[39]

Sunlit door or stair to the stars, Ida Mann eventually distinguished herself as the first woman professor in the University of Oxford (1944). In the meantime, she set off to enrol at the London School of Medicine for Women, wearing 'some sensible Saxone shoes'.[40]

Sensible shoes were a minimal requirement on the journey that lay ahead. Once having decided to embark on a medical career, the early generation of women doctors faced all manner of obstacles and trials. Isabel Hutton later reflected:

> How any of us had the courage to enter medicine at such a time is a mystery to me. We still studied under a good many disadvantages and observed that the woman doctor had to put up with very cavalier treatment by their male colleagues, who criticised, patronised or were even blatantly rude to them.[41]

As a young girl, she remembers, she had been fired with faith and optimism, never considering 'failure or the crossing of rickety bridges until I knew the way to skip lightly over them'.[42] Courage and faith were essential, as were hard work and a commitment to mastering subjects which the education of many girls had left unfamiliar or even untouched. Mary

Murdoch laboured alone in London lodgings, stinting on food and sleep until her health broke down, in order to prepare herself for preliminary study at the LSMW.[43] Frances Kenyon remembered feeling as if 'a great sea of incomprehensible physics and mathematics' lay between her and her goal to study medicine.[44] Octavia Wilberforce's trials seemed never-ending, as she struggled with parental opposition, the threat of disinheritance, failure after failure in the London University matriculation examination, followed by failure in anatomy and surgery at the LSMW.[45] Women in this generation were less likely to have benefited from a solid secondary education than those who followed, and had frequently to seek out private tuition or resort to evening classes to acquire basic competence in maths and science. Janet Vaughan took the Oxford entrance examinations three times before she managed to get in:

> First I failed in every single subject, then I passed in Latin Grammar and Arithmetic, and then my mother brought me up for the third time and we stayed at the Mitre and had a lot to drink – and for some reason I got through! I still wonder if they didn't mix my papers up with someone else's . . . [46]

She still found that she had much catching up to do in physics and chemistry, since all she had done was 'a little ladylike botany' at school.[47] Kathleen Norton had received a good training in classics at Clapham High School, but recalls that her teachers had to study alongside her when she announced that she would need to learn science in order to do medicine. She remembered that the 'poor wretched biology mistress' had considerable trouble in steeling herself to kill a frog.[48] Even in the interwar period several of my interviewees described how they had had to attend local boys' schools for basic instruction in science. Rosaline Howat, whose convent education had left her ignorant of chemistry, had to study at a preparatory school for Air Force Cadets in Blackpool before she could embark upon medical training at Manchester University; the science, she remembered, 'was like Black Magic to me'.[49] Two more of the women who qualified in medicine from Manchester in my questionnaire sample, both of whom had previously attended well-established girls' high schools, recorded that they had had to resort to 'Grimes College' and extra private tuition in order to get to grips with the chemistry, physics and mechanics necessary for entry.

Once having mastered the necessary science, the student moved on to anatomy, physiology, pharmacology and then the hospital-based, clinical part of her training. A moment of particular significance came when entering the Dissecting Room, and many accounts focus on this ordeal or heavily charged stage in the quest, a crucial *rite de passage*. One of my respondents covered her eyes and lapsed into silence when I asked her about this moment: it was, she said, too horrible for her to recall in any detail. Most were more blasée. Frances Kenyon described how a friend had urged her down to the Dissecting Room in the basement at King's,

> long before I was officially supposed to go. I got a pleasant thrill of horror at the boxes of dried up heads and arms and legs, out of which students fished their own bits each day to continue their dissection of muscles, nerves and other marvels of the human body. These had been preserved in formalin, and weren't at all human . . . [50]

Ida Mann commented that 'One's first corpse (subject) is always a bit of a nauseating shock.'[51] She records that she had been suffering from a recurrent nightmare in which a triangle of light was surrounded by meaningless dark forms

> One foggy evening in the Common Room, a second year student was lording it over us freshers. 'Why', she said, 'you children don't know what you're in for. Anyone game enough to come with me to the dissecting room?' I jumped up with a few others. We had never penetrated to the top of the building where anatomy was taught, and we felt a slight dread . . . [52]

Suddenly the meaning of her disturbing dream became clear:

> A large green door opened and I stopped dumbfounded. The London fog filled the long room. There was the triangle of luminous mist (the light from a shaded light-bulb hanging over a narrow zinc-topped table) of my recurrent dream. The light fell on the brown and twisted shapes which now resolved themselves into the formalinized bones and muscles of legs and arms and dried up clutching fingers.[53]

The shock left her 'rigid, silent and exulting', and she was never again to experience that particular dream.

Trials, tribulations and the crossing of rickety bridges in folk or fairy tales often came in threes, and this is often the case, it seems, in the narratives we are discussing. Janet Vaughan failed her Oxford entrance examinations twice, but was lucky the third time. Isabel Hutton considered herself 'wedded to her profession'. Thrice-tempted by love, she eventually succumbed to the marriage which would inevitably threaten her career. Octavia Wilberforce was disinherited by her father. She had failed her matriculation examination three times, and could not see how she would find the money to continue her attempts. Her friends the Buxtons offered to support her financially for three years. After that, Elizabeth Robins would play the role of 'fairy godmother' and offered the money to see her friend through. Omens and talismans played their part in sustaining our heroines in their quests. Isabel Hutton devotes a whole chapter in her autobiography to describing how, beset by doubts, she mused on the difficulties of studying medicine in a churchyard near her home in the Ochils. Sandy the gravedigger was busy about his work, and they talked of her plans to become a 'lady doctor'. He presented her with a skull, wrapped in a 'round ball of earth upon which great earthworms were writhing inquisitively'.[54] She washed the skull in a stream, superstitiously fearing to take it home. There was a violent storm that night, but next morning she found the skull where she had left it:

> there was my warrior safely cradled between the two rocks, the stream eddying round him; washed clean of every impurity, he looked grateful and seemed to smile good morning to me . . .[55]

She kept the skull with her over the years that followed, but towards the end of her life felt a mission to return him to his native soil.

Even the intrepid Ida Mann had recourse to her mystical signs, shrines and portents. When sitting examinations in South Kensington, she tells us,

> between papers I wandered into the Victoria and Albert Museum to do *puja* to the loveliest thing I could find. It was a glorious red lacquer vase about four feet high. I was to go and look at its serene and intricate beauty during each exam of the six and a half years ahead of me. It never failed me.[56]

However much emphasis on compassion, or on 'woman's mission' to other women, the study and practice of medicine was never easy to reconcile with late Victorian or Edwardian notions of femininity. There were some valiant attempts at reconciliation, more successful perhaps in novels of the period than in autobiographical writing or biography.[57] Biographers tried hard to represent their subjects as 'truly womanly' at heart. Mary Murdoch of Hull, for instance, was a tough, feminist practitioner who drove like a demon and relished many a political battle with public dignataries in her town. Yet Hope Malleson's biography of her struggles to emphasize her femininity: 'Our Lady Murdoch', 'radiant', of 'sunny disposition', loved by children and the poor. Clearly there is a tension here, and it is interesting to learn that Murdoch herself mused on the nature of similar tensions after reading a biography of Florence Nightingale. Writing to a friend in 1913 she pointed out that Nightingale had been 'no milk-and-water saint, but full of fire and forceful sayings', with a 'caustic pen', 'masterful in action', and an extremely powerful personality.[58] A similar awareness of the tensions involved in representing women as both feminine and powerful was apparent in a review which Lord Riddell wrote of Mary Scharlieb's autobiography in 1924. 'The pages breathe refinement', he wrote, and 'I almost sense the lavender and see the old lace', and yet 'the book is written by a woman of action, whose life has been a constant struggle and who has done great things.'[59]

Some of the life histories of women doctors tackled the problem head on. Ida Mann tells us that as a child, she had passionately wished to be a boy. She had been jealous of her brother Arthur, with whom she had shared a fantasy world based on their reading of Rider Haggard and the *Boy's Own Paper*. Her favourite stories were all about 'girls masquerading as boys so as to be able to enjoy adventure'.[60] Elizabeth Bryson described having felt very troubled as a girl: 'There was something which had to be faced', and she had struggled to understand what it was:

> I remember when I was three and had to choose between curls and trousers. I wanted both but gave up the trousers. Curls were becoming important again. I was nineteen. I still wanted both. And quite suddenly, it seemed, I knew that never again would my road of desire be simple and clear and straight.[61]

A sense of unease about gender is present in almost all the accounts of women doctors' lives. This could sometimes run very deep, particularly when sexual identity or affiliation seem to have been involved. Octavia Wilberforce found herself 'revolted' by an early proposal of marriage, the very physicality of it made her 'shudder'. She seems to have equated at least heterosexual physicality with a lower kind of animal passion and repeatedly emphasized her desire 'to keep free from being governed by my body', in effect, to transcend sex.[62]

The question of sexual preference is complex: we know that 'loving friendships' (such as Octavia Wilberforce's with Elizabeth Robins), cohabitation and 'Boston marriages' were fairly common in female medical circles, but life histories, whether autobiographical or biographical, are inevitably reticent or discreet. Christine Murrell, the first woman to be elected to the Council of the British Medical Association (in 1924) and to the General Medical Council (1933) lived and shared a practice with another woman doctor, Honor Bone, for around thirty years. Later the living arrangement expanded to include a third woman, Marie Lawson. Murrell's biographer, Christopher St John (herself a lesbian) had been chosen by Honor Bone, and the book was dedicated to both Bone and Lawson.[63] As Emily Hamer has observed, St John had 'a fine line to tread' between commemorating Murrell's achievements and somehow dealing with her sexuality and attachments.[64] 'Public' and 'private' were difficult to merge, and these difficulties are all too apparent in the text. Murrell is described as a 'virile woman' with a 'feminine' preference for colour and style in dress. We are told, in a particularly tortured passage, that she was not interested in sex:

She was not the kind of woman who has a natural chemical affinity with a man. It was possible that she was sexually underdeveloped or as I prefer to put it, too highly developed as a human being with a nice balance of male and female attributes and qualities, to be strongly sexed. But I think that this was rather a fortuitous help to a celibacy that she felt incumbent on her than its cause.[65]

Lord Riddell's biography of Louisa Aldrich-Blake exhibits similar problems in dealing with the gender and sexuality of his subject.[66] He emphasizes the 'masculinity' of her temperament and person. We learn that Louisa was called 'Harry' at school (Cheltenham Ladies' College), that she was known for her 'gentlemanly appearance' and that she excelled at boxing and cricket.[67] There is a somewhat desperate attempt to soften this as we are reassured that Louisa remained 'distinctly feminine' in her family relationships.[68] We are next told that Louisa had once confided to the author that had she not been able to build a career in medicine she would have liked to turn her hand to building roads.[69] Louisa was 'no champion of women', and she was 'admired, respected and feared' by men. She never had a love affair, seemingly, according to her biographer. Although she lived in the same house as her friend, Rosamond Wigram, they each of them 'went their own way'. In spite of her 'virile personality', we are assured that Louisa 'never aped the man, and never wished to be regarded as mannish. Indeed, she strongly objected to mannish women.'[70] Riddell's account, so problematic about gender, is a rich source for historical interpretation.

These texts are particularly troubled, but even where the subject was irreproachably heterosexual in inclination tensions around gender were inescapable. This can be illustrated with reference to two particular areas of 'feminine deportment', those of demeanour and dress. Hope Malleson tells us that as a student Mary Murdoch affected 'a severe style of dress and the plainest of hats', and this strategy of dressing to underplay 'femininity' and to signify serious purpose was one generally employed by women medical students at the time.[71] Elizabeth Bryson remembered that as a senior student in Dundee she had been asked to counsel a newcomer who was offending propriety 'by wearing her towsy hair adorned with splashes of pink and lavender ribbon'. It had been 'a ticklish task', and she observes that the student in question had married as soon as she had qualified, 'which left some of us thinking'.[72] Isabel Hutton sensed a double bind implicit in the dress codes amongst her peer group:

the plain dowdy women were on the whole preferred, for the men could then hoot with laughter and label them all as freaks, jokes or monsters. In fact, it was apparently impossible to be just an ordinary young woman. It was clear that the mannish suits and hob-nailed boots

71

were less frowned upon than lace on the petticoat. The men seemed surprised and annoyed that the attractive women could stay the course.[73]

Gladys Wauchope remembered that women studying at the London Hospital had been told what to wear: in order not to look frivolous 'it was decreed that we should wear three-quarter-length holland jackets of a severe style with large pockets'.[74] She recalled how Lord Knutsford (the Chairman of the Hospital) had expressed particular anxiety about the appearance of one good-looking student, and urged Wauchope 'not to let her wear white shoes'.[75]

Demeanour was equally important: it was essential for women to keep a low profile. Student culture in the medical schools was traditionally characterized by rowdiness rather than restraint. Christopher St John tells us that Christine Murrell kept a careful watch on her behaviour at the Royal Free, but was still involved in 'rags' of a kind.[76] Ida Mann, at St Mary's Hospital Medical School, found it difficult to restrain her exuberance. She remembered clambering over car-bonnets with the other students, collecting money on 'rag' days: 'It was grand', but the authorities were somewhat concerned.[77]

It has sometimes been argued that the rowdy exuberance of medical students represents a form of defensiveness, a response to the stresses and difficulties inherent in the nature of their tasks. This is hinted at in another of Ida Mann's descriptions, again of her work in the inner sanctum of the Dissecting Room:

> Our reorientation towards death and decay affected us in strange ways. We used to picnic in the Bone Room and used the orbits of an old skull as salt-cellars. One South African got some biltong from home and would sit perched on her dissecting stool gnawing at it while poking about among her subject's brown muscles which it so resembled. We made the most ribald jokes. We took pieces of skin, especially if tattooed, and stretched and dried them and tried to cover note-books with them, but this was seldom a success. We worked like mad, and to me the atmosphere of a dissecting room is the jolliest, funniest and most comradely of any I can think of.[78]

This is a difficult passage: there is a marked transition in tone here, from Rider Haggard, perhaps to Angela Brazil. Black humour is probably one of the commonest defences against or ways of coping with the taboos and violations of the Dissecting Room: easier to permit to men than to women at this time. In 1922 the London Hospital Medical College, which had first admitted women students during the war (in 1918) threw them out again.

One of the reasons given for the decision (and much debated in the newspapers of the day) was that coeducation in medicine made girls 'hoydenish'. Charles Pring, writing in *The Times* in 1922, elaborated this argument:

> the objection is that when young women consort with young men under conditions where ordinary delicacy and modesty are necessarily absent, the normal standard of conduct is lowered. No matter how choice the demeanour and character of the feminine neophyte, after a few months of the students' common room she becomes coarse, immodest and vulgar.[79]

Lord Knutsford disputed Pring's contentions, whilst conceding that it was 'very disagreeable and sometimes impossible' to teach 'certain matters' to a mixed class, and that there were 'reasons for this which are unprintable'.[80] Ida Mann studied at St Mary's, not at the London, and her autobiography was written in her old age. It was just as well that her account was not published between the wars, when normative prescriptions about feminine demeanour were so much at stake.

The First World War served as a catalyst for many women who have recorded that its events crystallized their own resolve and softened any parental opposition to the idea of medicine as suitable work for girls. Both Wauchope and Kenyon mention this. Kenyon took up nursing, initially, but was persuaded by one of her patients, a miner from Bolton, that she should train as a doctor when the war ended. Kathleen Norton, who studied at Oxford and St Mary's between 1918 and 1924, emphasized that her father, himself a doctor, had considered medicine 'too hard' for his daughter initially, but that he had completely changed his attitude during the war.[81] Women doctors received 'a good press' between 1916 and 1918, their efforts being applauded as part of the war effort, and a spate of articles drew attention to the field of widening opportunity that was believed to lie before them. The *Daily Mail* carried a headline 'Women doctors making good: a promising career', suggesting that an investment of £1,000 in training was well worthwhile.[82] Women who trained after 1920 or so appear less likely to have described their decision to study medicine in terms of a 'flash of revelation' or a conversion experience, and more in terms of having decided upon a sensible career alternative to nursing or teaching.

This was before, or in spite of, the 'backlash' of the interwar years, fuelled by fears of overcrowding in the profession. Such events left those women still studying or working in those schools and hospitals in a highly embarrassing and difficult position, as described by Wauchope, Wilberforce and Mann. When Wauchope was appointed to a house position at the London in 1922, the male residents complained and threatened their resignation.[83] Securing house officerships in leading hospitals was a step of key importance on the ladder to professional success in medicine. Such appointments were both highly competitive and barely remunerated during the period we are discussing. Hostility against women students at University College, the London and St Mary's Hospital Medical Schools was particularly focused on opposition to the idea of women in house appointments. The indignity of having to compete against women in this 'bottleneck' on the route to promotion would be removed if women were denied access to the schools in the first place.

Both Ida Mann and Kathleen Norton described the atmosphere at St Mary's in the 1920s as having become increasingly fraught and uncomfortable. In 1924 a petition signed by ninety-six men submitted that the presence of women students had led to bickering and bad feeling, and had ruined the School's reputation in rugby and athletics: the Board of Management were asked to call an end to coeducation.[84] Kathleen Norton described how male students at St Mary's resorted to a series of pranks and depredations on the women's common room.[85] Ida Mann was awarded a research studentship in 1924, officially to work in the Institute of Pathology under Sir Almroth Wright. Almroth Wright was an arch-misogynist, and she was made to understand that the award was conditional on her staying 'incommunicado' in the Anatomy Department at St Mary's, and never setting foot in 'the hallowed male territories of the Institute itself'.[86] These were years in which a number of women were driven to seek legal advice in order to clarify their situation as students in London medical schools, in terms of whether these institutions were bound to afford them facilities to complete their training.[87] These controversies over women's access to medical education exemplify what some historians have recently seen as a 'crisis in masculinity' in the interwar years.[88] A culture of masculinity which took shape and hardened, based on public school values, rugby and athleticism, and buttressed by freemasonry,[89] operated to the disadvantage of women, as we shall see further in Chapter 7 below.

Barriers, hurdles and oppositions were there in plenty, and any woman keen to study medicine still needed courage and a sturdy ambition. Ida Mann had both of these qualities in abundance. On one occasion she quailed. As a young house surgeon, she had been invited by her chief, Mr Frank Jules, to attend a dinner, 'I think of the Ophthalmological Society'. She found herself the only female guest, and both she and her host were covered with confusion:

> I felt overwhelmed (for the only time) by the all-pervading maleness and saw for once the enormity of my presumptuous ambition. But the horror had faded by the next day and I was not worried. I was just going to do all the proper things and I would inevitably get the appointments I wanted. Be damned to sex.[90]

Few women were as intrepid as Mann, but a 'feminine' temperament was no obvious advantage when conventions had to be kicked aside, or resolutely disregarded. 'Prohibitions only acted on her as incentives', wrote Hope Malleson of the young Mary Murdoch.[91] Murdoch's friend, Louisa Martindale, judged that few things were more important in the equipment of a female doctor than the possession of strong nerves.[92] Murdoch was the first woman in Hull to own and drive her own motor vehicle, and according to her friends, 'the world's worst driver', but she had nerves of steel. Louisa Martindale recalls how on one occasion,

> When she and I were ascending the hill up to Howarth, she got confused with the gears, the car slid backwards and, gathering speed, overturned at the bottom and flung us out. The petrol caught fire and it took six men to set the car on the road again. I was rather dazed and forgot to admire the scenery. 'Oh well, if you can't appreciate the scenery I shan't bring you out another time', she remarked.[93]

Cars, like clothes, carried symbolic attributes, and when Mary died in 1916, 'the deceased doctor's motor car . . . almost hidden in floral tributes', preceded the hearse in an elaborate funeral procession.[94]

Stories about Mary Murdoch's hair-raising adventures as a driver were legion. It is interesting that so many of the telling anecdotes which appear in the life histories of women doctors of this period focus on their driving, their love of powerful cars, and their fearlessness when they met with accidents or their cars came off the road. In these stories, driving seems to serve as a metaphor connected with a willingness to take risks, and the enjoyment of power and control. Gladys Wauchope waxed nostalgic about her first car, a 'round-nosed Morris Cowley' which was nicknamed Rosey, but reserved her real passion for the Talbot which followed it, and 'a great 30 h.p. Ford Mercury' which she drove for ten years after the Second World War: 'What power! It seemed to float on air.'[95] Wauchope's partner, Dr Florence Edmonds, had an Armstrong Siddeley, immaculately maintained by a chauffeur. Two intrepid women doctors, Janet Vaughan and Charlotte Naish, won the Ladies' Cup in the 1932 Monte Carlo Rally, in spite of losing an hour's time when they stopped to attend to the victims of a road accident.[96] Janet Vaughan acquired a reputation as an indomitable rally driver who 'crashed more times than she arrived, but was always undaunted'.[97] This tradition of women doctors with driving ambitions persisted. Professor Mary Pickford, a respected endocrinologist who died on her 100th birthday in 2002, was fondly remembered in an obituary as having driven a 1933 Rover saloon with non-functional shock absorbers over the cobbled streets of Edinburgh in the 1950s.[98] Josephine Barnes, as President-Elect of the Medical Women's Federation in 1966, was introduced as 'a perfectionist', who enjoyed 'good food, good wine, travel and fast cars'.[99]

Of all the qualities that were likely to jar with contemporary norms and conventions of femininity, perhaps the most discordant was the admission of a will to power, or the desire to take control. Louisa Aldrich-Blake (a skilled mechanic, whose motor car was ever 'a great joy'[100]) was never a communicative woman. Octavia Wilberforce related how on one occasion she had ventured to tease her Dean by asking her whether she thought women doctors needed more than a touch of the autocrat in their make-up if they were to achieve success. Aldrich-Blake allegedly 'grunted approval', and beamed. Women seeking power usually had to get it 'by mean ways', she suggested, 'but as a doctor you can be quite honest and open in your commanding'.[101]

A narrative of quest may end with arrival, and in a romance, folk- or fairy-tale struggle may be rewarded with success or a happy ending. How did these women who sought to study medicine experience their success in their quest or project to become qualified, and how was the moment represented in their own narratives or those constructed by biographers? For many of the earlier generation, the moment of triumph or celebration was quickly superseded by an awareness of further difficulties to be faced: opportunities for women were few and far between. Elizabeth Bryson and her friends had celebrated their graduation by visiting a clairvoyant.[102] Elizabeth had wanted to specialize in gynaecology but found herself 'up against a blank wall' when she sought the hospital experience which would be needed if she were to pursue this ambition. She embarked on research instead, graduating MD in 1907, but still found that salaried positions in hospitals were closed to her on account of her sex. 'What was the prospect before me?' she asked herself, ruefully, 'It appeared to be "the dawn of nothing".'[103] Her narrative ends at this point. Faced by the conspicuous lack of openings for women doctors at home, she applied for, and decided to take up, an assistant post in general practice in New Zealand.

A similar sense of anticlimax had accompanied Isabel Emslie's graduation. Her male colleagues, she recalled, experienced little difficulty in obtaining posts. Isabel, and those of her female contemporaries who did not particularly want to take up medical missionary work abroad, found that there were only a handful of posts open to them, most of these unpaid apart from 'one or two assistantships in big general practices in English industrial towns'. She found herself wondering why any of them had ever embarked 'upon such a hungry sea?'[104] The women had no choice other than to grasp at whatever posts were available to them, paid or unpaid, to mark time, and to fend off despair, in the hope that something would eventually come along.

As I have emphasized above, it was war that opened up opportunities for many of the first generation of medical women. In most of the earliest accounts, and in many of the narratives of the women who trained after them, there is a break in the story after graduation. The clear path of personal ambition may have led to a certain point, but the vagaries of chance and fortune then began to cloud horizons. The outlook for women seeking clinical experience in London, in particular, looked in many ways bleaker in the late 1920s and in the 1930s than it had appeared in 1918.[105] Even those women who had distinguished themselves as students frequently found difficulty in obtaining hospital appointments or lucrative positions in general practice. The search for a meaningful career, for some women doctors, assumed the status of another quest. For many, especially for those in the early generation who (like Isabel Emslie) chose to marry, the way forward was never clear. Life histories, unlike folk stories or fairy-tales, have no simple pattern.

Women who qualified in the 1930s faced many of the difficulties which had been experienced by their predecessors. As students, they were acutely conscious of representing a conspicuous minority in the highly masculine environment of the medical schools. Some women questioned the nature of this environment. The first issue of the Liverpool Medical Students' Debating Society newspaper, *Sphincter*, published in 1937, carried a letter from a woman student calling herself 'Jane Notsoplain', contending that the medical school was still 'run on lines suitable for, and in fact designed for men' which rendered life trying for the women, and submitting that the practice of medicine would benefit from 'a less trousered outlook'.[106] Statistics published by the University Grants Committee show that there were 130 women studying medicine in Liverpool on the eve of the Second World War, and 733 men. However, replies to Jane's letter showed that not all women sympathized with her viewpoint. Some of the women doctors who completed questionnaires in my study took pains to emphasize that they had never encountered any difficulty on account of sex. A woman who graduated from Manchester in 1939 insisted that 'There was *no* discrimination against women in Medicine at M/c Medical School and *no* discrimination in General Practice, either.' Similarly, a woman who qualified in Bristol in 1940 emphasized that 'There was really no sex dis-crimination in medicine in the 1930s student life in Bristol, though there were always a few men with a maddening attitude to women.' But there were others who offered sharply different perspectives, such as a con-sultant ophthalmologist who had also qualified in Manchester in the 1930s who recorded that she had been '*very much* discriminated against on account of being a woman'. Dr Celia Westropp, who went from Oxford to King's College Hospital in London for her clinical training, recalled that in 1938 there were still consultants who obdurately refused to teach any women students. The interpretation of memories of discrimination or perceptions of inequality can be a complex area for the historian.[107] The Second World War, like its predecessor, brought wider opportunities for women medical practitioners, as did the coming of the National Health Service thereafter.[108] But the gendered nature of experience and careers in medicine remained an issue. By the end of the century, proportions of female students had overtaken men in the medical schools, giving rise to a new set of concerns around older issues: were women driving men out of the profession?

Chapter Four

ا۵

Wasted investments and blocked ambitions?

Women graduates in the postwar world

Sinks, waste and drains

In the early 1950s, Judith Hubback, a graduate of Cambridge University and herself married with young children, set out to study 'the problem' of graduate wives and mothers. She admitted that the underlying assumption on which she based her enquiry was that 'an entirely domestic existence' was 'too limited for a highly educated woman'.[1] In 1953 she distributed some 2,000 questionnaires to married women graduates from a number of British universities, supplementing her sample with a 'control group' of 420 non-graduate wives. The questionnaire probed women's attitudes to work, career ambitions, domesticity and family life. Underlying Hubback's investigation was the theme of *waste*: was the housebound female graduate wasting her expensive higher education? Was the country as a whole wasting its resources by failing to exploit reserves of educated womanpower?[2]

Hubback saw her study as sharply relevant to contemporary debate over the aims and purposes of educating women. Such debates had been going on for many decades, of course, and indeed they had regularly accompanied women's entry into higher education. They were to prove particularly controversial in the postwar world, not only in this country but also abroad.[3] The frustrations of the housebound graduate mother were to become something of a *leitmotif* of the 1950s and early 1960s. They were most memorably expressed by Betty Friedan, whose representation and analysis of 'the problem that has no name', the 'deep malaise which gnawed at the happiness of so many American housewives' was published as *The Feminine Mystique* in 1963. Alongside Simone de Beauvoir's *Le Deuxième Sexe*, this became one of the key texts associated with the rise of 'second wave' feminism.[4]

The evidence of frustrated ambitions amongst postwar women graduates was piling up well before the publication of *The Feminine Mystique*. Hubback referred to 'the grit of discontent' which was so abundantly evident amongst educated women.[5] One of her respondents, a 33-year-old mother whose daughters were setting their sights on medicine and school-teaching wrote in 'rueful, almost cynical' tones wondering whether 'their careers, like my own, will end at the kitchen sink!'[6] Another respondent commented that 'Unfortunately, a university training appears to be running down the drain in the case of nine out of ten married women who are so often unable to make use of it and spend their time regretting the fact.'[7]

Publication of the findings of Hubback's study, initially in the form of a report for Political and Economic Planning entitled *Graduate Wives* in 1954,[8] then as a book, *Wives Who Went to College*, in 1957, fuelled controversy which was already appearing, fairly regularly, in the press. 'Is a bride (BA) wasting a degree?' asked the *News Chronicle* in April 1954.[9] The mother of an Oxford graduate submitted that her daughter's three years at university had cost them over £1,600: now she was marrying and throwing it all away. Her advice to other parents of attractive 18-year-old girls was to set them following a good secretarial course – at something like £90 per annum – rather than going to the expense of higher education. An avalanche of letters, both protesting against and sympathizing with this viewpoint followed.[10] Hubback's own collection of press cuttings (responding to her work and on related themes) shows that the argument remained in the public eye for most of the 1950s.[11] In an article which appeared under the title of 'Labour lost by love' in *The Economist* in June 1954, an anonymous reviewer of Judith Hubback's work concluded that:

> From the economic point of view, money spent on a girl's education is a long-term investment, and the material dividends are often paid in invisible ways, and may, it must be faced, be very small. But that is no argument against university education for women. Quite apart from the point that she *may* need a career, it is the undeniable human right of the able girl that her mind should have the opportunity to develop no less than that of the able boy.[12]

Then, at the end of the decade, controversy flared up yet again. In 1958 *The Times* had published an appeal for funds from the principals of the Oxford women's colleges, keen to draw public attention to the need to expand provision for female undergraduates in the university.[13] Their appeal met with a very mixed response. Some unsympathetic male respondents were derisive. There was intense competition for university places, conceded one such correspondent; but to allocate places to women whose concern for 'husband-hunting' outweighed their commitment to a serious long-term career was indefensible.[14] Letters from Keith Thomas, Jenifer

Hart and others strongly protested against this point of view.[15] Less than two years later, *The Guardian* published a letter from an Oxford graduate, Lois Mitchison, contending that the cost of educating women to degree level was difficult to defend, since most graduate women now married young, and 'only the very exceptional woman' was going to continue to work full time outside the home.[16] Graduate women were plagued by guilt, she submitted, and this guilt was a product of unreasonable expectations fostered by a highly academic training. It was time to review the kind of education offered to girls.

Families and careers were not always compatible, M J Jacks, a former Director of Oxford University's Department of Education, asserted that girls were marrying and becoming mothers at an earlier age than ever before, and this alone suggested the need to rethink the shape of their education.[17] Lois's mother, Naomi Mitchison, weighed in to argue against her daughter's viewpoint: if girls were denied access to a university education, she suggested, 'they will long for it'; as for domesticity, she herself saw no particular virtue 'in washing nappies, or even blocking up drains with disposables'.[18] Others maintained that the hyper 'intellectuality' of the graduate wife blinded her to 'the sensuous pleasures' of jam-making and furniture polish, insisting that the worst standards of cooking were always to be found in bookish homes.[19]

Was it easier 'to face the well-stocked sink with a well-stocked mind'?[20] In 1960 a writer in *The Woman Teacher* looked back on the controversy: 'Turn over the cuttings – so many of them – wives, mothers, babies, nappies, sinks (and sinks lead to waste . . .)', she mused.[21] This imagery of sinks, blocked ambitions, drained energies and wasted investments proliferated and permeated the whole debate about the higher education of women in the postwar world. Should girls be educated for domesticity or for the labour market? This question had been raised in a controversial polemic on *The Education of Girls* by John Newsom in 1948, earnestly investigated in a series of lectures and discussions at the University of Newcastle in 1952, and shaped a careful enquiry by the Women's Group on Public Welfare which was published in 1962.[22] There was little in the way of a consensus. 'The domestic ideal' was fraught with tension and undermined by challenge at the very moment of its construction and celebration. An awareness of this ambiguity in its appeal to women is central to our understanding of the social history of women in the 1950s and 1960s, and particularly pertinent to explaining long-term trends in women's take-up of university education.

Stagnation in the proportion of women students in universities: the 1930s to the 1950s

Women now outnumber men as students entering universities in the UK, but this by no means represents the culmination of a steady trend going back to women's first admission to universities in the late nineteenth century. In 1930 the proportion of women in the student population of Britain was around 27 per cent (25 per cent in England, 33 per cent in Wales, 32 per cent in Scotland). These proportions shrank slightly to an average of c. 23–24 per cent in the late 1930s, 'stagnating' at this level until the late 1960s. Even with the 'Robbins' expansion of higher education in this latter decade, the proportion rose slowly at first: to 28 per cent in 1968, 38 per cent in 1980.[23] But from then on the trend has seemingly become inexorable, with the proportion of women entrants overtaking men by the mid 1990s and representing more than half of student numbers by the end of the century.[24]

The decline in the proportion of women in the university student population in the 1930s did not go unnoticed by contemporaries,[25] but the reasons for the long period of 'stagnation' which followed up to the late 1960s have never been fully explored. Some commentators, such as Dame Kitty Anderson, who delivered her Fawcett lecture on 'Women and the Universities: A Changing Pattern' at Bedford College in 1963, simply ignored the trend, presenting instead a 'Whiggish' and reassuring interpretation of women's access to universities as a simple story of steady 'advance'. After depicting the years from 1902 to 1944 as a period of 'consolidation', Anderson argued that from 1944 onwards there was a widening of access to universities for both men and women together, which she described as a period of 'combined forces', in which there was no longer any need to think separately about the sexes in higher-education thinking or planning.[26]

This bland and inadequate description owed more, perhaps, to feminist optimism than to scrutiny of the data available from the University Grants Committee. The report of the Robbins Committee, published in the same year that Anderson delivered her lecture, drew attention to the fact that only a quarter of university students were female, and that the proportion of women varied widely according to type of institution. Only 10 per cent of Cambridge's students were female, 15 per cent of Oxford's: the proportion averaged at 35 per cent at smaller civic universities, 25 per cent at larger civics, and was around 30 per cent in Wales, Scotland and London. The Committee was well aware that at that time, 'the reserve of untapped ability' among young people was far greater among women than among men.[27]

Three years later, *The Times* published a perceptive article by E.M. Thomas pointing out that the proportion of women to men in British universities was lower in 1966 than it had been forty years ago, 'a surprising fact . . . tucked away' in data published by Robbins and brought to light again by Lord Franks' report on Oxford in that year.[28] Girls suffered from 'a cumulative series of disadvantages' in education, Thomas argued, and yet with the increased availability of state grants for university education (which were now equally available to girls and boys), as well as widening employment for women, this decline in women's share of university education was not easy to explain. There were several possible reasons. Probably most important, Thomas suggested, was the tendency of girls to marry at a much younger age. But there was also the fact that many women were going to teacher training colleges instead of university. Was this through choice, or was the decision forced upon them? The fact that some girls who were qualified for university chose training colleges instead, partly reflected issues of subject choice. The expansion of university places had best kept up with demand in science and technology, whereas women preferred to study arts and humanities.[29] But a preference for teacher training over university may also have followed from a realistic assessment of the labour market.

Discrimination in access and provision

Women made inroads into university education in both the First and the Second World Wars in Britain, but in each case there was evidence of a reaction shortly afterwards. This sequence was particularly clear in the case of the 1914–18 war. Women teaching and studying in the universities in the 1920s felt that their position was precarious. In 1924, Frances Melville (Mistress of Queen Margaret College in Glasgow since 1909 and President of the British Federation of University Women in the 1930s) wrote to a colleague, Phoebe Sheavyn (Senior Tutor to Women Students in Manchester), of the need to proceed carefully in relation to the interests of women students, since although it was (then) thirty years since women had been accepted as students in Glasgow, their presence was still regarded as 'experimental', and she felt that they were 'now in the midst of a period of abnormal reaction in the University, where women (were) concerned'.[30]

This reaction was most marked in the older universities, where male dons were given to lament the presence of women as undermining the status and dignity of their institutions. When Oxford conceded degrees to women in 1920, it was widely expected that Cambridge would follow suit. Instead, Cambridge's refusal to grant degrees and full membership to women, in 1921, was accompanied by scenes of misogyny and rowdyism reminiscent of the 1890s, and a mob of undergraduates barged into Newnham with catcalls and shouts of 'We won't have women'.[31] A Royal

Commission of the following year (the Asquith Commission) sanctioned Cambridge's determination to remain 'mainly and predominantly a "men's university", though of a mixed type'. It was recommended that the number of women students should not exceed 500, which would fix the proportion of women to men at around 1:10 of the student body.[32] In Oxford, Joseph Wells, Warden of Wadham, urged similar restrictions, alongside dark threats that unless the feminine presence was reined in in Oxford 'our young men will prefer the other place'.[33] In June 1927, Oxford voted in favour of limitation: the five women's 'societies' (not yet permitted the status of 'colleges') were not to admit more than a total of 840 students, fixing the proportion of women to men at about 1:6 in the university.[34]

The postwar reaction against women students was particularly marked in the case of the medical schools, a subject which will be explored in some detail in Chapter 7. Under wartime conditions, in 1916, the University of Edinburgh finally agreed to make provision for teaching women medical students (previously, women had been confined to extramural schools, and the university accepted no responsibility for teaching them, acting as an examining body only). Oxford and Cambridge both opened their medical examinations to women in 1916/17. Under pressure from the University of London and from public opinion, seven of the London medical schools had agreed to admit women students (though in the case of St George's, for the duration of the war only). The situation proved short-lived. By 1928 five of the schools had reverted to an all-male entry. There were protests and strong reactions against women medical students in both University College and King's, although here, these Colleges' relationship to the University of London helped to check a full reversal of policy: both institutions decided to admit very limited numbers of women (ten to twelve students annually) to clinical instruction instead.[35]

The attitude of the London medical schools had a knock-on effect on the numbers of women studying medicine in both Oxford and Cambridge, in that those studying medicine in the women's colleges experienced great difficulty in finding placements for the clinical part of their training. In 1937 the Medical Women's Federation investigated this situation, and learned that in the case of Lady Margaret Hall, in Oxford, for instance, four out of five able women applicants for medicine were rejected because of the difficulty in finding placements for women in the London schools.[36] The secretary of the Oxford Society of Home Students also submitted that the number of women studying medicine in Oxford was kept artificially low for this reason.[37] Figures from the University Grants Committee for 1937/8 suggest a total of fifteen women students of medicine each in Oxford and Cambridge as compared with 193 and 428 men in each institution respectively.[38]

Medicine was not the only subject in which universities discriminated against the admission of women between the wars. The numbers of women admitted to dental and veterinary schools were also kept artificially low in these years. In the case of the latter this was partly because it was argued that women were unsuited to work with horses and larger animals (although it was seen as acceptable for them to treat smaller, domestic pets).[39] And ironically (given the small numbers of women keen to study the subject at the time), engineering faculties were often unreceptive to the idea of admitting women. When (in 1932) it was rumoured that King's College London intended to enrol female students, there was uproar. A petition signed by over two hundred past and present students carried the day and the women failed to appear.[40]

It is difficult to quantify the extent of this direct discrimination, but there is no doubt that it was seen as acceptable by many. Alison Gaukroger and Leonard Schwarz have pointed out that even after the Second World War, Sir Raymond Priestley, Vice-Chancellor of the University of Birmingham, had no compunction in admitting to discrimination against women, stating in his report to Council for 1945 that

> The proportions of men to women have changed less than would have been the case had the University not adopted a self-denying policy. We are convinced that the pre-war proportion was about right and that any considerable increase in the proportion of women would so change the character of the University as to act to the detriment of both men and women students.[41]

During and after the Second World War there was growing pressure on the medical schools, Oxford and Cambridge to make more adequate provision for the women who wanted to study in these institutions. In 1944 London University's Senate voted by a large majority for 'opening all London medical schools to men and women on terms of equal opportunity', and began corresponding with the schools on how to implement this.[42] The decision was given added clout by the report of the Goodenough Committee on medical education in the same year, noted in the previous chapter, which not only declared in favour of coeducation, but recommended that public funding should be conditional on its implementation.[43] The schools had little choice but to comply. However, the admission of women (or, in the case of the previously all-female Royal Free Hospital School, of men) by no means implied instant parity between the sexes in access to medical education. 'Quotas' soon became ceilings, and an uneasy combination of direct and indirect discrimination against women applicants continued through the 1950s and 1960s.[44]

A similar combination of direct and indirect discrimination ensured that the numbers of women in Oxford and Cambridge remained low through the same period. Again, there was pressure on these institutions from those who argued that the acceptance of public funding required that they make proper provision for women students. In a letter to the UGC dated 28 June 1946, Cambridge conceded that 'it would be in the national interest' to admit more women students and, after the war, University Ordinances were amended to allow the proportion of women to rise to one-fifth of the total of men.[45] However, the University's Committee on Women Students was riven with dissent. Expressions of the need for a third women's college in the university were strongly opposed by Professor Hollond, who expressed himself doubtful about whether any 'able' women were in fact excluded from the university under existing conditions.[46] Plans for a third foundation stalled, much to the frustration of many on the committee. But the situation was not made any easier by the fact that much of the opposition to a third foundation came from the existing women's colleges. A number of women academics from Newnham and Girton, for instance, wrote to the Vice-Chancellor in 1952 suggesting that it would be a 'disservice' to bring more women 'of modest general ability' into Cambridge, when they 'would find an education better fitted to their needs elsewhere'.[47] This kind of attitude, explicable in part by the desire to retain a 'protectionist' monopoly over the best women candidates, reflected a conservative – or defensive – elitism on the part of some in the women's colleges, which persisted well into the second half of the century.

The institution of a third women's college in Cambridge was eventually agreed in 1952, although it was stipulated that the number of women admitted should not exceed one hundred. New Hall came into existence in 1954. The following year, Cambridge's Registrar sent a letter warning the College against assuming that it could make any plans for expansion.[48] This ambivalence on the part of the University authorities in Cambridge – 'public' concession of the need to make more provision for women, combined with 'private' discouragement of any attempt to actually do so – was characteristic in the postwar years (and indeed continued into the 1970s).

In 1960 Cambridge removed the quota restricting the numbers of women students: Oxford had abandoned its quota three years previously. But in Oxford, as in Cambridge, the leaders of the women's colleges were rather less than whole-hearted in their desire for expansion: as the historian Janet Howarth has emphasized, they were sometimes sceptical about whether the demand from able schoolgirls would justify extended provision. There was also the question of funding: at a time when the question of the value of a university training for women was so hotly contested in the press, appeals for benefactions met with something of a mixed response, and there were few wealthy women keen to step forward with large endowments.[49] While colleges remained single sex, and there were so few women's colleges, the numbers of women remained low in both Oxford and Cambridge. The vexed issue of coeducation – and the tortuous politics of its introduction – will be examined in the second half of this book.

In considering gender differences in access to higher education before the 1970s we need also to be aware of women's participation in teacher training. The postwar expansion of the teacher training colleges (later designated 'Colleges of Education') was dramatic. In 1938/9 there were some 13,000 students in teacher training colleges in Britain: by 1964 the target number of places in the colleges was 111,000. In 1972/3 there were 131,000 students in training in the UK.[50] In 1960 the two-year certificate was replaced by a three-year course, but this carried far less status than a university degree. Whereas women represented (on average) one-quarter of the university student population in the universities, in teacher education the proportions were reversed, over 70 per cent of the training college population being female. Many observers were beginning to question this situation.[51] The academic reputations of these colleges – of which there were around 180 in 1970 – were very variable, and it was estimated in 1963 that whilst a university place cost c. £660 per annum, the cost of a place in training college was a mere £255 p.a. To many it appeared that women were being offered higher education on the cheap.[52] However, colleges offered a broad curriculum, often of the liberal arts kind, which appealed to those women less attracted to the specialised honours degree courses in many universities. Much of the expansion in university places after the war had been in science and technology, rather than in arts and social science, where there was keen competition for places. We should further remember that the most likely destination for all women graduates was teaching: an awareness of this would doubtless have influenced many female school-leavers in their choice of higher education.

Aspirations and employment

In the early years of the twentieth century, employment opportunities for women graduates outside schoolteaching had been very limited. A proliferation of advice offered to 'the educated woman' in numerous careers publications and by advisory bureaux partly reflected the feminist desire to widen professional opportunities for the woman graduate, but catered, at the same time, for an obvious need: in addition to the woman graduate, many unmarried women from modest middle-class backgrounds (including 'impecunious gentlewomen' of the kind represented in George Gissing's 1893 novel, *The Odd Women*) found themselves desperate to secure paid work.[53] In 1912, the Central Bureau for the Employment of Women's Students' Careers Association published a pamphlet, *Openings for University Women other than Teaching*, valiantly assembling a list of possibilities and reassuring its readers that opportunities *were* opening up and that loan funds for further training were available, but the inventive list of possibilities (including 'horticulture and bee-keeping in the colonies' and 'the management of steam and hand-laundries') hardly made for an optimistic reading.[54]

Educated women found more scope for work during the 1914–18 war, but many of these opportunities then disappeared in the 1920s and 1930s. Competition for teaching posts in secondary schools forced some graduates (of both sexes) into elementary school classrooms. A shortage of posts in relation to the numbers applying for them led the Board of Education to announce a 10 per cent reduction in grants for teachers in training in the universities from 1933, an economy which particularly affected women.[55] The Central Bureau for the Employment of Women reported itself as besieged by requests for advice and assistance in securing posts in these years.[56] With financial backing from Newnham and Girton Colleges, the Cambridge University Women's Appointments Board was launched in 1930,[57] and a new organization, the Women's Employment Federation (which had its roots in the employment services offered by the London Society for Women's Suffrage during the war), came into existence in 1933.[58] Ray Strachey chaired the Cambridge University Women's Appointments Board from its inception until 1939 and also served as organizing secretary of the WEF. Under her indefatigable leadership, both organizations sought to provide advice, to disseminate information, and to work for a widening of opportunities for the educated woman.[59]

Albums of press cuttings compiled by the WEF during the 1930s convey a gloomy picture of the prospects of the woman graduate.[60] Headlines from newspapers all over the country drew attention to the plight of 'Girls doomed to blind alley jobs after expensive education', 'Training tragedies', 'Varsity girls behind the counter', 'Starting work in debt: girl graduates hit by economic crisis', and so forth. A university education might be worthwhile in itself, warned a writer in the *Daily Despatch* in 1934, but it was not to be seen as an investment by parents, who should certainly not count upon their daughter being able to recoup the cost of her training. Dire stories were told: one sad girl graduate living in a Bayswater women's hostel calculated that she would be 32 years old by the time that she had repaid her debts.[61] The *Evening News* (19 March 1936) reported that

> Universities are every year turning out young women who have taken degrees and mastered half the 'ologies', but only the lucky few are able to find openings suitable to their attainments . . . Cases are known of girls with brilliant university records who are in blind alley posts at £3 or £4 a week.[62]

Ray Strachey ploughed on, doing her best to reassure women graduates that work was available to the determined amongst them who were undaunted by the prospect of further training,[63] but lists of 'training opportunities' regularly supplied by the CBEW (including, from 1927, apprenticeships in 'Angora Rabbit Wool Farming' as well as the perennially advertised opportunities for training in Laundry Management) must have dampened many spirits.[64] Even the optimistic Strachey felt it necessary to warn her readers that a degree carried 'little commercial value', and that 'from the strictly practical angle, there is not so much to be said for a university education'.[65]

Nonetheless, the women who ventured upon a university education in the 1930s usually did so in the hope that it would improve their prospects in life. In this sense they looked upon a degree as an investment rather than a 'consumption good', and there is no lack of evidence that their parents and families, many of whom had to make considerable financial sacrifices in order to support them through college, hoped that a degree would provide a route to well-paid and secure employment. In my survey of 500-plus women who graduated before 1939 (described in Chapters 1 and 2), just under one-third of the 500 women recorded that their higher education had been made possible by scholarships from the Board of Education which committed them to teaching as a career. Many of the sample confessed that they had felt little inclination for teaching, but were unable to find career openings elsewhere. Stories of frustration and disappointment were commonplace, particularly amongst those who had graduated in scientific subjects and could find no vocational outlet for their skills before the war. A number recorded being reduced to secretarial work. Dr Edith Merry, who had trained at University College London, remembered that a colleague, unable to see any hope of making a living as a doctor in the late 1930s, had taken a two-year post as a children's nanny after qualifying.[66] A long list of women confessed to having had early ambitions to be something other than a schoolteacher: a diplomat, a solicitor, a research chemist, business manager, veterinary surgeon, etc., but most had been disappointed. The outbreak of war in 1939 eased the situation somewhat, providing more opportunities for some, especially those women with a training in medicine.[67] However a count of all the women graduates in my sample who chose (or were reduced to) teaching at some stage of their careers revealed that over two-thirds of the total fell into this category.[68]

The impact of the Second World War in freeing jobs for educated women ushered a new tone into the literature of the careers advisory agencies. The annual report of the CWAB in 1941 was infused with buoyancy, recording the many openings for women graduates in national service and administration, the call for women to replace masters in boys' schools, the opportunities for women workers in new fields. It was reported that 'it was impossible to satisfy' the demand for women chemists, physicists and mathematicians with an interest in engineering.[69] But again, the ending of the war brought reaction. In December 1948 it was reported that, although nearly all of the women graduates of that year had been 'absorbed in employment' or 'were taking further training courses', their employment 'was not in all cases satisfactory as regards status, salary and prospects'.[70] In the early 1950s the reports of the CWAB emphasized the continuing difficulties experienced in finding jobs that were satisfactory in terms of status and prospects, and bemoaning 'the wide differentiation between the men's and women's salaries'. Women students were repeatedly advised to think of a university degree as 'mental training' rather than as a vocational goal.[71] Irene Hilton (who became organizing secretary of the WEF in 1949) regularly responded to parents who asked whether a university education was worthwhile for a girl who had no intention of teaching in cautious, measured terms. A university education conferred many advantages, she pointed out, but it was only suitable for girls with scholarly interests, and it was most certainly not a vocational training. Equally, 'the training' a girl would receive at university should produce 'certain qualities of mind and outlook which (could) be used to advantage in any profession – including the most important one of managing a home and family'.[72]

Hilton's words of advice in this respect appeared regularly throughout the 1950s in the WEF's annual editions of *Careers: a memorandum on openings and training for girls and women*.[73] Her remarks were carefully chosen. From the end of the war onwards the careers agencies had begun to emphasize the problem of 'the marriage risk'. As we have seen, the public debate over whether a university education for girls was worthwhile, which had so prominently featured in newspapers in the 1930s, was rekindled in the 1950s, albeit in a slightly different (and harder-edged) form. At a time when competition for university places was becoming ever keener (a situation very different from the 1930s) this debate became heated and acrimonious. Women were indeed marrying younger, and the arguments about 'wastage' could be and were adduced to defend discriminatory admissions policies such as those in the medical schools, where women applicants were admitted in much smaller numbers (and usually with higher qualifications) than men.[74]

The issue of whether women graduates could be accused of 'wasting' their expensive education must have seemed cruelly misplaced to those who were all too well aware of the limited opportunities they had had for exploiting academic qualifications in the labour market.[75] Data on the first destination of university graduates were first collected nationally in 1957/8, but not considered very reliable until the 1960s.[76] In 1960 the Cambridge Appointments Boards decided to carry out their own survey of the work taken up by graduates: aware of the fact that men's and women's patterns of employment were radically different, it was deemed necessary to use different questionnaires for the two sexes.[77]

The survey carried out on behalf of the women's board focused on the careers of women who had graduated from the Cambridge women's colleges in 1937/8 and 1952/3.[78] The results showed that, although the majority of single women were in full-time work, only 43 per cent of the married women from the earlier cohort were in paid employment, and an even smaller proportion, 35 per cent, of the younger married women graduates were in paid work.[79] However, many of those in both age groups indicated that they would like to return to work when family responsibilities permitted. One of the problems was, as the Board had emphasized in its annual report ten years earlier, and continued to emphasize throughout the 1950s and 1960s, that older women graduates faced near-insuperable problems in finding suitable work. This was attributed, variously, to the prejudices of employers and to competition from the rising numbers of male graduates coming from an expanding university system.[80] There had been an increase, in the early 1960s, in the proportion of women graduates going into teaching: over half of the 1937/8 women graduates and just under half of the 1952/3 cohort were working as teachers.[81] Opportunities in industry scarcely existed, and employer prejudice against women was rife.[82] The CWAB files contain material (unfortunately closed) on the Board's relationships with Shell between 1941 and 1955. In 1961 it was reported that Shell had recently turned down all women candidates submitted for interview and 'had caused considerable discouragement to students'.[83] The CWAB report for 1962 concluded somewhat wearily that:

> organisations prepared to make use of the services of graduate women are beginning to divide the employment offered into two kinds, (1) a short-term period of work, accepting as inevitable the early marriage rate and consequent withdrawal into private life, and (2) non-pensionable, unestablished posts without real responsibility, for the over 40s who are prepared to forego promotion prospects. This is a very serious development from the point of view of the woman graduates – and there are still many – who seriously hope to pursue a career.[84]

Crompton and Sanderson have analysed the way that the contradictory messages received by women about their roles in the family and the workplace after the Second World War helped to sustain a somewhat unstable 'gender order' and sexual divisions in the labour market.[85] The contradictions were certainly rife. Surveys of women's working lives, and of the attitudes to work of women graduates, proliferated in the 1950s and 1960s.[86] In the British Federation of University Women's survey of *Graduate Women at Work*, for instance, Constance Arregger returned to the twin themes of wasted ambitions and wasted 'womanpower', urging a change of policy on the part of employers, a change of heart on the part of women. Employers were urged to be open-minded and flexible, women were urged to take a long-term view of their social contribution and to see beyond the short-term imperatives of their domestic and family lives.[87] In the meantime, women blamed employers, employers blamed women.

The trend to early marriage

One of the major concerns of those writing on the education of girls and women in the 1950s and 1960s was 'the early marriage problem'.[88] Observers could have little doubt about the trend for women to marry younger, which had set in before the war, but became even more dramatic thereafter. In 1921, 14.9 per cent of brides had been under 21 years old when they married, by 1965 this proportion had risen to 40 per cent. In 1960 the proportion of girls married under 18 years of age reached nearly 6.0 per cent (as compared with 1.6 per cent in 1936–40, and just under 5.0 per cent in 1959); of girls under 20 years of age the proportions married in 1960 and 1959 were 26.4 per cent and 25.2 per cent, as compared with 11.4 per cent in 1936–40.[89] This tendency to marry at a very young age was particularly marked amongst girls from working-class families, but it was also noticeable amongst middle-class girls.[90] The median age for women to marry reached its lowest point (around 21 years) in 1966–7.[91]

Women were also becoming mothers earlier than before. In each year of the 1950s around 27 per cent of all teenage brides were pregnant at their weddings.[92] Those who were not were likely to start their families soon after marriage. Michael Schofield's study of *The Sexual Behaviour of Young People*, carried out in the early 1960s, highlighted 'the tremendous prominence of marriage as an immediate goal in the lives of many teenage girls', and also drew attention to the fact that unmarried girls were reluctant to use contraceptives themselves, nor were they generally insistent on their partners doing so.[93]

The desire to marry young (over a third of the younger women in Schofield's sample wanted to marry before they were 21 years of age) discouraged girls from staying on at school and making long-term educational and career plans. Kathleen Ollerenshaw commented that, increasingly, it was becoming the fashion 'for a girl to step from the school choir to the church altar, and to discard her prefect's badge for a wedding ring'.[94] At the time she was writing, three-quarters of all girls left school at the age of 15.[95] Both the Crowther Report in 1959 (on the education of those aged 15–18) and the Albemarle Report the following year (on the Youth Service) had made reference to early marriage and the changing pattern of women's lives, suggesting the need for schooling and social provision to accommodate to these trends: both of these reports added fuel to the controversies over the proper aims of women's education.[96] The National Union of Women Teachers deplored the idea of marriage being

a. By age range (000s)

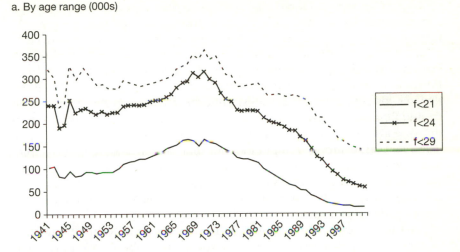

Source: *Annual Abstract of Statistics*, various years.

b. By age bracket (000s)

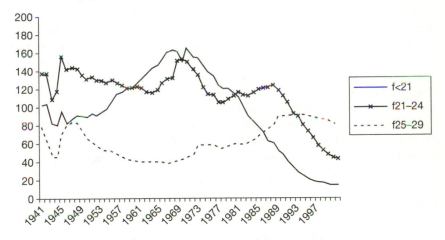

Figure 4.1 Numbers of women marrying, England and Wales

Source: *Annual Abstract of Statistics*, various years.

seen as a career for women. Feminists exhorted girls to take a longer-term perspective and a more active role in designing their futures.[97]

There was an increasing tendency to divide women into two categories: the majority, for whom marriage loomed large and education was something of a diversion from 'the real world', and a scholarly minority, who might be relied upon to continue the 'bluestocking' tradition. But even the second group were no longer immune from the 'marriage risk'. 'Marriage for women today is a hazard, as far as university education is concerned,' conceded Ollerenshaw, 'almost in the category of war service.'[98] Marriages at university, 'though officially frowned upon', were not uncommon.[99] In evidence which she submitted to the Robbins Committee on Higher Education, Lady Ogilvie (Principal of St Anne's College, Oxford) confessed that she thought marriage amongst undergraduates 'a grave error', which should be discouraged by those in authority, even to the extent of with-drawing grants.[100] She conceded that this might be seen as encouraging 'extra-marital relations', but pointed out that unless 'a completely ostrich-like attitude is adopted, it must be admitted that such relations exist on a wide scale already'. Chastity she considered crucial 'to a woman's integrity and happiness', but 'to urge early marriage as a cure for incontinence' was irresponsible and unwise.[101]

The trend to early marriages was increasingly seen as a stumbling block by careers advisers working with women who were about to graduate and leave university. How could they persuade employers to invest in the training of women when so many were likely to interrupt their careers soon after marrying, and particularly after the birth of a first child? We have seen these considerations shaping the reports of the Cambridge Women's Appointments Board discussed previously.[102] There was endless discussion of 'women's two roles' and 'the dual career model', whereby women left paid work for the period when they were occupied with childbearing and raising small children, but hoped to return to employment and resume their careers later in life.[103] However, the loss of experience and expertise which might be expected to accrue from the early years of professional employment was a serious issue which could not be ignored. Stories of employers quizzing potential female employees about their matrimonial intentions were common in the 1950s and 1960s, as were stories of women attending interviews having taken off their engagement rings.

Predicaments of the woman student in the postwar world

The postwar years, then, constituted a period characterized by much ambivalence about the purposes and value of higher education for women. Sexual divisions were sharp, both in the labour market and in the home. There was evidence of continuing discrimination in university admissions and policies, and marked double standards were still the norm in the disciplinary policies and procedures of many higher education institutions of the day. From late Victorian times, female students had been subject to more restriction on their liberty than their male peers: a stringent surveillance of women's sexual behaviour, with more serious penalties for 'misdemeanour', persisted well into the 1960s (these issues will be returned to in the next chapter). In this context it is scarcely surprising that women students might be unsure of their goals, diffident and unfocused about their ambitions, and uncertain about the relevance of their studies to their lives. Advocates of women's higher education might deplore the tendency to early marriage, but for many women students the prospect of making a good marriage soon after graduation might appear a sensible investment in their future.[104] University was, after all, a good place to find a husband. The outlook in terms of career ambitions was much less clear.

Autobiographical accounts of this period illustrate something of this, as do novels exploring the theme of university life for women in the period. Women 'cooped up' in the women's colleges of Oxford and Cambridge frequently expressed a sense of existing on the margins of an extensive kind of male, public-school world. In Lois Day's depressingly bleak novel, *The Looker In* (1961), the central character, deeply confused by the 'role models' of academic woman and housewife, enters a women's college with high expectations, only to find herself disillusioned.[105] As in Rosamund Lehmann's earlier novel, *Dusty Answer*, she finds herself out of place and marginalized in the university.[106] In Andrea Newman's *A Share of the World* (1964) and Margaret Forster's *Dames' Delight* (also 1964), women students agonize over sex and relationships, show uneasy commitment to their academic work, and find themselves completely stumped about what to do when they graduate, attracted neither by teaching nor secretarial work, which appear their only options.[107] 'I wish I could do Finals in Life, Love and Sex' confides one character in Newman's novel.[108]

There is a wonderfully telling expression of this predicament in Penelope Lively's novel, *Spiderweb* (1998).[109] The novel centres on the relationship between two friends who met in Oxford in the 1950s. The central character, Stella, nurses scholarly inclinations, in strong contrast with her friend, Nadine, who is determined to find a husband and to marry before the age of 23. Before leaving Oxford, Nadine makes for the University Appointments Board. On confessing her preference for an early marriage, rather than a long-term career, she finds herself subjected to a frosty disapproval from the female careers officer, who advises a secretarial course. Nadine achieves her come-uppance with a chilly stare of her own, objecting that she had not embarked on such an expensive education simply to become a secretary.[110]

In her recent autobiography, *The Centre of the Bed* (2003), Joan Bakewell recalls that when she studied in Cambridge in the 1950s, 'No one spoke of careers, job prospects or earning potential.'[111] She married shortly after graduation, and found her career options limited. There was little joy from the CWAB in the Trumpington Road. Like others among her female contemporaries, she was attracted by the idea of working in broadcasting, but found that women were considered unsuitable as newsreaders or even as general trainees: 'It wasn't merely discouraging: it said to me and thousands of other women that in the postwar world the heights of public life were to be largely a male preserve.'[112] A couple of years later, house-bound with a baby daughter, she found that her 'mind was turning to porridge'. 'I didn't know it then, but thousands of women graduates across the world who'd bought into the postwar fantasy of the idyllic home and family were restless, too.'[113]

Chapter Five

❧

Gaining places
The rising proportion of women students in universities after 1970

The resurgence of feminism in the 1970s encouraged new interest in the history of women's participation in higher education. In 1978 the *Times Higher Education Supplement* published an article by Tessa Blackstone in which she drew attention to the fact that the proportion of women students in universities had been higher in the mid 1920s than in any other five-year interval until 1975/6.[1] She argued that more work was needed if we were to understand the long period of stagnation in the 1950s and early 1960s, but suggested that the expansion of working-class participation in higher education since the war may have worked against any increase in the proportion of middle-class girls going to university. This seems unlikely, although her second line of explanation, which was that the expansion of teacher training colleges after the war provided an alternative form of higher education for girls, had much more purchase. There can be little doubt that the dramatic cuts in teacher education of the 1970s, and the large-scale institutional changes of the last quarter of the century which saw the closure of many of the colleges of education or their amalgamation into the new polytechnics (later to become new universities in their own right) did much to redirect girls' choices in higher education.[2]

The issue of long-term trends in the proportion of women in universities in the UK was addressed by Jones and Castle in 1986,[3] and by Blackburn and Jarman in 1993.[4] Jones and Castle presented a somewhat generalized account of 'changing social expectations' through a period of 'moderate but uneven growth in the female share of undergraduate enrolments' between 1920 and 1980, but added little to a more finely tuned understanding of trends. Blackburn and Jarman offered a highly sophisticated and careful analysis of the data, highlighting two periods in the last century (the first from 1955 to 1959, the second in the years of rapid expansion in higher education following the Robbins Report) when women appear to have lost ground or to have made 'surprisingly' little gain in their share of university places. They suggest that between c. 1948 and 1970, women tended to lose out during periods of expansion in universities, and to gain during contractions, 'with the net outcome unclear'. After about 1970, however, women steadily gained ground, 'unaffected by the pattern of expansion or contraction'.[5] They argue, broadly, that changing expectations about the role of women in society, a widening of women's choice of subjects of study, and their anticipation of more favourable labour market opportunities, must all have played a part in this.[6]

We can now look back over a period of some thirty years' sustained increase in the proportion of women students in universities: they now represent well over half of all undergraduates. The tide has turned, and more and more voices are raised in concern about the 'underperformance' or under-representation of men in higher education.[7] Are women 'taking over' the universities? In an article published in the *Times Higher* in October 2003, entitled 'Who's the Weaker Sex Now?', Alan Smithers (then Professor of Education at the University of Liverpool) was quoted as having offered two explanations of the trend. In the first place, girls had overtaken boys in their performance in school; second, girls were no longer leaving school early and thinking in terms of a short period of employment before marriage – instead they were looking towards careers for themselves.[8] But there is a sense in which these remarks describe rather than explain the dramatic changes of the last few decades. This chapter will address these changes in more detail.

There are a number of problems in the way of any precise delineation of the upward trend of women's participation in universities over the last century. These problems relate to institutional changes and changes in methods of collecting data; there is also the complication that some series refer to Britain, others to the United Kingdom, and data for England, Wales and Scotland are sometimes but not always disaggregated. Data for the period after the early 1990s are not always consistent with previous sets, not least because the collection of educational statistics was being privatized at that time. A graph showing changes in women's shares of all UK full-time university education between 1919 and 2001 is included here for reference, but needs to be treated with some caution.

The graph shows the proportion of women enrolled for full-time study from 1919 to 2001. Figures for Oxford and Cambridge were not included in the returns before 1922/3: the small proportion of women in those universities at that date accounts for the noticeable drop (some 3 per cent) in the proportion of women immediately after that date. The effect of the Second World War is clear but temporary: the departure of men accounts first for a rise in the proportion of female students, but this is entirely offset after the war. The proportion of women in the late 1960s was little if any

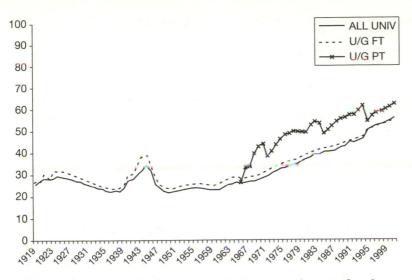

Figure 5.1 Proportion of students in UK universities who were female, 1919–2000

Sources: 'Returns from Universities and University Colleges (UGC) (various names, annual); 'Statistics of Education: vol. 6, Universities' (annual, 1966–79); 'University Statistics: vol. 1, Students and Staff' (annual, 1980–94); 'Higher Education Statistics for the United Kingdom' (annual, 1992–); 'Students at Higher Education Institutions' (annual, 1994–).

Note: All figures are percentages of the respective totals who were female.
ALL UNIV: All university students (British to 1952, thereafter UK).
U/G FT: Full-time undergraduate university students (ditto).
U/G PT: Part-time undergraduate university students (UK, since 1965).

higher than in the mid 1920s. However, the fact that the Colleges of Advanced Technology (CATs) as well as Heriot-Watt College in Scotland, were first included in returns for universities in 1964/5 accounts for a decline in female shares at that time. This makes it difficult to decide whether the growth trend in women's participation began in the 1960s or somewhat later. In view of the decline from the level of the mid 1920s, there is some justification for tracing the turning point to the early 1970s. Thereafter, the rise in female share is almost unbroken, though slowing slightly during the difficult years of cutbacks in the 1980s. The impact of the 'new universities' of the 1960s was important, as will be discussed below. The transformation of the polytechnics into the 'new universities' of the 1990s brought a further boost to women's shares, which first rose above the 50 per cent figure in 1996.

Women and the 'new universities' of the 1960s

The new universities of the 1960s proved particularly attractive to women. They offered broad curricula, particularly in the arts, and carried no tradition of gender segregation or discrimination against female students. In the representation of these institutions in the press (including the student press) and in ephemeral and promotional literature of the time, the contrast with the older universities is striking. The cover of Warwick University's first students' handbook, in 1966, featured a wistful-looking blonde in a mini-skirt leaning against a signpost in a rural setting, the signpost marked simply 'university'.[9] The University of Sussex's *Guide to Applicants*, *1966/7* carried a cover illustration of an attractive young girl, deeply absorbed in a book (inside, a photograph captioned 'An interview for admission' featured the economic historian Barry Supple, smiling encouragingly at a female student).[10] A series of articles on new universities in the newspaper *Student Life* included a piece on East Anglia (March 1968) illustrated with a photograph of three long-haired girls with high boots and even higher hemlines descending steps near the library. Another, on Lancaster, in November that year, showed five fashionably dressed young women coyly smoothing their hairstyles whilst earnestly discussing the contents of some textbook on the concrete steps of the campus.[11] The 'dollybird' was effectively part of the branding image of the new university.

There was glamour in this, and a break in the long tradition whereby female students were caricatured as down-at-heel bluestockings sporting hairy tweeds and hopeless hairstyles. In February 1961, the *Observer* noted that more than half of the 400 applicants for fifty places at the new University of Sussex, scheduled to open its doors in October, were female.[12] The headline 'Girls plump for new university college' provoked some (anonymous) versifying: '. . . A girl-student used to be skinny,/ And was also considered a frump,/ But here, in this town loved by Prinny,/ We should heartily welcome "girls plump". . . .'[13] (with much more in the same vein).

In the 1950s and early 1960s those with a special interest in the education of girls had urged the need for universities to consider the structure of their degree courses in the light of girls' aspirations. Too few girls went on to higher education, insisted Kathleen Ollerenshaw, in *Education for Girls* (1961), largely because 'the provision for women at universities is at present inadequate'.[14] In 1959 just over ten thousand girls left school having satisfied the entry requirements for university, but fewer than half of them went on to study for a degree. She believed that a broader curriculum would do much to remedy this.[15] 'If the universities were to provide the right courses', she thought that there was little doubt that demand from women would necessitate a level of provision closer to that for men.[16] Such a claim was not new. It had often been suggested that, whilst single honours subject specialization might be appropriate for intending teachers, the breadth of some traditional 'pass' degrees better equipped women for the labour market. J.J. Milne, Senior Tutor to Women Students at the University of Birmingham from 1926 to 1951, had long argued along these lines. In her annual reports to Birmingham's Council and Senate between the wars, for instance, she had regularly suggested that a large proportion of the women in the University's Faculty of Arts 'ought to be tempted to prepare for some form of civic administration, the Civil Service, etc.; they ought to have in the University an encyclopaedic training, bearing some relation to the world of today', instead of being straitjacketed into narrowly specialist courses.[17] Similarly, the annual reports of the Cambridge Women's Appointments Board in the late 1950s and early 1960s had noted the difficulties faced by women graduates interested in social work: at that time none of the first degree courses offered in Cambridge 'was sufficiently wide in social studies' to be considered an acceptable background for such work.[18]

The evidence submitted to the Robbins Committee on Higher Education in 1962/3 included a closely argued memorandum from the Association of Headmistresses calling for more broadly based degree courses ideally combining 'two or three fields of study integrated to form a coherent whole'.[19] The new University of Keele was applauded for its innovative 'foundation year', allowing students an introduction to both science and arts. The Headmistresses declared 'emphatic and widespread approval of the plans (then) being initiated in the University of Sussex' and hoped that other universities would experiment along the same lines.[20] Similarly, E.M. Thomas (whose 1966 article in *The Times* was mentioned in the previous chapter), applauded Sussex's decision to abandon traditional subject-based departments in favour of inter-disciplinary 'schools of study', which were already proving very popular amongst girl school-leavers.[21]

The new universities certainly did attract large numbers of women applicants. In Ollerenshaw's (1967) book, *The Girls' Schools*, she pointed out that 'Sussex University has proved so attractive to women that there has to be discriminatory selection in the arts subjects to prevent the student population from becoming predominantly female.'[22] In 1962 Sussex boasted one of the highest proportions of women students (well over 50 per cent) recorded in a British university, although this proportion was to shrink once the science schools became established over the next few years.[23] In his history of the University of East Anglia, Michael Sanderson observes that, although the appeals brochure published in 1962 in connection with the foundation of that institution featured rather idealistic drawings of young men, there was an immediate flood of applications from women school-leavers.[24] In Autumn 1963 the *Eastern Daily Times* reported that, 'Women undergraduates will outnumber men by almost two to one when the first term of the new University of East Anglia at Earlham,

Norwich, opens on October 7.'[25] Fifty-one out of the first seventy-nine graduates of East Anglia were women.[26]

As we saw in the previous chapter, the Robbins Report had noted that the proportion of women in different universities had varied (in 1961/2) from 10 per cent at Cambridge and 15 per cent at Oxford to an average of 25 per cent in the larger civic universities, 35 per cent in the smaller civics and in London, Wales and Scotland.[27] The two new universities then included in the 'smaller civic' category, Keele and Sussex, returned their proportion of women students as 43 per cent and 67 per cent respectively.[28] By 1966/7, figures published by the UGC indicate clearly that the new universities were playing a key role in the process of widening opportunities for women (see Table 5.1).

Aside from a brief mention of the intense competition amongst girls for places in Oxford and Cambridge, there was scarcely any mention of women students in the section on universities included in Anthony Sampson's *Anatomy of Britain* (1962).[29] The edition of that text which was published three years later (*Anatomy of Britain Today*) highlighted the success of the new universities, particularly Sussex, 'with its debs and political daughters'; a success which Sampson credited with breaking up 'the Oxbridge monopoly'.[30] In *The New Anatomy of Britain* (1971) Sampson opined that 'Sussex soon enjoyed special publicity as a kind of glamorous Brighton finishing school full of pretty girls and avant-garde intellectuals'.[31] But by the time that *The Changing Anatomy of Britain* appeared, in 1982, the glamour and fashionable modernity associated with Sussex and other new foundations was fading.[32] Ollerenshaw had pointed out that severe restrictions on the numbers of women who could be accommodated in Oxford and Cambridge in the 1960s meant that applications to the two universities were seen as hardly worth the effort by many able girls.[33] They flocked to the new universities instead. As will be seen in later chapters, a

Table 5.1 Student numbers in the 'new universities' of the 1960s, men and women

University	Men	Women	Women %
East Anglia	906	632	41.1
Essex	588	356	37.7
Keele	869	643	42.5
Kent	838	637	43.2
Lancaster	783	428	35.3
Sussex	1641	939	36.4
Warwick	724	411	36.2
York	791	606	43.4

Source: UGC returns for 1966/7; own calculations.

sense of losing out on the country's reserves of highly able girls was undoubtedly one of the factors which propelled the rush towards 'coresidence' in Oxbridge in the 1970s.

The sexual revolution and the woman student

The previous chapter drew attention to the trend to early marriage in the postwar world and highlighted the concerns of educational authorities and careers advisers who contemplated this demographic trend and assumed that it would continue. Questions of propriety, and in particular the sexual behaviour of young people, had long exercised university authorities who regarded themselves as *in loco parentis* where students were concerned, at a time when the age of majority (21) was not reached until most students had graduated.

The behaviour of women students had always been subject to rather more scrutiny than that of their male peers.[34] In the mid 1930s, D.W. Hughes had observed that 'University education for women is not yet the same thing as university education for men; there is rather less freedom in it.'[35] Well into the twentieth century, many if not most universities operated different disciplinary structures and regulations for the two sexes, and this was particularly marked in Oxford and Cambridge. Even after the 1939–45 war, for instance, the principals of the women's colleges in Oxford had to be applied to for formal permission before their female charges could join mixed clubs or participate in social events organized by male societies.[36] Permission was by no means automatic: a request that women be allowed to attend meetings of the Oxford University Rhythm Club, in 1946, for instance, was met with some suspicion, not least on account of the elaborately mock-deferential tone of the request itself (which emanated from the young Kingsley Amis).[37] A letter from the future historian J.C. Holt in the same year, seeking permission for women to attend meetings of the Stubbs Society, met with easy approval, but the suggestion of a 'Dance Club', in the following year, encountered opposition.[38] An interest in parliamentary history, presumably, was a better guarantee of good behaviour than jazz or the dance-floor.

Many women students resented what they saw as 'petty' rules and restrictions on their behaviour, or chafed against 'the double standard' in matters of personal and sexual freedom. In her autobiographical *Promise of a Dream* (2000), Sheila Rowbotham describes what she remembers as the 'archaic' and anxiety-inducing regulations that governed the lives of women students at St Hilda's, in Oxford in the early 1960s:

> Not only did the Oxford regime induce hypocrisy and fear, it was also manifestly unfair. The penalties we faced in the women's colleges were

much more severe than those governing male sexuality . . . In my first year, Cathy, a wiry, small, dark-haired girl whom I knew slightly, was found in bed with her boyfriend in St Hilda's by a don. She was kicked out of college, lost her grant and could not get into any other university. He was sent away from his college for two weeks, 'rusticated'. The institutional injustice was blatant and the issue was personal behaviour not some distant cause. This could so easily have been me.[39]

Scarcely surprisingly, students often felt that their women tutors looked upon sexual expression as incompatible with scholarship. A.S. Byatt has submitted that 'the mind–body problem of an intellectual woman in the 1950s was . . . one of rigorous conflict':

In those days the body required sex and childbearing, and quite likely the death of the mind alongside. My thesis supervisor, Helen Gardner, truly believed that women scholars should be nuns, renouncing the body for higher things.[40]

The issue was not simply a question of respectability, or the concern to avoid scandal in an era of less 'permissiveness', because the idea of a woman student wanting to marry before graduation, or the idea of a married woman student living in college, could equally provoke discomfort or anxiety amongst college authorities.[41] Some women graduates of this generation record that they needed – or felt that they needed – to ask permission of college authorities if they wanted to marry before completing their studies; some even recalling that their fiancés were subjected to close scrutiny from college principals as to whether they were acceptable choices, or socially up to scratch.[42]

Equally, the fear of unwanted pregnancy was real enough in the minds of women students, their parents and the university authorities of the time. Reflecting upon her student years in Oxford in the 1950s in her recent autobiographical study, *A House Unlocked* (2001), the novelist Penelope Lively recalled that this fear haunted the minds of many of her contemporaries:

. . . in those pre-Pill days grim tales of clandestine abortion haunted us all. There was much scared and private counting of days and watching of the calendar. Each of us knew, or knew of some girl to whom it had actually happened: that awful realization, the nausea, the panic. This was no climate of sexual liberation – it is strange now to think that the sixties were only ten years off. But it was a climate of new expectations and assumptions for women graduates.[43]

The fear of pregnancy, and the traumatic experience of illegal abortion, feature prominently in novels about women students' lives during the period. Andrea Newman's *A Share of the World* (1964), Margaret Forster's *Dames' Delight* (1964, 1966, 1968), Margaret Drabble's *The Millstone* (1965), Judith Grossman's *Her Own Terms* (1988) and Hilary Mantel's *An Experiment in Love* (1995) all deal with the complexity of these issues and the seeming intractability of the problems faced by young women who were increasingly given to challenging the traditional association of scholarly pursuits with celibacy.[44] The tone of these novels is bleak and claustrophobic, the experience of abortion sometimes serving as a metaphor for stifled hopes, loss of direction, a confused sense of purpose and identity.

In 1968 the University of Kent's magazine, *Fuss*, featured a cartoon depicting anxious-looking parents facing their daughter's teacher over a desk, asserting that they 'would like Brenda to go to the university with the lowest pregnancy rate'.[45] Well into the 1960s, the fear of unwanted pregnancy which shadowed the lives of women students was echoed in the minds of many parents and university authorities. The role of 'moral tutor' was not an easy one at this time. In 1969, Anthony Ryle, of Sussex University's Student Health Service, published a book entitled *Student Casualties*, in which he argued that 'the problem of the unwanted pregnancy . . . contributes to the pool of student casualties to quite a marked degree'.[46] In spite of the fact that contraceptive advice was more easily available to the young unmarried student than ever before, Ryle contended that 'a distressing proportion of women students' – he estimated around 10 per cent – became pregnant during the three years that they were studying at university.[47] Ryle's careful analysis of the situation drew attention to the ways in which the female student often experienced conflict between her sexual identity and student life in a way 'unknown to her male contemporaries'.[48]

Three years later, a study of the sexual behaviour and contraceptive practice of unmarried female students at the University of Aberdeen, published in the *British Medical Journal*, revealed that 'a disturbingly high' proportion of women students 'seemed content to maintain a high level of sexual activity with no form of contraception'.[49] Contraceptive advice was held to be freely available from Aberdeen's Student Health Service and from general practitioners locally: the authors of the study suggested that shyness, ignorance, embarrassment and a fear of moral censure seemed to explain this behaviour. In an editorial comment in the journal ('Sex and the single girl') it was suggested that 'Many single girls, thinking of approaching their doctor for contraceptive advice, fear they will be given a lecture instead.'[50] Of the 684 female students who responded to a questionnaire in the study, 49 'thought they might be pregnant', 6 were pregnant, and at least another 55 appear to have already had at least one abortion.[51] These findings were reinforced by the research carried out by Schofield for his second study, published in 1973, on *The Sexual Behaviour of Young Adults*, which emphasized that premarital sex was increasingly seen as normal by both young men and women, particularly amongst more educated, middle-class groups.[52] Students, living away from home, had more opportunity for experiment in this respect, but Schofield claimed that in spite of easier access to contraception, they were particularly at risk: rates of unwanted pregnancy, terminated by abortion, were high amongst the student population.[53]

The pill became generally available in Britain from 1961. It has been estimated that there were something under half a million users by 1964: this had increased to well over two million by the mid 1970s.[54] A demand for information about contraception and abortion became very evident in the student press in the late 1960s and early 1970s. These were years that witnessed something of a proliferation of new publications aimed at the student market nationally, as well as local papers. Richard Branson's magazine, *Student* (1968–70), went even further, in claiming an international audience.[55] Issue no. 2, published in the summer of 1968, offered an informative article on contraception, noting that:

> Some 'enlightened' universities are now providing contraceptive advice at their own student health centres. At least six university health centres are prepared to provide contraceptives for women students. Some others will make them available without officially publicising the fact, and some will prescribe them on the production of an engagement ring.[56]

The article also gave information on the progress of the reform of the abortion law and considered the ways in which this would affect students. In the same year, the magazine announced that it was setting up its own 'Student Advisory Centre', claiming, one year later, that at least half of a deluge of enquiries that it had received from worried students were from girls needing advice on abortion and contraception.[57] The spring issue of *Student* in 1969 featured a striking cover illustration of a young, naked, pregnant woman, and offered a thoughtful article on student mothers who had decided to try to continue their studies whilst going ahead with pregnancy and childbirth.[58] In the same issue Dr Faith Spicer set out 'to answer the questions of a student whose girlfriend has suffered from an unwanted pregnancy', which she concluded by expressing her conviction that more effective, easily available contraception would greatly diminish the need for students to have recourse to abortion.[59] Features like this were extremely common in local student newspapers during these years. In February 1971, for instance, the *Leeds Student* included an article on 'Unwanted pregnancies', illustrated with a drawing of a pregnant woman in cap and gown with the legend 'Failed' underneath it, as well as graphic depictions of condoms and packets of the pill.[60]

The unease about student sexuality and 'permissiveness' which infused many of the debates about mixed halls of residence and the 'coresidential' college during the 1960s and 1970s often focused around the 'problem' of the pregnant woman student. In 1965, Churchill College in Cambridge mulled over the question of whether to admit women, and arguments for and against such a change were exhaustively aired.[61] On the negative side, there were those who predicted that that coeducation would 'inevitably lead, in a proportion of cases, to unwanted pregnancy', the consequences of which might damage the reputation of the college in the eyes of parents and schoolmasters.[62] It was suggested that this might also mean a lot more worry for tutors. Four years later, when the admission of women had been agreed, a college subcommittee recorded that they had been reassured by evidence 'from the ladies' colleges' that they might 'expect few pregnancies and abortions' and that they did not feel that it was necessary to frame rules to deal with such eventualities. It was reported that 'the general practice at Newnham and Girton' was for girls who became pregnant to 'go away and have their babies and return to take their degree', which seemed 'perfectly reasonable' to the committee.[63]

Fertility rates fell dramatically between 1964 and 1981, with the most rapid fall in the five-year period from 1971 to 1975.[64] The lowering of the age of majority to 18 in 1969 relieved university authorities of any responsibility for policing the sexual morality of the student, male or female, and the seemingly perennial friction over gate hours and visitors in college bedrooms rapidly faded. 'Coresidence' became 'normal' by the end of the 1970s, and was quickly accepted as such, as we will see in some of the chapters to follow.[65] Female students were increasingly seen as students, rather than as an alien species, prone to reproduce as soon as any disciplinary arrangements slackened. The availability of the pill, together with access to (legal) abortion following the Abortion Law Reform Act of 1967, allowed women increased control over their own fertility, which was central to a longer-term view of their own futures. There was much more scope for education and career planning. The trend to earlier marriages, which had been one of the fundamental reasons for the setting up of the (Latey) Committee on the Age of Majority in 1967, was halted; indeed it went into reverse. As Hera Cook has convincingly argued, an understanding of the way in which sexuality became separated from reproduction is central to our understanding of women's lives in modern history.[66] The 'sexual revolution' played a crucial role in reshaping the experience and aspirations of the woman student.

Feminism and equal opportunities

The battle for equal pay and equal opportunities for women had a long history, which can be traced back to (at least) the beginning of the twentieth century.[67] In the years after the Second World War, steady pressure was exerted by feminist organizations such as the Fawcett Society, the National Council for Civil Liberties, the Six Point Group and the Status of Women Committee.[68] These campaigning organizations were invigorated by the rise of 'second wave' feminism in the 1960s, and their efforts were supplemented by newer organizations such as the Women in Media group.[69] There was a growing consensus between political parties that action against 'sex discrimination' was necessary. In 1968 Edward Heath, as leader of the Conservative Party, invited Anthony Cripps, QC, to head a committee on the legal status of women, and this committee produced a report, *Fair Shares for the Fair Sex* in 1969, which made many recommendations for change.[70] 1968 was also the year in which Joyce Butler introduced an 'Anti-Discrimination' bill in the Commons: this was to be the first of a succession of bills over the next few years. Barbara Castle's energies and persistence, combined with pressures from the unions (and growing awareness of the implications of European legislation) brought the Equal Pay Act on to the statute book in 1970: its provisions were to take effect from 1975. In 1971, Anti-Discrimination Bills were introduced by William Hamilton (in the Commons) and Baroness Seear (in the Lords). Seear's bill was opposed on second reading, but subsequently referred to a Select Committee of the House. Hamilton's bill, reintroduced in the Commons one year later, was also referred to a Select Committee of the House.[71] Both Lords' and Commons' Committees collected ample evidence relating to pervasive discrimination in the UK, and both came out in favour of legislative intervention to address the problem.[72] In 1973 the Conservative government announced its own plans for legislation on sexual equality.[73]

Margaret Thatcher, as Secretary of State for Education and Science, confessed that she found 'great difficulty in grasping the practical element of discrimination in education' and was of the opinion that there was 'virtually no' scope for legislation applying to schools.[74] She was committed to the defence of single-sex schools and colleges and chary of any idea of interfering with university autonomy in respect of admissions policies. However, well-argued expressions of the need to tackle direct and indirect discrimination in education (as well as in training and employment), together with vigorous lobbying by women's groups and individuals (such as Margherita Rendel), ensured that the Conservative administration included education in preparations for a consultative document on sexual discrimination in 1973.[75]

In relation to higher education, three topics stood out as demanding particular attention. There had long been criticism of university medical school admissions policies. Many of these schools operated quotas when it came to admitting women students, and this practice was widely considered a clear example of direct sex discrimination. A second bone of contention was the question of grants to women students who were married to non-students, which were 40 per cent lower than those of single students irrespective of husbands' earnings. The third issue was the hugely vexed one of single-sex colleges.

The more 'direct' forms of discrimination inherent in regulations governing grants to married women students and in medical schools admissions policies proved easier to address than the issue of the single-sex colleges in Oxford and Cambridge. Though evasive about whether they actually operated quotas to limit the admission of women students, many of those heading the medical schools, as well as the British Medical Association (BMA) itself, offered a defence of such a 'policy' in terms of the 'wastage' of qualified women doctors who married and were lost to the profession.[76] (The Royal College of Veterinary Surgeons argued along similar lines.[77]) The evasiveness in correspondence with officials at the Department of Education and Science (DES) about the implications of planned equality legislation makes for amusing reading. The Select Committee of the House of Lords took some trouble to try to establish whether discriminatory admissions policies were practised by the individual medical schools and to determine their extent: a few confessed to quotas of between a quarter and a third for women; others prevaricated.[78] Evidence later supplied by the 'Joint Four' (i.e. the joint executive committees of the Association of Headmasters, Headmistresses' Association, and Associations of Assistant Masters and Mistresses) – and a list of quotas for the various schools supplied by the Women in Media group, ostensibly originating from the Careers Research and Advisory Centre – suggested that the practice of limiting the intake of women medical students was indeed widespread; and that the proportion of places allotted to women might be as low as 15–20 per cent in some schools.[79]

Neither the Conservative nor the Labour administration which replaced it (in 1974) was prepared to tolerate this situation, which had caused resentment for many years. The UGC and the CVCP were urged to advise the medical schools to abandon quotas and to cease to discriminate against women students in this way.[80] In February 1974, the Royal College of Veterinary Surgeons wrote to the DES, submitting that women veterinary practitioners had a 'shorter working life' than their male counterparts and noting that some of the college's education committee felt that it was 'in the national interest' to operate quotas limiting female intake into the profession, in spite of moves to equal opportunities. J.H. Thompson, at the DES, replied with a carefully phrased letter, asking for confirmation that policies on the admission of women to veterinary schools were *not* subject to quota restrictions, and that the suggestion that they *should be* was not *a formal proposal that they should*. This prompted, of course, a somewhat wriggling reply.[81]

The situation regarding the single-sex colleges and the legality of their practices under forthcoming legislation was extremely confused. Margaret Thatcher had regarded it as 'out of the question' to take any action which would outlaw these institutions.[82] Letters from heads of both men's and women's colleges, pointing out that their statutes required their governing bodies to remain all-male or all-female, and asking for clarification of the position, began to arrive at the DES following the publication of the Conservative Government's *Green Paper on Equal Opportunities* in 1973.[83] Some feminists (Pauline Hunt, Catherine Belsey) responded to the consultative document, suggesting that the government needed to take action against single-sex colleges if they were genuinely committed to equality.[84] Of course there was no shortage of those (of both sexes) prepared to argue differently. A submission from the Colleges' Committee in Cambridge urged caution, and the need to preserve a mixture of colleges, both single-sex and coeducational. The position of women in the university had improved, it was suggested, and to compel colleges to go mixed could only be detrimental to their position.[85] Others contested this. The JCR Presidents of ten Oxford colleges, and the Cambridge Students' Union, wrote urging the government *not* to exempt colleges or their fellowships from any sexual equality legislation.[86]

But both politicians and officials at the DES fought shy of any direct confrontation with Oxford and Cambridge. Some 'let-out' clauses for the Oxbridge colleges were thought necessary if a bill was to succeed. The problem was less that of the continued legality of institutions catering for the education of one sex (which was not seriously challenged), but more that of the impact of the employment provisions of any sex discrimination legislation on the appointment of college fellows. At one stage it was suggested that 'fellows' might be regarded as members of a corporation rather than as contractual employees, in which case their appointment might be exempt from the employment provisions of the new legislation.[87] However, attempts to draft legislation in such a way as to placate the colleges and leave the right loopholes proved a serious challenge. Something of the flavour of this was apparent in a communication by the Department's Legal Adviser, G.E. Dudman, when, asked to find a wording which would allow the colleges let-out clauses, he responded in some consternation to W. K. Reid:

> I am afraid that your second request defeats me. I assume that the decision taken by ministers is to exclude (without actually saying so) the members of governing bodies of the colleges of collegiate universities (including, therefore, presidents, principals and masters as fellows, but excluding lecturers and tutors, to say nothing of the

administrative staff). But I cannot think of any formulation of principle (iv) on page 11 of the draft instructions that would come anywhere near achieving this bizarre result. Indeed, I cannot think of any draftable principle that would justify discrimination on the governing body whilst prohibiting it amongst the teaching staff.[88]

Correspondence in DES files from January/February 1974 reveals gentlemanly co-operation between Cambridge's Vice-Chancellor (Professor Linnett), Oxford's University Registrar (Geoffrey Caston) and J.H. Thompson as they tried to work towards solutions. Professor Linnett's attempt to help with phrasing the new legislation drew forth more exasperation from the beleaguered Dudman, who expostulated:

It may be that we must allow the Vice Chancellor of Cambridge to determine our policy (on the principle that in 1974 it is the crowd which decides whether a batsman is out); but we ought not to allow him to do our drafting for us.[89]

There were numerous thorny issues in relation to the formulation of equality legislation and its implications for single-sex colleges, and it is not possible to trace all the ramifications of these issues here. But it should be remembered that the problems faced by those with responsibility for drafting the legislation were encountered at a time when Oxford and Cambridge themselves were grappling with the vexed issue of coresidence. This situation will be explored in much more detail in the second half of this book. These debates over the desirability of coresidence, or of colleges 'going mixed', spanned the years from 1964 through to the 1980s, and indeed are still alive (in respect of the question of whether the remaining women's colleges should admit men) today. Crucially, the controversies of the 1970s were rehearsed at a time when there was mounting public concern over the fact that Oxford and Cambridge remained bastions of male privilege, offering limited opportunities for women students and even more limited opportunities for the career aspirations of women academics. As will be seen in Chapter 8, many in the women's colleges fought tooth and nail against coresidence, partly on the grounds that they would be likely to lose their better students to the more prestigious male colleges. However, scope for the expansion of the women's colleges had been shown to be limited, and it was increasingly evident that, if more space was to be made available for women to study in these universities, the men's colleges had to open their doors to women.

J.H. Thompson, at the DES, had had the foresight to recognize this, observing in a note to a colleague that:

There is of course, a basic contradiction between requiring all universities to provide equal facilities and maintaining the position of

111

the single-sex colleges at Oxford and Cambridge. The two propositions are seemingly inconsistent unless someone founds a great many new women's colleges.[90]

In retrospect, it is clear that government discussions around the formulation of equal opportunities legislation and the passing of the Sex Discrimination Act in 1975 had an important impact on the rate and pattern of institutional change in Oxbridge. Single-sex colleges could seek exemption from certain provisions in the Act, but the position remained extremely complex and the force of its potential impact varied between colleges, according (for instance) to terms of foundation. Some of the strategies which were adopted in both universities to regulate and order the process of change (such as Oxford's 'limited experiment' in co-residence, or quotas for admission by sex) were of dubious legality under the new legislation. G.J. Warnock, Principal of Hertford College, had foreseen something of this in 1976; writing in the *American Oxonian* on 'The coresidence question' he concluded that:

> In effect, the Sex Discrimination Act has taken away from both colleges and the University the freedom to decide and to control, in certain respects, what their future is to be. Which is, of course, exactly what that Act was intended to do.[91]

As we have seen, in the first half of the twentieth century, women's limited participation in 'elite' forms of higher education, notably the medical schools, and the Universities of Oxford and Cambridge, had had important implications for their position in higher education generally. The implications were both quantitative and symbolic. In the mid 1950s just over half of those studying in English universities had been students in Oxford, Cambridge and London (c. 33,000 of a total of 62,000 in 1953/4).[92] The proportion of women in these three universities was well below that of the provincial or civic institutions. In the case of London this reflected the quotas operated by the big London medical schools (other than the Royal Free), which admitted a heavy preponderance of men. Both Oxford and Cambridge had maintained quotas in respect of the overall proportion of women in their student bodies before 1957–60 (although Cambridge reserved the *right* to restrict the numbers of women students until 1987). In practice, the fact that colleges in Oxbridge were single-sex, and that there were so few colleges for women, ensured that the numbers of women admitted remained low. The expansion of higher education generally, and the rise of the new universities, meant that by the 1960s those studying in Oxford, Cambridge and London represented a smaller proportion of the student body than previously (34.6 per cent of the total for Great Britain in 1962/3, 26.8 per cent by 1966/7, and 25.5 per cent by 1967/8).[93] After

1975 student numbers in London, Oxford and Cambridge were beginning to show less of an imbalance of gender, and the proportion of women admitted in these universities continued to rise through the final quarter of the century.

Changing employment opportunities for women graduates

In 1964 the DES agreed to fund two studies which would provide information on graduate careers: the first of these related to those who had embarked on higher degrees and was carried out at the University of Essex (by E. Rudd and S. Hatch).[94] The second and larger investigation focused upon first-degree graduates and was led by R.K. Kelsall at the University of Sheffield. Postal questionnaires were sent to a large national sample (more than ten thousand in all) of those who had graduated in the academic year 1959/60. The results of this investigation were summarized in two publications, *Six Years After* (published in 1970), and *Graduates: the sociology of an elite* (1972).[95] Both Annette Kuhn and Anne Poole, who worked with Kelsall on the study, showed an interest in gender differences and paid particular attention to the plight of the woman graduate. The final chapter of the 1972 publication (written by Anne Poole) was entitled 'Captives by choice?' Poole argued that the evidence on women graduates showed that highly educated women were 'greatly restricted in their occupational achievements by prevailing conditions which bear little relation to their training and capabilities': following in the tradition of earlier researchers such as Judith Hubback and Constance Arregger (whose work was discussed in the previous chapter) she contended that this represented waste on an alarming scale.[96]

The study led by Kelsall showed that six years after graduation the majority of women graduates were married and that more than half of these had no paid activity whatsoever.[97] Those still at work were heavily concentrated in education. Very few women went into industry or other professions, and only a handful (36 as compared with 618 of the men) had made it into managerial-level posts.[98] The proportion of women who had gone into schoolteaching significantly exceeded the proportion that had expressed any desire to teach upon graduation.[99] Poole showed that opportunities available to the woman graduate, restricted from the outset, were further narrowed and constrained by social class, marital status and the arrival of a first child. Social conditions, and the ideology of motherhood and domesticity, were in her view much to blame. But the writing is infused with impatience and frustration: Poole cannot understand why graduate women are not more critical of their lot, and why they appear to show so little resentment of the social conditions which restrict their lives.[100] A more optimistic tone creeps in when she writes of the frustrations of middle-aged 'empty nesters': women who, no longer fully occupied by the needs of their families, indicated that they would welcome a return to work.[101] But she is unhappy with this 'two phase model' of women's working lives, much discussed in the 1950s and 1960s, because it effectively barred them from acquiring the foundation of training and experience necessary, in many careers, to success. More hope was to be derived, Poole suggested, from the rise of 'women's liberation groups' among contemporary undergraduates, and from the attitudes and 'militancy of young women who are currently at university'.[102] These might prove a force for real social change.[103]

The expansion of teacher training in the 1960s had ensured that by far the majority of women entering all forms of higher education continued to enter the teaching profession. Contemporary anxieties about teacher shortages and the 'wastage' of women teachers through marriage ensured that girls and young women were given every encouragement to consider a future in the classroom. Many female school-leavers opted for training college rather than university, and a large proportion of female graduates embarked on a one-year teaching certificate after graduation.[104] The University Grants Committee began regularly publishing statistics on the first employment of university graduates in 1963. The data for those graduating in 1961/2 revealed noticeable differences between the destinations of male and female graduates. Amongst graduates in arts and social studies, over one-third (34.5 per cent) of the women proceeding with further training went on to train for teaching, as compared with 17.9 per cent of the men.[105] The proportion of women who actually went on to teach (since formal training was not required of graduates at this time) would have been even larger. Of those graduating in pure and applied sciences, again, amongst those taking further training, the proportion of women training for teaching greatly exceeded that of their male counterparts.[106] The proportion of women arts and social science graduates taking up employment in education in 1961/2 was 48.7 per cent (compared with 19.9 per cent of men); in respect of female graduates in pure and applied science it was 43.3 per cent (compared with 19.7 per cent male graduates in pure science, 2.8 per cent in applied science).[107] Data for 1965/6 showed that over a quarter (28.7 per cent) of all the women first-degree graduates who embarked on further training went on to teacher training, as compared with only 9.9 per cent of the men.[108]

This was all depressingly familiar. At a meeting of the Cambridge Women's Appointments Board in 1965, Sir Maurice Dean had concluded that 'all considered, it might be found that women gained rather poor jobs'.[109] Was, then, a university education still something of a 'wasted investment' in the case of women? Around the same time as the Kelsall study, Maureen Woodhall, at London University's Institute of Education, set out to try to answer this question.[110] A higher education, she argued, increased a woman's earning capacity and also her propensity to remain in the labour market. Some allowance had to be made for 'non-market work', for indirect benefits, and for 'psychic income'.[111] But discrimination remained rife in the labour market. It was difficult to construct a powerful case against the 'wasted investment' argument in strictly economic terms, and Woodhall, like Anne Poole, was reduced to urging the need for a change in traditional attitudes. Changes in education, training and employment, the eradication of discrimination in the labour market, and matters of pay: all these were necessary for 'an increase in the social and private returns to investment in women's education'.[112]

In the 1970s the situation began to change. Crompton and Sanderson have suggested that two factors were crucial in helping to break down traditional gender divisions in the graduate labour market. On the one hand, there were drastic cuts in teacher training (see Figure 5.2), on the other there was the impact of the equality legislation of that decade: the Sex Discrimination Act together with the Equal Pay Act forced changes in both attitudes and practice.[113] The effect of the savage cuts in teacher education, they suggest, 'bumped' women into other forms of training and graduate employment such as commerce.[114] The influence of second-wave feminism and discussion of equality legislation made employers begin to look twice at advertising opportunities for men and women graduates separately when organizing their recruitment programmes. Carolyn Morris (formerly Robb), in the early 1970s an officer of what was then Sussex University Appointments Advisory Service, remembered that women students were beginning to complain when employers on 'the milk-round' specified vacancies according to sex.[115] A joint universities and polytechnics appointments services working party on equal opportunities for women campaigned against this practice.[116] In 1974, the Cambridge Women's Appointments Board combined with the Men's Appointments Board to offer a common service. First-destination data for 1976 showed a drop in the proportion of graduates entering teacher training, and significantly, this was most marked amongst women (from 25.9 per cent in 1974/5 to 21.0 per cent in 1975/6 of the total undertaking vocational training).[117] The tide was beginning to turn.

A marked fall in the proportion of university graduates training for schoolteaching was a feature of the 1980s (a 42 per cent drop in the proportion of those going on to further training in 1984/5 as compared with 1980/1, with another decline of 11 per cent recorded in the following year).[118] By 1990 women graduates were still more likely than men to embark upon teacher training, but the proportions had shrunk dramatically. Men were still much more likely to enter industry than women (40 per cent of male graduates, 17 per cent female). Male graduates tended to take up scientific and engineering work (33 per cent) and financial and

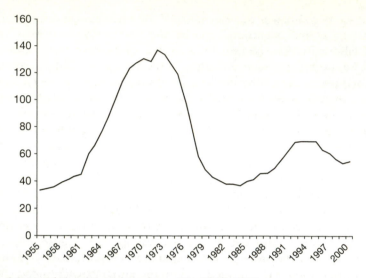

Figure 5.2 Numbers in initial teaching, UK, 1955–2000

Sources: 'Education Statistics for the UK' (annual); 'Higher Education Statistics for the UK' (annual, for recent years).

Note: Numbers in thousands, female plus male, UK all years.

legal work (17 per cent), whereas female graduates were more likely to go into teaching (18 per cent) or into personnel, medical and social work (22 per cent). However, the proportions entering commerce were roughly the same for men and women graduates (28 per cent men, 28.9 per cent women). Rather more women graduates (24.7 per cent) than men (17.2 per cent) went into public service.[119] But there had been significant shifts away from the pattern of the 1960s and earlier, and the old high road into teaching had narrowed. In 1992/3 it was recorded that, for the first time, the proportion of women university graduates going into permanent employment had drawn equal with that of their male counterparts.[120]

From 1994/5, data on the first destination of graduates were collected by the Higher Education Statistics Agency (HESA) for the higher education sector as a whole: this change, together with differences in categorization and presentation of data makes comparison with the early series very difficult. In 1994/5 it was suggested that women graduates seemed 'more inclined to take unpaid, part-time or temporary employment'.[121] By the end of the century HESA reported a 'fairly close parity' between the proportions of men and women entering different occupational categories, although a smaller proportion of women than men entered 'professional' occupations, and more women than men were taking up clerical and secretarial posts.[122] Even so, women were making substantial gains in some areas: given the long history of opposition to women in medical education, for instance, the fact that female entrants into the profession were outnumbering males by the early 2000s represents a remarkable transformation.[123] Discussions of women's 'two phase' career model had begun to sound outmoded as early as the 1980s, as increasing numbers of women graduates indicated a determination to stay in post: juggling home and family, and facing many of the obstacles of the women who had gone before them, but unwilling to contemplate (or unable to afford) a retreat into the home. But there can be no ground for complacency. By the end of the century it was clear that women's 'successes' in higher education were failing to translate into a fully equivalent measure of success or material reward in the labour market. Graduate starting salaries were lower for women than for men, and this gap even widened, slightly, at the end of the 1990s.[124] This divergence between average graduate salaries for men and women widened further in the five years following graduation. It has been argued that the present pay gap – of around 15 per cent – is only in small part attributable to the difference in the pattern of subjects studied by men and women in universities.[125] Over the course of a working life a woman graduate can expect to earn some 12 per cent less than her male counterpart.[126] The value of a university education, seen purely as a monetary investment, is still considerably less for women than for men. And for many women, combining parenting and paid work continues to prove a taxing and daunting prospect, particularly given the culture of long hours extant in many workplaces today.[127]

Part II
Coeducation and culture

Chapter Six

ða

Siege mentalities

Laying siege, storming citadels, bastions falling: the discursive narratives of both the history of women's entry into higher education in Britain since the mid nineteenth century, and indeed accounts of gender relations in universities in more recent history, are replete with the tropes of the battle-field. In its day, the call to arms served to rally the troops, to exhort women to struggle: access to education, like the franchise, was a unifying goal in 'the feminist campaign'.[1] That the language of campaigning should have permeated the historiography is unsurprising, but as Mary Beard observed in a review of Edward Shils' and Carmen Blacker's *Cambridge Women*, a fiction which attempts to 'enlist' us in 'a single vision of pioneering struggle' conceals as much as it reveals, and sometimes seems designed to prevent us from telling a story in any other kind of way.[2] There are at the very least two stories that might be told, for instance, about women's acceptance as members of Oxford and Cambridge Universities over the last century and more. On the one hand there is a 'triumphant' narrative of widening opportunities achieved through unremitting struggle. On the other, there is an account which emphasizes gradualism and patience, the achievement of 'degrees by degrees', and the incremental effect of worthy feminine demonstrations of academic competence, tactful perseverance and good manners.[3] Both kinds of narrative contain 'truths'. The aim of this chapter is not to consider the merits of one narrative or another, still less to adjudicate between them, but to approach the subject of the 'gender politics' of higher education since Victorian times as a cultural historian, attentive to language, image and metaphor. This will sketch, in broad outline, a context for the chapters dealing in finer detail with the politics of and discussions around coeducation which follow in the second half of this book.

The Princess, and *Castle Adamant*

Writing in the *News Chronicle* in 1934, Winifred Holtby expressed frustration with the continuing pattern of segregation between the sexes prevalent in Oxford: the photograph of a young women student which illustrated her text bore the caption 'Eve in the home of lost causes'. 'We are all apt to forget,' she wrote

> that only 87 years ago the poet Tennyson, wishing to invent a purely fantastic fairy story, conceived the startling and ludicrous notion of a women's college.[4]

Tennyson's 'fairytale', mock-heroic poem, *The Princess*, was first published in 1847, at a time when ideas and controversies about the nature and purposes of 'female education' were much in the air.[5] The poem itself has always generated controversy. It has served as a source of inspiration to some who have worked to extend educational opportunities for women. In late Victorian times the poem was often 'staged' by students in the new women's colleges, for instance, and to this day the line from the poem where Princess Ida proclaims 'Girls,/ Knowledge is now no more a fountain seal'd:' serves as the motto of the Girls' Day School Trust (originally founded in 1872).[6] On the other hand, there have always been feminists who objected to the poem: Emily Davies, for instance, deplored its popularity, and in the 1960s the critic Kate Millett memorably anatomized it as 'candy coated sexual politics'.[7]

The poem dramatizes the 'wild dream' of a separatist women's college, the troubled relations between the sexes of the Victorian period being transposed into a pseudo-medieval setting. It attempts to resolve what would later be designated as 'the woman question' by setting up an idealized version of 'separate spheres', emphasizing sexual difference and the interdependence of men and women. The feminist project of Ida and her colleagues is brought under siege from without and within, both in and by the text. The Prince (Ida's rejected suitor) and his friends array themselves in women's clothing to 'infiltrate' the college. The Prince's male chauvinist father gathers troops to prepare to storm it. The college is undermined from within as young girl students show too much interest in sex and babies, and women teachers with no real authority indulge in catty rivalries with each other. In the end the feminist vision collapses, besieged by unreconstructed patriarchy (the Prince's father), liberal paternalism (the Princess's father), sensitive new manhood (the Prince), and a whole riot of supposedly natural feminine traits such as the desire for babies, the urge to heal wounded soldiers and the yearning for a strong supporting shoulder.

The Princess, aptly subtitled *A Medley*, is a bizarre blend of heroism and farce; lyrical and highly erotic in places, it plays with gender identity in an uninhibited way which some critics have found intriguing and others absurd.[8] There is something there for everybody. Ida (reminiscent of Wonderwoman or Xena, Warrior Princess), her hair long and black, a single jewel on her brow burning 'like mystic fire', strides about flanked by leopards and Amazonian handmaidens (the 'daughters of the plough'). She is attracted to the Prince, who suffers from epileptic seizures, sports long golden ringlets, is dressed in 'woman's gear', and serenades her singing falsetto.

It is possible that Winifred Holtby's reference to the 'ludicrous notion of a woman's college' was based on her response to Tennyson's poem itself. As an ex-student of a woman's college (Somerville College, Oxford) she would have been aware of the history of the women's foundations in the older universities, and of their uphill struggle for recognition: she would have known that a mixed, or 'co-residential' college would have been a historical impossibility in nineteenth-century Oxford or Cambridge. It is equally probable that reference to Tennyson's poem had become mediated, by this time, by the impact of Gilbert and Sullivan's comic opera, *Princess Ida, or Castle Adamant*, which was first performed at the Savoy Theatre in 1884.[9] If there were elements of the ludicrous in Tennyson's text, these were amplified loudly in the later version. Here the comic potential inherent in the idea of women students denied contact with men were camped up in a feast of burlesque and *double entendre*. Girl students are rusticated for playing with chessmen and doodling perambulators, the true identity of men in drag is revealed when they are found hiding cigars in their needle-cases. We are invited to snigger at the vision of young ladies 'matriculating'; and the idea of a women's college is presented as a total absurdity, one of the Prince's companions lewdly volunteering to 'teach them twice as much in half an hour outside it'.[10] Whatever attempts might be made to rescue or to reappropriate any radical meaning in *The Princess* were pretty much doomed thereafter.

Laying siege: ridicule, misogyny, revenge

In 1897 and again in 1920, when the question of women's entitlement to degrees was debated in Cambridge, there were scenes of rowdyism and expressions of deep-rooted misogyny.[11] On the battlements of Senate House in 1897, onlookers watched as a dummy of a woman student riding a bicycle, her buttocks grotesquely padded in straw-filled breeches, was lowered from a window in Caius College into the street. The news of the women's defeat on this occasion incited a roaring crowd of under-graduates to storm to the gates of Newnham, where the women dons evidently appealed to their 'gentlemanly instincts' to leave them be: the men returned to their fireworks and bonfires in the centre of town. The defeat of the women's claims in 1920 produced a similar reaction: but this time a mob descending on Newnham rammed the beautiful bronze-flowered gates of the college with a handcart, badly damaging the lower panels.[12]

Ridicule, misogyny and revenge were combined in such scenes; revenge because the women were represented as having dared to try to invade male 'territory'. A.D. Godley, later Public Orator of the University of Oxford, penned a 'Fragment' in Greek Tragic form to commemorate events in Cambridge in 1897.[13] Entitled 'The 1713 against Newnham', it dramatizes women students receiving the news of their defeat against a background of firecrackers. They collapse into lamentations until a male supporter arrives: with much word play about gates he tells them to 'shut up'; they are both 'shut in' and yet 'shut out' of the university:

> I ask you, ye intolerable creatures
> Why raise this wholly execrable din,
> O objects of dislike to the discreet?
> Six hundred persons also sixty-two
> (Almost the very number of the Beast)
> Have voted for you, and defend your gates
> Moreover, mark my subtle argument: –
> When gates are locked no person can get in
> Without unlocking them; your gates are locked
> And I have got the key: so that, unless
> I ope the gates, the foe cannot get in
> This statement is Pure Reason: or, if this
> Is not Pure Reason, *I* don't know what is.

At this point the men hammer on the gates: the women try to console themselves:

> Never mind! A time is coming when despite of all their Dons
> We shall sack the hall of Jesus, and enjoy the wealth of John's!

But the idea of any such challenge is immediately rendered comic as the women prepare to march into battle with their 'chaperons in front'.

In the years between the wars the women's foundations in Oxford and Cambridge existed in an atmosphere of uneasy tolerance, feminine encampments on the margins of a male-dominated university and society. The recollections of some of the men who were undergraduates at this time suggest that they were scarcely aware of the women's colleges' existence.[14] But misogyny was often fierce: in Oxford, where women had been admitted to degrees after the First World War, moves to control the numbers of women in the university were fuelled by the argument that should

Oxford become too 'feminized', young men would opt for the more 'virile' environment of Cambridge (where women were not admitted to full membership until 1948).[15] In 1926 the Oxford Union voted in favour of a motion that 'the Women's Colleges should be levelled to the ground'. A statute limiting the proportion of women in the university (to around one-sixth of the numbers of men) was passed in 1927.[16]

Christopher Hobhouse's book on Oxford, published in 1939, furnishes examples of the potent mixture of misogyny and ridicule with which the women's foundations were so often besieged between the wars.[17] Women students are described as an unattractive breed decking themselves 'in hairy woollens and shapeless tweeds', their hair braided into 'stringy buns':

> Their domestic background is equally repellent. Instead of a quiet pair of rooms, guarded by an impenetrable 'oak' upon a secluded staircase, each girl has a minute green-and-yellow bed-sitter opening off an echoing shiny corridor. Instead of deep sofas and coal fires they have convertible divans and gas stoves. Instead of claret and port, they drink cocoa and Kia-Ora. Instead of the lordly breakfasts and lunches which a man can command in his own rooms, they are fed off warm cutlets and gravy off cold plates at long tables decked with daffodils.[18]

There are a number of observations that can be made about this kind of description, which is worth comparing with Virginia Woolf's much cited passages on Newnham ('Fernham') in *A Room of One's Own*.[19] Woolf's text was published ten years earlier than Hobhouse's book. The purpose of the writing of course is quite different: where Hobhouse sneers and expresses contempt, Woolf writes as a feminist to explain what she sees as the depressing and deplorable poverty of the women's college. Nonetheless, her language and imagery prefigure Hobhouse's, the reference to cold gravy, old green-and-yellow vegetables, cheap meat, dry biscuits, 'stringy' prunes. The idea of 'stringiness' appears twice; once in labouring the awfulness of the prunes ('an uncharitable vegetable (fruit they are not), stringy as a miser's heart and exuding a fluid such as might run in misers' veins . . .') and again in the same paragraph to conjure the image of poor women in a muddy market clutching string bags for their cheap purchases.[20] As in Hobhouse's writing about 'stringy buns' and unappetizing food, suggestions of meanness, repression, celibacy and a lack of fulfilment infuse the representation of the women's college as a most unattractive (indeed unpalatable) institution. As a feminist 'defence' of women's entitlement to higher education, there is a definite tension in Woolf's writing: discursive weapons are hazardous, and can sometimes misfire.

Women students might be portrayed in an unflattering way, but the most concentrated abuse was levelled at those teaching in the women's colleges, depicted as second-rate, embittered and small-minded. 'Spinsters almost to a woman, the female dons present a terrifying caricature of the medi-aeval tutor,' wrote Hobhouse, contending that they goaded their charges into a stupor of mechanical compliance and sometimes breakdown.[21] 'Oxford women are at the mercy of a spinster-autocracy,' asserted Keith Briant, in *Oxford Limited* (1937).[22] This 'spinstocracy' spun webs of petty restriction and cluttered rule books; then lay in waiting for pretty young girls to infringe the regulations so that it could 'pounce'.[23] Too small-minded and repressed for any judicious exercise of authority, the 'spinstocracy' treated young women like 'female convicts on parole'.[24]

Fortifications and gate-hours

With such Gothic grotesquery in mind we might recall the physical structure and architecture of the Oxbridge male college as well as the turrets and gargoyles of Royal Holloway in Egham. Many colleges were built like fortifications, with their muniment rooms and machicolated parapets. As Keith Thomas has observed in a chapter of the *History of Oxford University*, 'college walls were fortified with spikes, railings and broken claret bottles to prevent night-time invasion'.[25] Of course masculine prowess might be defined by the very ability to negotiate these defences through night-climbing or the daring scaling of defences. In Tennyson's poem, the narrative framing device is provided by a group of college lads who boast of such deeds:

> . . . but we, unworthier, told
> Of college; he had climb'd across the spikes,
> And he had squeezed himself betwixt the bars,
> And he had breath'd the Proctor's dogs . . .[26]

Similar traditions of misrule and daring had evolved in many of the civic universities around the turn of the century. These often took the form of male students 'raiding' women's hostels and halls of residence, and serenading the inmates of these 'dovecotes' or 'hen-coops', before making off with 'trophies' in the form of door-knockers, bits of garden statuary and the like.[27] But the playfulness of such traditions lost something of its appeal in the new century. Keith Thomas has pointed out that the ex-servicemen who returned to Oxford after 1945 were ill inclined to tolerate restrictions on personal liberty such as a prohibition on their entering pubs, or college gate-hours.[28] During the 1950s there was a tendency for the rules – at least tacitly – to be relaxed. From the start of the 1960s the student press was featuring articles attacking 'antiquated college regulations'. In *Cherwell*, in 1961, Harold Lind protested against the notion of colleges seeing themselves as being *in loco parentis*:

The clearest example of this is the rule enjoining all young gentlemen – and even more stringently, all young ladies – to return to college by midnight at the latest, failing which the unfortunate latecomer, like a wretched variant of Cinderella, will find himself the victim of a fairy curse in the form of a fine or a gating.[29]

Colleges, he maintained, the majority of which were 'fortified in a manner reminiscent of a mediaeval citadel', could only be put into 'this state of siege' because of a heavy-handed paternalism. Here are the beginnings of a tendency for male undergraduates to make common cause with their female counterparts in besieging authorities (instead of seeing themselves as being under siege from each other). But there was no doubt in the male mind that the female dons were more 'dragon-like' than their own college custodians. Lind continued:

The lengths to which SCRs can carry stupidity is usually best illustrated by the women's colleges, which have never had the salutary shock of receiving their undergraduates toughened by national service, and most of whose dons are still spiritually in the era when nice young ladies were expected to imitate every quality of a wax dummy except its low melting point.[30]

There were women students who prided themselves on ignoring gate hours and 'climbing in', of course. Dilys Powell had been 'rusticated' for standing on the roof of a cab in Walton Street and climbing into Somerville in the 1920s.[31] Expressions of resentment over 'gate-hours' were increasingly heard from women students in the early 1960s. Anne Bavin, a graduate of St Anne's College, declared in the *New Statesman* (1961):

This artificial restriction of freedom reaches some ludicrous lengths. St Anne's College was caged in last year by barbed wire, making the inhabitants feel, so they said, like a collection of broody hens, and the new college gates were topped by a murderous set of spikes to discourage late night entrances.[32]

Any humour here was muted: Bavin's article, entitled 'The second class sex', was basically an attack on the women's colleges. The latitude and easy tolerance of mild misdemeanours in men's colleges was denied to their female counterparts, she contended; many women dons were narrow and unworldly in outlook with little understanding of their students' goals. 'There is something absurd about a community of women which one does not find in a community of men,' suggested one (female) critic of the women's colleges in the early 1960s. Perhaps coeducation was the answer in the long term?[33]

Storming the bastions of reaction

As the 1960s progressed, student resentment of 'gate-hours' and other disciplinary restrictions grew more vocal: 'At 5 to 12 men become Cinderellas and run for "home",' protested one writer in *Cherwell* in 1963:

> If by ill luck or design they don't make it they have a good chance of being maimed on the medieval barricades. Why are gates locked at all? . . . Is it too unreasonable to expect to be treated like big boys and girls?[34]

'Spiked student falls from gate,' proclaimed a headline in the same newspaper, drawing attention to a second-year student who suffered an unfortunate accident whilst trying to climb into Pembroke College one year later.[35] A glance through the index to *The Times* under the headings of Oxford and Cambridge University for 1964 ('Students to pay for spikes in Bodleian' or 'Worcester College: walls greased to stop late students') gives an insight into the tensions of these years.

Guest hours ('Men hours') in women's colleges were a constant source of friction. 'On a week-day in Somerville 8.30 p.m. is the dividing line between propriety and promiscuity,' alleged the writer in *Cherwell* quoted above.[36] 'Longer hours in bird cages,' rejoiced another (male) student journalist in 1964, celebrating the fact that St Hilda's and Lady Margaret Hall had now relaxed restrictions to allow women students to keep their visitors until 10 p.m.[37]

Women in Oxford were 'mollycoddled' like 'Roedean third formers,' 'cocooned in the Victorian mother-love of their colleges,' jeered one male journalist.[38] Others lamented the plight of the male undergraduate in Oxford or Cambridge, where female company was in such short supply, contrasting this 'unnatural' situation with what was claimed to be the much more healthy situation in the newer universities where the balance between the sexes was more equal. Women had an unenviable lot in Oxford, pointed out one such writer, 'trying to combine the vast amount of work which is expected of them because of their privileged position with the attempt to satisfy the social and emotional needs of six thousand growing boys'.[39] There was a need to increase the numbers of places for female students in the university, it was often argued, not only on grounds of equity, but in the interests of the social and emotional balance of the undergraduate male.

'Single-sex education is one of the last bastions of petty paternalism within Oxford and has to go if we aspire to an adult existence,' declared Simon Sedgwick Jell in an article 'Storming the bastion of reaction: co-education', published in *Isis* in 1970.[40] The 1970s were a decade in which radical students, both men and women, were pretty much united in favour of coeducation and 'the mixed college'. JCR after JCR expressed themselves unhappy with 'sexual apartheid' and segregation.[41] The proponents of 'the mixed college' in these years may have waded into a minefield, but they survived to win the war.

'Selling the pass', or 'grabbing the best girls'

In the early decades of the twentieth century it had been a matter of pride for many of the newer civic universities in Britain to claim that they 'made no distinction of sex'. This was far from being the case; plenty of distinctions remained in these institutions in terms of access, disciplinary and social arrangements, as a previous study of mine has shown.[42]

There were no all-male colleges in the University of London, although segregation remained a feature of many of the London medical schools before 1944 (this will be the subject of the next chapter). There were four all-female colleges in London in 1939: Bedford, Royal Holloway, Westfield, and King's College of Household and Social Science (later reconstituted as Queen Elizabeth College in 1953), but by the mid 1960s all these had decided in favour of coeducation.[43] (These changes will be explored more fully in Chapter 8.) Janet Sondheimer, historian of Westfield, entitled her (1983) history of the college, *Castle Adamant in Hampstead*, some twenty years after its portals had been breached by men.[44] 'Chambord by the Thames: men to invade women's stronghold,' announced the *Times Educational Supplement* when Royal Holloway converted to coeducation in 1962.[45] However, the principle of segregation remained enshrined in the historical legacy of single-sex colleges in Oxford and Cambridge at this time, elite institutions with a cultural status which impacted on the whole university 'system'.

Between the 1960s and the 1980s the change in these institutions was dramatic. By the end of the 1980s there were no single-sex male colleges left in either Oxford or Cambridge. In Cambridge, Girton admitted male undergraduates in 1979, leaving Newnham, New Hall and Lucy Cavendish admitting only women. In Oxford three of the formerly women's colleges had 'gone mixed' by the end of the 1980s: Somerville (until 1994) and St Hilda's remained all-female. The purpose of this chapter is not to explore the various reasons for these changes, nor to try to explain the troubled politics of these years, which will be elaborated in Chapters 8 and 9 below. Here I want to emphasize the extent to which many of the authorities in single-sex colleges felt *besieged* by demands for coeducation. Whilst there can be no doubt that many of the Fellows of male colleges felt beleaguered by the demands of their Junior Common Rooms, and by the provisions of the Sex Discrimination Act of the mid 1970s (which made 'quotas' for the admission of women, for instance, illegal), it was some of the Principals and Fellows of the women's colleges who probably felt most 'under siege' from the 1970s onwards.

The first serious proposal that a male college should seek to address the shortage of places for women in Oxford came from New College in 1964 (see Chapter 8 below).[46] In the event this proposal foundered in that the requisite majority of two-thirds of the college's governing body in favour of statutory changes was not forthcoming.[47] The events of 1964 inspired a comic muse to pen a poem 'Selling the pass', which appeared in the *Oxford Times* for that year (see appendix to this chapter), replete with images of portals breached and bastions and crenellations crumbling. New College's librarian, who was credited with the idea of admitting women, was represented as having made himself highly unpopular amongst many of his colleagues:

> They said 'Queer manners makyth man'
> And gloomy port went round
> They blamed the wise Librarian
> Abused him and reviled
> But he picked up his Vogue and disingenuously smiled
> Because he numbered this among his most successful ploys: –
> A College that creams off the girls
> Will (ergo) cream the boys.

This was precisely the point. The situation had changed markedly from that of late Victorian times when women students could be regarded as an embarrassment, and tolerated only when segregated in women's colleges round the edges of a male-dominated university. Women students, more particularly the clever ones, were now a *resource*. To admit them was increasingly seen as likely to improve the academic status of colleges with comparatively low rates of highly able applicants; at the same time it became apparent that well-qualified men were increasingly liable to favour entry into mixed colleges. Those principals of the women's colleges who looked uneasily upon the opening of the men's colleges to women were all too aware of this, and they feared for their own entry, particularly in those departments (such as science and maths) where the supply of able women was seen to be limited.

In both Oxford and Cambridge the authorities in women's colleges tried to dampen and defuse enthusiasm for coeducation. The women's colleges were seriously threatened, and they found themselves again on the defensive, though in a very different context from that of the period before the Second World War. They feared the loss of their best students, that the older foundations (in a much used phrase of the time) would 'skim the cream'; they feared that, should they admit men, the best male students would shun 'a women's college' (and that they would be 'left with the dregs'); they feared for the position of women students in colleges with a 'male ethos', and they feared, in short, for their very survival.[48]

In an article 'Women breach Oxford defences' published in the *Times Higher Education Supplement* in 1974, Ian Bradley alluded to Gilbert and Sullivan's Princess Ida once again, contending that many girls set their sights on a mixed college out of 'sheer dread of spending three years in an all-female institution'.[49] The women's colleges, he submitted, were going downhill as it became apparent that all the 'more extrovert and exciting girls' were electing for the mixed colleges. He sensed 'a distinct aversion to men' among applicants to a women's college. 'The real revolution' would come, he suggested, when the women's colleges opened 'their Holloway-like gates' to men.[50] The reference to 'Holloway' is significant, conjuring images of the sanatorium or prison as much as the college in Egham. Misogyny, mental disturbance and confinement are coded together in a single cultural reference to the women's college.

Although the women's colleges continued to plead for 'a moratorium' or breathing space for adjustment, through some kind of 'orderly queue' or controlled phasing of the process whereby men's colleges opened their doors to women in both Oxford and Cambridge in the 1970s, by the end of the decade many of those in the men's colleges were impatient with such demands. As will be detailed in Chapter 8, Oxford University had originally sanctioned an 'experiment' whereby five formerly male colleges had been given licence to admit women undergraduates from 1972. In 1977 the University's Council resolved to withdraw from any further attempt to 'hold the ring' and to leave the question of 'going mixed' to the colleges. One opponent of this policy feared that this would be 'the starting pistol for a race in which the colleges would try to beat all the others in grabbing the best girls for themselves'.[51] What followed was indeed something along these lines. Attempts to agree an orderly transition were doomed in both Oxford and Cambridge as what some in the women's colleges regarded as 'rogue male' colleges broke ranks and decided, simply, to go ahead and admit women without submitting themselves to any more protracted and frustrating negotiations. The 'rogue colleges' in both universities submitted that complexity and delay in implementing coresidence was counterproductive, confusing and discouraging to applicants, and sending out very mixed messages about whether women students were welcomed in Oxbridge.[52]

The phrase 'Grabbing the best girls' featured as the page title to the section dealing with Oxford and Cambridge Universities in Anthony Sampson's *Changing Anatomy of Britain* in 1982.[53] As Jenifer Hart observed, the motives of those in the men's colleges anxious to go mixed were diverse, sometimes altruistic and egalitarian, sometimes based on institutional self-interest: some may have been spurred by thinking it 'their duty to rescue girls' from 'inferior women tutors and the convent atmosphere of women's societies'.[54] St Georges, galloping to save maidens from the dragon-dons? Were the women's colleges plundered and doomed? In the end, those in the women's colleges who deplored the moves towards coeducation were probably moved by a similar mixture of motives: institutional self-interest might be combined with a genuine anxiety about the kind of experience young women would be likely to have in a college overwhelmingly dominated (at the senior level at least) by men. Women held few senior positions in either Oxford or Cambridge and their colleges could not compete (in terms of resources and prestige) with the older male foundations. The sense of being threatened was real enough. These themes will be explored further in Chapters 8 and 9.

Masculine strongholds: last ditch resistance

Resistance to the idea of admitting women to the London medical schools and to the men's colleges in Oxford and Cambridge was staunch and vehement, but not powerful enough, ultimately, to withstand the forces of change. From the 1960s, pressure was also mounting against other forms of gender segregation in universities in the UK. After a series of battles and campaigns in each institution, women were admitted to membership of both the Cambridge Union Society and the Oxford Union in 1963. The idea of separate male and female student unions and societies had been abandoned in most universities before this date.[55] In Glasgow, however, there was strong student resistance to the idea of a mixed union. Women joined the Queen Margaret Union Society (a legacy of the women's college which had formerly existed in the University[56]). Male students might join the Glasgow University Union, an institution originally founded on the model of the Gentleman's Club, which had a dyed-in-the-wool reputation for hard drinking and other forms of masculine excess. In the 1970s the GUU gained particular notoriety for its entertainment of 'ladies of artistic merit' (i.e. strippers).[57] The state of its bar was legendary. There was concern, in the university, about whether such formal and enforced segregation was in fact legal after the Sex Discrimination Act of 1975. In 1979, Queen Margaret College Union voted to admit men.[58] The election of a popular and openly gay male student president soon after this led to an interesting situation in the student community whereby the GUU's reputation for unreconstructed blunt (and often deplorably intolerant) masculinity hardened, and many men of a more liberal, egalitarian and tolerant outlook joined the former women's union.[59] Newspaper articles regularly reported men in the GUU 'manning the barricades' and fighting off any attempt on the part of feminists to 'storm the bar'. The GUU finally submitted to pressure from the university authorities to admit women (but emphatically with 'ill grace'), in 1980.

All-male hostels and halls of residence were some of the last male strongholds in universities in Britain. Woolton Hall, a residence of the University of Manchester, was a case in point. From its inception, the hall had prided itself on its 'Oxbridge' public-school and rugby playing character, its high table, and its noisy traditions of competitive drinking, water- and pudding-throwing at dinner, and its rampaging raids on other halls and hostels. Again, the rise of feminism and the advent of equal opportunities served initially to harden this character. In the 1980s, the hall's discipline book shows its warden up against the showing of 'blue films of the "raw meat" variety', announced as 'cultural evenings' in the JCR.[60] The university's plan for Woolton as a mixed hall of residence seems to have been in part inspired by the hope that women would provide a 'civilising influence'.[61] When this future was announced, some of the students planned an appeal to Prince Philip to avert such a fate. To no avail: yet again the press resounded with notices of 'one of the last bastions' of masculinity falling.[62]

La lutte perpétuelle?

Even a cursory glance through the educational press of these decades will yield a surfeit of headlines about gates being opened, citadels stormed, bastions breached and so forth, and the same imagery is etched into the historiography. 'The male bastions succumb at last,' declares a title heading to one of the later sections of *Women at Cambridge: a brief history*, published to mark the fiftieth anniversary of the formal admission of women to degrees in the University in 1998.[63] Coeducation has triumphed, and very few segregated institutions remain in British universities today. Those that do survive are largely for the female sex. At the time of writing, there are a very few women's halls of residence in universities around the UK and four remaining colleges in Oxford and Cambridge admitting only women.[64]

In concluding her chapter on women in the twentieth-century volume of the *History of Oxford University*, Janet Howarth points out that the transition to mixed colleges can be interpreted in two ways. One might choose to represent the women's colleges as having been undermined and effectively 'doomed' by the changes. Or one might celebrate the changes as representing a widening of opportunities for women and a 'triumph' for feminism.[65] There can be little doubt that the transition to mixed colleges was highly effective in increasing the proportion of places available for women undergraduates in both Oxford and Cambridge, bringing this closer to the proportion of places available for men. There were many scholars in the women's colleges who from the outset welcomed the opening of the men's colleges to women as a move in the right direction, and recognized that their own institutions would also have to change.[66] Considerations of this kind encouraged Girton to open its doors to men in 1979, and in Oxford, St Anne's, Lady Margaret Hall and St Hugh's did likewise; then, after much debate and amid public controversy, Somerville admitted its first male students in 1994.[67]

Being perceived as 'holding out' against the admission of men has left the remaining women's colleges in an unenviably defensive position, constructed as 'under siege' in newspaper headlines, and facing conflicting pressures from within and without.[68] When Somerville's governing body took the decision to admit men at the beginning of the 1990s, they found themselves doing battle with their own junior members as well as a significant section of the public.[69] For the case for protected 'women's spaces' has not disappeared. Reports and surveys in the last quarter of the twentieth century repeatedly drew attention to the plight of women students and teachers in Oxford and Cambridge: both universities remain male-dominated institutions with a deplorably poor record in promoting women: there has been some change, but not enough.[70] The battles continue, but they are increasingly waged from within the mixed colleges, rather than from a 'segregated' base.

If this chapter has overly laboured the imagery of the battlefield, my defence is that 'siege mentalities' have been so embedded in the discursive construction of the subject as to render it inevitable. There are, after all connections (if not literal correspondences) between language and history. Perhaps historical circumstances will shift in the course of this new century to make possible a 'linguistic turn' premised on a sense of fairness and co-operation between the sexes in academic life. This would entail a different ideal, based on different politics, but is perhaps not altogether removed from Tennyson's vision in *The Princess*.

APPENDIX

'Selling the pass'

(An anonymous poem by 'M.S.' published in the *Oxford Times*, 3 July 1964.)

The Warden's brow was sad
And the Warden's speech was slow
He gazed from Alma Mater's walls
Towards the female foe
That, wave on charging wave, advanced
And ebbed to charge anew
And for the many win a place
Reserved for far too few.

Out spoke the wise Librarian
A master-man of ruse
'Nuffield may think to buy them off
It's not the slightest use
To every man there cometh
The knowledge soon or late
That women are too much for him
So, ope the College gate.

'Our crenellations crumble
Our bastions are thin
We cannot keep them out,' he said
'Well then, invite them in
For what can we do better
To shorten fearful odds
Than share with ninety lovely girls
Our cloisters and our quads?'

The Warden heaved a sigh
And flung the portal wide
And ninety maidens stared amazed
Then fought to get inside.
The cream of all the maidens
The toughest and the best
O, dark and bitter were the thoughts
In Alma Mater's breast.

Then girlish laughter echoed
Up each New College stair
Complacently the Warden sniffed
The bath-salts in the air
But in the other SCRs
What donnish teeth were ground
They said, 'Queer manners makyth man'
And gloomy port went round.

They blamed the wise Librarian
Abused him and reviled
But he picked up his *Vogue*
And disingenuously smiled
Because he numbered this among
His most successful ploys:-
A College that creams off the girls
Will (ergo) cream the boys.

Chapter Seven

Women students and the London medical schools, 1914–1939

The anatomy of a masculine culture

Chapter 3 focused on the ambitions and experiences of women who sought an education which would qualify them for careers in medicine. The purpose of this chapter is to look more closely at controversy over coeducation in the London medical schools before the Second World War. E. Moberly Bell, in her work *Storming the Citadel*, regarded the arguments put forward by those schools which decided against admitting women as 'probably not taken very seriously by those who put them forward', suggesting that they were 'merely the pretexts to conceal some deep-seated, probably sub-conscious, determination to keep women out of the profession.'

> It was probably some deep primitive masculine instinct, which forbade them to admit women to any sort of equality demanding that they should confine themselves to serving their lord and masters and bearing their children.[1]

She comes pretty close to asserting a model of simple patriarchal backlash, which is an explanation that I shall consider more closely later in this chapter. Moberly Bell's history was based largely on the archives of the Royal Free Hospital School of Medicine, and on the journals, notes and papers of the Medical Women's Federation. She appears to have made less use of the records held in other London schools, and one of my aims here has been to consult these in as much detail as possible. In what follows, I shall aim firstly to supply a more detailed narrative of events and chronology, unravelling some of the issues and politics involved. I will consider the attitudes of the schools themselves and of the University of London, the stance taken by the Medical Women's Federation, and the responses of feminists and the national press to what was widely described as 'The sex war' in medicine in the 1920s and 1930s. Finally I want to consider the light that the gender politics involved in the controversies throw upon our understanding of masculinity and professionalism in the period.

The system of provision for medical education in London when war broke out in 1914 was unusual in that women students were confined to a separate school, the London (Royal Free Hospital) School of Medicine (before 1897 the London School of Medicine for Women). In the late nineteenth century, separate schools of medicine for women had also been founded in Edinburgh and in Glasgow and it has sometimes been argued that the existence of these schools served to delay the integration of women students into university classes in medicine in both cities.[2] Broadly speaking, by 1914, most universities outside London provided 'coeducational' facilities for medical training. Separate classes (most often in anatomy) and sexually segregated dissecting rooms were sometimes defended on grounds of 'delicacy' or modesty. And mixed classes certainly continued to provoke mixed feelings on the part of many teachers. (The Acting Dean of the Faculty of Medicine at Leeds University, for instance, told investigators from the University of London in 1916 that he was 'absolutely averse from the medical education of women', but that since his university admitted them as students, he could see 'no good or useful reason against treating them on equal terms and along with the men'.[3]) The University of London found itself in an anomalous and somewhat compromising position: it prided itself on having been the first British university to have opened its degrees to women and yet none of the medical schools of the university except the London School of Medicine for Women (LSMW) would actually admit them as students.[4] By 1915 women were being urged to rally to the nation's need and to train as doctors, and yet it was obvious that the facilities for their training, in London, were wholly inadequate. The LSMW was full to bursting, whilst some of the other schools, depleted of male students in wartime, were almost empty. What could be done?

In 1915 the University of London Senate appointed a subcommittee to consider the problem. This took evidence from the Deans of all the schools of the University in the Faculty of Medicine and other witnesses. It also addressed questions about coeducation to medical schools outside London. The first part of a report from this subcommittee was submitted to Academic Council in May 1916. The committee emphasized that it was 'the policy of the University to afford equal opportunities to all students without distinction of sex'; and stated that they could find 'no valid objection' against the coeducation of men and women students of medicine.[5] They conceded that there might be 'some difficulty' in instructing women on the subject of 'diseases peculiar to men', but did not consider this insuperable.[6] They reported that the deans of the schools feared that their male students would object to the admission of women on the grounds that women were 'keener in their work' than men and edged to the front at demonstrations. There was also the objection that women 'were unable to contribute to the athletic life of their school'. Nonetheless, the committee reasserted its strong leaning in favour of the schools reconsidering their entry policies. The university itself had no power 'to take executive steps' in the matter except in the case of the Departments of Anatomy in King's College and University College, both of which were informed that their exclusion of women students was 'inconsistent with the University of London Act and the University Statutes'.[7]

Events moved quickly at this point, as the second part of the subcommittee's report (submitted to Academic Council a few months later) made clear. Outside London, the University of Edinburgh finally decided to admit women to full membership of the Faculty of Medicine, and it was announced that the separate School of Medicine for Women in Edinburgh would close.[8] Things were changing in London, too, and the subcommittee was able to report with some satisfaction that Charing Cross, St Mary's, and King's College London had followed St George's Hospital Medical School in opening their facilities, to varying extents, to women.[9] The subcommittee concluded with the suggestion that their report should be circulated to the schools, with the suggestion that the university should make arrangements for a conference on the question of the medical education of women in London, with the aim of reaching a general agreement on the question of admission.[10] This conference took place in January 1917. The proceedings were published; they show little in the way of any consensus, but provide a good deal of insight into contemporary attitudes.[11]

By 1918 seven of the previously all-male schools had decided to admit women. Four schools remained all-male (St Bartholomew's, Guy's, St Thomas's and the Middlesex). St George's was the first to admit 'lady students', in strictly limited numbers, and for the duration of the war only.[12] (Five women were admitted in 1915, and the student registers record nineteen female entrants in the period as a whole.[13]) Charing Cross was more liberal: R.J. Minney, historian of the hospital and its medical school, records that the numbers of male students had declined dramatically by 1915, and it became a necessity to admit women:

> They came swarming in. Within a few weeks the male students were mere dots amidst the fluttering skirts and flowing hair in the lecture theatre.[14]

Dr Fenton, the Dean of the School, expressed magnanimity, arguing that coeducation was the logical conclusion of women's campaign to enter the medical profession, and that it was to the advantage of everyone that it should come about.[15] The school and hospital had been 'thrown open to women students on the same conditions as men', and 'no distinction' would be made in 'teaching, hospital practice or discipline' between the sexes. Dr Fenton was commended for his perspicacity and his sympathy for women students' aspirations by the Oxford Women's Suffrage Society, whose Press Secretary, J.P. Margoliouth, penned an article in the *Oxford Times* on these events.[16]

Like Charing Cross, both St Mary's and the Westminster Schools of Medicine had found themselves suffering from the exodus of male students in wartime. (According to Westminster's Hospital Gazette, *The Broad Way*, by 1915 there was a solitary male student in the college.[17]) Both institutions decided to admit women in 1916. In the case of St Mary's, the decision was coupled with an agreement with the LSMW to take a number of this school's students annually for clinical instruction only.[18] The annual intake, originally of less than twenty students, soon rose, although these numbers showed considerable fluctuation from year to year between 1916 and 1924.[19] In the case of Westminster, the number of female entrants appears to have been very small.[20]

At the London Hospital Medical College the decision to admit women was delayed until 1918, when the Minutes of the House Committee record a 'general feeling . . . that the time had come when – whether we liked it or not – women students must be admitted to the College'.[21] It was suggested that up to thirty-five or forty women could be accommodated annually, for the clinical part of the course only. Miss Margaret Basden was appointed tutor to the women students, at a salary of £50 p.a.[22] Later estimates show that about sixty-eight women were admitted to 'The London' between 1918 and 1922.[23]

The Minutes of the London Hospital Medical College record that the University of London's Senate 'learnt with gratification' of the college's decision to admit women, 'a step which is in entire conformity with both the wishes and the policy of the University'.[24] The Subcommittee on the Medical Education of Women Undergraduates could feel that its urgings had had some effect by 1918, especially when both King's and University Colleges moved, albeit somewhat tardily, to accommodate women. In 1916 the King's College Delegacy decided that it was prepared to admit up to twenty women, annually, to the Department of Anatomy.[25] Two years later, at a special meeting of the Medical Board, it was decided to approve the admission of women students to the King's College Hospital Medical School.[26] University College eventually conceded women admission to the Faculty of Medicine in 1917, and the following year they were allowed entry into the University College Hospital Medical School.[27]

In the course of discussion at the conference, which was held under the auspices of the University of London in 1917, the deans of the medical schools had inquired of the Vice-Chancellor whether it was the university's aim to see women admitted to the London Schools permanently, or merely on a temporary basis whilst the war lasted. Without hesitation, Sir Alfred Pearce Gould replied that the university wished to see them permanently admitted.[28] The Dean of St George's Hospital Medical School had observed that arrangements for the education of women at his school had worked 'with perfect harmony and success'. Women had 'belonged to the athletic clubs, and no trouble had arisen out of the sports'. Female students 'attended the medical societies, saw cases, read papers just as the men students did'.[29] Nevertheless, he emphasized that the school's acceptance of women was for the period of the war only, and this was indeed the case: the names of women students disappear from the register after 1919. Dr Fenton, the Dean of the Charing Cross Hospital Medical School who has been mentioned above, argued that although his school regarded the admission of women as 'in the nature of an experiment', he thought it would be very difficult for a school, 'having once opened its doors to women to find any logical reason for closing them again'.[30] In the events of the next decade or so, logic was to play less than a governing role.

The first challenges to women's new-found gains came in 1920, at University College and at the London Hospital. Unfortunately, it has proved impossible to find the Minutes of the University College Hospital Medical School Committee, and what follows has been taken from W.R. Merrington's history of the hospital and its medical school (which was published in 1976).[31] Merrington records that in October 1920 a movement supported by students who were ex-servicemen gathered momentum and demanded that the school call a halt to the admission of women. The letter which these students sent to the committee claimed that 'Public School and Oxford and Cambridge men' would prefer to train at Guy's and St Bartholomew's while these eschewed coeducation, and feared that University College Hospital would gain a damaging reputation as 'the teaching Women's Hospital of the Metropolis'. Worse, many of the male students were alarmed at the prospect of women getting house appointments:

> We need hardly point out, gentlemen, the intolerable position of an ex-serviceman who has, perhaps, as his House Surgeon over him a girl of twenty-two . . .[32]

The controversy which ensued showed that women students were not without their supporters as well as opponents, among the college and school authorities: nevertheless a meeting of the Medical School Committee in November 1920 passed a resolution limiting the number of female entrants for the following session to twelve. From 1921 on (and in effect until 1944) the small group of women privileged to undergo clinical training at UCH were to feel somewhat on the defensive.

In attempting to unravel the sequence of events which led to women's exclusion from the London Hospital Medical College between 1920 and 1925 the historian has the advantage of much more evidence, since these events are clearly detailed in the Minute Books of the college and of the house committee. In March 1920, a decision was made to limit the numbers of women students to 10 per cent of the entrants annually and to reconsider the whole issue of their admission after 1923.[33] It seems that effectively, however, the authorities had already decided to revert to an all-male policy. A subcommittee was appointed by the college board with a brief to collect evidence on the effects of coeducation on the welfare of the college, but this seems to have been a mere gesture, an attempt to collect ammunition to defend a cause that had already been determined. The one-page report submitted in October 1921 was flimsy in the extreme, based on impressionistic evidence and hearsay. It simply contended that 'Cambridge men' thought of 'The London' as 'almost entirely a woman's school' and that 'at a recent meeting of the Medical Council almost everyone present had some instance to give of students going elsewhere through their aversion to co-education.'[34] The college's intake of Oxford and Cambridge men, it was argued, had gone down from an average of 17.8 per annum before the war to 13 in 1921/2. The Medical Council, College Board and House Committee all resolved that no more 'lady students' be admitted from 1921.

The reaction against women's presence in the London did not end there. There was still the vexed question of whether women who had received their clinical training in the college were eligible for the coveted house appointments which would extend their training. In January 1922, Dr Gladys Wauchope was appointed House Physician to the firm of Drs Hutchinson and Rowlands. There was 'a very strong opposition' to her appointment as Lady Resident: the male residents protested bitterly that women were not suited to such appointments, and that they would damage the welfare of the college and its athletics. They went so far as to threaten resignation over the issue.[35] Lord Knutsford, as Chairman of the Hospital and of the House Committee, drew upon all his resources of tact on this occasion. He seems to have assured the men that time was on their side, but that while women were still in the course of their training in the college it was only fair that they should be considered for house positions. Such appointments would only be made 'with extreme care', and when women were considered absolutely suitable.[36] Resignations were averted, but even then, the bad feeling persisted. In February 1923 Miss Gibson and Miss Glyn-Jones were appointed as Receiving Room Officers. The residents' response was recorded in the House Committee Minutes: they emphasized their understanding that

> The appointment of women to Resident posts is the logical outcome of a pledge, and that while here they should be on equality with men;

but since it has been determined to refuse further admission of women *as students*, this liability will be strictly limited, as regards number, to the obligations of honour, and *no more*.[37]

In June 1923, Margaret Basden's appointment as tutor to women students in the College was terminated.[38] There were a few more splutterings of ill-feeling in the following year. By 1925 the College Minutes record discussions over the future use of the now-vacated women's common room,[39] and the men went quietly about their business.

By 1924 the spotlight on controversy over coeducation had shifted to St Mary's. Here again, the archives permit of a detailed reconstruction of events. The story has recently been told in an (unpublished) dissertation by James Garner, who drew upon the school's plentiful archives.[40] 'The women's side' of events can further be explored from files which the St Mary's Hospital Women's Committee lodged with the Medical Women's Federation, now preserved in the Contemporary Medical Archives Centre at the Wellcome Institute.[41] Garner has shown that the agreement which St Mary's Hospital Medical School had made with the LSMW in 1916 had led to many tensions between the two institutions. From 1920 onwards, antipathy towards women students in the school mounted, mainly amongst ex-servicemen, but fuelled by the intractable misogyny of Sir Almroth Wright, an anti-feminist of almost legendary status already encountered in Chapter 3 via Ida Mann; Wright was alleged to have 'hated students of any sort' but reserved a particular loathing for women.[42]

In February 1924, a petition signed by ninety-six men was addressed to the Medical School Committee claiming that the presence of women in the school had led to bickering, bad feeling and 'athletic paralysis'. Most men, it contended, disliked serving under women house officers and on mixed firms, which was not conducive to the smooth running of the hospital.[43] The committee referred the petition to the Hospital's Board of Management, intimating, at the same time, that there was a good deal of support amongst the staff for the men's petition. The staff were not undivided on the issue and a counter-petition, signed by thirteen male doctors, was also forwarded to the Board of Management, taking issue with the contentions elaborated in the first petition one by one and suggesting that

> the anti-feminine feeling among the men students is largely worked up by a few enthusiasts and is not the result of mature consideration by the majority.[44]

In the meantime the women students in St Mary's countered with a Memorandum of Protest, signed by 183 out of the 236 women who had been admitted to the school, in which they described themselves as 'dismayed and distressed beyond expression' to have their case so judged in their absence, particularly in view of their awareness of the fact that it was only the admission of women in 1916 that had saved the school from bankruptcy.[45] The atmosphere amongst the students became charged and tense. Kathleen Norton, who had come to St Mary's from Oxford for her clinical training in the 1920s, recalled a series of incidents in which male students threw squibs under chairs and added salt to the teapots in the women's common room.[46]

There followed a period of intense wrangling and great confusion over the college's position. A meeting between the Dean (Dr C.M. Wilson) and the women students in the library on May 24 failed to reassure the women or to clarify the situation. Wilson gave an awkward speech emphasizing financial difficulty in the college (according to notes made by one of the women at the meeting), confessing that 'we have got into a hopeless mess'[47] (whether he meant financially, or in terms of politically loaded negotiations is unclear). According to the same source Wilson 'appealed that the matter should be allowed to die down', complaining that the 'men students thought he was against them, and so did the women.'[48]

Having no idea where they stood, the women students busied themselves collecting money as well as moral support; probably hoping that an endowment of scholarships for female students would strengthen their position. A total of £810 was collected from past and present students, and in June 1924, the Secretary of the Women Students' Committee (M. Herford) wrote to the Dean offering the money 'as a token of loyalty' and in appreciation of the decision to keep the St Mary's 'character as a mixed school'.[49] Wilson replied rejecting this 'generous offer' of a bursary fund, on the grounds that the Board of Management had 'come to no final decision concerning co-education'.[50] The women wrote again, later in June, asking for clarification of the situation. But by this time they knew that the battle was lost. In July, Joan Ross, the Chairman of the St Mary's Women's Committee, packed up the collection of letters, memoranda, newspaper clippings and pledges of financial support that had accrued over the last few months and parcelled them off to the Medical Women's Federation, noting the women's desire that the documents should be entrusted to some 'permanent and corporate body' where they might be preserved for posterity.[51]

Aside from University College Hospital, which as we have seen offered twelve places to women students annually, St Mary's reversion to an all-male entry left only Charing Cross, Westminster and King's College Hospital Medical Schools still 'coeducational'. In the case of Charing Cross and Westminster, it has not proved possible to reconstruct the details of the reversal in policy, because the Medical School Committee Minutes are missing from the archives of Charing Cross for the period 1922–8 and none could be located for the Westminster School before 1933. Both of these institutions decided against taking any further women students in 1928.

The Medical Board of King's College Hospital Medical School recorded its decision to reconsider a mixed entry of students in 1927.[52] In February 1928, at a Special Meeting held at Sir Lenthal Cheatle's house in Harley Street, the Board reported that they had sought legal advice in the matter and that:

> It was agreed by the unanimous vote of the twenty-four members of the Board present at this meeting that the Medical Board is of the opinion that the best interests of KCHMS will be served by not admitting women in the future.[53]

However, the situation at King's was complicated by the relation of the college to the University of London. We have seen how the events of 1915–17 had led to the Senate appointing a subcommittee on the medical education of women undergraduates which had reported in favour of coeducation. This subcommittee had reported again in 1923, following the London Hospital Medical School College's decision not to admit any more women.[54] At this point in time female medical students were eligible for clinical instruction at Charing Cross, King's, St Mary's, Westminster and University College Hospitals as well as at the Royal Free, and so the sub-committee was able to reassure the Senate that there was in fact adequate provision for women in London.[55] By 1928, the situation was very different. The subcommittee produced its third report in 1929. It reiterated that its members were 'unable to see any valid argument on the merits against the provision of co-education in medicine', emphasizing again that 'the prepossession of the University is in favour of such co-education'.[56] They conceded that maybe 'the advantage is not felt so much by men students', but on balance they judged that 'the advantage to the women outweighs any possible loss to the men'. However the subcommittee was forced to recognize that its powers of intervention were limited and that co-education, if it was to succeed, must be voluntary. They concluded that in their view there should be three types of clinical education: (1) for men only, (2) for women only, and (3) for men and women. An additional recommendation was that the Vice-Chancellor be requested to invite the medical schools (other than UCHMS and the Royal Free) to consider the possibility of admitting a quota of women students 'as a means of giving effect to the policy of the University as set out in the Report'.[57]

Even before the publication of this Report in 1929 the Principal of King's College, Dr Halliday, had urged the Board of Management in the College Hospital to reconsider its decision to bar entry to women. At first the Board were obdurate in refusing to re-open the issue. However, in December 1929, the Minutes of the Committee of Management record that following the request of Dr Halliday, five women students from King's College might be admitted to the Medical School. A period of some wrangling and obstructionism seems to have ensued. But by November 1930, it was agreed that the Dean of the Medical School might be given discretion to admit 'a limited number of women' and that for the present he would be advised to limit the number to ten women, annually.[58]

The feminist response to these events was of course one of outrage. Feminists were not slow to claim that women doctors had spearheaded advances in all those branches of medicine which particularly concerned women and children. Articles in *Time and Tide*, following the London Hospital's reversal of policy in 1921/2 and that of St Mary's in 1924, urged women to think twice about any subscription to hospitals which excluded women students.[59] At a meeting in Women's Service House in October 1924, Lady Barnett delivered a powerful speech condemning the actions of the London Hospital and St Mary's, and the meeting resolved to redouble efforts to give money to those hospitals that continued to admit women for clinical instruction.[60] October 1924 saw the Jubilee Celebrations of the London School of Medicine for Women, which had begun with an intake of fourteen students in 1874, but by 1924 had 400 women enrolled. Women were urged to subscribe to the LSMW as a mark of loyalty to the feminist cause. The news that three more medical schools had decided to bar women in 1928 swelled indignation further. In a letter published in *The Times* on 30 March 1928, Nancy Astor, Mrs Corbett-Ashby, Elizabeth Macadam and Lady Rhondda insisted that women as taxpayers had the right to demand that women be given equal opportunities in medicine and a fairer share of hospital appointments.[61] A campaign gathered momentum, and in 1928 representatives of most of the leading feminist organizations came together under the auspices of the National Union of Societies for Equal Citizenship (NUSEC) to form a 'Joint Committee to Promote Equal Opportunities for Women with Men in the Medical and Hospital Services'. This group published a detailed Memorandum on the subject in the same year.[62]

The Medical Women's Federation (which had been founded in 1916) was rather more cautious in its response to the closures. This was partly because the MWF had a policy of avoiding affiliation with any non-medical bodies and tried (not always realistically) to steer clear of political issues and to concentrate on medical matters. Correspondence in the MWF archives makes it clear that many of the women associated with the struggle in St Mary's felt let down and betrayed by what they considered the lukewarm support offered by some of the Federation's Officers, especially those with loyalties to the all-female LSMW who were believed to be sceptical about the value of coeducation.[63] Indeed Marguerite Kettle (trained at St Mary's and later assistant editor of *The Lancet*) wrote to Louisa Martindale in October 1924 expressing her 'deep disappointment at the MWF not publicly identifying itself with the cause of the women at St Mary's', and confessing that she felt very much like resigning over the issue.[64]

Following the news that three more schools were closing their doors to women in 1928, the London Association of the MWF pressed for the appointment of a committee to consider how the Federation might best respond.[65] At a meeting in July, Christine Murrell reported that Letitia Fairfield and Annis Gillie had been asked to represent the views of the Federation to the University of London's subcommittee on the medical education of women undergraduates, which had been asked to report on the situation in the light of the recent closures.[66] The Federation was busy collecting statistics and other information for the use of the subcommittee, and she felt it advisable to wait for their report before taking further action. The tensions which had been apparent within the Federation in 1921/2 threatened a reappearance when Keren Parkes, representing the women currently working at King's College Hospital, reported that her colleagues were getting 'rather impatient' at the suggestion that they should wait and see what happened: there were some who were finding the Federation's policy of 'masterly inactivity' very difficult.[67] But the truth was that the MWF had very little power to influence the course of events. Catherine Chisholm wrote to Violet Kelynack (Secretary of the MWF) in July 1928, confessing that it was 'very difficult for the Federation to do anything effectively' and adding that 'of course we all know that well-meant efforts may bring disaster'. At the same time she conceded that 'of course the youngsters think we are doing nothing, and it seems hard.'[68]

It is interesting to note that the Federation's subcommittee on co-education voted 'by a large majority' in April 1928 *against* a motion that its policy should be 'to work for the opening of all hospitals to men and women alike'. But it was agreed that 'every effort should be made to obtain the re-admission of women to medical schools which had at any time admitted women'.[69] As it turned out, this became more of a stance than a plan of action. In 1929 the MWF subcommittee judged the Report of the University of London's subcommittee in 1929 'very fair',[70] and from 1929 onwards the MWF reverted to a rather passive role. Its subcommittee on coeducation was turned into a 'watching committee', rather than being invested with any more positive brief. When the issue of women's access to clinical training became rather more pressing, in the 1930s, the Committee reacted to pressure from individuals such as Professor John Ryle, in Oxford, who were becoming increasingly concerned by the problems in placing women students, rather than initiating its own interventions.[71] The Federation was resolute, throughout the 1920s and 30s, in deprecating any attempt by feminist pressure groups to lobby against subscriptions to hospitals which withheld training from women.[72] Hardly surprisingly, its caution in this and other respects fostered a certain amount of frustration amongst some of its own members as well as in wider feminist circles.

Although it is no easy matter to generalize about public opinion through the controversies of 1921–30, newspapers at both the national and local level demonstrated intense interest in the debates. Correspondence from individuals could be acrimonious in the extreme, but the impression one gets from published articles and editorial reports is one of strong sympathy with the women's cause.[73] A plethora of articles carried the headlines of a 'Sex war in medicine' and the rhetoric of 'the battlefield' was sustained throughout the period from the 1914–18 war to the 1930s. Celebration of 'a new army of women doctors' around 1915–16 gave way to a discussion of 'invasion', 'overcrowded territory' and fears of women 'undercutting' male professionalism in the early 1920s. If the field was indeed over-crowded, several observers suggested that the medical schools should raise their standards of entry and let the women compete on merit with the men. Correspondents took issue with 'the medical Tsars' and lamented 'the dead hand of Harley Street', deriding the 'silly excuses' of those who argued that women detracted from rugby or athletics, and deeming the suggestion that 'delicacy' prohibited men studying anatomy and physiology along with women as 'ridiculous' and contemptible.[74] Resorting to the same rhetoric as the women's opponents the *Birmingham Post* declared that the closure of three more medical schools to women in 1928 represented a 'curious departure from national ideals of fair play'.[75] The notion that married women, in particular, were unsuited to the profession gained little popular support. 'If a married woman doctor is not a suitable person to treat the illnesses of women and children, then who is?' asked the *Northern Telegraph* in 1924.[76] With public opinion running so high it was not surprising that the University of London, with its proud tradition of having pioneered women's access to higher education in the late nineteenth century, found itself in such a difficult situation, or that the report of the Senate's subcommittee in 1929 demanded of the medical schools that 'no communication of any kind be made to the Press except on the authority of the Vice-Chancellor'.[77]

So how can the historian best understand the intensity of the London medical schools' opposition to women? This intensity is not in doubt. An editorial article in the *Guy's Hospital Gazette* in 1930 commented with acerbity on King's College Hospital's agreement to re-open clinical training to 'a limited number' of women in that year, rejoicing that in his own school, at least, 'the woman student is banned like the leper, her name is anathema on all but a few devoted tongues.'[78] And nearly a decade later, a leading article in the same publication insisted that Guy's men were largely unanimous in their attitude to the question of women students:

> although we are not articulate about the problem . . . we are agreed that we do not want them . . . We voice the sentiments of the majority when we say, without heat, that we do not want women to share our clinical studies here with us. It is not easy to say, without being unkind or frivolous, just why we feel this way; but then we all have so many firm beliefs on various matters that defy logical elucidation.[79]

Whether in defiance of logic or not, what follows in the rest of this chapter represents an attempt to elucidate this stance.

The most comprehensible explanation of the medical schools' reaction against women students is in terms of simple backlash, the reassertion of patriarchal prerogatives after the war, in the first instance, and in the context of competition for employment during the later 1920s. We have seen that Moberly Bell's account made use of this explanation. In recent years the work of historians such as Margaret and Patrice Higonnet and Susan Kingsley Kent has amplified our understanding of the interwar years as characterized by an attempt to reconstruct sexual difference as one of the constituents of a stable social order.[80] This work of 'reconstruction' can be seen to have been fuelled by representations of a 'sex war', in which men set out 'to reclaim territory' which women were perceived to have 'usurped' during the 'unnatural' conditions of wartime. The language used in the popular press coverage of the events of 1915–30 certainly lends some support to these interpretations, although as we have seen, the articles themselves frequently demonstrated a marked sympathy with the aspirations of women doctors.[81]

There can be no doubt that the mood of many ex-servicemen who returned to medical education in London between 1916 and 1920 was characterized by unease and volatility. Ida Mann, employed as a physiology demonstrator at St Mary's Hospital Medical School in 1917, recalled this vividly. She found herself

> Suddenly faced with a gang of hard-faced youths, mad enough at being sent back to school, but madder still at finding that they were to be taught by a girl. I set up the Practical class. The work the first day consisted of making a nerve-muscle preparation of a frog's leg and getting a tracing of the contractions produced by a mild electric shock. It was a fiddling, finicking, exacting job for everyone. They looked daggers at me and one huge black-browed boy made for the door. I stood in front of it.
>
> 'Have you finished?' I said.
>
> He swore at me 'Damn and blast you. Look, five days ago I was killing Germans. How the hell can you expect me to spend the afternoon tying little bits of cotton and wire to a dead frog?'[82]

Young men who viewed the state as having expended the lives of so many of their comrades were unlikely to have looked upon the prospect of interrupted careers and what they perceived as the sacrifice of career opportunities with anything approaching equanimity. Christine Heward has emphasized the ways in which middle-class parents sacrificed often scarce resources in a determined attempt to secure those educational advantages which would allow their sons professional status and independence.[83] Wars posed a real threat to such parental projects, even where the sons' lives were spared.

We have seen in Chapter 3 how hostility against women students at University College, the London and St Mary's Hospital Medical Schools was particularly focused on opposition to the idea of women in house appointments. The fear of female competition in house appointments was exacerbated by the fact that many men considered the prospect of studying or working under female authority an unbearable affront to their dignity. The petition from the male students at University College Hospital in 1920 instanced 'the intolerable position of an ex-serviceman who has . . . as his House-Surgeon over him a girl of twenty-two'.[84] Although women were not admitted to the medical school at Guy's Hospital during this period, a letter which was published in the *Guy's Hospital Gazette* in March 1939 raised the spectre of a 'wretched man' having to 'cook supper for the woman house-surgeon and female registrar, by whom he is taught, and account for his expenditure to the lady dressers'.[85] An article that appeared earlier in the same journal had elaborated the dystopic vision still further, in deprecating the attitudes of women 'thrusting into the affairs of men':

> Considering what power is wielded by some of the Sisters, we are terrified at the thought of a female Visiting Physician. In twenty years we would be a matriarchy, with a few degenerate and despised males hanging on to the Surgeon's apron-strings.[86]

There are a number of observations that can be made here. The vision of infantilization or emasculation brings to mind the very similar rhetoric used by the National Association of Schoolmasters in campaigning against women's authority in schools in Britain during the interwar period. Margaret Littlewood has drawn our attention to the ways in which the NAS dramatized representations of 'the castrating effects' of 'spinster authority' on schoolboys, instancing the testimony of a delegate to the NAS conference in 1936, who declared that he had 'witnessed the process of nipping out by Miss Teacher of the budding shoots of young manhood'.[87] Christine Heward's analysis of public school education in the first half of the present century has highlighted the importance of a popular psychology which saw masculinity as depending upon a revolt against the mother and all she represented as 'babyish, cissy or womanish'.[88] There are many parallels between the gendered structures of authority in schoolteaching and in medical education during the period, and the structures and ethos of medical education came very close to those of a classical boys' public school.

Power and authority in hospitals, as in schools, was both gendered and quasi-familial. Matrons and Sisters might be powerful, but had clearly defined subordinate roles. Deans of the medical schools and the honorary surgeons and physicians involved in teaching were powerful enough, but often referred to familiarly by the students as 'Daddy', 'Grandad', or

'Uncle'.[89] The authoritative stance was often one of a stern or benevolent paternalism, shading, as the students grew towards professional competence, into a shared 'gentlemanly' code of honour. Where male students appealed against female admissions to their deans and the boards of management in the 1920s the tone was often governed by intimations that gentlemen's agreements or codes of honour had been threatened by their esteemed patrons, and in some cases the tone verged towards that of filial complaint. Both Lord Knutsford at the London Hospital and Dr Wilson (later Lord Moran) at St Mary's adopted stances (at least in some contexts) of lofty but harassed paternalism, giving the impression that they were trying to sort out squabbles between siblings. We may recall from what was said earlier Dr Wilson's embarrassed meeting with the women in the Library at St Mary's in 1921, when he complained that the men 'thought he was against them, and so did the women'. Expectations of patronage, 'mentorship' and *noblesse oblige* could be strong, and all added to the sense of betrayal which was clearly felt by some ambitious young men who saw women elected to house appointments. A sense of gentlemanly obligation might work both ways, in that when a doctor left the hospital for general practice, he was expected to refer any suitable cases needing specialist treatment to his 'old chiefs' or those honoraries who had taught him.

Medicine, like schoolteaching, could be viewed as a 'caring profession' and it might be argued that connotations of caring implied femininity and made for a particular sensitivity to gender and sexual difference within the profession. Doctoring (male) had to be clearly differentiated from nursing (female). Frances Margaret Kenyon (later Taylor), who undertook her clinical training at King's College Hospital in 1922, recalled a particularly embarrassing moment in her memoirs:

> William Gilliat, later to become Sir William, obstetrician to the Queen, was questioning me: 'Miss Kenyon, let's suppose that you have just delivered a woman of her baby and the after-birth. What would you do next?'
>
> 'Give her an Egg Flip', I said, confidently, having seen nurses do just that.
>
> 'A *WHAT*?' demanded the great man, when he could get his breath back, 'A *WHAT*?' When I explained, he reminded me with icy sarcasm that I was trying to learn to be a doctor, not a nurse. He never forgot my idiotic answer.[90]

Medical school education was a project which for many was inextricably linked with gender. St Mary's trained 'St Mary's Men', Guy's Hospital produced 'Guy's Men' and so forth. It is at this point that the schools' obsession with athletics and rugby came into play.

It is difficult to exaggerate the importance of athletics, team sports and particularly rugby in the culture of the medical schools. Outside observers, contemporaries and later historians have all manifested scepticism about the logic of the medical schools' objection that the admission of women students would endanger their rugby, but the emotional purchase of this contention cannot be swept aside. Dame Josephine Barnes, who studied medicine at Oxford and then at University College Hospital in the 1930s, recalled that 'Rugby was almost a religion' in the London Medical Schools at that time.[91] James Garner has described how for Charles McMoran Wilson, the aforesaid Dean of St Mary's Hospital Medical School from 1920, military and sporting values gelled to shape a vision of 'the right sort of chap' whom he envisaged as the best guarantee of the school's reputation in the profession and the future.[92] It is not without significance that in a special edition of the *Guy's Hospital Gazette* which commemorated the bicentenary of the hospital and the centenary of its medical school in 1925, Alfred Allport's emotionally charged history of the Rugby Club represented by far the biggest section in the book.[93] It is an epic in the truest sense, a narrative celebrating generations of heroes embodying the school's conception of its past history and character. It is also a hymn about the male body, its heroes taut with 'bone, muscle and sinew', such as 'Fripp, a powerful hard-working forward weighing 13 stone and as hard as nails', or E.T. Shortland, 'at his best, a powerful bullocking forward'.[94]

A scrutiny of the sporting and athletic columns in any medical school publication of the interwar years (save the magazine of the LSMW) yields much the same impression: they are celebrations of masculine prowess, charged with anxieties about competition and performance. There were constant exhortations against 'slacking' as men were urged to exert themselves in a virile effort to secure what Joanna Bourke has neatly designated as the triumph of the 'team spirit' over the 'tame spirit'.[95] The presence of women, it was widely feared, might all too easily signal defeat. In March 1928, the *Daily Mirror* quoted the misgivings of 'a well-known Harley St doctor' implacably opposed to the idea of mixed schools, who insisted that:

> Whenever women are present, the male students, instead of turning to athletics, which keep the place together and create a valuable *esprit de corps*, turn to social distractions. They tend to become what are called in the Navy 'poodle fakers', that is, fellows who like parties more than games.[96]

Women might be just about tolerable if they confined themselves to the role of *spectators*, when (whether in the operating theatre or on the sports field) their role was essentially one of admiring male *performance*. Frances Kenyon's scrapbooks, illustrating her years as a student at King's College

Hospital in the 1920s, are packed with newspaper cuttings and photographs of the college rugby team in action, detailing the scores of matches against Mary's, the London and Bart's. It is interesting to learn that she attributed her election as Senior Woman Student in the college in 1921 to the fact that she had absented herself from the premises on the day of the poll, having 'gone to watch a Rugger match at Twickenham'.[97] This ensured her status as 'a good sport'. (She went on to marry a fellow student, G.F. Taylor, early described in a clipping in the scrap-book as 'a very sound player who trains hard and plays hard. He is always on the ball . . .')

The sporting columns in the *Broad Way* (the Westminster Hospital Gazette), record brooding dissatisfaction with the hospital's none too impressive record in the 1920s. The school was still admitting women students at this juncture and a correspondent lamented that the women's 'sporting instincts' and performance were putting the men to shame.

> The men have displayed an apathy and lack of camaraderie that is disappointing, and they can take to heart, unpleasant though it may be, the example set by the lady students. One male student refused to play hockey on the ground that the game was too rough: one is left wondering whether this was but a feeble attempt at humour or merely the natural result of the . . . almost invertebrate attitude of the men towards an essential side of hospital life.[98]

'Men can be men,' observed Deborah Cameron, 'only if women are unambiguously women.'[99] This observation probably goes some way towards explaining the growing unease, in some educational and medical circles, with women's growing interest in sport in the 1920s. I have described elsewhere how a controversy erupted in King's College London in 1922 when the professorial board tried to impose a ban on mixed sports. The principal explained the authorities' fears that women's participation threatened to reduce the annual sports day to a mere social event, that women's athletics were considered 'unseemly' and that 'athletic excellence was only obtainable in sports for men'.[100] The popularity of boat-racing amongst university oarswomen (and students at the LSMW) precipitated similar controversy in the 1920s. The majority of women doctors briskly dismissed the misgivings of those such as Sir James Crichton-Browne, who warned of the deleterious social effects of 'a loss of feminine grace'.[101] Viewed from a distance, however, these debates in the 1920s lend substance to the title of Mariah Burton Nelson's recent book, *The Stronger Women Get, The More Men Love Football*.[102]

The opposition to women's admission to the London medical schools, however persistent, was never total, and I should not end without pointing out that the policy of male exclusiveness was opposed by a significant number of men who believed that coeducation in medicine was both professionally desirable and that it represented an elementary form of social justice. It was not always easy to maintain such a stance amongst colleagues who felt that proud traditions, fellowship, professional identity, status and loyalties and even the natural order of things would be threatened by letting the women in.

In 1961, Becker, Geer, Hughes and Strauss introduced their study of student culture in the University of Kansas Medical School, *Boys in White*, by declaring that, since the medical profession in America remained 'overwhelmingly male', they would focus on the process 'of boys becoming medical men'.[103] The lack of any reference to gender in the text which follows is, from a present day viewpoint, rather startling. On page 324, the reader finds the following:

> If there is such a thing as male culture, one element of it certainly consists of an injunction always to have an eye out for a pretty girl.[104]

There is little more. This chapter will, I trust, have shown that there was indeed 'such a thing as male culture' in English medical schools, at any rate in London between the Wars, and that it certainly merits anatomizing.

'Apostates' and 'Uncle Toms'
Challenges to separatism in the women's college

Some who wish the College to retain its present character are in the habit of saying that those who advocate change are apostates – in the sense that they are men who come into a women's college and then agitate to alter its character.

> (O.R. McGregor, Reader in Sociology, University of London, Discussion in Bedford College Council, July 1962)[1]

As supporters of the New College proposal we regard the views of the women's colleges as presented to the Franks Commission as narrowly conceived. They are what the Negroes in the United States call *'Uncle Toms'* – *good negroes who know their place in a white man's world*.

> (John Vaizey, Fellow of Worcester College, Oxford, Editorial comment in the *Oxford Magazine*, 11 March 1965)

In Chapter 4 it was suggested that for women in universities the early postwar years were in some respects a period of stagnation, and of 'wasted ambitions' for many able girls. Several of the separate women's colleges established in Oxbridge and London in the late nineteenth and early twentieth centuries had acquired status and reputation: it is scarcely surprising that many of those who worked to improve provision for girls sought to build upon their proud traditions and to expand from this existing base. Erosion of the separatist tradition might be seen as a major threat to the institutions and achievements of late Victorian feminism.

In this chapter I explore some of the reasons for the bitterness that sometimes surfaced in debates over the role of the women's college, by focusing on allegations of *betrayal* made by protagonists of women's higher education. The vehemence of the accusations reflected a deeper mistrust between women and men over the safeguarding and furtherance of women's educational interests. There was no simple division between men and women over the desirability of coeducation: positions were complex and need to be understood in different institutional settings. I shall look first at the erstwhile women's colleges in the University of London, and in particular at Bedford, where male proponents of coeducation were labelled by some as 'apostates', then turn to the University of Oxford, where senior women uneasy about coeducation were accused of behaving like 'Uncle Toms', and represented as defending narrow institutional claims rather than the wider interests of women in higher education. It may be noted here that such debates were by no means confined to these universities and colleges, and surfaced also (for instance) in single-sex halls of residence of civic universities around the same time.

By 1914 most English universities had seen fit to advertise themselves as 'coeducational' institutions, or as making 'no distinction of sex' in matters of admissions, appointments and educational policy. Such descriptions should not be accepted too literally, since patterns of gender differentiation persisted well into the twentieth century.[2] Towards the close of the nineteenth century, reluctance to grant women degrees in Oxford and Cambridge, and continuing male unease at coeducation, had fuelled discussions about whether there should be a separate 'women's university' in the south of England, based at Royal Holloway College.[3] The scheme came to nought, and was opposed by leaders of women's education who objected strongly to segregation on the grounds that a 'women's university' would be regarded as second-rate. Although rejecting the idea of a separate *university*, many feminists remained convinced of the importance of separate women's *colleges*, since they believed that institutions controlled by women offered them opportunities for self-government and self-determination too easily lost in mixed institutions.[4]

Bedford College had been founded by Elizabeth Jesser Reid in 1849, and had played a pioneering role in opening opportunities for the higher education of women. Mrs Reid was determined to ensure that her college would be governed by Ladies as well as Gentlemen: according to Margaret Tuke, it was Reid's 'distrust of men in their attitude to female education' that led her to stipulate that the fund she bequeathed for the higher education of women would be administered by female trustees.[5] The University of London was in fact the first university in Britain to open its degrees to women (in 1878). University College, in Gower Street, opened most of its classes to women in the same year and has laid claim to being the first coeducational university institution in the country.[6] By 1939 all of the colleges of the University of London (though not all of the medical schools associated with the university) accepted women students. Four colleges at that time accepted women students only: Bedford, Westfield, Royal Holloway and King's College of Household and Social Science (from

1953, Queen Elizabeth College) at Campden Hill. But by 1965 all of these institutions admitted students of both sexes and London could properly describe itself as a 'coeducational' university.

In Oxford and Cambridge the first moves towards 'coeducational' or 'mixed colleges' at the undergraduate level came much later. As late as 1970 the pattern was still that of what the student press of the time dubbed 'sexual apartheid', of separate 'men's colleges' and 'women's colleges'.[7] The ensuing rush to coresidence is described below.

These events radically altered the social character of elite institutions of higher education in the United Kingdom, and the speed at which they took place is quite remarkable given the conservatism of many of the institutions involved, particularly men's colleges with a history going back over several centuries. Seen from one angle, a tradition of gender segregation collapsed 'in a flash', and once a few colleges decided to admit women, 'the rest followed like falling skittles' in the competition to 'grab the best girls for themselves'.[8] There was more to it than this, of course, and whilst some observers, both male and female, rejoiced in what they saw as a new phase of integration and widening opportunities for women, there were others in the women's colleges who looked on with mixed feelings and even consternation: if the brightest girls were lured by the glamour of the wealthy, old-established men's colleges, what would happen to their own institutions? Would the women's colleges betray their foundations by admitting men at a time when women were still far from representing half of the university student population in the UK? These preoccupations and the key figures who espoused them are the subject of this chapter.

Segregation or new opportunities?: the University of London colleges

Around the turn of the twentieth century, first Bedford, then Royal Holloway, and finally Westfield became schools of the newly constituted teaching University of London, exclusively for women students. Of the three institutions, Bedford had the strongest reputation, and this was to be consolidated under the leadership of Margaret Tuke (Principal, 1907–29). Tuke was attracted to Bedford as a single-sex college in London, where, she recorded, 'the position of women was, I understood, assured in the University.'[9] Interestingly, she compared this with what she considered to be the less satisfactory situation she had experienced as Tutor to Women Students in a supposedly 'coeducational' environment at the University College in Bristol: there she had felt 'an outsider', as a woman with no place at all in college government.[10] Even so, none of the London women's foundations was in anything like an invulnerable position. Soon after becoming Principal, Tuke was asked to consider the amalgamation of

Bedford into University College, London (a proposal fiercely opposed by the Reid Trustees).[11] And a couple of years later, the more recently established King's College for Women was dismembered (in accordance with the recommendations of the Haldane Commission), part of it reconstituted as a Household and Social Science Department, the rest of the women being absorbed into the hitherto male precincts of King's College London in The Strand.[12]

Proposals for coeducation in respect of the three remaining women's colleges were first seriously discussed at Royal Holloway, a somewhat isolated small community of women housed in a glorious faux-French château in rural Englefield Green, near Egham. Here the first proposals to admit men were enshrined in a report of 1944 commissioned by the governors to consider college policy after the Second World War.[13] Evidence and statements of opinion were solicited from a very wide range of sources and authorities.[14] The Post-War Policy Committee was unable to reach unanimity on the question of admitting men – the college's Principal, Janet Bacon, was strongly opposed to what she saw as an unwarranted departure from the founder's intentions ('Englefield Green,' she opined darkly, 'is not a suitable environment for a coeducational experiment with the adolescent'[15]). A majority of the committee, nevertheless, took the position that 'segregation at the University stage is now becoming out of date', and recommended that Holloway be converted into a mixed college.[16]

This recommendation could not of itself effect policy. The 1950s were in some ways a period of stagnation for the college.[17] Towards the end of the decade members of the Academic Board put pressure on the College Council to implement change, arguing that the segregation of women students was no longer 'in the best interests of university education' and that the science departments in the college were experiencing a serious decline in applicants.[18] The final decision to admit men as undergraduates to Royal Holloway College was not made until 1960.[19]

Even then, funds remained a problem. There was no guarantee of the resources that would be needed to build accommodation for male students. Caroline Bingham points out that, even after the passing of the Act which enabled Royal Holloway to admit men in 1962, the college was unsure about where the extra funds would come from.[20] An earlier Acting Principal of the University of London had suggested the sale of the college's picture collection to finance the building of a male hostel.[21]

In 1956 both Westfield and Bedford Colleges had received tactfully worded letters from the University of London noting that at a recent meeting with the University Grants Committee it had been suggested that 'the time had now come to consider whether segregation was not an anachronism'.[22] The UGC was represented as being 'delighted – and possibly a little surprised' to find that the women's colleges had not immediately 'ruled out' the possibility of admitting men when they had broached the subject on visits.[23] Westfield's response to this communication was somewhat equivocal; its Council was divided on the desirability of reconstituting the college as a mixed institution, although the idea of 'experimenting' by admitting men to newly established science departments gained general support.[24] This 'experiment' was not implemented, however, owing to concerns about its dubious legality under the existing charter.

In 1958 Sir Douglas Logan, Principal of the University of London, penned a 'Personal and Confidential' note to Sir Keith Murray at the UGC confessing that, 'I am not making much headway with the problem of the admission of men to the women's colleges.'[25] There was also the question of the necessary legal changes: Bedford and Westfield were incorporated by Royal Charter, while alteration to Royal Holloway's Trust Deed called for an Act of Parliament.

The question of the college becoming 'bisexual' came before Westfield's Council again in 1963. In a Memorandum supposedly summarizing the arguments on both sides, but massively weighted in favour of the college admitting men, the Chairman of Council argued that the decision had to be made before the college could outline constructive plans for the future.[26] He contended that most of the academic staff, as well as student opinion, were on the side of admitting men. The university and the UGC, 'though meticulous in their observance of the independence of the college', clearly favoured coeducation. Lest any Mrs Grundy lurked in the wings, he assured Council that there was no danger of a 'heterosexual hostel'.[27] The moral problems existing at Westfield, he feared, 'were very great', but he thought that these would become less rather than more in a mixed rather than a segregated college (he presumably thought that the men would 'protect' the women). Westfield's College Council resolved to admit men in 1963.[28]

Bedford and its 'apostates'

This left Bedford. Records of the discussions which took place in Bedford's Academic Board and Council following the University's letter of 1956 show concern – even consternation – and controversy over suggestions that the college might consider admitting men. The response at that date was to the effect that, although the college would not want 'to close the door' against change, it was felt that it was still necessary to uphold the principle for which it was founded.[29] There was much concern about safeguarding the number of places for women students (especially in science) alongside a concern that opportunities for women in senior posts were few in mixed colleges. A further approach from the university, in 1960, about whether the college would like to be associated with 'enabling legislation' which would permit it to admit male students, received a negative response from

159

the Council.[30] By 1962, however, there were stronger forces within the college marshalling for change.

In 1962 Bedford's Academic Board was asked by a group of Faculty to reopen discussions about the admission of men. Eleven members of the Board (nine men, two women) submitted a strongly worded memorandum to Council contending that changing circumstances demanded an 'urgent reconsideration' of the issue.[31] It was argued that the continued segregation of women could no longer further Mrs Reid's vision of equality for women and would represent 'an attempt to provide for the needs of tomorrow within the framework of a past that has died'.[32] Students – and many academic staff – were alleged to prefer mixed institutions, and to dislike a single-sex, 'psychological atmosphere congenial only to those emotionally harnessed to the past'.[33] The authors of the memorandum warned that 'public policy' and the UGC favoured coeducation. They pointed out that the medical schools had had to respond to this preference lest they forfeit grant support. There was a note of threat in the suggestion that the college rethink now lest it should find itself in a similar position in future.[34]

Between March 1962 and July 1963, correspondence, discussions and memoranda proliferated as the controversy about admitting men deepened. Those making the case for the college remaining single-sex argued that women were still far from enjoying equal opportunities with men in higher education as either students or teachers, and hence that the college still had a crucial role to play.[35] The size and shape of the departments in the college, it was suggested, should reflect demand from women students rather than the perceived needs of men.[36] There was evidence that Bedford was still attractive to highly qualified women and the college made an important contribution to postgraduate work. Women still faced discrimination in employment, and the college both recognized and challenged these distinctions.[37] In short, those opposing the admission of men submitted that,

> As the oldest of the women's university colleges in this country, and the biggest and most central of the women's colleges in London, [Bedford had] a high reputation, a distinctive role, and special tasks in the contemporary world.[38]

The college was nearly torn apart by this controversy over its future. Two men in particular, B.C. King (Professor of Geology) and O.R. McGregor (Reader in Sociology), were the most vocal of the advocates of the case for a mixed college. They claimed that student opinion (as evidenced by the College Union Society's submission to the Robbins Committee) favoured 'a normal society' and looked upon segregation as an anachronism.[39] King and McGregor cited evidence from authorities such as Kelsall, Moser and

Furneaux in support of the argument that women students no longer suffered from 'discrimination' in entering universities: the fact that they represented a clear minority of the university student population was held to be irrelevant because it was claimed that women applicants enjoyed a higher rate of success in their applications than their male peers.[40] This brushing aside of the question of 'discrimination', together with the assumption of masculine subjectivity which was built into sections of the King/McGregor arguments, was unlikely to appeal to the other side.

Eventually, a majority of the college's non-professorial staff expressed themselves in favour of admitting men; by a narrow majority, the Academic Board came down on the same side.[41] After much agonizing, Council's decision to set in motion the changes that would reconstitute Bedford as a mixed college was taken in July 1963.[42] Bedford's academic staff in the early 1960s was around 34 per cent female, 66 per cent male.[43] The lines of division over the issue had by no means been clearly drawn according to sex – there were men and women in both camps. However, it would appear to have been the case that the arguments in favour of a mixed college had been articulated most powerfully by men, and that there were many on the college staff who saw this as a form of betrayal.[44] Oliver McGregor recognized that colleagues who fought to retain Bedford's character as a women's college saw those like him who advocated change as 'apostates – in the sense that they are men who come into a women's college and then agitate to alter its character'.[45] He defended himself against such accusations by representing himself as 'an ardent male feminist', insisting that he suffered from no misgivings in the 'wish to see this change on feminist grounds'.[46] Others saw things very differently.

Segregation at Oxbridge to the 1960s

In 1934 the feminist writer Winifred Holtby had penned an article in the *News Chronicle*, asking the question 'Should women go to Oxford?'[47] Her photograph of female students in Oxford, with the caption 'Eve in the home of lost causes', mentioned in Chapter 6 above, was set against an image of women graduates in London, titled 'A friendly group of London's less segregated Eves'. Students in London, and in universities elsewhere in Britain, found it difficult to comprehend why segregation of the sexes was so extreme in Oxford and Cambridge, she proclaimed: why, at this point in time, should so much fuss be made about the presence of women at the older universities?

Compared with the University of London as a whole, both Oxford and Cambridge were universities profoundly structured by sexual difference. In Oxford, the women's 'societies' had only recently been accorded 'college status'.[48] In both universities, the women's colleges ranked well below the men's in terms of wealth and prestige. In the 1950s and early 1960s, the heads of the women's colleges, much experienced in the difficulties of fundraising, were ambivalent about expansion, and early suggestions for coeducation came from the men's colleges.

The question of the relationship between men and women in the 'Ancient Universities' of the country was even more complex than at the colleges of the University of London, and had never seemed likely to be resolved by logic alone. In the last paragraph of an article describing the first 'serious' attempt by an Oxbridge men's college (New College) to become coresidential, Geoffrey de Ste Croix touched on the delicate question of a potential conflict between the interests of women in the university (broadly defined) and the institutional interests of the existing women's colleges. It might be that these latter would have to be sacrificed to the former, he suggested, in spite of a recognition of the fact that 'the very existence of the women's colleges at Oxford is due to long and stubborn male resistance to the presence of women in the University.'[49]

The centuries-old traditions and masculine privileges of the Oxbridge colleges slowed the acceptance of women as students in both universities. That women students should be confined to separate halls and institutions, preferably away from the centre, was never at first questioned. Both universities sought to contain the female presence, not least by limiting the numbers of women students. When Oxford conceded degrees to women in 1920, there was an expectation that Cambridge would do likewise. But Cambridge 'held out', determined to remain 'mainly and predominantly "a men's university", though of a mixed type'.[50] The number of women students in Cambridge was not to exceed 500, which would fix the proportion of women to men at around 1:10 of the student body.[51] The decision fuelled the fears of those in Oxford who predicted that young men would be attracted to Cambridge rather than Oxford as the more 'virile' (and hence prestigious) institution, free from the (terrifying) possibility of feminine government. Oxford reasserted its maleness in 1927 with a Limitation Statute: the five women's 'societies' (not yet permitted the status of 'colleges') were not to exceed a total of 840 students, which would fix the proportion of women at about one-sixth of the student body.[52] Limitations on the numbers of women students persisted in Oxford until 1957 and in Cambridge until 1960 (although in the case of Cambridge the university reserved the right to limit the number of women students until as recently as 1987).[53]

In both universities the idea of segregation by sex was taken for granted by so many as to seem part of the natural order of things. The idea of women 'seeking to invade' men's colleges was usually dismissed as mere absurdity.[54] As bedmakers, cooks and cleaners, of course, their presence could be tolerated, but even as guests they were often unwelcome. A woman who had studied at St Hilda's between the wars recalled that one of the ways in which many men's colleges signalled an unwillingness even to acknowledge the presence of women guests was by refusing to provide lavatories for them. This meant that tea parties and other social occasions could cause acute embarrassment – one 'host' (in Exeter College) was alleged to direct his female guests to a slop bucket in his bedroom which his scout would be called upon to empty the next day.[55] Nor could women dine in the majority of men's colleges. Offering congratulations to Professor Dorothy Hodgkin on her Nobel Prize in 1964, John Vaizey reflected that there were only three men's colleges in Oxford which would allow her in as a guest at dinner.[56]

With the possibilities for expanding existing women's colleges limited, Dacre Balsdon, a fellow of Exeter, speculated gloomily on the alternatives. In *Oxford Life* (1957) we are introduced to Mr Botteaux, who is writing a novel about the University a hundred years into the future. The speculation is that the government requires Oxford to make more provision for women. Coeducational colleges are opposed by women dons on the grounds that they would lose their jobs, because men don't like being taught by women and women prefer being taught by men. It is decided that one male college should go female. Each college exerts itself to find reasons why it should not be chosen. The college with the best lavatories draws the short straw. The dons of the doomed college dispose of college property to avoid it falling into the hands of the women. Methodically they drink through the contents of the entire cellar, in a last desperate orgy of regret. With all the drink inside them they decide that they simply cannot tolerate relinquishing the college to women and burn it down instead. At the last moment comes a reprieve – the government decides that a new women's college can be built, but it is too late: no buildings, wine or investments are left.[57]

Coresidence in Oxbridge, 1964–1994

After the Second World War, women concerned about the lack of provision for female students in Cambridge campaigned for 'a third foundation', and New Hall came into existence in 1954.[58] In 1958, a number of women's organizations made representations to Winston Churchill urging him to consider opening the new college to be founded in his name in Cambridge to women as well as men.[59] Churchill's private secretary, Jock Colville, intervened swiftly, warning Sir Winston that 'a proposal for a coeducational college would be like dropping a hydrogen bomb in the middle of the university.'[60] Similarly, in Oxford, suggestions that the newly founded St Catherine's College might admit both sexes were quickly dismissed as likely to foment too much controversy.[61] Nonetheless, in the climate of Robbins and postwar schemes for the expansion of higher education, both Oxford and Cambridge were increasingly sensitive to criticism focused on the fact that they offered so few places to women.[62]

It is generally recorded that the first 'serious' suggestion from an all-male college that it might begin to tackle the shortage of places available for women in Oxford by opening its doors to a number of female undergraduates came from New College in 1964.[63] Discussions of the possibility of a college or colleges going 'coeducational' were in the air at the time, although they were usually dismissed as unrealistic. Nevertheless, Oxford's student newspaper, *Cherwell*, carried a headline speculating about whether Worcester would be the first college in Oxford 'to go co-ed' in May 1963, alleging that 'an influential minority' in the Senior Common Room, including the recently elected economics tutor John Vaizey, were in favour of such a plan.[64] Vaizey, formerly Director of London University's Institute of Education, had been a member of the Labour Party's Study Group on Higher Education, and was known to be concerned about the acute imbalance between places for men and women in Oxford and Cambridge.

The ratio of men to women undergraduates in Oxford at the time was just over 5:1 (at Cambridge it was 9:1).[65] It was the realization that this was increasingly unacceptable to 'public opinion' and policy-makers at the time of the Robbins investigations, as well as the inequities of the situation, which fed speculation about coeducation.[66] The chances of securing funding for the foundation of another women's college in Oxford looked bleak (New Hall had found fund-raising an uphill task).[67] The predicament led Henry Bell, a tutor and Librarian of New College (referred to in the poem quoted in Chapter 6 above), to the suggestion that the college might admit women, in 1963.[68] Bell's colleagues, knowing him as a conservative, were stunned (the Warden of that time later explained that Bell thought that 'women got on better when taught by men').[69] But many were persuaded, and in June of the following year the College's Governing Body passed a resolution declaring its wish to amend its statutes in order to admit women.[70]

The reasoning behind the Governing Body's decision was made public in a lucid and carefully argued article on 'The admission of women to New College' by de Ste Croix, which appeared in the *Oxford Magazine* in October 1964.[71] The argument which had weighed most, he contended, stemmed from the conviction that the numbers and proportion of women in Oxford were far too small. There was also a belief that university education ought to be 'fully mixed', and that communities of both men and women would generate less 'emotional and sexual tension'. Finally there were legitimate reasons for believing that academic standards in the college would benefit from the admission of women students, since as things stood so many highly qualified and able women failed to secure places in the university, whereas less able male applicants found admission easier. He well understood that the fears of the women's colleges were that they would lose their best applicants if New College were allowed to 'skim the cream': however he knew of no evidence to suggest that the 'pool' of able women in the country was so limited as to give substance to these fears. The Robbins Report had abundantly demonstrated the need for a steep rise in the provision of university places. If mixed colleges proved much more attractive to applicants than their single-sex predecessors, then the women's colleges themselves had the option of 'going mixed'.

For a variety of reasons (including opposition from the women's colleges and, in the event, a failure to secure the requisite majority amongst its fellowship to allow for a change in statutes), the proposal did not come to fruition at that time.[72] The pattern of what the student press of the day came to refer to as 'sexual apartheid' persisted through the 1960s, and it was not until the following decade that mixed colleges at the under-graduate level became a reality. In Cambridge, Churchill, King's and Clare Colleges began 'a limited experiment' in admitting women in 1972. In both universities there were attempts (ultimately unsuccessful) to phase and control the process of change in what was represented as the interests of the women's colleges, anxious lest they lose their best students to the wealthy and prestigious male foundations.[73]

Oxford's 'Uncle Toms'

In the general brouhaha and explosion of controversy in Oxford, Cambridge and the national press that peaked in the 1970s over the desirability of 'coresidence', the onus for objections to 'the mixed college' was routinely placed on the shoulders of the Oxford women principals.[74] While this may be fair, it is important to recognize that right from the beginning, those in the men's colleges who were uneasy or unhappy about schemes for admitting women were all too happy to be able to represent their position in terms of 'chivalrous' regard for the interests of the women's colleges.

Many of those (both men and women) who had been keen to see the numbers of women in the university increased and who had looked upon the New College initiative as radical, generous and 'progressive' were bitterly disappointed. John Vaizey, as editor of the *Oxford Magazine* in the mid 1960s, made space for their views, and his accusation of the woman principals as behaving like 'Uncle Toms' was made in this context.[75]

The views of the three woman principals who submitted evidence to the Franks Commission (Janet Vaughan, Lucy Sutherland, Mary Ogilvie), together with those of Kathleen Kenyon (Principal of St Hugh's) and Mary Bennett (who succeeded Kathleen Major as Principal of St Hilda's in 1965), can be explored in both their public statements and in the files of correspondence from this period.[76] Janet Vaughan's response to the New College proposals was somewhat equivocal, in that she was aware that some of Somerville's fellows welcomed the proposals as a move towards equality for women.[77] Lady Ogilvie and Dr Sutherland were more hostile. Both were at pains to emphasize that the status of the women's colleges and their establishment as self-governing institutions in the university were of very recent origin, and it was only in the last few years that they had been freed from the statutory restrictions on their numbers which had been imposed to restrict their expansion and to limit the 'feminine presence' in Oxford. If the proportion of women students in the university was going to increase, they thought that the existing women's colleges should be given the chance to expand their numbers before other strategies were considered.[78] However it was clear from the beginning that both Mary Ogilvie and Lucy Sutherland were highly sceptical about the possibility of attracting more able women students: neither found reassurance in the arguments of those who pointed out that far more highly qualified women candidates for admission than men were turned away. Many girls set their sights on primary and infant teaching, nursing and other non-graduate occupations, argued Dr Sutherland, and this and a marked trend towards earlier marriages disinclined them for the rigours of an Oxford degree.[79] Even if more women were qualifying for university entrance, many were attracted to the 'perhaps less exacting' general courses in the new universities. Planning for a very modest expansion of places for women seemed in her view the sensible option.

There is no doubt that these views were taken seriously by Lord Franks, appointed by the university to consider its future in the light of the Robbins Report, who warned the warden of New College that any 'rapid action' in the matter of men's colleges admitting women 'would inflict great damage on the existing women's colleges'.[80] Hence the Franks Commission has subsequently been described as having 'smothered' or sidestepped initiatives towards coeducation.[81] The stance which appeared to have been taken by the women principals was widely criticized in the local and national press; Vaizey's portrayal of them in the *Oxford Magazine* as 'Uncle Toms' was echoed by articles in *The Guardian* and *The Times*.[82] An article by E.M. Thomas in *The Times* suggested (as had de Ste Croix) that perhaps the interests of the once pioneering women's colleges in Oxford and Cambridge no longer ran 'parallel with the interests of women's education'.[83] *The Guardian* argued that any damage which might have been done to the women's colleges in the event of men's colleges opening their doors to women ranked as nothing against the injustice suffered 'by countless women now denied admission to two leading universities'.[84] The situation in Oxford was compared unfavourably with that in London, and (in a veiled attack on the Oxford principals) Elizabeth Chilver, the new principal of the newly coeducational Bedford College, was described as having 'too much common sense to keep the flags of segregation unfurled in Regent's Park'.[85]

Some women teaching in Oxford felt the need to challenge the representation of the women's colleges as being the stumbling block for coeducation, and wrote to make public their support of the New College and any similar initiatives in opening men's colleges to women. Peter Ady (St Anne's) found the arguments for mixed education 'overwhelming', even if they entailed 'the eclipse of the women's colleges'.[86] Antoinette Pirie (Somerville) argued that fears of there being a shortage of well-qualified women applicants were exaggerated, and that the supply of good female candidates was increasing year by year (her argument was backed by some convincing statistics).[87] In 1964 sixteen women scholars (among them Mary Warnock, Dorothy Hodgkin, Helen Gardner, Bridget Hill and Alice Stewart) wrote to the *Observer* to make it clear that the women's colleges contained many who favoured 'joint education' as a way forward.[88] Four years later thirty-three women were signatories to a letter in the *Oxford Magazine*, again aiming to dispel the belief that the women's colleges were 'the fiercest opponents' of the admission of women to men's colleges, and putting it on record that they would welcome some such scheme.[89]

Losing control

The pressure for coresidence increased in the later 1960s. Strong arguments in favour of opening men's colleges to women were voiced by students and Junior Common Room committees.[90] In Oxford, the stance of women principals, individually, reflected some ambivalence as well as continuing anxieties. Collectively, something of a 'united front' seems to have been orchestrated by Lucy Sutherland, who was diplomatically discouraging in response to enquiries from other colleges (Wadham, Queen's, Brasenose), exploring the possibility of going mixed in the late 1960s.[91] By 1970, representatives of those men's colleges with such an interest began meeting to co-ordinate strategy.[92] In 1971 Lucy Sutherland conceded (in a letter to the Vice-Chancellor) that although she was 'personally against the development' she had to recognize that 'the tide in favour of it was too strong to stem'.[93] Her main object would be to try to prevent 'short-term dislocation' to the women's colleges and also to protect the interests of those women accepted into the men's colleges.

The direction of the 'tide' may have been clear at this point but the next two decades towards the end of the twentieth century saw anything but a smooth crossing. The politics of these years – personal, sexual and institutional – were highly complex. A plan for limited female quotas in certain Oxford colleges was opposed by those who thought that the scheme did not go far enough, as well as those who saw it as going too far. It bore the 'seal of approval' of the women principals.[94] In debate in Congregation, Kathleen Kenyon of St Hugh's made it plain that a scheme without 'safeguards' for the women's colleges would forfeit the co-operation of the women's colleges:

> The whole idea of co-residence must surely then drop, for I hope that we can take it that no men's college will be sufficiently ungentlemanly to go forward ruthlessly over the collective dead bodies of the women's colleges.[95]

The scheme was accepted, but resentments smouldered. In an article entitled 'Oxford's October Revolution' in the *Daily Telegraph*, in 1974, Marguerite Alexander quoted the views of a fellow of Wadham who judged that too many concessions had been made to the women's colleges, but noted that 'we gave them everything to establish the principle. Later we can negotiate our own terms.'[96]

In both Oxford and Cambridge the heads of the women's colleges played something of a double game, uneasy about being seen to oppose schemes which would widen access for women, but horrified at the possibility of losing their best candidates to the men's colleges. In both universities (in Oxford, through the Hebdomadal Council, in Cambridge through the Colleges' Committee) the women's colleges argued for protection; a slowing down, a 'moratorium', an orderly phasing of what they saw as the unchivalrous rush of the men's colleges to go mixed.

In Oxford, after tortuous discussions and negotiations, the 'working parties' on coresidence (co-ordinated at different stages by Wadham and Jesus Colleges) evolved into a Committee on Coresidence (appointed by Council), which produced a report and worked out a plan for a controlled 'experiment' in coresidence, which was put to Congregation in May 1972.[97] The scheme allowed five men's colleges (Wadham, Jesus, Hertford, Brasenose and St Catherine's) to admit a quota (20 per cent) of women students over the next three years.[98] No further changes would be countenanced before a review of the situation had been carried out, in 1977. However, tensions built up amongst colleges chafing to 'go mixed' before the review of the experiment in 1977. The University's 'right' to withhold approval for statutory changes in colleges in terms of the admission of women rested on 'moral' force. In the meantime, the passage of the Sex Discrimination Act in 1975 complicated an already complex situation.[99] By 1977 the Hebdomadal Council was reluctant to act as 'honest broker' (in a situation of dubious legality) any longer.[100] If there were those in the women's colleges who feared a 'disorderly rush' towards coresidence, many in the men's colleges feared the same, and that there would soon be no all-male colleges left ('There really is a danger that the pendulum will snowball and throw out the baby with the bathwater in a mass stampede!' opined a fellow of Merton in Congregation[101]). Mixed metaphors aside, a disorderly rush is what eventuated.

There were parallels as well as differences in the situation as it developed in Cambridge, where the heads of the three women's colleges, Girton, Newnham and New Hall, were similarly exercised by the implications of men's colleges opening their doors to women. Cambridge was in some ways a more insular and patriarchal environment than Oxford: the university had been the last in England to grant degrees to women and to accept them as full members of the university in 1948. The proportion of women in the university was subject to statutory limitation in the postwar years; an Ordinance limited the numbers of women *in statu pupillari* to a ceiling of one-fifth of the average annual number of resident men.[102] The proportion of women in the undergraduate population in Cambridge in 1952 was around the lowest in the country. Pressure to make more room for able women applicants grew, and as in Oxford, 'the solution' to many observers seemed to lie in opening the male colleges to women. Muriel Bradbrook, Mistress of Girton, later recalled that the news that Churchill, King's and Clare were to admit female students had thrown her into consternation: 'I felt . . . this great liner had struck an iceberg because we had lost our monopoly.'[103] From 1973 onwards a Standing Subcommittee (of the Colleges' Committee) on the Admission of Women (later 'Equal Opportunities') in Cambridge attempted 'to phase the men's colleges' lemming-like rush towards the sea of coresidence'.[104] Tensions mounted, as in Oxford: the women's colleges hoped that an orderly, slow process would allow them a breathing space to adjust, whilst some of the men's colleges felt frustrated by what they saw as 'a moratorium' on change. Rosemary Murray, Principal of New Hall (and Vice-Chancellor of the University after 1975), argued for a slow increase in the number of places for women, arguing that the pool of able women was limited.[105] Others deplored this position, and called for a more public and wholehearted commitment to equal opportunities. Alan Cottrell, Master of Jesus, argued strongly that a policy of restricting admission to women so as to follow rather than stimulate demand was not likely to attract more women to Cambridge.[106] As in Oxford, the attempt at an orderly 'queue' broke down, as it became clear that the majority of applicants (both women and men) favoured the mixed colleges.

Mistrust and 'betrayal'

Before the mid twentieth century, the very idea of admitting women students into men's colleges in Oxford or Cambridge had been just about unthinkable. One way of understanding the move towards mixed colleges is that women students, now 'accepted' in these universities, were increasingly seen as a resource. In an article on St Hilda's College which appeared in the *Telegraph Magazine* in 1995, Marilyn Butler was represented as having reflected that:

We knew the men's colleges just wanted our bright girls. They were quite unscrupulous, they just packed in a superfluity of good women and made no effort to accept them. They thought the girls were an asset as dolly-birds, but didn't want to know them as academic and powerful colleagues. They weren't trying to equalise, they didn't want to admit women as Fellows. When I hear them say 'Well, we've got women in now, and d'you know, it doesn't make any difference', I think that's the most sinister utterance they could make.[107]

The politics and relationships between men and women in higher education since around 1850 had often been characterized by mistrust. Elizabeth Reid's determination that her college should be governed by Ladies as well as Gentlemen – a fairly radical concept at the time – had been a political decision. The opponents of Bedford's going mixed in the 1960s saw those who pressed for the change as betraying the Trust and Mrs Reid's intentions.

Their stance was countered by those who argued that historical conditions had changed and that 'women's best interests' were no longer served by continuing segregation. Such controversies were to become all too familiar as the separate women's colleges in Oxford and Cambridge wrestled with decisions about whether to admit men over the next few decades. The accusation of the Oxford women principals in the 1960s as behaving like 'Uncle Toms' was based on the belief that they could not be trusted to act in the interests of women then debarred from an Oxford education. The position of the women principals was indeed a defensive one, but history, and their own experience, accounts for this. It was far from inevitable that coeducation should have been seen as a form of 'betrayal', but historical experience helped to shape such accusations.

It is difficult to see how the numbers of women undergraduates in either Oxford or Cambridge could have been raised to anything like a respectable proportion without the men's colleges going mixed. The anxieties of those heads of the women's colleges who believed that the supply of intelligent and well-qualified women students who might seek an 'Oxbridge' education was so limited in the 1970s look unduly pessimistic today. However it is worth remembering that the advocates of Bedford's 'going mixed' in the 1960s often shared their prejudices, arguing that social and demographic factors exerted a brake on the numbers of women applying for degree-level and postgraduate study.[108] But as one observer in the 1970s emphasized, the stance of those in the women's colleges who were fearful of the consequences of coresidence could not be dismissed simply as 'morally questionable paranoia', or an attempt to defend narrow institutional interests at the expense of opportunities for women more broadly defined. 'While the world in general offers women an unequal deal,' she contended, 'they would be advised to hold on to their strongholds.'[109] The misgivings of Mary Ogilvie, Janet Vaughan and Lucy Sutherland – and many others who were uneasy about the opening of men's colleges to women – stemmed in part from concern about what kind of experience young women would have in colleges controlled by men and characterized by male traditions and a masculine ethos. They were equally concerned about the position of women teachers, fearing that fellowships and senior positions in the colleges would continue to be monopolized by men.

A key advance came when Marilyn Butler became Rector of Exeter College, Oxford – long a 'men's college' – in 1993. As appointments of women to senior posts in Oxford and Cambridge become more commonplace we may see an erosion of the kind of discursive construction of gendered interests ('them and us') evident in the remarks attributed to Professor Butler which were quoted above, representations which have shaped the past of these institutions and in particular the troubled history of coeducation. Only when women share equally with men in the teaching, learning and governance of the mixed college, might one expect accusations of betrayal, alongside the legacy of mistrust, to be relegated to history.

Chapter Nine

ᏕᏍ

Troubled identities

Gender, status and culture in the mixed college since 1945

Questions of gender, prestige and identity have been closely entwined in the history of educational institutions.[1] It will have become clear from earlier chapters that controversy over coeducation in British universities has a long and complex history, and that debates over the potential of 'mixed colleges' to further or safeguard 'women's interests' were particularly bitter in the context of the dramatic institutional changes in higher education after the Second World War.

There was much contention between those who believed that the interests of women were best served by female-governed or single-sex institutions and those who sought equality through institutional integration. Here I probe more deeply into the troubling of identity involved in the history of the mixed college. Academic and collegiate institutions previously defined by gender and serving to construct male or female identities needed to redefine themselves in the context of coeducation.

To recapitulate: in 1914 women were still not admitted to the high-status medical schools of Edinburgh and London, they were not entitled to graduate in the University of Oxford before 1920, and full acceptance as members of the University of Cambridge was withheld from them until 1948. Segregation by sex remained the norm in these 'elite' areas of provision: in London and Edinburgh, women were relegated to their own, all-female medical schools, and in Oxford and Cambridge separate colleges for men and women (with marked differentiation in wealth and prestige) were the rule. The twentieth century saw a near total abandonment of this pattern of segregation by sex. As it ended, there were no all-male colleges left. Three colleges in Cambridge still admitted only women (Newnham, New Hall and Lucy Cavendish). In Oxford, only St Hilda's College remained all-female.

An end to segregation in London, 1914–1965

The controversies and vexed events of the years during and after the First World War made it clear that the London medical schools felt their status undermined by the female presence, which they regarded as inimical to sporting prowess and masculine camaraderie. But a series of subcommittees appointed by the university to consider the problem of the medical education of women in London felt differently, and consistently reported in favour of coeducation. By 1944 the University Senate voted by a large majority for 'opening all London medical schools to men and women on terms of equal opportunity', and set about corresponding with the schools on how to bring this into effect.[2] This decision was given further clout by the report of the Goodenough Committee on medical education in the same year, as detailed in Chapter 3 above.[3]

Thus far, it becomes clear that the University of London's support of coeducation was associated with expanding opportunities for women. But in the context of a general shortage of university places after the Second World War, support for coeducation was equally likely to be associated with the perceived need to find more places for men. The women at the Royal Free Hospital School of Medicine had no choice other than to recognize this:[4] a directive to implement coeducation could scarcely exempt an all-female medical school, and the first male students entered its portals in 1947.[5] The men scarcely rushed in: an editorial in the school's magazine in 1947 noted that, 'while the women have disappeared from the title of the school the men can hardly be said to have appeared', and that the authorities may as well have retitled the institution 'The London (Royal Free Hospital) School of Medicine for Women and Two Men'.[6] The number of male students increased slowly. The June 1953 issue of the magazine commented with gentle irony that:

> we are sure that the ladies will forgive the men of this College for maintaining a none-too-secret notion, that the one sure way to steady progress and increasing eminence of the Medical School (the objective of the progress, and the nature of the eminence is not always clear) is the raising of the number of male students as rapidly as possible.[7]

A pair of male students similarly breached the feminine precincts of Queen Elizabeth College a few years later, in 1953, but the number of men seeking admission to what was after all a college associated with 'household science' did not appreciate significantly until the introduction of a new BSc (General) degree in 1957.[8]

This left the three single-sex institutions in London: Royal Holloway, Westfield and Bedford, whose debates over coeducation have been detailed in the previous chapter. Discussions came to focus around perceptions of losing places for women at the expense of bringing in men. Even when some commitment had been made to change, events moved slowly.

Gender and status in the London colleges

Many of the more obvious ways in which gender and status were linked will be apparent from the foregoing accounts: it was the London medical schools' concern with their elite status, and the belief that this status would be undermined by any association with femininity, that led them to resist women students so determinedly and for so long.

If segregation was represented as an anachronism, and as an obstacle to widening opportunity for women, what were the implications for women's colleges? If an association with femininity diminished status, would an association with maleness strengthen prestige? Here, issues became much more complex. In the case of the London women's colleges 'going mixed', there were certainly many who believed that this would be the case.

Several of those who gave evidence to the Post-War Policy Committee at Royal Holloway expressed the view that the admission of men would improve both the academic and social tone in what had become a rather second-rate institution. According to the minutes of a meeting held by the Committee in 1944, for instance, the Vice-Chancellor of the University of London submitted that Royal Holloway's Trust Deed, in his private opinion, 'should be burnt'.

> When the college was founded the education of women was in its infancy. It could, he thought, be argued that the best education for women was coeducation. By and large, men students were better than women students. This was certainly so in his own subject. The admission of men would raise the standard – not, of course if they were 'rabbits', but if they were average men, the standard would certainly be raised in physics. He could not, of course, speak for Arts.[9]

There was a pervasive view of the college as a feminine backwater, a vestigial version of the vision cherished by Ida in *The Princess*.[10] It was not only the male witnesses who thought this way. A number of witnesses argued that the presence of men would 'invigorate' the women. Lynda Grier, Principal of Lady Margaret Hall, Oxford, asked during the collection of evidence about the differences between men and women students in their approach to study, contended that even the stupid men she taught had more 'mental audacity' than the women, who were schooled to be 'more sponge-like and docile'.[11] Even Margery Fry (a former Principal of Somerville) confessed to a fear of 'over-femininity' were the college to expand as a single-sex institution.[12]

In the cases of Westfield and Bedford, as at Royal Holloway, the advocates of coeducation envisaged the admission of men as a way of raising academic standards, particularly through strengthening admissions on the science side, in allowing the expansion of postgraduate work. In the Memorandum of the Chairman of Council in 1963 referred to in Chapter 8, the need to address the national call for an expansion of places in higher education, particularly on the science side, was seen as crucially important.[13] Again, it was suggested that the segregation of women was an anachronism. He argued the need to attract 'scientists of distinction' to the teaching staff; these were likely to be men, who would want to teach male students and to foster research which women students were increasingly unlikely to undertake. The Chairman considered that a refusal to admit men 'might imperil the very existence of the College as an independent institution'.

Much was also made of demographic factors such as a tendency to earlier marriage, which, it was argued, not only explained why the demand for university places from women would be less than from their male peers, but also militated against women carrying out research or applying for academic posts.[14] Defenders of the women's colleges protested that they were more likely than mixed colleges to take these problems seriously and to seek ways of encouraging women to combine family and professional life. Against that, at Bedford, O.R. McGregor and B.C. King argued similarly to the Chairman of Council at Westfield, emphasizing that the trend to earlier marriage disinclined women from postgraduate work.[15] A university teacher needed 'to feel that he is helping to prepare men for their work in the world as well as women for theirs' claimed one manifesto, whose authors wanted to see Bedford 'a School of the University aiming at absolutely the highest possible standards', rather than 'a service to the underprivileged . . . working to compensate women for their "lack of male advantages"', 'a university in microcosm' rather than 'a girls' day-college'. Both the anxieties about status, and the aspirations, are clear.[16]

Gender and status at Oxbridge

Given the limitations on women student numbers and the elite position of Oxbridge in British society generally, competition for places in the women's colleges had been much fiercer than in the men's before the new threat of coresidence had arisen. Thus in spite of their lowly position in male-dominated universities, the academic status of the Oxbridge women's colleges, nationally, was high. We have seen how the climate of expansion in higher education in the early 1960s led to criticism of Oxford and Cambridge as not making sufficient provision for women students.

The desire to offer more opportunities to women was coupled with a concern about application rates: Oxford was seen to be attracting fewer (male) applicants per place than many of the newer universities, and even losing ground to the older, provincial foundations.[17] The language deployed in the endless debates about coresidence in these years indicates an overwhelming concern with academic status, competition and elites. The women's colleges feared that the men's colleges would 'skim the cream' of their entry, and that they were motivated by what the Principal of St Hilda's dubbed the 'stupid-men-out-clever-girls-in argument'.[18] The Principal of St Hugh's argued in Congregation that, if mixed colleges were a success, there was 'a real risk that we shall drop back again into being second-class citizens'.[19] These arguments failed to convince those scholars in the women's colleges who welcomed proposals for coeducation. Antoinette Pirie (Somerville), Peter Ady (St Anne's), Jenifer Hart (St Anne's) and Margaret Paul (LMH) vigorously contested the idea that the supply of able women candidates was so limited, arguing that girls' performance at A-level had been improving dramatically in recent years.[20]

Sooner or later each of the women's colleges had to confront the dilemma of whether to respond to the rapidly changing circumstances of these years by admitting men. As early as 1971 Girton had applied for 'enabling powers' to admit men should this come to be accepted as the best way forward (the Sex Discrimination Act of 1975 raised the possibility of such an 'Enabling Statute' proving compelling[21]). But in both universities it was recognized that the problems facing women's colleges contemplating the admission of men were not symmetrical with those of men's colleges considering the admission of women. In Oxford, Council's Committee on Coresidence in 1972 had queried whether

> mixed colleges, being formerly women's colleges [would] be likely to attract men of good quality, given that they would continue for many years to be predominantly governed by women and that they did not have facilities (including sports facilities) customary in men's colleges?[22]

When this report was debated in Congregation the Principal of St Hugh's (Kathleen Kenyon) put the question more bluntly: why, she asked, did the women's colleges not counter the movement for opening the men's colleges to women by going mixed themselves?

> The answer is of course that quite apart from the fact that the ostensible object of this exercise is to increase the number of women at Oxford, we should get the dregs. Only men who failed to make the grade at a men's college would try to creep in in this way, and only a man who saw no hope of getting a fellowship elsewhere would accept one at a college where it would require an effluxion of time of some thirty years before petticoat government disappeared.[23]

Her remarks did not go unchallenged. In a lucid intervention in the debate, Margaret Paul drew attention yet again to the abundant supply of talented young people in the country, both women and men, pointing out that the former women's colleges in London seemed to have maintained academic standards once they had admitted men.[24] But Kathleen Kenyon's remarks reflected widespread anxiety and a profound sense of insecurity in the women's colleges, a fear of being reduced yet again to 'second-class citizenship', easily enough explained by history.

To those involved in the controversies around 'coresidence' during these years the discussions and debates seemed interminable. Seen through the longer lens of history, events moved with extraordinary rapidity. Once a few male colleges decided to admit women, it quickly became apparent that their popularity increased among male students, and the academic quality of their entrants improved. Women students, once an embarrassment, had become both resource and bait. By 1988, when Magdalene admitted its first female students, there were no all-male colleges left in Cambridge. Oriel was the last of the male colleges to admit women in Oxford, in 1985. Of the women's colleges, Girton College, Cambridge, admitted men in 1979. St Anne's and Lady Margaret Hall in Oxford did so in the same year; St Hugh's admitted male undergraduates in 1986; Somerville, after much publicized disputes with its student body, went mixed in 1994.[25]

Gender and culture

The separate histories of men's and women's colleges in Oxbridge had led to profound differences in their organization and culture. Male student culture in both Oxbridge and the medical schools had been long associated with rowdiness, drink and deeds of derring-do. Challenges to authority (Deans and Proctors), though usually ritualized and contained, were both frequent and frequently tolerated as part of the construction of masculinity, part of the 'natural order of things'. Women's colleges had a history of keeping a low profile, of trying to earn respectability through good behaviour and avoiding any head-on challenges to social convention. They inherited a legacy of rules and restrictions that were only very slowly beginning to be relaxed in the aftermath of the Second World War. In this period male students, whose masculinity had been confirmed by National Service, were apt to pour ridicule on the strictures of the women dons and to scoff openly at the predicament of the female students whom they regarded as either mollycoddled or subject to intolerable restrictions on their freedom.[26]

The post-war years, and particularly the 1960s, saw increasing student complaints against 'paternalism' and conflict with university authorities over 'gate-hours' and other attempts to regulate the relationships between the sexes in Oxford and Cambridge (as elsewhere). The social and moral authority which university authorities were able to exercise over students as 'minors', that is, under the age of 21, became increasingly contested and was effectively undermined by the Family Reform Act of 1969 which lowered the age of majority to 18.[27] The Act both reflected and reinforced changing standards of sexual morality, easing the way towards the acceptance of mixed colleges. One of the arguments frequently adduced by the opponents of coresidence earlier in the 1960s had been that parents would object, and that the 'moral problem' of women living alongside men would require college fellows to shoulder an unwelcome burden of supervisory and moral responsibility for the 'good behaviour' of the young.[28] Institutions exploring the possibilities of coresidence in the late 1960s, such as Churchill and King's in Cambridge, often conducted elaborate inquiries into the experience of mixed halls and hostels in universities elsewhere in Britain.[29] Crombie Hall in Aberdeen, a 'mixed' hall of residence which had opened in 1960, was deluged by requests for information during this period. T.E. Lawrenson, an early Warden of Crombie Hall, testified reassuringly to the fact that young people behaved well in a mixed environment, there was no upsurge of immorality, and rather less 'destructive horseplay' than was apt to erupt in an all-male residence. If there was some loss of 'male camaraderie', he confessed, there were much better opportunities for Scottish country dancing.[30] The Warden of University House (also mixed) in Birmingham, similarly reassured the Senior Tutor of Churchill College that in her experience coresidence diminished the 'gang hooliganism' common in men's halls, as well as the 'secretiveness and hysteria' too often present in an all-female environment.[31]

Students pressing for coresidence seized on such evidence. By 1970 the JCRs in nineteen Oxford colleges were alleged to have declared 'in favour' of going mixed.[32] Exponents deplored what they saw as the unnatural, unhealthy, unbalanced 'monastic/army camp atmosphere' of the all-male college, claiming that it exacerbated social and sexual tensions and inhibited adulthood.[33] In Cambridge, women students' action groups in the early 1970s perceived single-sex colleges as 'discrimination', identifying equal opportunities with the opening of male colleges to women, a tendency which led to uneasy relationships with some women dons.[34] Although the exponents of coresidence may be held to have been more vocal than its opponents, particularly in the student press, there can be little doubt that 'student opinion', both male and female, was strongly in favour of co-education at this point in time. The fact that applications to mixed colleges quickly began to overtake those to single-sex institutions confirms this. Both proponents and opponents of the mixed college spoke of 'the tide of history' or the 'tide of public opinion' being strongly in favour of coeducation,[35] and plans to receive the opposite sex were set in motion.

The cultural impact of such accommodations varied. The admission of women by King's, Clare and Churchill in 1972 proved less 'eventful' than was hoped by the journalists who hung around Cambridge hoping for a story. There was a great deal of anxiety in some quarters about what women would want or need. One college bursar gloomily likened the admission of women to the 'letting of cats into a dogs' home'.[36] There was much fussing about sanitary arrangements – were the bathrooms adequate? Worse, what about incinerators for sanitary products? Some colleges set out to provide long mirrors and ironing boards, sometimes earning themselves the riposte from feminists who asserted that women wanted equal rights rather than 'a pandering to their stereotyped feminine needs'.[37]

There might be last-ditch displays of masculinity from the 'unreconstructed'. In Queens' College, Cambridge, for instance, the JCR committee organized a 'stag night' with strippers on the eve of admitting women students. This provoked a retaliatory but 'peaceful' demonstration by feminist groups.[38] An article in the student press in 1979 quoted members of St Catharine's College, who conceded that they had no objection to the college admitting women 'so long as they do our washing'.[39] When Magdalene College, Cambridge's last 'male bastion' (and with a reputation for being 'roisteringly' so), finally decided on coresidence in 1988, some members sported black armbands but were allegedly discouraged by authority from their original plan to walk through the town carrying a coffin.[40] An earlier edition of the *Varsity* handbook had alleged that Magdalene tended to treat women guests 'like tarts in some frontier gold-rush town'. Ten years later one of the first female students admitted averred that her male colleagues seemed 'nice and friendly', even the armband wearers, who she suggested 'were in mourning' for an older ideal of femininity rather than expressing their implacable hostility to change.[41]

The admission of male students to former women's colleges provoked, if anything, more elaborate preparations. Probably the most vexed issue was that of providing the sports facilities considered the life-blood of the male. In the 1940s the Royal Free Hospital Medical School had recognized that it had overlooked the importance of 'rugger' for male applicants and had set about urgent negotiations with Guy's Hospital for shared facilities. To survive as a coeducational venture, suggested one female observer, they needed 'to simulate the men's colleges where "sport" may be more important than medicine'.[42] Contemplating coresidence in the late 1970s led Girton to build a squash court, and after only partial success in negotiating shared sports facilities with other colleges, to press ahead for a rugby field of its own. Provision was also made for 'a new bar complex with a dart board', shaver sockets, and some extra long beds.[43] Some disgruntled female students complained that more effort had been expended in making the men comfortable than had ever been forthcoming for the women.[44]

An observer in the Cambridge student paper, *Stop Press*, reported that fewer than ten of the first intake of fifty-four first-year men in Girton had included the college in the list of preferences on their application form. She pointed out that they had encountered a good deal of ridicule from other men in the university. They had tended to meet this with uncompromising displays of masculinity, putting their energies into establishing a rugby club, setting up equipment for a discotheque and 'manning' the JCR. One of the men whom she had interviewed for the article had complained of 'the endless portraits of academic women with big jaws' in Girton, another had ostentatiously remarked to 'a girl who came to fetch sherry glasses as I left, "By the way, I've got some ironing"'.[45] In an article written for *The Old Haileyburian*, another of Girton's male 'pioneers' recorded his experiences for his old school contemporaries: he had felt 'intimidated' among so many women at first, he confessed, but the college was changing fast. The men had bonded together and made a significant impact, the college authorities had done all they could to make them feel comfortable. He was no longer intimidated by female company, 'in fact it [was] a constant nourishment for my ego.'[46]

Women's colleges admitting male students usually ensured that there were significant numbers of men in senior positions to welcome them. In this sense, they prided themselves on being more fully coeducational than the former men's colleges admitting women, where the fellowship tended to remain overwhelmingly male.[47] The men who first entered women's colleges may have suffered anxieties about their status, but soon set about trying to alter the culture and conventions of the institution. Conversely, the first female entrants to previously male colleges enjoyed high status in the public eye. In an article which appeared in the *Times Education Supplement* in 1974, one writer described a casual conversation with a 'young lady' en route to Oxford. 'Where?' he asked, confessing himself having been 'all set to make a witty and probably slightly derogatory remark about St Hilda's or Somerville'. 'Brasenose,' she replied, taking the wind out his sails and silencing him, 'politely filling the awkward gap where the witty response should have come with a blow by blow account of how she put her tutor at his ease during the interview'.[48] However, many of the first female students to enter wealthy, prestigious male colleges felt privileged and often rather overawed: grateful for what they initially perceived as 'equal opportunities' with their male peers. It was by no means uncommon for (male) senior members of the former men's colleges to assert that the advent of women had left the 'essential character' of the college completely unchanged.[49]

Troubled identities

For many feminists, this insistence on the part of some of the former male colleges that nothing had really changed was precisely the problem, since it raised the spectre of what Lady Ogilvie, Principal of St Anne's College Oxford in the 1960s, had described as essentially 'a men's college with some women in it'.[50] Looking back on the history of mixed colleges in Oxford in 1995, Marilyn Butler observed ruefully that, whilst the men's colleges had been keen enough to admit bright girls as undergraduates, they had failed to accommodate them as academics and powerful colleagues, and there had been little progress in admitting women as fellows.[51] This was true in both Oxford and Cambridge. In Cambridge, a study published in 1988 by the University Women's Action Group (CUWAG) drew attention to this:

> Promising women students are admitted, but their talents are not allowed to develop to their fullest capacity; women of high ability graduate, but they are not directed towards research; experienced and capable women are appointed as staff, but their expertise and value is not recognized by permanent contracts or promotion.[52]

The report concluded that the university was 'failing in its obligation as an educational institution' by 'cheating' women, and cheating itself, in wasting valuable human resources.[53]

One college particularly responsive to criticism of this kind was King's College, Cambridge; as we have seen, one of the earliest to 'go mixed'. Between 1988 and 1998 the college made serious efforts to consider the predicaments and experiences of its female members in supporting research and activities, which led to three interesting publications. In 1988–90 a piece of 'practically orientated' research was commissioned into the position of women in the university (and particularly in King's itself) from Andrea Spurling.[54] Her report identified key obstacles to women's 'academic success' in a male-dominated environment and generated a mass of interesting insights into the gendered culture of the college. This research had practical outcomes in that it led to the college setting in motion an equal opportunities policy. However, the sections on language, ritual, status and identity in the report showed the pervasiveness of (albeit unintentionally) a structuring of sexual difference.[55] In 1993 the college celebrated twenty years of coeducation with a conference and series of workshops addressing the question 'Is King's still a male college admitting women?'[56] A number of pertinent topics were investigated, alongside the experiences of women teachers and students. Germaine Greer challenged the meeting by expressing doubt about whether there was anything to celebrate, contending in her usual vigorous style that it was 'useless to attempt to take over an institution predicated upon male relationships and values', and that coeducation was a 'misplaced goal'.[57] In an interesting attempt to draw attention to the 'symbolic order' of the college, the many portraits of male worthies festooning the walls were given temporary paper coverings, sporting feminist observations and reflections.[58] A third project testifying to the college's continuing process of self-examination and reflection on the subject of its coeducational identity involved a question-naire survey of the experiences of its women graduates. Co-ordinated by Joanna Norland, this resulted in the publication of a report entitled *Her Generation* in 1998.[59]

Both the experiences recorded by the first female entrants to men's colleges, and those of the first men to enter women's colleges, show a troubling of identity around gender and status. According to a (female) journalist, writing in *The Times* in 1994,

> the way that the first men admitted into women's colleges behaved has passed into Oxford legend: they shouted, they drank, they vomited in the dean's flowerbed, they clumped, they took over all the key positions on undergraduate committees . . .[60]

Representations of this kind were matched by the stories of (male) writers about women:

> It only needed a beginning of term stroll through the porters' lodges, where Habitat bags and vanity cases were piled up against the usual trunks, to reveal that things were going to be very different,

observed Ian Bradley in the *Times Higher Education Supplement* in 1974, alleging that one girl had arrived at Hertford College with a wardrobe, dressing table and cooker, to the alarm of the Domestic Bursar who had 'hitherto regarded requests for an extra chair as a major nuisance'.[61]

Clearly many such stories were apocryphal, but they reveal something of the difficulties of transition. The argument that the former women's colleges became more 'genuinely mixed' in offering equal opportunities at both junior and senior levels has substance; the tendency of the former men's colleges to remain, in essence, men's colleges admitting female undergraduates but with very few women in positions of authority posed continuing problems of identity for women members. This troubling of identity has sometimes been expressed in 'demands' for equal oppor-tunities policies, designated 'women's tutors', and women's common rooms. Whilst never underplaying the sense of privilege expressed and enjoyed by women admitted to prestigious colleges, some researchers have shown concern about the evidence of damaged self-esteem, frustration and disappointment that they have nonetheless encountered amongst some of the women who have graduated from these institutions.[62]

A troubling of identity at both the individual and the institutional level was not confined to the mixed college in this period. The women's colleges which 'held out' against going mixed suffered from continuing problems of policy and public image. The women principals who, as seen in Chapter 8, had used what power they had to discourage and slow the transition to coresidence had attracted considerable public opprobrium. They had often been perceived as privileging their own elite institutional claims above those of women more generally.[63] As it became apparent that the mixed colleges were attracting excellent candidates of both sexes, those in the women's colleges who had feared that the former men's colleges would 'skim the cream' felt their anxieties justified.[64] However, articles in the press suggesting that this was indeed what was happening were likely to elicit angry replies and denials.[65] The dilemma was acute at times, and in the midst of what she and some of her colleagues perceived as 'a takeover bid', a beleaguered Principal of St Hilda's complained that she felt that many in Oxford would be greatly relieved if the women's colleges would 'somehow or other vanish into thin air'.[66]

By the time that Somerville came to admit men in 1994 it is clear that the remaining women's colleges were facing a barrage of problems. Although Somerville's decision was opposed by its student body, there is little doubt that the popularity of the women's colleges (measured in terms of the proportion of first-choice applicants) was declining. There were also legal and financial problems to be faced.[67] Although there was no shortage of those prepared to mount a reasoned and spirited defence of the role which single-sex colleges might still play in promoting opportunities for women, articles in the press posed with depressing regularity the question of whether these colleges had lost their 'allure' or had been reduced to the status of 'anachronism'.[68] Somerville's historian, Pauline Adams, has suggested that the very fact that Somerville and St Hilda's could be seen as 'havens' for women in a male-dominated Oxford tended to isolate them from the initiatives and campaigns to improve women's status that were coming from the mixed colleges, and that a large part of the Governing Body's concern for change 'was to join the battle on behalf of women where the action was now perceived as being keenest'.[69]

Girton College's archives hold a tape-recording of Muriel Bradbrook, reflecting on the decision to go mixed at the end of the 1970s. Her observations are punctuated by sighs. She speaks of a sense of having been 'amputated from the past'. Traditions had been broken, but the past was past and could not be regained. The sense of troubled identity, the feeling of loss and regret, is almost overwhelming. But not quite. She rallies, composing both herself and a different narrative. Emily Davies, she reminded her interviewers, had established a tradition:

... what they did, we did, and if the men went mixed, we must go
mixed. This, I think, is part of our real tradition and we had . . . we had
to swallow it.

Was it the rewriting of history or the prospect of the future that was hard
to 'swallow'? The future that Bradbrook fleetingly envisaged, a college in
which men and women would work as colleagues on an 'equal footing',
was not, after all, so unpalatable. The sense of powerlessness, of having
no choice, of being swept away by 'the tide of history' was understandably
less so.

Gender, culture, power

In 1969, John Gray, then a student at Exeter College, Oxford, wrote a
notably comprehensive and vigorous manifesto in favour of the mixed
college, in which he observed that sexual segregation hardly conduced to
that transmission of a common culture which had been identified by the
authors of the Robbins Report as one of the aims of higher education.[70]
Heralding what he saw as 'The disintegration of Oxford's male monopoly'
in the *Times Higher Education Supplement* three years later, Robert
Jackson (Fellow of All Souls and a future Minister with responsibility for
education) observed that:

> The Oxford Colleges are forms of community surviving from the pre-
> industrial age. In the Nineteenth Century they lost their Anglican and
> clerical monopoly. Now the process has worked through to attack their
> masculine exclusiveness.
>
> We must not too readily condemn the Oxford dons of an earlier
> generation who confined women to their own colleges and organised
> them in a female monopoly which answered – and often parodied –
> their own monopoly of masculinity. The cultural order in which they
> lived was one in which the sovereign virtues were considered to be
> male. Underlying all the other collectivities of British society in their
> time were the two great communities of sex. Within them, clear and
> distinct identities were marked out.[71]

Jackson contended that the breakdown of this pattern of segregation in
the academic communities of Oxford and Cambridge according to sex
represented both a 'liberal revolution' and a profound cultural change: the
Report of the Oxford University Committee on Coresidence, he claimed, a
'slender but devastating (12-page) volume' should be seen as 'a document
in the tradition of Voltaire's remark, that only short works change the
world'.[72]

Before the 1970s, the segregation and containment of women in Oxford and Cambridge buttressed the masculine hierarchy, structuring gender identity and underlining the separate cultural and historical traditions of men and women in this privileged educational milieu. The links between gender, status and power were complex, but some understanding of the interplay between them is fundamental to our grasp of the institutional history of higher education in both Oxbridge and London over the twentieth century. The triumph of the mixed college may be seen as a necessary condition for men and women to be able to act as equal partners in and beneficiaries of a common academic culture; a necessary, but not yet sufficient, condition for equal opportunities and full integration. For at the same time, it must be conceded that some of the 'battles' that had been uneasily 'resolved' or deferred by segregation remain to be fought.

Chapter Ten

&.

The student rag

OED: An act of ragging; *esp.* an extensive display of noisy disorderly conduct, carried on in defiance of authority and discipline. Now usually a programme of satirical revues, frivolous stunts etc., organized by students to raise money for charities.
(*Univ. slang*) To annoy, tease or torment; to annoy or assail in a rough or noisy fashion, to create wild disorder . . .

Cheeky Guide to Student Life (Brighton, 2003):

Rag Week is a tradition that dates back approximately 200 years. Its main purpose is to raise money for local or national charities (Rag is an acronym for Raising and Giving), but you'd be forgiven for thinking that it was just a flimsy excuse for loads of people to dress up as gorillas and schoolgirls, sit in baths of baked beans and get legless.[1]

My interest in the history of the student rag, deriving from a longer-term concern with changes in student culture and identity, gained a particular stimulus from the availability of the Pathé News archives, which became accessible online in 2002. An initial search on the subject revealed extensive footage of student rag activities in university towns throughout Britain and Ireland through the interwar period and up to the 1970s. 'Rag' and student carnivals were important popular spectacles, and the archive film footage, together with the contemporary 'voice-over' commentaries, yield fascinating insights of three kinds: the events in themselves, their audience and the cultural representations of the time.[2] Interpretation is not always straightforward: some aspects of the student rag – the costumed participants (many in drag) on a parade of floats, rattling collecting-tins; the pram-races, pantomime slave auctions and the like – are instantly familiar and recognizable from work on the carnivalesque following

Bakhtin, such as Peter Stallybrass and Allon White's analysis *The Politics and Poetics of Transgression*, published in 1986.[3] We see enacted the inversion of hierarchy, the assertion of identity through definition of 'the other', a celebration of liminality and the transitoriness of the student state. But there are other aspects – such as the pervasiveness of imagery from the Ku Klux Klan in student rags before 1939 – that are harder to understand.[4] What follows is a preliminary exploration of the history of student rag as an organized event in British universities over the past century, which will show how a study of the subject can throw light on gender relations and shifts in student culture and identity, as well as the changing relationships between students and society during this period.

Origins

'Rag' festivities drew upon a variety of traditions. There was nothing new about episodes of misbehaviour amongst young men *in statu pupillari*. In his memorable Stenton Lecture of 1975, Keith Thomas turned his attention to traditions of 'barrings-out' and ritual misrule in educational settings since the seventeenth century.[5] Licensed episodes of misrule might be associated with rites of passage, or with traditions of merrymaking and saturnalia amongst young artisans and mechanics.[6] Such events might be seen in part as reaction against the discipline and deprivations of student life. 'Ragging' in universities took a variety of forms: there were barrings-out and barrings-in in nineteenth-century Oxford and Cambridge, sometimes as protest against unpopular tutors or fellows, at other times associated with pranks and drunken revels. There were 'rags' to celebrate graduation, or the inauguration of rectors or vice-chancellors. There were 'rags' which involved the systematic roughing-up of fellow student rooms, and traditions whereby parties of male marauders serenaded female student hostels at night and made off with door-knockers. The accumulation of 'trophies' in this way, together with particularly daring acts of defiance and derring-do, served to construct masculine student identity and to cement bonds of camaraderie. Universities in Scotland cherished traditions of student assertiveness and misrule around rectorial elections. Medical students everywhere were notorious for drinking and roistering, although they sometimes competed in this respect with engineers. Competition was important: between individuals, between colleges, between engineers and medics.[7] Masculine prowess and proud traditions were forged together, and colourful stories of preposterous misbehaviour, gross inebriation and large-scale damage fondly enshrined in student memory and passed on through generations.[8]

In *Redbrick University* (1943) 'Bruce Truscot' claimed rather snootily that 'rags' were 'an invention of Oxford or Cambridge', but that the tradition had been vulgarized by the plebeian activities of students in the provinces:

'Rags', an invention of Oxford or Cambridge – nobody knows of which and neither claims precedence – are in those universities joyful, spontaneous things, sometimes carried by high spirits to excess but nearly always characterised by a deep, sometimes even a subtle, sense of humour. Aping Oxford and Cambridge, in days when they had less individuality than now, the modern universities took over the rag, of which they appreciated the horseplay but missed the humour . . .[9]

However, in the course of an interesting chapter on 'Rowdyism' amongst Oxford undergraduates in the 1950s, Norman Longmate pointed out that the older universities boasted

no lasting period of licensed riot comparable to the 'Rag Week' of some provincial universities, when undergraduates, reinforced by the rougher elements from other universities, will scour the city in gangs, proving their manhood by the furtive theft of Belisha Beacon tops or public notice boards, and when the general public are victimized and insulted under the pretence of raising funds for the local hospital.[10]

The large-scale, organized rag activities and processions that feature in much of the Pathé news archive were not rooted in the 'Oxbridge' tradition: rather they represented one of the few traditions of student life that emerged from universities in the North of Britain around the turn of the twentieth century.[11] There was much cross-fertilization of institutional forms and patterns, however, with bonfires, processions, pitched battles between rival groups of undergraduates (involving much throwing of flour, soot and rotten fruit), kidnapping of college mascots and the like associated with rag activities throughout universities in Britain.

'Rag Weeks' in Manchester and Liverpool had their origins in student excursions to theatres and to the pantomime in the late nineteenth century. In Liverpool, in 1888, a procession of students marched to attend an opera at the Royal Court Theatre: their rowdy behaviour led to condemnation by the Principal, and it was not until 1897 that a similar procession took place, this time of 400 'Varsity men' in fancy dress, who marched through the city to attend a performance of 'Babes in the Wood' at the Shakespeare Theatre.[12] From then on, 'Pantonight' became an annual event, organized by the Students' Representative Council (from 1905, the Guild of Undergraduates).[13] In Manchester, an annual 'Shrove Tuesday' pantomime visit is recorded from 1896, when 'College men' would process to the Prince's Theatre.[14] Having arrived at the theatre the students would join in choruses (sometimes being allowed on stage by the managers of the theatre for this purpose) and they would present bouquets to the cast. By the end of the century the organization of the Shrove Tuesday procession and pantomime visit was being delegated to a special committee comprised of 'Four Arts men, four on the Medical side'.[15] In 1898 the procession assembled in Coupland Street under a banner 'Guide Our Youth'. Between 500 and 700 students in fancy dress descended on the Comedy Theatre singing college songs. Following the performance, baskets of flowers, bunches of violets and chocolates were presented by the students to the women *artistes*; bouquets of cauliflowers, carrots and turnips to the male leads. There was an elaborate expression of thanks to the theatre managers 'for the liberties and licence' granted to the students on this occasion.[16]

University authorities were somewhat divided in their attitude to these events. Principals welcomed the evidence of fellowship and community feeling, which they deemed essential in the building-up of 'tradition' and institutional confidence.[17] But there was also the question of town–gown relationships: local townspeople might relish the spectacle provided by student revellers, but the potential for rowdyism was ever-present. In Liverpool, university staff (including the Vice-Chancellor) attended the pantomime along with students in 1906, and the students were congratulated on having behaved in an exemplary fashion.[18] From the outset, 'Varsity men' were quick to blame 'local youth' (from whom they attempted to distance themselves) for any disturbances: in Manchester, the student press reported that processions to the Prince's Theatre 'were accompanied by the usual rowdies, who call themselves students but are not'.[19] In 1904, however, when Manchester's procession turned into something more like a mob, a student reporter accused fellow students who had forgotten 'that they had left the nursery', irresponsible 'children, who took the name of Owen's College with them'.[20]

Manchester's celebrations proved a triumph in 1907, an occasion described in the student press as 'a day of fierce delight'. Huge crowds allegedly greeted the procession with 'roars' of appreciation. Between three and four hundred men with blazing torches joined the parade, costumed as monks, skeletons, pierrots, 'painted Indians' and 'heathen Chinee'. Disciplines and 'trades' were in evidence, with 'chemical students . . . in benzene rings', engineers in overalls with hammers. The police were reported as having commended the 'gentlemanly way' in which college men disported themselves.[21] A correspondent in the *Manchester University Magazine* expressed the hope that the university authorities would soon see fit to recognize 'the Shrove Tuesday Demonstration' as 'a real College Rag' and to make the day into a student holiday in future years.[22] The hope materialized, and in 1910, the *MUM* reported that 'the Great Rag' was now 'officially recognised as a University Institution' and a college holiday.[23] In 1914 the *MUM* included a special 'Shrove Tuesday Supplement' entitled 'Carnival'; it included photographs of revellers in their fancy dress alongside lists of jokes and humorous asides, and can be seen as one of the earliest examples of (and possibly the first) 'Rag Magazine'.[24]

These early examples of college rags were essentially the activities of 'Varsity men': female students were onlookers rather than participants in the process whereby young men rehearsed new student identities which involved distancing themselves from children/women/non-whites and the working class. The costumes selected by male revellers lampooned and ridiculed the social groups implicitly recognized as 'outsiders' in this process of establishing a male student identity.[25] Men paraded as babies and fat matrons (the pram race was a favourite in student rags); they postured in drag as schoolgirls and suffragettes, blacked themselves up as Indians, Hottentots and Zulu warriors. Women were not allowed to don fancy dress or to join the carnival processions in Manchester and Liverpool at this time. In the discursive tone of the student press of the day, a 'student' was assumed to be male, and there were endless jokes about the prim and proper behaviour of 'girl-students' or 'women-students' who were often represented as marginal or outsiders in the community. It could be difficult for women to puncture this tone of voice. One female student, for instance, who contributed an article to the *MUM* describing the Shrove Tuesday Rag 'From a girl's point of view' (under the pen-name 'Bien Amusée') in 1912, observed that 'At the theatre we were struck by the good behaviour of the students.'[26] Men sat separately from women students in the theatre performances of the 1890s and 1900s. In Liverpool, male students appropriated the upper circle, and the women were consigned to the pit, although this arrangement was later reversed on safety grounds.[27] In another piece in the *MUM*, 'Shrovetide – a feminine review' in 1913, a 'mere woman' confessed that, as such, she 'was not initiated into the mysteries of Shrove Tuesday', she could write only as a spectator. 'As far as we know, or are concerned,' she commented, 'the men get the best of the fun. We look on, as of course we can only do.'[28]

There was a general suspension of rag activities in universities during the First World War, but such celebrations were resumed with vigour thereafter. The interwar years witnessed the flowering of the carnival/rag tradition: such activities were not confined to students, and many towns appear to have introduced annual civic carnivals during the 1920s, a phenomenon which still awaits the attention of students of leisure and cultural historians.[29] Even before the war, student carnivals had proved a popular public spectacle: Liverpool's 'Panto' parade of 1914 had been 'bioscoped' and played to audiences at the Lime Street Picture House.[30]

Stallybrass and White have described how:

> Carnival is presented by Bakhtin as a world of topsy-turvy, of heteroglot exuberance, of ceaseless overrunning and excess where all is mixed, hybrid, ritually degraded and defiled.[31]

An article in Manchester University's student paper the *Serpent* in 1920 conveys something of this spirit of renewal and exuberance which fuelled the Shrove Tuesday celebrations of this period. With a loquacity rivalling the event itself, the writer confessed that any description of Shrove Tuesday must be inadequate, for

> How to capture and enclose in print that of which the essence is elusiveness and impalpability? How reduce to the cohesion of a balanced sentence that which is a riot of joyous lunacy, a madcap fling of fantastic incoherence?[32]

Once a year, he continued, 'the drab industrial North' enjoyed 'a gorgeous day of topsy-turveydom', 'transformed into a playground of irresponsible youth' by students in 'a surging mass of motley' dressed as convicts, profiteers, minstrels, pierrots and jesters, 'niggers and flappers', 'a kaleidoscopic phantasmagoria' of a procession snaking its way through the city.[33] The article implies an analysis of modernity and cultural forms very close to some of the insights later developed by Bakhtin.

An important new feature of student rag activity and carnival after the First World War was its association with fund-raising and local charity. Collections for the unemployed and particularly for local hospitals became a focus and supplied legitimation for masculine exuberance and disorder. Liverpool students began collecting for local hospitals during 'Panto Night' in 1920.[34] The rattle of collecting tins became common during processions, and the sale of rag magazines (published with support from local businesses, who paid for advertising space) proved an important source of funds. Liverpool students published a special edition ('Panto Number') of their university magazine, *Sphinx*, in 1925. (This later became *Pantosfinx.*)[35] Manchester's Carnival Supplement developed into *Rag Rag* in 1924, its editorial introduction emphasizing that the purpose of Shrove Tuesday was to raise money for hospitals: 'the great cloak of charity which we hope will cover the multitude of our sins'.[36] It became common for rag magazines to feature a letter signifying support for rag activity from vice-chancellors, lord mayors or other civic dignitaries, who would commend the students for their charitable efforts, sometimes posing as 'lords of misrule'.[37]

These developments of student rag activity quickly spread throughout universities in the UK. The local origins of 'rag' or carnival in Glasgow and Birmingham, for instance, were slightly different and arguably somewhat later than in Manchester and Liverpool. The organization of a large-scale bazaar to raise money for the building of a student union in Glasgow in 1889 provided the impetus for fancy dress and a torchlight procession, but 'Infirmaries Day' (subsequently 'Charities Day') as an annual event in the university calendar dated from just after the First World War, in 1920.[38] This involved processions, an annual revue ('College Pudding'), and an annual rag magazine, which took its name from the College song (*Ygorra*).[39] In Birmingham, from the late nineteenth century, students enjoyed a robust tradition of 'ragging' and tomfoolery on degree days, and as in other universities, they regularly resorted to 'ragging' as a way of welcoming noteworthy visitors,[40] but the first 'University Hospital Carnival' in Birmingham took place in 1921.[41] A street collection on this occasion yielded £2,000, and it was not long before patrons of a hospital in nearby Wolverhampton were urging Birmingham University students to mount a carnival procession in that town in order to raise funds, chartering special free trains for the purpose, and providing lorries that could be decorated for the procession.[42] The first issue of *Carnival*, Birmingham University's rag magazine, appeared in 1926, its editorial introduction acknowledging a debt to Manchester:

> We are not original in our idea. Such a magazine has been produced before, in Manchester, and was a great success. May the influence, probably infernal, which presides over such matters, show that Birmingham is not far behind.[43]

Birmingham's first 'carnival magazine' sold 28,000 copies; the following year there were sales of around 67,000 copies. In 1928 a print run of 100,000 was ordered.[44] The interwar editions of *Carnival* sported beautifully drawn colourful paper cover designs: inside, alongside messages of goodwill from university and civic dignitaries and advertised routes for the procession, there was the medley of humorous articles, gags, cartoons and advertisements for local business which was by then becoming established as standard fare in such productions.

Competitive masculinity: the flowering of the rag tradition between the wars

As was pointed out earlier in this chapter, competition was an important element in student rag. There were competitions for the best costume and for the best float. There were competitions between students in different departments or faculties, and there was rivalry between different colleges and universities in terms of who could raise the highest sums of money for hospitals and charities. In London, traditional rivalry between King's and University College fuelled regular skirmishes between the male students of these institutions who would send out raiding parties to kidnap and damage and mutilate each others 'mascots' ('Reggie the Lion' in the case of King's; 'Phineas' in the case of UCL).[45] Skirmishes became associated with a certain amount of dressing up and parading in fancy dress, and descended into pitched battles on certain occasions, such as November 5 and annual sporting events on the Mitcham playing field.[46] Photographs and film footage of battles in King's or UCL quad in the 1920s and 1930s show male students assembling with much pageantry prior to pelting each other with rotten fruit, flour and soot. On November 5 these events would culminate in gigantic bonfires.[47] These images show that combat was a masculine performance: sooty, mud-covered wrestlers writhe and head-butt as flour bags burst among them: meanwhile the women students sit in neat, ostensibly decorous rows along the steps, observing.[48]

In Liverpool, institutional rivalry between students of medicine and engineering took the form of battles at the start of the 'pre Panto Rag' for the possession of a mascot called 'Sister Jane', originally a rag doll dressed as a nurse.[49] Supplies of ammunition were assembled in the form of bags of flour and soot, fish heads and rotten vegetables, together with stink bombs manufactured by chemistry students. The President of the Guild, formally robed and carrying 'Sister Jane', would mount the rostrum (usually a handcart), a pistol would fire, and the battle commenced. The doll was usually dismembered in the scrum, and 'Sister Jane' went through a number of incarnations before the university authorities stepped in to ban the affair as too rowdy in 1929.[50]

Such contests of masculinity amongst students in the 1920s gained something from the presence of ex-servicemen, who were frequently observed to supply an added edge to roistering and rough play. In the context of complaints about the allegedly offensive contents of Birmingham University's rag magazine, in 1933, it was reported in the press that the university authorities were considering a ban on further sales. A correspondent calling himself 'Nearly Forty' wrote to the *Birmingham Mail*, submitting that:

> As one who had the privilege of being an undergraduate when the population of the university consisted of ex-servicemen, in post-war parlance, 'He Men', I have often been disappointed by the mild tone of the younger set who followed in our footsteps.[51]

In the *Birmingham Post* in 1926, students were reported as having accused university authorities of insulting them by trying to make them behave 'like good little boys': they argued that rag activities in Glasgow and Manchester had been much more successful in raising money for charity because in those universities the authorities treated students like adults.[52] The language is interesting because in addition to complaining that it was inappropriate for Birmingham University authorities to treat students like 'infants' or 'hooligans', male students showed themselves desirous of distancing themselves from both non-university students and women. 'We are members of a great university, not students at a technical school, but a corporate body, with a will of our own,' a spokesman asserted, suggesting in addition that the style of street collection in carnival needed stiffening: 'Many of us are too ladylike in our manner . . . collectors should be more forceful in their methods, and systematically invade the suburbs.'[53] Students tended to regard their adult male identity as being at stake when the authorities tried to control or to restrict their annual rag activities.

We have seen that male student revellers frequently sported drag and arrayed themselves as schoolgirls, mothers, babies in prams, 'lady doctors' and suffragettes: forms of inversion and parody which, in traversing boundaries, served to reinforce dominant student identity as young males. This concern to establish status as adult males had repercussions on gender relations within the student body. Between the wars most university authorities expected and required different standards of behaviour from men and women. There were separate men's and women's unions in many institutions, segregated forms of accommodation and often different disciplinary codes.[54] In both Manchester and Liverpool the authorities showed considerable opposition to the idea that women should dress up or join processions, although there seems to have been little concern about them acting as sellers of magazines or collecting for charity. In Manchester, the *Serpent* records that in 1927 the women students 'transformed themselves into smiling Hebes and skivvies' by running a cafe on Shrove Tuesday, although the Chief Constable appears to have had some doubts about women involving themselves in even such a quintessentially feminine venture a few years later.[55] Similarly, in Birmingham, in 1932, the 'women medicals' advertised a 'carnival cafe' with the slogan: 'Don't be ill when you eat.'[56]

In Manchester, the Vice-Chancellor's discipline files show that wardens of the women's halls of residence were far from relaxed about allowing their charges to share in the Shrove Tuesday celebrations of the 1930s.[57] Their opposition was reinforced by complaints by local headmistresses about the behaviour of the male students on these occasions. In 1932, for instance, the VC received a complaint from the Headmistress of Manchester High School for Girls who alleged that men students dressed as devils and rattling collecting tins had been invading classrooms just before prayers or examinations, reducing the girls to 'a state of seething excitement and some confusion'.[58] In 1931 the VC may have been reassured by a letter from the Women Students' Union to the effect that they had circulated a 'Rag Questionnaire' amongst themselves, which showed that 'the vast majority' of the women were averse to joining the men students in the rag procession that year. Nevertheless, two years later, a Miss Morris, Rag Secretary of the Manchester University Women's Union, reported that the VC had actually been approached for permission for the women students to join the procession, although she had not yet received his reply.[59] In 1935 there was lengthy discussion about whether women might collect in costume without joining the procession. Those in favour clearly felt the need for extreme caution, aware that 'public opinion and the press would pounce' on anything suggestive of misconduct.[60] They expressed themselves willing to co-operate with the VC and the Chief Constable in drawing up and policing a dress code, and promised that they would not appear on the streets in fancy dress after 6 o'clock in the evening.[61]

It is interesting to note just how contentious an issue this was, not only in terms of the women students' relations with 'authority', but also in terms of divisions between the students themselves. Mabel Tylecote, whose history of women's education at the University of Manchester was published in 1941, reported that there were 'classic' and recurrent disputes between the men's and women's unions over the Shrove Tuesday rag between the wars.[62] Some of the men were keen to keep the procession an all-male affair, and many of the women accepted this, whilst others resented being treated as 'subsidiaries' rather than 'partners' in the rag. In 1937, the *Serpent* published a letter from one Georgie Chester asserting that:

> The one and only near-riot ever recorded in the women's union was caused by yours truly, when in February 1935 I went so far as to put in the form of a motion . . . the desire of several members that we should accept the MU's invitation to collect in fancy dress on Shrove Tuesday. Had we proposed to stage a mass-production Lady Godiva procession we could hardly have caused greater horror and consternation amongst the ranks of the 99.999 percent pure of the WU! What a clamour! What imputations were laid at our door! Dress up? Better to undress! There was no precedent for such a thing! Moreover, Manchester women students were English Ladies, and these, I was pointlessly informed, do not indulge, as it seems some of their foreign comrades would desire to do, in public display.[63]

Attitudes had softened, it seems, by the following year. In 1938 the Women's Union resolved to have its own lorry in the procession, which would feature 'Rag Queens', and there were also plans for a beauty contest, subject to the VC's mounting no objection.[64] Similarly, in Liverpool, a few intrepid women students defied the authorities' unease about dressing up for the Panto procession that year.[65]

Photographs and images from film archives show that women did participate in rags elsewhere in the UK during the 1920s, but that this was often contested. In London, in 1929, an incident whereby female students from UCL and King's became involved in a 'scrimmage' on the Mitcham sports ground and emerged covered in mud, attracted adverse press commentary and strong disapproval from A.S. Paul and E. Goodyear, the Tutors to Women Students in each institution. According to the *Star*, which reported these events, 'Most people . . . felt [that] the women's function should be to attend in full force, merely to cheer the men on.'[66] Concern about what was and was not appropriate behaviour on the part of the woman student mounted rapidly in Glasgow in the following year, when

'Twenty of the prettiest girl-students' in the university advertised their intention of setting up 'a kissing shop', selling kisses at sixpence a go to passers-by, in order to make money for Charities Day. Their entrepreneurship provoked a vehement protest from a cleric in the North of England about the degradation of womanhood and the insult to public order, decency and the reputation of a great university.[67] There was no shortage of observers ready to blame women for male misbehaviour in rag activity: they were often accused of 'leading the men on'.[68]

Frankensteins

The size and scale of student rag and carnival events grew rapidly between the wars and succeeded in raising very large sums of money for charity. In 1939, for instance, the Manchester and Salford Medical Charities Fund acknowledged that Shrove Tuesday collections between 1922 and 1938 had poured a total of £100,000 into their coffers: a commemorative tablet was installed in the Royal Infirmary in recognition of the students' efforts.[69] The organization of such events became a mammoth task, as rag days swelled into rag weeks, alongside a proliferation of activities in addition to torchlight and daytime processions. In Liverpool, these involved a 'pre Panto ball', as well as a 'Grand ball'. Events were staged with film crews in mind; in the 1930s these involved the Paramount Newsreel Company, British Movietone News and Gaumont News, in addition to the Pathé coverage. Birmingham's student carnivals in the 1920s involved dances, cabaret and a wireless concert. Ten years later these were supplemented by an ox-roast, a fair, jazz and police bands, an 'ice gymkhana' and car competition (the prize being a De luxe Austin 7 donated by Lord Austin). 'Immunity badges' were sold in addition to rag magazines: these were purchased by those who thereby exempted themselves from the harassment of students with collecting tins. The planning of carnival routes and the division of towns and suburbs into 'collecting districts' required something akin to the strategy of a military campaign.[70]

From an article headed 'Carnival warning note: Carnival Frankenstein' which appeared in the *Birmingham Mail* in 1927 we learn that Birmingham's Principal, Grant Robertson, felt 'obliged to utter a note of warning and misgiving', fearing that the annual carnival for the hospitals threatened 'to become a dangerous Frankenstein'.[71] He conceded that the event functioned as a safety valve for letting off high spirits in an admirable cause and the spirit of civic philanthropy, but pointed out that the event was now effectively sabotaging students' hopes of serious study for the first four weeks of the autumn term, urging students 'to reduce the next saturnalia to reasonable proportions'.[72] His views were echoed by the VC in Manchester a few years later, who submitted that the Shrove Tuesday celebration had grown to a size and level of elaboration never contemplated by its founders and beyond the tolerance of either civic or academic authority.[73]

Students in Birmingham appear to have had some sympathy with their Principal's viewpoint. Some felt that the city expected too much from them, and they resented the pressure to organize and to think up endless new ideas, particularly when their efforts drew criticism from members of the public and some civic authorities, who regularly complained about the tasteless quality of stunts and carnival gags.[74] Complaints over the content of the carnival magazine in 1933 led to its withdrawal, and precipitated a University Council meeting with the Guild of Undergraduates in which the students voted against staging a carnival in 1934. Interestingly, this led to a barrage of complaints in the press and from the public, berating the students for a lack of civic responsibility and public duty.[75]

With the outbreak of war and the departure of many young men for service there was again a suspension of rag activity in most universities, although Birmingham mounted an 'austerity version' of the carnival procession in 1942, a solitary horse and cart replacing the mile-long procession of floats in pre-war years, and the Mass Observation Archive contains a detailed description of an evidently rather depressing rag held by students at the University of Sheffield in November 1940, when rain as well as wartime exigencies dampened spirits.[76] 'Bruce Truscot' opined that it was time to bury the whole tradition:

> After the War, perhaps, the hospitals, taken over by the state, will no longer need support paid for so dearly in a less tangible currency than money. In any case, it may be confidently hoped that the Organized Rag, together with its official organ the *Rag Mag*, will be buried as deep as Hitler and more quickly forgotten. While the ebullience of youth fully merits the sympathy of the mature, organized ebullience is merely revolting, not least to those who feel themselves its victims.[77]

Postwar developments

Developments following the Second World War initially failed to offer those of Truscot's persuasion any peace of mind, however, and immediately after the war the spirit of rag reignited with a vengeance. In 1946 the *Birmingham Gazette* reported that 'The city rained cash on the Carnival' of that year, and that the students had raised over £10,000, while the *Birmingham Mail* declared that 'Carnival breaks all records'.[78] Mindful of the bad press associated with the event before the war, the *Birmingham Post* declared solemnly:

The students of Birmingham University have merited the cordial congratulations of the city. By renewing the spirit of carnival, hidden behind the solemn stage of the war years, they brought merriment into local life on Saturday in a very big way.[79]

1947 was another good year, with Birmingham students raising £14,342.[80] The 'car competition' proved a highly effective fundraiser, and was copied by students elsewhere in the country. In 1951 Birmingham set its sights even higher, adding an 'air carnival' to the festivities, with parachuting and flying displays at Elmdon. The advent of the National Health Service lessened the dependence of the hospitals upon student fundraising, but there was certainly no shortage of independent charities or local good causes grateful for donations. Rag and carnival committee membership now carried serious entrepreneurial responsibility, and a national 'Rag Organisers' Conference was held at Sheffield University in 1951, where students learned from each other's efforts across the country.[81] Some argued that the majority of students were becoming 'apathetic' and that the time had come to employ professional fundraisers.[82]

Towards the end of the 1950s the tide turned in Birmingham. Although £14,645 was raised in 1956, there were problems with 'hooliganism' at a 'midnight matinee' in a local cinema, which led to a warning from magistrates. The 1957 carnival flopped.[83] An editorial in the *Guild News* contended that the whole event had grown out of hand, and had strained relationships between staff and students in the university to breaking point. Carnival had become 'a bullying, money-grabbing and immoral bore'.[84] There was a radical pruning of events, and in 1959 Birmingham's Senate and Council insisted upon changing the timing of the annual rag/carnival from November to June, in order to limit interruption to study at the beginning of the academic year.[85] The event never really recovered.

These developments were paralleled elsewhere. In 1954 the University of London's Senate directed college authorities to ban rag processions on November 5 and to draw students' attention to the 'undesirability' of intercollegiate rags, which often resulted in 'wanton and unnecessary' damage, warning that participation in such activities would henceforth be regarded as 'a serious disciplinary offence'.[86] In Manchester and Liverpool, Shrove Tuesday and Panto activities of the 1950s became increasingly associated with misbehaviour which attracted a hostile press. In 1952, police were pelted with flour, smoke and stink bombs, and tramcars were pulled off wires in Manchester, leading to a press demand 'Give these students a public spanking', alongside letters of complaint objecting that students were not fit subjects for state grants or for deferment from military service.[87] There were unfavourable class comparisons, one correspondent averring that the young people who have only attended elementary schools have elementary common sense and decency which seems to be lacking in schools of higher education.[88]

Student miscreants were similarly admonished by the *Liverpool Evening Express* in 1954:

> You should realise that if a gang of youths from Scotland-road or West Derby-road behaved like some of you they would be called juvenile delinquents and hauled before the magistrates. And I tremble to think what would happen to a crowd of young soldiers doing their National Service who took it into their heads to invade a theatre with stink bombs and flour.[89]

In 1956 students in the northern universities were given serious warnings against kidnapping and raiding parties, following an episode in which Manchester students made off from Liverpool with a valuable painting by Augustus John.[90] In 1958 hostile coverage in the press swelled to a crescendo when students in Liverpool, many of them engineers, reportedly wrecked a pantomime staged at the Royal Court Theatre, starring Tommy Steele and for the benefit of pensioners and crippled children.[91] After rag scenes described as 'disgusting' by the Chief Constable in Liverpool, in 1961, a special committee of the University Senate decided on a complete ban of Panto processions for the following year, referring the whole question of rag activities to a Discipline Committee.[92] A cartoon in the student *Guild Gazette* of that year depicted a morose young man with collecting tin and 'Panto' legend on his coat and a knife through his back, with policemen and academics turning away, under the caption 'Society in general is intolerant to [*sic*] us.'[93]

The 1960s

It is undoubtedly true that there was less tolerance of student rag in the late 1950s and 1960s: the atmosphere and attitudes had changed on both sides. It was no longer so common for students to seek the active encouragement of authorities: to process to the Town Hall to address the Lord Mayor as the 'Lord of Misrule', or to persuade VCs or Principals to write encouraging prefaces for rag magazines. Rag had become less of a collusive ritual within a consensual value structure. This should be seen in the context of a new mood of student protest against 'paternalism' and the unacceptable face of authority in academic life. Given the political concerns of student activists and widespread unease about war in Vietnam, a tone of playfulness was less in evidence than were charters of demands and assertiveness about student rights.

There were suggestions in Birmingham, Manchester, Liverpool and elsewhere that new forms of social service were more appropriate than rag or carnival. Students initiated the building of an adventure playground in Handsworth, for instance, held musical evenings in old people's homes, and began schemes for decorating homes for unmarried mothers in Birmingham.[94] In Liverpool, similarly, there were programmes of community service, projects for the homeless, efforts to provide for children and the elderly.[95] Such activities drew upon a tradition whereby women students had long involved themselves in charitable activities, settlement work and the like, and were less gendered in nature than the traditional rag.[96]

However, the new universities and reorganized institutions of the second half of the last century tended to lay claim to the traditions of rag as part of the assertion of student identity. It is significant that at Royal Holloway College in Egham the tradition of rag really took hold only once men were admitted as students in 1964. In earlier years, women students at Holloway had made some attempt to mount processions and collections in nearby Windsor, and there had been earnest discussions about the adoption of a college 'mascot' in the form of a stuffed bear, but photographs indicate that the RHC 'rag' had been a very tame affair.[97] Men quickly took the lead in the organization of Holloway's rag activity, and a rag magazine, *Hollocaust*, was soon offering the standard diet of 'sexist' jokes and jibes against women.[98] Michael Sanderson observes that students at the new University of East Anglia introduced rag celebrations in the 1960s, which began promisingly but after the 'troubles' of 1968 soon became 'a disastrous liability'.[99] In the late twentieth century there were attempts to co-ordinate rag activity between the various colleges in large towns such as Birmingham and Liverpool, but organizational difficulties and longstanding rivalries between different institutions meant that these ventures met with mixed success. The rag tradition undoubtedly survived the century, but the large-scale cultural performances and celebrations of the interwar years were no more.

How can the historian best understand this change? One has to consider the changing status and experience of students in the community. Ferdynand Zweig, who investigated the social attitudes of students in Oxford and Manchester Universities at the beginning of the 1960s, depicted them as living an austere existence with an undercurrent of anxiety about money and the cold war. He suggested that most students worked hard and had conservative aspirations: secure jobs and stable family lives were their main hopes for the future.[100] The 1960s brought important changes in student funding, with the introduction of 'mandatory' grants for school-leavers qualified for university; in addition to this, the adoption of the recommendation of the Latey Committee on the age of majority meant that, by the end of the decade, 18-year-old students were legally 'adults'.[101] These changes took place against a background of student unrest and manifestations of 'protest' which many contemporary authorities in higher education were hard pressed to understand, and some regarded as distinctly pathological.[102]

'Student power' and the call for 'revolution' were indicative of a new mood in universities: a radical questioning of previously shared values and the rejection of traditional hierarchies and deference. A consequence of this was that 'youth culture' became perceived as a 'counter culture', rather than being associated with rites of passage or a transitional state.[103] Authorities contemplated actual rather than simulated rebellion, the possibility of serious revolt. Yet in some ways there were continuities of tradition. Keith Thomas observed that the strike and the 'sit-in' both had their roots in the 'barring-out' ceremonies of the seventeenth century noted above.[104] In *The Rise of the Student Estate in Britain*, Ashby and Anderson confessed themselves fascinated by the effect of the 'sit-in' on student participators:

> Unless there is fear and danger, *the whole atmosphere is one of carnival* [my italics]. Everybody knows that the sit-in has no future; it is like a cruise at sea: for a few hours hundreds of young people . . . find gaiety and companionship. Although it is in a densely crowded room, sleeping bags on the floor, graffiti on the walls, beat music on the gramophone, there is a sort of Arcadian euphoria.[105]

If the sit-in and strike drew upon traditions of 'barring-out', and the experience of at least some of the participants in these forms of protest bordered upon the carnivalesque, there were of course also ways in which the 'pop culture' or 'counter-culture' of the 1960s was riddled with elements of carnival. In the Pathé news coverage of the Isle of Wight pop festivals, one can see echoes of the rag processions referred to earlier in this chapter.[106] The exuberance of the 'flower-children', musicians dressed like minstrels or clowns, the record covers of 1960s LPs (the Beatles' 'Sergeant Pepper' album, for instance, designed by Sir Peter Blake), the 'psychedelic' motifs of popular art, are all in some sense highly resonant of the student processions and performances of an earlier period.

It may be no coincidence that as student protests waned in the 1970s, the student rag revived, albeit with a weakening of local traditions and in a watered-down form. As cultural performance, the lead in the organization of street processions and annual carnival had passed by the end of the century to different social groups: the residents of Notting Hill in London, of Handsworth, Perry Bar and Sparkhill in Birmingham. However, the dramatic rise in the number of university students after Robbins, and the creation of many more universities (first the 'new' universities of the 1960s, subsequently the even 'newer' universities created by the institutional changes in higher education as the twentieth century drew to its close), ensured that something of the tradition of rag would be kept alive. The organization of a student rag might be seen as part of the identity of the newer institutions, alongside the university mace, crest and Vice-Chancellorial regalia. Trawling through the internet certainly provides some evidence for the suspicion that the newest universities take the institution particularly seriously. And (in stark contrast to the attitudes of many university authorities during the 1960s) we find some vice-chancellors adding performance in Rag Week to league table scores and institutional deliverables: at the University of Loughborough's Degree Congregation in July 2003 the Vice-Chancellor boasted to students and their parents that Loughborough Students' Rag

> has had its best year ever, raising more than £300,000 for local and national charities, bringing the total for the last eight years to well over £2m – well ahead of any other University.[107]

Nevertheless, the nature and composition of the student population in the UK has changed dramatically since the 1920s. The rag festivities, the carnivals, processions and pantomimes of the first half of the last century served to construct and to celebrate local communities of students as well as a particular kind of masculine, white, middle-class, late-adolescent or early-adult transitional student identity. The dressing-up as women, and the parodies of feminism and femininity; the blacking-up as nigger minstrels, sheikhs, gollywogs and Eastern potentates (parodies of ethnic difference and Orientalism) were part of this identity construction. The stereotypes were not seriously challenged before the 1970s. Although the contents of 'rag mags' had regularly attracted censure for impropriety and for trespassing beyond the bounds of good taste in the 1950s and 1960s, complaints about the racism and sexism inherent in rag publications and performances in the 1970s and 1980s were of a different order. These complaints, moreover, were increasingly less likely to be voiced by disgusted clerics and local dignitaries and more by other students themselves. In Glasgow, for instance, the National Union of Students conducted a long campaign against beauty contests in Charities Week and attempted to ban sales of *Ygorra* on account of racism and offensiveness to women from 1973 and through the 1980s.[108] Students at several higher educational institutions in Glasgow refused to sell the magazine, leading to strained relations over the whole organization of Charities Appeal and Rag Week.[109] The undergraduate community, now swollen to encompass a large percentage of the 18–24 year age group, was no longer homogeneous; it included a sizeable proportion of mature students, as well as students from a diversity of social and ethnic backgrounds, and an ever-increasing proportion of women. The student rag has survived into a new century, but it can be argued that it has lost some degree of cohesion and coherence as a popular cultural form.

Conclusion

Historians and social scientists generally agree that a reshaping of understandings about gender, together with radical changes in the relationships between men and women, constituted one of the most dramatic aspects of social change in twentieth-century Britain. Many have been quick to point out that these changes have led to new problems and dilemmas for both sexes. Feminist historians have emphasized that the gains to women in terms of new freedoms and opportunities for self-determination, however important, have not always been equally apparent for women from different social backgrounds; they also point to new problems and tensions that have arisen from or been exacerbated by change.[1]

As emphasized in the introduction to this volume, both universities themselves and the nature of student experience have also undergone profound changes over the last century. The popular image of the student has changed equally dramatically; from the earnest, bespectacled 'Varsity' male with his college scarf of the postwar years, through the long-haired beatniks and student radicals of the 1960s, the aimless and scruffy denizens of 'Scumbag University' portrayed in the popular television series *The Young Ones* in the 1980s, and again, to the more career-conscious, self-financing (and usually debt-ridden) 'customers' of higher education today. Most of the stereotypes have been male, although over half the student population today is female. Most of the stereotypes are of the young, although many students today are classified as 'mature' students, and in the last quarter century or so, a significant proportion of adults returning to study have been women who 'lost out' on opportunities for study earlier in the life cycle.[2]

The improvements in women's status over the last century would not have been possible without educational change, and women's increasing participation in higher education has acted as a driving force for more general change. Access to universities was a key issue for feminists in the nineteenth century. They sought higher education as proof of intellectual capacity: they fought for opportunities to practise medicine, and they wanted to improve their chances in teaching. Improvements in educational provision for middle-class girls and women were intimately related to 'first-wave' feminism and to the struggle for the vote. Rising levels of aspiration and educational achievement amongst women, following the extension of secondary schooling after 1944, and extensions of university provision from the 1960s, were crucially important in the rise of 'second-wave' feminism in the late 1960s and 1970s.

Other factors were equally important. Demographic change, associated with increasing control over fertility, acted as both cause and effect of educational change. We have seen that in the 1950s, over three-quarters of girls left school at 15, and many aimed to marry before they were legally classed as adults at 21 years of age. An increasing proportion were indeed marrying younger than ever before, and whilst feminist educationalists deplored the tendency, educational policy-makers sought to accommodate what they believed to be a new fact of life. They were mistaken, of course, and from the 1970s the trend halted, then went into reverse. The advent of new forms of contraception, together with the availability of legal abortion, allowed women more control over their lives. The terrible fear of conceiving an illegitimate child that had haunted young women in the 1950s and early 1960s receded. Sexual activity before marriage became the norm, as did later marriages, particularly amongst the higher-educated: indeed an increasing proportion of young adults rejected the idea of marriage altogether.

When the Second World War broke out in 1939 women represented about a quarter of the student population in universities in Britain. The proportion of women had shrunk somewhat during the Depression, alongside declining opportunities in medicine and schoolteaching during the 1930s. Pressure to accommodate returning servicemen after the war brought a period of confusion in higher education, making it difficult to discern long-term trends; however, the 1950s and early 1960s were years of stagnation in respect of women's share of university education, although there was a considerable expansion of opportunities for female school-leavers in colleges dedicated to teacher training. It has become something of a cliché of historiography to represent the decade of the 1950s as one of domestic tyranny for women, the 'nadir of feminism', years in which suburbia and the nuclear family triumphed. More recently, historians have been eager to challenge the simplicities of this analysis, but it is important not to lose sight of some of the constraints and oppressions of the period.[3] These included the afore-mentioned fear of unwanted pregnancy and the stigmatization of unmarried motherhood and illegitimacy, the associated bullying of some adoption agencies, 'shotgun weddings', the rows over early marriage without parental consent, the 'runaway marriages' in Gretna Green, the tight-lipped disapproval of divorce, or of mothers who worked outside the home.

The clear distinction between male and female worlds proclaimed by the primary school reading books of the day had their counterpart in the gendered structures and divisions of much of the educational world and especially the more elite forms of higher education. In Oxford and Cambridge, women were confined to separate colleges, where both students and women academics were ruefully aware that they occupied something of a peripheral place in the male-dominated academic community of these ancient universities. The female colleges offered some advantages in that they offered a protected, congenial space for some women, and they represented a proud tradition associated with the pioneering feminism of an earlier period. Even so, others felt 'hedged in' by such segregated arrangements, which perpetrated forms of distinction and inequalities that could be galling in the extreme. When Professor Dorothy Hodgkin was awarded the Nobel prize for her work in chemistry in 1965, Oxford academic life was so riddled with sex distinction, that there were only three 'men's colleges' where her male colleagues could invite her to dine.[4] An increasing number of highly intelligent and well-qualified female school-leavers chose not to apply to universities where the odds were against their being offered a place. Women were similarly discouraged from applying to leading medical schools in the 1950s and 1960s, since the operation of stringent quotas militated against their chances of success.

The tide began to turn in the late 1960s, as we have seen in Chapters 4 and 5 of this book. The 'new universities' of the 1960s treated male and female students more equally, and offered exciting new programmes of study that proved particularly attractive to women. A new generation of well-qualified female school-leavers took advantage of these new opportunities, and it was their unwillingness to accept traditional forms of discrimination that helped to fuel the critique of second-wave feminism in the late 1960s and beyond. The proportion of women students in universities began to rise steadily from 1970, a trend reinforced by the impact of government policy on teacher training and the cuts and mergers which decimated the colleges of education at this time. The steady increase in the proportion of women taking advantage of higher education coincided with the demographic changes brought about by new forms of contraception and the widespread adoption of the pill. An exact sequence of causality is near impossible to determine but the trends were interrelated and, as described in Chapter 5, the sexual revolution had an important impact on both attitudes towards, and outlooks of, the woman student.

As the numbers of women students rose, their presence began to exert a more powerful influence on student culture and in the academic community. The demise of the single-sex colleges in Oxford and Cambridge, with the shift to coresidence, represented a troubled but crucially important transition, and has been discussed at length throughout Part II of this book. This made possible the equalization of the numbers of men and women in these elite institutions of higher education, and had a profound cultural and symbolic purchase which was recognized by many contemporaries. We have seen how Robert Jackson, for instance, in 1972 a Fellow of All Souls, recognized that the tradition of single-sex colleges had served to buttress a cultural order demarcated by 'the two great communities of sex', within which 'clear and distinct identities were marked out', and in which there was no doubt that the 'the sovereign virtues were considered to be male'.[5] The advent of coresidence could not (and certainly did not) ensure instant equality for women students or Fellows in the formerly male colleges, and many feminists have been disappointed by the pace and levels of change. But it is difficult to see how progress towards equality could have been made without coeducation in the older universities, which must be accounted a precondition if not a sufficient condition of change. The increasing numbers of women students in universities throughout the UK in the last quarter of the twentieth century, the demands of second-wave feminism, and the impact of equality legislation from the 1970s onwards, all served to highlight forms of gender differentiation which were no longer acceptable to many in academic life, setting in train curriculum change (associated with gender critiques of traditional disciplinary approaches and the rise of women's studies), changes in provision for students' needs (such as the establishment of crèches and nursery provision), and many other challenges to masculine hierarchies and a male-dominated academy.

The proportion of women students in universities rose and has continued to rise. We have seen that the proportion of female undergraduates reached 50 per cent in 1996, and by the end of the century women students were clearly outnumbering men. According to figures published by the Higher Education Statistics Agency, women took 58.8% of first-year places in higher education in 2004/5. In many of the debates over access to higher education, the concern with social class has obscured what can be seen as the most dramatic 'success story' of the last fifty years, the widening participation of women. It can be argued that female school-leavers have more than 'closed the gender gap', and it was scarcely surprising that the 1990s witnessed an efflorescence of concern close to moral panic about male 'underachievement'.[6] Women steadily increased their share of places, even beginning to outnumber male students in the medical schools,[7] which we have seen were once protected male spaces in which an informal curriculum of athletics and rugby underpinned notions of academic excellence. The tide of publications with titles akin to 'women outside the ivory tower/sacred grove' or 'on the margins of academe' has receded since the 1980s; indeed a recent book by Jocey Quinn, *Powerful Subjects*, is even subtitled *'are women really taking over the university?'* Quinn answers her own question resoundingly in the negative, maintaining that in many ways curricula have remained unresponsive to any feminist critique, and emphasizing that a high proportion of female students does not guarantee a shift in power or change in the university hierarchy.[8]

Nevertheless, the historical evidence presented in this book shows that the gendered nature of university life has changed radically since the 1950s. Women students are no longer a conspicuous minority, hedged in by separate institutional arrangements and special provisions, alternately despised or gently ridiculed as 'lady-students' or 'undergraduettes'. Women are more likely to be seen simply as students, alongside their male peers. Few would suggest these days that women are ruled by biology, rather than intellect. Women do very well academically, and may be perceived as 'model students', 'outperforming' the men, who are sometimes perceived as lacking in application and commitment to study. Male and female students live alongside each other in halls of residence and other forms of student accommodation; they join the same societies and share opportunities for student journalism and representation in union affairs. Few would defend the need for segregated men's or women's student unions in the UK today.[9] Rag activities are no longer a quintessentially male performance: where these continue, women play as active a role as the men. Women students may have contributed to the reshaping and reform of rag after the 1970s, as discussed in the previous chapter of this book.[10] There were also ways in which young women were increasingly subject to the influence of traditionally male aspects of student culture such as competitive heavy drinking and various kinds of horseplay.[11] Pressures on women to share in these masculine rituals of college life were particularly strong in the formerly male colleges of Oxford and Cambridge, but they were present to some extent in most university environments.

There are other aspects of university life where gender divisions remain deeply etched and give continuing cause for concern. Gender differentiation in subject choice continues to be a problem, with women still a minority of students in applied science, engineering and computing. These are subjects which confer particular advantage in the labour market. Wage differentials between male and female graduates remain worrying. Towards the end of the last century there were even signs that these were increasing. Higher education may still be seen as a better investment for men than for women, particularly if women choose to interrupt their careers by having children, and particularly if they have previously incurred large amounts of 'student debt'.[12] This book has concentrated on students rather than teachers: even so, the aspirations of more academically minded students are likely to be affected by their perceptions of opportunities for teaching and research in higher education. The career opportunities for women teachers in universities have improved considerably since the 1970s. Nonetheless, women continue to be underrepresented particularly in science, at senior levels, and in the higher-status institutions. Universities are increasingly subject to a managerial and audit culture, which some would regard as heavy handedly controlled by workaholic males. There is a tendency for teaching to be delegated increasingly to part-time staff, or to 'non-research' faculty on temporary, short-term contracts: many of these are women. On a pessimistic note, one might suggest that the status of university teaching continues to decline: as universities become more like secondary schools, women can be expected to increase their share of faculty posts. Women teachers, as well as students, have established a share in university life, but gender divisions and inequalities in higher education are not simply the stuff of history.

ક્ર

Notes

Introduction

1 Higher Education Statistics Agency, http://www.hesa.ac.uk/presspr83.htm. Throughout this book, I shall normally use the forward slash to indicate the academic year, so 1937/8 (say) relates to the period from Autumn 1937 to the end of Summer 1938.
2 Higher Education Funding Council, *Young Participation in Higher Education*, Bristol: HEFCE, Jan. 2005, p. 10.
3 A.H. Halsey, *Change in British Society*, Oxford: Oxford University Press, fourth edition, 1995, p. 162.
4 The educational commentator Peter Wilby, in an article published in *The Observer*, 'How to end this elitism', 28 May 2000, p. 28, asserted that 'Entry to the two ancient universities remains as socially selective as it was 30 years ago.' If one considers gender, as well as social class, this is an astonishingly inaccurate assertion. Examples of mounting concern for boys' underachievement in higher education include the following: Alison Goddard, 'Who's the weaker sex now?', *Times Higher Education Supplement*, 31 Oct. 2003, p. 8; Wendy Berliner, 'Where have all the young men gone?', *Times Higher Education Supplement*, 18 May 2004, pp. 18–19; Gaby Hinsliff, 'Now women are storming last bastion', *The Observer*, 15 Aug. 2004, p. 3.

1 Going to university in England between the wars: access funding and social class

1 Jennie Lee, *This Great Journey*, New York and Toronto: Farrar and Rinehart, 1942.
2 Lee, *This Great Journey*, pp. 47–8, 56–9.
3 Patricia Hollis, *Jennie Lee: a life*, Oxford: Oxford University Press, 1997, p. 17.
4 R.D. Anderson, 'Universities and élites in modern Britain', *History of Universities*, 1991, vol. 10, 230–6.
5 R.D. Anderson, *Universities and Elites in Britain since 1800*, Basingstoke: Macmillan, 1992, p. 23.

6 Anderson, 'Universities and élites in modern Britain', p. 234.

7 England's nine 'other' universities, with the dates of their charters were: Birmingham (1900), Bristol (1909), Durham (1832), Leeds (1904), Liverpool (1903), London (1836), Manchester (1903), Reading (1926), and Sheffield (1905). The University Colleges, with their dates of foundation, were Exeter (1901), Hull (1926), Leicester (1922), Nottingham (1903) and Southampton (1905). For more complete and annual data, see Chapter 5 below.

8 W.H.G. Armytage, 'Flexner to Truscot: the stocktaking phase of civic university development, 1930–1944', *Universities Review*, 1953, vol. 26, pp. 5–6.

9 W.A. Kotschnig, *Unemployment in the Learned Professions: an international study of occupational and educational planning*, London: Oxford University Press, 1937.

10 Kotschnig, *Unemployment in the Learned Professions*, p. 121; Armytage, 'Flexner to Truscot', p. 6.

11 K. Lindsay, *Social Progress and Educational Waste: being a study of the 'free place' and scholarship system*, London: Routledge, 1926, p. 193.

12 D.V. Glass and J.L. Gray, 'Opportunity and the older universities', in *Political Arithmetic, a Symposium of Population Studies*, edited by L. Hogben, London: Allen and Unwin, 1938, p. 419.

13 Anderson, *Universities and Elites in Britain since 1800*, p. 53. In *The Decline of Privilege: the modernization of Oxford University*, Stanford CA: Stanford University Press, 1999, Joseph A. Soares argues that after the First World War, the 'not very academic sons of wealthy gentlemen were bumped aside by meritocratic scholars often from middle- or working-class homes' (p. 9), but nevertheless recognizes that even in 1938, 'state school alumni contributed only 19 percent of Oxford's freshmen' (idem). Of course, by no means were all of the latter from modest homes. The decline of the 'gentleman commoner' in Oxford between the wars is discussed in some detail by Daniel Greenstein in B. Harrison (ed.), *The History of the University of Oxford, vol. VIII: the twentieth century*, Oxford: Clarendon Press, 1994, pp. 52–9.

14 L. Doreen Whiteley, *The Poor Student and the University: a report on the scholarship system, with particular reference to awards made by Local Educational Authorities*, London: George Allen and Unwin, 1933, pp. 19, 30.

15 R. Hoggart, *A Local Habitation (Life and Times*, 1: 1918–1940), London: Chatto and Windus, 1988, pp. 184–5.

16 'B. Truscot' (E. Allison Peers), *Redbrick University*, London: Faber and Faber, 1943, p. 21.

17 Truscot, *Redbrick University*, p. 20.

18 Truscot, *Redbrick University*, p. 20, note 1.

19 Some replies came in a long time later, and were not included in the response rates, though some of their interesting comments are included in the discussion below.

20 J. Hall and D. Caradog Jones, 'The social grading of occupations', *British Journal of Sociology*, 1950, vol. 1, pp. 33–40. See also C.A. Moser and J. Hall, 'The social grading of occupations', in D.V. Glass (ed.), *Social Mobility in Britain*, London: Routledge, 1954.

21 E.M. Becket, *The University College of Nottingham*, Nottingham: Henry Saxton, 1928, p. 54. Becket quotes from a Treasury Inspectors' Report of 1901/2 which noted that 'Nottingham University College stood at the head of all English university colleges in the number of students who entered from elementary schools and that the opportunities offered to young working men of promise were very

considerable.' 'We think', stated the Inspectors, 'that the College exhibits the nearest approach of all colleges we have visited to a People's University' (p. 54). There are no women from Nottingham in the sample.

22 Truscot, *Redbrick University*, p. 20, note 1.

23 Anderson, *Universities and Elites in Britain since 1800*, p. 56.

24 Whiteley, *The Poor Student*, p. 29.

25 University Grants Committee, *Returns from Universities and University Colleges in Receipt of Treasury Grant, Academic Year 1937/8*, London: HMSO, 1939, p. 5. Brian Simon estimated that before the war, 'just over half of the students in the modern universities originally went to elementary schools'; see *A Student's View of the Universities*, London: Longmans, Green and Co., 1943, p. 42.

26 Board of Education, *Interim Report of the Consultative Committee on Scholarships for Higher Education*, London: HMSO, 1916, Cd 8291, vol. VIII, p. 56.

27 Whiteley, *The Poor Student*, pp. 59–61. For more detail on costs see C. Dyhouse, *No Distinction of Sex? Women in British universities 1870–1939*, London: UCL Press, 1995, pp. 27ff.

28 C.L. Mowat, *Britain between the Wars, 1918–1940*, London: Methuen, 1968, p. 490.

29 University Grants Committee, *Return from Universities 1937/8*, Table I.

30 In view of the Data Protection legislation, names have been given in this text only where the respondents specifically ticked the box in the questionnaire permitting me to do so.

31 A. Oram, *Women Teachers and Feminist Politics, 1900–39*, Manchester: Manchester University Press, 1996, pp. 23–38.

32 Mrs Fisher, née Billington, father died in France serving in First World War, mother living on army pension supplemented by taking in lodgers. Mrs Fisher obtained a first class degree in history at Bristol in 1921.

33 Mrs Cresswell, née Goodridge, father employed by North Somerset Electricity Supply Company in charge of a village sub-station in Somerset. Obtained her degree (honours geography) from Bristol in 1939.

34 Letter from Mrs A. Fletcher, 24 Oct. 1998.

35 G.S.M. Ellis, *The Poor Student and the University: a report on the scholarship system, with particular reference to awards made by Local Educational Authorities*, London: The Labour Publishing Company, 1925, p. 3, also p. 9.

36 Board of Education, *Interim Report*, p. 65, para. 119.

37 Whiteley, *The Poor Student*.

38 Board of Education files on State Scholarships, ED 54, nos. 34, 35 and 37 (National Archives).

39 Whiteley, *The Poor Student*, pp. 33–5.

40 National Archives, ED 54, no. 37: Letter from Assistant Mistresses' Association dated 20 May 1930 and comments, memorandum relating to interview with Headmistresses, 18 Jan. 1921, and Headmasters, 9 May 1933.

41 National Union of Teachers, *Higher Education Bulletin*, 1925, p. 4; Dyhouse, *No Distinction of Sex?*, pp. 31–2.

42 Lord Haldane, 'Foreword' to Ellis, *The Poor Student*, p. vi.

43 Ellis, *The Poor Student*, p. 10.

44 Whiteley, *The Poor Student*, pp. 23–5.

45 Ellis, *The Poor Student*, p. 9.

46 Edith Morley (ed.), *Women Workers in Seven Professions: a survey of their economic conditions and prospects, edited for the Studies Committee of the*

Fabian Women's Group, London: George Routledge and Sons, 1914, pp. 82–136; Whiteley, *The Poor Student*, pp. 118–41.

47 Dyhouse, *No Distinction of Sex?*, p. 31.

48 J.B. Thomas, 'The day training college: a Victorian innovation in teacher training', *British Journal of Teacher Education*, 1978, vol. 43, 249–61; Dyhouse, *No Distinction of Sex?*, pp. 19–22.

49 J.B. Thomas, 'Day training college to Department of Education', in J.B. Thomas (ed.), *British Universities and Teacher Education: a century of change*, London: Falmer Press, 1990, p. 26.

50 W.H.G. Armytage, *Civic Universities: aspects of a British tradition*, London: Benn, 1955, p. 256.

51 Board of Education, *Annual Report for 1923/4*, London: HMSO, 1925, p. 28.

52 Board of Education, *Memorandum on the Board of Education Estimates 1923/4*, London: HMSO, 1923, p. 18.

53 Board of Education, *Statement of Grants Available from the Board of Education in Aid of Technological and Professional Work in Universities in England and Wales*, London: HMSO, 1911, Cd 5762, vol. lix, p. 17.

54 Morley, *Women Workers in Seven Professions*, pp. 11–12.

55 Simon, *A Student's View*, p. 46.

56 Board of Education, *Regulations for the Training of Teachers*, London: HMSO, 1918, Cd 9170, Appendix B, pp. 55–7.

57 Board of Education, *Regulations for the Training of Teachers*, London: HMSO, 1920, Appendix B, pp. 73–5.

58 W.A.C. Stewart, *Higher Education in Postwar Britain*, Basingstoke and London: Macmillan, 1989, pp. 25–6.

59 Whiteley, *The Poor Student*, p. 78.

60 B. Castle, *Fighting All The Way*, London: Macmillan, 1993, p. 40.

61 Whiteley, *The Poor Student*, p. 30.

62 In 1926 Kenneth Lindsay (*Social Progress and Educational Waste*, p. 193) estimated that less than three-quarters of 1 per cent (0.73 per cent) of elementary school children reached universities.

63 Whiteley, *The Poor Student*, p. 24.

64 This was one of the late returned responses excluded from the tables, since King's was not targeted in the survey for women.

2 Men and women in higher education in the 1930s: family expectations, gendered outcomes

1 J. Floud, 'The educational experience of the adult population of England and Wales as at July 1949', in D.V. Glass (ed.), *Social Mobility in Britain*, London: Routledge, 1954, esp. pp. 112–16; A.H. Halsey, A.F. Heath and J.M. Ridge (eds), *Origins and Destinations: family, class and education in modern Britain*, Oxford: Clarendon Press, 1980, pp. 181–9, 206; M. Sanderson, *Educational Opportunity and Social Change in England*, London: Faber and Faber, 1987, p. 42; R.D. Anderson, *Universities and Elites in Britain since 1800*, Basingstoke and London: Macmillan, 1992, pp. 47–58.

2 Halsey *et al.*, *Origins and Destinations*, p. 206.

3 Anderson, *Universities and Elites*, p. 53; H. Perkin, 'The pattern of social transformation in England', in K.H. Jarausch (ed.), *The Transformation of Higher*

Learning, 1860–1930: expansion, diversification, social opening and professionalisation in England, Germany, Russia and the United States, Chicago, IL: University of Chicago Press, 1983, p. 218.

4 H. Perkin, *The Rise of Professional Society: England since 1800*, London: Routledge, 1989, pp. 248–50; M. Sanderson, *The Universities in the Nineteenth Century*, London: Routledge, 1975, p. 20; M. Sanderson, *The Universities and British Industry, 1850–1970*, London: Routledge, 1972, pp. 98–9.

5 Anderson, *Universities and Elites*; see also the same author's *Education and Opportunity in Victorian Scotland, Schools and Universities*, Oxford: Oxford University Press, 1983.

6 R.D. Anderson, 'Universities and élites in modern Britain', *History of Universities*, 1991, vol. 10, p. 238.

7 M. Pugh, *Women and the Women's Movement in Britain 1914–1959*, Basingstoke and London: Macmillan, 1992, p. 288.

8 Anderson, *Universities and Elites*, p. 23.

9 Ibid., p. 57.

10 Brian Simon, *A Student's View of the Universities*, London: Longmans, Green and Co., 1943, p. 46.

11 C. Heward, *Making A Man of Him: parents and their sons' education at an English public school 1929–50*, London: Routledge, 1988, p. 77 and *passim*.

12 R. Hoggart, *A Local Habitation* (*Life and Times*, 1: 1918–1940), London: Chatto, 1988, pp. 184–5.

13 J. Howarth and M. Curthoys, 'The political economy of women's higher education in late nineteenth and early twentieth century Britain', *Historical Research*, 1987, vol. 60, no. 142, 208–31.

14 J. Howarth and M. Curthoys, 'Gender, curriculum and career: a case study of women university students in England before 1914', in P. Summerfield (ed.), *Women, Education and the Professions*, Leicester: History of Education Society Occasional Publications, no. 8, 1987.

15 R.L. Miller and B.C. Hayes, 'Gender and intergenerational mobility', in G. Payne and P. Abbott (eds), *The Social Mobility of Women: beyond male mobility models*, Basingstoke: Falmer Press, 1990, pp. 61–3.

16 Ibid., p. 62.

17 Heward, *Making a Man of Him*, p. 77.

18 J. Copley, *Autobiography*, vol. 1, 'Mother and Father', p. 165 (unpublished Mss).

19 On this theme see (for instance) Carolyn Steedman's 'Introduction' to K. Woodward, *Jipping Street*, London: Virago, 1983.

20 B. Jackson and D. Marsden, *Education and the Working Class*, Harmondsworth: Penguin, 1962, p. 97. See also A. Miles, *Social Mobility in Nineteenth and Twentieth Century England*, Basingstoke and London: Macmillan, 1999, pp. 151–2, for comments on mothers as 'inculcators of ambition'.

21 Sanderson, *The Universities and British Industry*, p. 325.

22 A total of 56.7 per cent of the 504 women took arts degrees, 37.8 per cent science degrees, and 5.6 per cent studied medicine.

23 Board of Education, *Annual Report on the Education and Training of Teachers*, London: HMSO, 1932.

24 W.H.G. Armytage, *Civic Universities: aspects of a British tradition*, London: Benn, 1955, p. 256.

25 Ministry of Education, *Report of Working Party on the Supply of Women Teachers*, London, HMSO, 1949.

26 My evidence supports the conclusions reached by Michael Sanderson in respect of the buoyant demand for male graduates in aircraft and aeronautics, gas and electricity, electrical engineering and research in industrial chemicals and pharmaceuticals before and after the Second World War. Sanderson, *The Universities and British Industry*, pp. 284, 313.

27 J. Hubback, *Graduate Wives*, London: Political & Economic Planning, pamphlet no. 361, 1954; J. Hubback, *Wives Who Went to College*, London: Heinemann, 1957.

28 Collection of press cuttings and reviews relating to *Wives Who Went to College* held by J. Hubback.

29 On marriage and social mobility see A. Heath, *Social Mobility*, Glasgow: Fontana, 1981, ch. 4.

30 H. Phelps Brown, *The Inequality of Pay*, Oxford: Oxford University Press, 1977, p. 254.

31 For the idea of demand for higher education spreading like an infection, or as snowballing, see R. Layard, J. King and C. Moser, *The Impact of Robbins*, Harmondsworth: Penguin, 1969, pp. 16–17.

3 Driving ambitions: women in pursuit of a medical education, 1890–1939

1 Isabel Hutton, *Memories of a Doctor in War and Peace*, London: Heinemann, 1960, p. 2.

2 Idem.

3 The Medical Register lists registered rather than practising registered doctors. For some of the problems involved in calculating the numbers of practising women doctors see Mary Ann Elston, 'Women doctors in the British health services: a sociological study of their careers and opportunities', unpublished PhD thesis, University of Leeds, 1986, pp. 41–64.

4 Salary estimates from V. Biscoe, *300 Careers for Women*, London: Lovat Dickson Ltd, 1932, p. 147.

5 E. Moberly Bell, *Storming the Citadel: the rise of the woman doctor*, London: Constable, 1953.

6 Ibid., p. 174.

7 Ibid., p. 191.

8 Elston, 'Women doctors'. Theoretical issues about gendered exclusionary strategies are discussed in A. Witz, *Professions and Patriarchy*, London: Routledge, 1992.

9 *Daily Telegraph*, 3 Oct. 1916 (see Press Cuttings, Medical Women, vol. 5, p. 77, Archives, Royal Free Hospital).

10 Press Cuttings, Medical Women, vol. 6, part 1, Archives, Royal Free Hospital.

11 In addition to Moberly Bell, *Storming the Citadel*, see also C. Blake, *The Charge of the Parasols: women's entry to the medical profession*, London: The Women's Press, 1990; Thomas Neville Bonner, *To the Ends of the Earth: women's search for education in medicine*, London and Cambridge, MA: Harvard University Press, 1992.

12 See, *inter alia*, Anne Digby, *Making a Medical Living: doctors and patients in the English market for medicine, 1720–1911*, Cambridge: Cambridge University Press, 1994; C. Lawrence, 'Incommunicable knowledge: science, technology and the clinical art in Britain 1850–1914', *Journal of Contemporary History*, 1985, vol. 20, 503–20; M. Jeanne Peterson, 'Gentlemen and medical men: the problem of

professional recruitment', *Bulletin of the History of Medicine*, 1984, vol. 58, 457–73.

13 Witz, *Professions and Patriarchy*, p. 102; Elston, 'Women doctors'.

14 See, for instance, Flora Murray, *Women as Army Surgeons*, London: Hodder and Stoughton, 1920; L. Leneman, 'Medical women at war, 1914–1918', *Medical History*, 1994, vol. 38, 160–77.

15 The literature pertinent to these issues is huge. I have found the following particularly useful in thinking about the content of this chapter: M.J. Corbett, *Representing Femininity: middle-class subjectivity in Victorian and Edwardian women's autobiographies*, New York and Oxford: Oxford University Press, 1992; J.W. Scott, 'The evidence of experience', *Critical Inquiry*, 1991, vol. 17, 773–97; Carolyn G. Heilbrun, *Writing A Woman's Life*, New York and London: The Women's Press, 1988.

16 Elston, 'Women doctors', pp. 130–1.

17 M. Murdoch, 'Practical hints to students', 1904 (Address delivered at London School of Medicine for Women); reprinted as Appendix (pp. 166–80) in Hope Malleson, *A Woman Doctor: Mary Murdoch of Hull*, London: Sidgwick and Jackson, 1919, p. 178.

18 There is a set of scrapbooks containing newspaper cuttings relating to 'Medical Women' in the archives of the Royal Free Hospital. Volumes 2 and 3 (c. 1878–1903) contain a large selection of articles of this type.

19 Ibid. See especially Arabella Kenealy, 'How woman-doctors are made', *The Ludgate*, May 1897, vol. IV, New Series, 29–35.

20 Ibid., 33.

21 Idem.

22 Heilbrun, *Writing A Woman's Life*, p. 20.

23 Ibid., p. 25.

24 Nancy K. Miller, quoted in ibid., p. 18.

25 I. Mann, *The Chase*, 1972, p. 1. (Typescript autobiography in Archives of St Mary's Hospital, London.) There is a published version of this autobiography, edited by Ros Golding, which was published in Australia by Fremantle Arts Centre Press in 1986. The text in the published version has been much abridged and all references here are to the unpublished typescript original.

26 G.M. Wauchope, *The Story of a Woman Physician*, Bristol: John Wright and Sons, 1963, pp. 27–8.

27 V. Propp, *Morphology of the Folktale* (ed. L.A. Wagner), Austin: University of Texas Press, 1968.

28 C. Dyhouse, *Feminism and the Family in England 1880–1939*, Oxford: Blackwell, 1989, pp. 14–28.

29 Malleson, *A Woman Doctor*, p. 16.

30 O. Wilberforce, *Octavia Wilberforce: the autobiography of a pioneer woman doctor* (ed. P. Jalland), London: Cassell, 1989, p. 20.

31 Wauchope, *The Story of a Woman Physician*, p. 20.

32 F.M. Kenyon, *Memoirs*, unpublished typescript, n.d. (c. 1969), vol. 1: 1894–1927, pp. 96–99. (My thanks to her granddaughter, Mary Clare Martin, who has allowed me access to these memoirs.)

33 Ibid.

34 Mann, *The Chase*, pp. 81, 88–92, 94.

35 Wilberforce, *Octavia Wilberforce*, pp. 33–4.

36 Mann, *The Chase*, p. 98.

37 Ibid., p. 97.
38 Ibid., pp. 99–100.
39 Ibid., pp. 100–1.
40 Ibid., p. 101.
41 Hutton, *Memories of a Doctor*, p. 39.
42 Ibid., p. 3.
43 Murdoch, 'Practical hints to students', pp. 21–2.
44 Kenyon, *Memoirs*, p. 134.
45 Wilberforce, *Octavia Wilberforce*, pp. 57–81.
46 Quoted in L. Caldecott (ed.), *Women of Our Century*, London: Ariel Books, BBC, 1984, p. 109.
47 Ibid.
48 Dr K. Norton, interview with author, Oct. 1996.
49 Dr R. Howat, interview with author, Dec. 1996.
50 Kenyon, *Memoirs*, p. 146.
51 Mann, *The Chase*, p. 122.
52 Ibid., pp. 108–9.
53 Ibid.
54 Hutton, *Memories of a Doctor*, pp. 23–4.
55 Ibid., p. 105.
56 Mann, *The Chase*, p. 105.
57 See, inter alia, 'Graham Travers' (Margaret G. Todd), *Mona Maclean: medical student*, Edinburgh and London: Blackwood, 1892; Annie Swan, *Elizabeth Glen, M.B.: the experiences of a lady doctor*, London: Hutchinson, 1987; L.T. Meade, *Mary Gifford, M.B.*, London: Wells Gardner, Darton and Co., n.d.
58 Malleson, *A Woman Doctor*, p. 53.
59 Lord Riddell, review of M. Scharlieb, *Reminiscences*, in *John O'London's Weekly*, 12 Apr. 1924.
60 Mann, *The Chase*, p. 16.
61 E. Bryson, *Look Back in Wonder*, Dundee: David Winter and Son, 1966, p. 161.
62 Wilberforce, *Octavia Wilberforce*, pp. 27–9.
63 Christopher St John, *Christine Murrell, M.D.: her life and her work*, London: Williams and Norgate, 1935.
64 E. Hamer, *Britannia's Glory: a history of twentieth century lesbians*, London: Cassell, 1996, pp. 124–6.
65 Ibid., p. 126.
66 Lord Riddell, *Dame Louisa Aldrich-Blake*, London: Hodder and Stoughton, n.d. (1926?).
67 Ibid., pp. 15–16.
68 Ibid., p. 13.
69 Ibid., p. 19.
70 Ibid., p. 24.
71 Malleson, *A Woman Doctor*, pp. 24–5.
72 Bryson, *Look Back in Wonder*, p. 190.
73 Hutton, *Memories of a Doctor*, p. 40.
74 Wauchope, *The Story of a Woman Physician*, p. 45.
75 Idem.
76 St John, *Christine Murrell*, pp. 28–9.
77 Mann, *The Chase*, p. 177. On 'rags', see Chapter 10 below.
78 Ibid., pp. 122–3.

79 Charles H. Pring, 'Women medical students', *The Times*, 9 Mar. 1922.
80 Lord Knutsford, 'Women medical students: "hoydens" in the schools, the difficulties of mixed classes', *The Times*, 14 Mar. 1922.
81 Dr K. Norton, interview with author, Oct. 1996.
82 *Daily Mail*, 29 Aug. 1917.
83 Wauchope, *The Story of a Woman Physician*, pp. 48–9.
84 James Garner, 'Sex and Sensibility: the admission of women to St Mary's Hospital Medical School', unpublished dissertation for Intercalated BSc Course, Wellcome Institute for the History of Medicine, 1994, pp. 88–9. The petition is preserved in the Archives at St Mary's Hospital (MS/AD46). See also J.S. Garner, 'The great experiment: the admission of women students to St Mary's Hospital Medical School, 1916–1925', *Medical History*, 1998, vol. 42, 68–88.
85 Dr K. Norton, interview with author, Oct. 1996.
86 Mann, *The Chase*, p. 187.
87 See, for instance, W.R. Merrington, *University College Hospital and its Medical School*, London: Heinemann, 1976, pp. 237–9, which describes Gwen Hilton (née Hill) consulting a lawyer to prepare a case urging the continued admission of women to the College Hospital in 1920. The London Hospital Medical College Minute Book (vol. 12) contains an entry for 15 Feb. 1922 indicating that Dr Alice Bloomfield had considered starting legal proceedings against the College for rejecting her application to study for the Final Fellowship Course (FRCS). (Archives of London Hospital).
88 The idea of 'a crisis in masculinity' is discussed in J. Bourke, *Dismembering the Male: men's bodies, Britain and the Great War*, London: Reaktion Books, 1996; see also J.A. Mangan and James Walvin (eds), *Manliness and Morality: middle class masculinity in Britain and America, 1800–1940*, Manchester: Manchester University Press, 1987; M. Roper and J. Tosh (eds), *Manful Assertions: masculinities in Britain since 1800*, London and New York: Routledge, 1991; M.R. Higonnet, J. Jenson, S. Michel, and M. Collins Weitz (eds), *Behind the Lines: gender and the two world wars*, New Haven, CT and London: Yale University Press, 1987; and S. Kingsley Kent, *Making Peace: the reconstruction of gender in interwar Britain*, Princeton, NJ: Princeton University Press, 1993.
89 Freemasonry is not the easiest subject for the historian to research, but see, for instance, R.M. Handfield-Jones, *A History of the Sancta Maria Lodge No 2682, 1897–1960* (Pamphlet in Archives of St Mary's Hospital, 1960) for some idea of the strength of the movement in that particular hospital.
90 Mann, *The Chase*, p. 191.
91 Malleson, *A Woman Doctor*, p. 8.
92 L. Martindale, *The Woman Doctor and Her Future*, London: Mills and Boon, 1922, p. 131.
93 L. Martindale, *A Woman Surgeon*, London: Gollancz, 1951, pp. 158–9.
94 Malleson, *A Woman Doctor*, p. 163.
95 Wauchope, *The Story of a Woman Physician*, p. 74.
96 Personal communication, John Davenport.
97 Ibid.
98 Obituary in *The Independent*, 23 Aug. 2002.
99 Scrapbook collected by Dr Mabel Lindsay relating to history of Medical Women's Federation, p. 213 (in Greater Manchester County Record Office).
100 Riddell, *Dame Louisa Aldrich-Blake*, p. 78.
101 Wilberforce, *Octavia Wilberforce*, p. 75.

102 Bryson, *Look Back in Wonder*, p. 204.
103 Ibid., p. 219.
104 Hutton, *Memories of a Doctor*, p. 102.
105 In 1918 Emily Forster published a little book entitled *How to Become A Woman Doctor*, London: Charles Griffin. On p. 48 she declared, 'The war suddenly opened practically all doors to women doctors: and once women have entered any sphere of labour they have remained. There never has been a "going backward" where the woman worker is concerned.' As we have seen, such optimism was somewhat misplaced.
106 *Sphincter*, Autumn 1937, vol. 1 no. 1, p. 9, Liverpool University Archives.
107 See, for instance, S. Aiston, '"I didn't look at it that way": oral history and the historical study of women at the University of Liverpool, 1944–1960', *History of Education Society Bulletin*, May 1999, no. 63; C. Dyhouse, *No Distinction of Sex? women in British universities 1870–1939*, London: UCL Press, 1995, p. 153.
108 See, for instance, Liverpool Medical History Society, 'Women in medicine during world war II, twelve eye-witness accounts with an introduction by Carol Dyhouse', 1997.

4 Wasted investment and blocked ambitions? Women graduates in the postwar world

1 Judith Hubback, *Wives Who Went to College*, London: William Heinemann Ltd, 1957, p. 11.
2 Ibid., for Hubback's methodology see pp. 15–23, for her questionnaire, pp. 161–2.
3 See papers presented at panel entitled 'The restless fifties: expectations and realities for graduate women in the UK, Australia and the USA', European Social Science History Conference 2004, Berlin; A. Mackinnon, 'University women shaping the future in the fifties and early sixties'; Linda Eisenmann, 'Women and post-secondary education in the post world war two United States: expectations and behaviour'; Pat Thane, 'Graduate women in 1950s Britain'.
4 Betty Friedan, *The Feminine Mystique*, London: Gollancz, 1963; Simone de Beauvoir, *The Second Sex*, London: Cape, 1953.
5 Hubback, p. 79.
6 Ibid., p. 124.
7 Ibid., p. 76.
8 Judith Hubback, *Graduate Wives*, London: Political & Economic Planning, no. 361, 1954.
9 'Is a bride (BA) wasting a degree?', *News Chronicle*, 22 Apr. 1954, p. 6.
10 'What a buzz of angry BAs', *News Chronicle*, 24 Apr. 1954, p. 6; 'Now the BA wives have their say', *News Chronicle*, 27 Apr. 1954, p. 6.
11 My thanks to Judith Hubback for kindly allowing me to consult the collection of press cuttings related to her work.
12 'Labour lost by love', *The Economist*, 26 June 1954, p. 1036.
13 'University places: making more room for women', *The Times*, 20 June 1958, p. 11. Letter signed by Lucy Sutherland, Janet Vaughan, Kathleen Major, Mary Ogilvie.
14 Letters from S. John Rogers, Sir Shane Leslie, *The Times*, 24 June 1958, p. 9.
15 The Times, 26 June, p. 11 and 27 June 1958, p. 11.
16 Lois Mitchison, 'The price of educating women', *The Guardian*, 8 Jan. 1960, p. 4.

17 M.L. Jacks, 'Education of girls: why a new approach is needed', *The Times*, 6 Jan. 1960, p. 11.
18 *The Times*, 15 Jan. 1960, p. 7.
19 Letter from Mary McLean, *The Times*, 18 Jan. 1960, p. 6.
20 Joyce Neath, quoted in the Women's Group on Public Welfare, *The Education and Training of Girls*, London: National Council of Social Service, 1962, p. 10.
21 Amy Treece in *The Woman Teacher*, Feb. 1960, pp. 179–80.
22 John Newsom, *The Education of Girls*, London: Faber, 1948; Education Department of King's College, Newcastle upon Tyne, *The Education of Girls*, Newcastle, 1952; Women's Group on Public Welfare, *The Education and Training of Girls*.
23 R.D. Anderson, *Universities and Elites in Britain since 1800*, Basingstoke and London: Macmillan, 1992, pp. 23 and 27; the figures and long-term trends are discussed in more detail in Chapter 5.
24 The proportion of female full-time undergraduates in the UK first rose above 50 per cent in 1996. See Chapter 5.
25 See, for instance, L. Doreen Whiteley, *The Poor Student and the University: a report on the scholarship system*, London: George Allen and Unwin, 1933, pp. 23–5; D.W. Hughes, *Careers for Our Daughters*, London: A. & C. Black Ltd, p. 293.
26 Dame Kitty Anderson, *Women and the Universities, A Changing Pattern*, Fawcett Lecture, Bedford College, University of London: 1963, pp. 10–14.
27 *Report of Committee on Higher Education* (Robbins Report) 1961–3, Appendix Two (A), *Students and their Education*, Cmnd 2154 – II, pp. 24–6; Appendix One, *The Demand for Places in Higher Education*, Cmnd 2154 – I, p. 82.
28 E.M. Thomas, 'A problem of talent', *The Times*, 19 May 1966, p. 17.
29 Ibid. On this theme see David Edgerton, 'The masculinisation of science: gender, class and big science in Britain around the Second World War', in *The Transformation of an Elite? Women and higher education since 1900*, papers presented at conference held at University of Cambridge to mark the fiftieth anniversary of women's full membership in the University, Sept. 1998, pp. 165–82; also Michael Sanderson, *Educational Opportunity and Social Change in England*, London: Faber and Faber, 1987, pp. 133–4.
30 Correspondence between Phoebe Sheavyn and Frances Melville, 22 Feb. and 15 Mar. 1924, in Glasgow University Archives (DC 233/2/6/2/17)
31 A. Phillips (ed.), *A Newnham Anthology*, Cambridge: Cambridge University Press for Newnham College, 1979, pp. 150–1; T.E.B. Howarth, *Cambridge Between Two Wars*, London: Collins, 1978, p. 42.
32 *Report of Royal Commission on Oxford and Cambridge Universities* (Asquith Commission), 1922, Cmd 1588, p. 173.
33 J. Wells, 'Statement of Support for Limitation Statute', July 1927, Limitation of Numbers File, Archives, Somerville College.
34 V. Brittain, *The Women at Oxford, a fragment of history*, London: George G. Harrap, 1960, p. 172.
35 C. Dyhouse, 'The citadel storms back: women's medical education in Britain 1900–1939', in *The Transformation of an Elite?* (see note 29, above).
36 Letter from J. Orr Ewing dated 21 Apr. 1937, in archives of Medical Women's Federation, Contemporary Medical Archives Centre at Wellcome Institute for the History of Medicine (Coeducation Files, Box 2 File 3, 1919–1938).
37 Ibid., letter dated 23 Apr. 1937.

38 University Grants Committee, *Returns from Universities and University Colleges in Receipt of Treasury Grant for the Academic Year 1937/8*, London: HMSO, 1939, p. 14.

39 J.M. Cooke, 'Women and the Professions, 1890–1939', unpublished DPhil thesis, University of Sussex, 1997; M. Brancker, 'The rise of women in the profession 1: the 1930s', *In Practice*, 30 Sept. 2002, vol. 24, no. 8, pp. 474–8.

40 W.O. Skeat, *King's College London Engineering Society 1847–1957*, London: King's College Engineers Association, 1957, p. 56.

41 *Report of the Vice-Chancellor and Principal to the Council for the calendar year 1945*, University of Birmingham Archives, 7/ii p.12, quoted by Alison Gaukroger and Leonard Schwarz in 'A university and its region: student recruitment to Birmingham, 1945–1975', *Oxford Review of Education*, 1997, vol. 23, no. 2, p. 187.

42 *Report of the Special Committee on the Medical Education of Women in London*, University of London Senate Minutes, 1944; copy in National Archives, MH 71/72.

43 Ministry of Health, *Report of Inter-Departmental Committee on Medical Schools* (Goodenough Committee), London: HMSO, 1944, pp. 99–100.

44 See, for instance, submission by 'The Joint Four' (Joint executive committee of Associations of Headmasters, Headmistresses, Assistant Masters, Mistresses) to (Merrison) Committee on Regulation of Medical Profession, copy in National Archives, ED 188/322. There is interesting material documenting the continuing difficulties faced by girls keen to train for medicine before and after 1945 in MH 71/58 and MH 71/60.

45 University of Cambridge, *University Committee on Women Students, 1949–1971*, Cambridge University Library (UA R 1795 A-E), draft committee report of Jan. 1950, cites letter to UGC dated 28 June 1946.

46 Ibid., Professor Hollond's opposition to idea of a third college for women, 22 Feb. 1950 (1795/49).

47 Ibid., file C, letter to Vice-Chancellor dated 23 Jan. 1952 signed by M.C. Bradbrook, J. Caton Thompson, D.A.E. Garrod, M.T. Hollond, D.M. de Navarro, H.G. Steers, J.M.C. Toynbee.

48 Ibid., letter from Registrar to Lady Whitby, 17 June 1955.

49 Janet Howarth, 'Women', in Brian Harrison (ed.), *The History of the University of Oxford: vol. VIII, the twentieth century*, Oxford: Clarendon Press, 1994, esp. pp. 358–9, 373–4.

50 W.A.C. Stewart, *Higher Education in Postwar Britain*, Basingstoke and London: Macmillan, 1989, esp. pp. 125–36, 184–99; David Hencke, *Colleges in Crisis: the reorganisation of teacher training 1971–7*, Harmondsworth: Penguin, 1978, pp. 27–73.

51 See, for instance, Stella Greenall, 'Women and higher education', London: National Union of Students Education and Welfare Department, 1966, p. 15, copy in National archives (LCO 17/11); Linda Tinkham, 'Learning one's lesson', in A. Cockburn and R. Blackburn (eds), *Student Power: problems, diagnosis, action*, Harmondsworth: Penguin, 1969, pp. 82–98.

52 R. Crompton and K. Sanderson, *Gendered Jobs and Social Change*, London: Unwin Hyman, 1990, p. 55.

53 George Gissing, *The Odd Women*, London: Lawrence and Bullen, 1893; on careers advisory magazines and journals in the early twentieth century, see Cooke, 'Women and the professions, 1890–1939', pp. 32–9.

54 Students' Careers Association, Central Bureau for the Employment of Women,

Openings for University Women other than Teaching, London: Harmsworth and Co., 1912.

55 Board of Education, *Annual Report on the Education and Training of Teachers*, London: HMSO, 1932.

56 See Annual Reports of Central Bureau for the Employment of Women published in *Women's Employment*, 1903–75 (Women's Library).

57 Until women were admitted to full membership of the University of Cambridge in 1948, the Cambridge Women's Appointments Board was conducted by the two women's colleges from offices in London. The archives of the CWAB are held in the University Library (ref. APTB).

58 Joan M. Anderson, *Fifty Years' Service: a short history of the work of the National Advisory Centre on Careers for Women*, 1983 (copy in Women's Library). The Women's Employment Federation became the National Advisory Centre on careers for women in 1970. The archives of the WEF are in the Women's Library. See also Brian Harrison, *Prudent Revolutionaries: portraits of British feminists between the wars*, Oxford: Oxford University Press, 1987, pp. 175–8 for the background to the formation of the WEF.

59 Harrison, *Prudent Revolutionaries*.

60 WEF Albums of press cuttings (1–6) in Women's Library,

61 Eleanor Dunbar, 'A mortgage on youth', *Daily Despatch*, 29 Jan. 1934, in WEF press cuttings album.

62 Ibid.

63 Ray Strachey, 'Prospects for university girls', in *Careers and Openings for Women: a survey of women's employment and a guide for those seeking work*, London: Faber and Faber, 1935.

64 Detailed lists of training opportunities were a regular feature in the CBEW's paper, *Women's Employment*. The Lady Rachel Byng's 'Thistledown Angora Wool Farm' at Winkfield, Windsor advertised for 'Lady Apprentices' from the late 1920s.

65 Strachey, *Careers and Openings for Women*, p. 168.

66 Author's interview with Dr Edith Merry, 8 Sept. 1995.

67 A theme which emerged strongly at a day conference organized by the Liverpool Medical History Society in 1997. See 'Women in medicine during world war II, twelve eye-witness accounts with an introduction by Carol Dyhouse', Liverpool Medical History Society, 1997.

68 See Chapter 2.

69 Cambridge Women's Appointments Board, *Annual Report for year ending Dec. 31, 1941*, Cambridge University Library, APTB 4/3.

70 Ibid., *Annual Report for year ending 31 Dec. 1948* (APTB 2/1–22)

71 Ibid., *Annual Report for year ending 31 Dec. 1955*; see also papers for meetings of Board, APTB 5 61–3.

72 See sequence of editions of *Careers: a memorandum on openings and trainings for girls and women* in WEF archives, the Women's Library (Box 498). Quotations in the text are from the 1961 edition, p. 9.

73 Ibid.

74 The concern over the 'wastage' of women doctors through marriage had a long history and remained a controversial issue through the 1950s and 1960s. See M.A. Elston, 'Women doctors in the British health services: a sociological study of their careers and opportunities', unpublished PhD thesis, University of Leeds, 1986, pp. 385ff. Women doctors argued that the 'wastage' was exaggerated and that there was a pressing need for more flexible conditions of work in order for women to

combine family and career successfully. See (for instance) Jean Lawrie, Muriel Newhouse and Patricia Elliott, 'Working capacity of women doctors', *British Medical Journal*, 12 Feb. 1966, 1, pp. 409–12. By the early 1970s deans of medical schools were wary about making any public admission of operating 'quotas' on female admissions or defending these on grounds of the 'wastage' of women doctors through marriage, but see (for instance) correspondence between A.B. Gilmour (Secretary to the British Medical Association's Board of Science and Education) and W.K. Reid at the Department of Education and Science, 13 Dec. 1973, Papers relating to Consultative Document on Sex Discrimination (ED 188/322), National Archives.

75   There is an interesting account of one woman graduate's frustrations in this respect in the University of Kent's campus magazine, *Fuss*, in 1969: see Dagmar Prichard-Jones, 'For girl graduates [.] it's back to square nought', *Fuss*, May 1969, vol. 1, no. 4, pp. 25–6.

76   By 1963 'it was felt that the returns were sufficiently comprehensive and had achieved sufficient validity to warrant their publication' (S.L. Bragg, foreword to Central Services Unit for Careers and Appointments Services, *First Destination of University Graduates 1975/76*, Manchester: Central Services Unit, p. 3).

77   Cambridge Women's Appointments Board, archives in Cambridge University Library, APTB 5, 61–63.

78   Christine Craig, *The Employment of Cambridge Graduates*, Cambridge: Cambridge University Press, 1963, p. 67.

79   Ibid., pp. 68–9, 79–84.

80   CWAB Minutes, 16 Nov. 1963 (APTB 5/73–75).

81   Craig, *The Employment of Cambridge Graduates*, p. 72.

82   Ibid., p. 78. See also Nancy Seear, Veronica Roberts and John Brock, *A Career for Women in Industry?* London: Oliver and Boyd for the London School of Economics and Political Science, 1964. Introducing the volume, Seear pointed out that the findings suggested that 'the really ambitious career girl might well not be attracted by the present position of women in industry' (p. 3). Margherita Rendel's article, 'Do women have trouble getting jobs?', *New Society*, 27 Aug. 1964, pp. 17–18, drew attention to employers' discrimination against women.

83   CWAB Archives, reference in papers for 1961 (APTB 5/67–69). The closed files of correspondence between the CWAB and Shell, 1941–1955, are APTB 11. At a meeting on 4 Nov. 1961 it was noted that the secretaries of the CWAB and the Oxford University Appointments Committee had interviewed Miss Thorne of Shell and 'it was agreed that no particular effort should be made to put up women candidates for Shell appointments unless the situation seemed to have changed very radically' (APTB 5 61/3).

84   CWAB Archives, *Annual Report for year ending Dec. 1962* (APTB 5 73/5).

85   Rosemary Crompton and Kay Sanderson, *Gendered Jobs and Social Change*, London: Unwin Hyman, 1990, pp. 47–64.

86   See, *inter alia*, Alva Myrdal and Viola Klein, *Women's Two Roles*, London: Routledge and Kegan Paul, 1956; Constance E. Arregger (ed.), *Graduate Women at Work: a study by a working party of the British Federation of University Women*, Newcastle-upon-Tyne: Oriel Press, 1966; Pearl Jephcott, with Nancy Seear and J.H. Smith, *Married Women Working*, London: Allen and Unwin, 1962; M. Collins (ed.), *Women Graduates and the Teaching Profession*, Manchester: Manchester University Press, 1964; R.K. Kelsall, *Women and Teaching*, London, HMSO, 1963; F. Zweig, *Women's Life and Labour*, London: Gollancz, 1952.

87 Arregger, *Graduate Women at Work*, p. 127.

88 See, for instance, 'Early marriage as a threat to girls' ambitions' (Report of Presidential address to Easter Conference of National Union of Women Teachers, *The Times*, 20 Apr. 1960), p. 8.

89 Statistical Evidence submitted to the Committee on the Age of Majority (Latey Committee), 1967, in National Archives, RG 48/3089; see also the Committee's *Report*, London: HMSO, 1967, Cmnd 3342, Appendix 8, pp. 196–7; E. Grebenik and G. Rowntree, 'Factors associated with the age of marriage in Great Britain', *Proceedings of the Royal Society*, 1963–4, vol. 159, pp. 178–202.

90 Griselda Rowntree, 'New facts on teenage marriage', *New Society*, no. 1, 4 Oct. 1962, pp. 12–15.

91 Hera Cook, 'The long sexual revolution, British women, sex and contraception in the twentieth century', University of Sussex DPhil thesis, 1999, p. 273.

92 Rowntree, 'New facts on teenage marriage', p. 12.

93 M. Schofield (in collaboration with John Bynner, Patricia Lewis and Peter Massie), *The Sexual Behaviour of Young People*, London: Longmans, 1965, pp. 124, 107.

94 Kathleen Ollerenshaw, *Education for Girls*, London: Faber and Faber, 1961, p. 38.

95 Ibid., p. 107.

96 See, for instance, Amy Treece, 'Fifteen to Eighteen', *The Woman Teacher*, Jan. 1960, vol. XLI, no. 2; Feb. 1960, vol. XLI, no. 3; 'The Crowther Report', March 1960, vol. XLI, no. 4. Ministry of Education, *Fifteen to Eighteen, A Report of the Central Advisory Council for Education (England)*, (Crowther Report), London: HMSO, 1959; Ministry of Education, *The Youth Service in England and Wales* (Albemarle Report), London: HMSO, 1960.

97 J.M. Collins, Presidential address to National Union of Women Teachers, Easter Conference, Buxton, 1960 published in *The Woman Teacher*, vol. XLI, no. 6, May 1960, see esp. p. 225; Arregger, *Graduate Women at Work*, p. 127; 'Stunted schooldays', editorial in *Women's Employment*, 20 May 1955; Women's Group on Public Welfare, *Education and Training of Girls*, pp. 96–7, 109.

98 Ollerenshaw, *Education for Girls*, p. 143.

99 Ibid., p. 38.

100 M. Ogilvie, 'Notes on some problems of the education of girls at university level', Evidence submitted to Robbins Committee on Higher Education, National Archives, ED 118/111.

101 Ibid., p. 2.

102 See notes 79, 83 above; 'Jobs for the girls?' *The Times*, 15 Feb. 1960, p. 13, which quotes the views of Kay Baxter of the CWAB.

103 The idea of 'the dual role' is mainly associated with the title of the book by Alva Myrdal and Viola Klein, *Women's Two Roles*.

104 As Pat Thane has pointed out, marriage might be looked upon as a more secure option for women between the 1920s and the 1950s than either before or afterwards. See P. Thane, 'Girton graduates: earning and learning, 1920s–1980s', *Women's History Review*, 2004, vol. 13, no. 3, p. 353.

105 Lois Day, *The Looker In*, London: Jonathan Cape, 1961.

106 Rosamond Lehmann, *Dusty Answer*, London: Chatto and Windus, 1937.

107 Andrea Newman, *A Share of the World*, London: Bodley Head, 1964 (this edition London: Panther, 1965); Margaret Forster, *Dames' Delight*, London: Jonathan Cape, 1964.

108 Newman, *A Share of the World*, p. 134.

109 Penelope Lively, *Spiderweb*, London: Viking, 1998, this edition Harmondsworth: Penguin, 1999.
110 Ibid., pp. 180–1.
111 Joan Bakewell, *The Centre of the Bed*, London: Hodder and Stoughton, p. 89.
112 Ibid., pp. 114–16.
113 Ibid., p. 140.

5 Gaining places: the rising proportion of women students in universities after 1970

1 Tessa Blackstone, 'Success or failure?', *Times Higher Education Supplement*, 8 Sept. 1978, p. 11.
2 R. Crompton and K. Sanderson, *Gendered Jobs and Social Change*, London: Unwin Hyman, 1990, pp. 55–8.
3 Jennifer Jones and Josephine Castle, 'Women in UK universities, 1920–1980', *Studies in Higher Education*, 1986, vol. 11, no. 3, 289–97.
4 Robert M. Blackburn and Jennifer Jarman, 'Changing inequalities in access to British universities', *Oxford Review of Education*, 1993, vol. 19, no. 2, 197–215.
5 Ibid., p. 208.
6 Ibid., p. 209.
7 Alison Goddard, 'Who's the weaker sex now?', *Times Higher Education Supplement*, 31 Oct. 2003, p. 8. See also Wendy Berliner, 'Where have all the young men gone?', *Education Guardian*, 18 May 2004, pp. 18–19.
8 Goddard, 'Who's the weaker sex now?'
9 University of Warwick, *Students' Handbook, 1966*, in University of Warwick Archives (UWA/PUB/S/HB/1).
10 1966/7 *Guide to Applicants*, University of Sussex Archives.
11 *Student Life*, Mar. 1968, vol. 1, no. 3, pp. 12–13 for East Anglia; Nov. 1968, vol. 2, no. 1 for Lancaster. See also Nov. 1967, vol. 1, no. 1 for Kent, illustration of 'three swingers from the swinging university', p. 1.
12 'Girls plump for new university', *The Observer*, 26 Feb. 1961, p. 12.
13 Typescript of anonymous poem 'Girls plump for new University College', laid in with publications in Box 50, University of Sussex Archives.
14 Kathleen Ollerenshaw, *Education for Girls*, London: Faber and Faber, 1961, pp. 134, 135.
15 Ibid., pp. 141–2.
16 Ibid., p. 144.
17 See, for instance, Jane Johnston Milne, 'Report from the Senior Tutor to Women Students', addressed to Vice-Chancellor, University of Birmingham, Feb. 1929, p. 4, in University of Birmingham Archives.
18 Cambridge Women's Appointments Board, *Annual Report for Year Ending 1964*, p. 3 (Cambridge University Library, University Archives, APTB 2/11)
19 Association of Headmistresses, 'Memorandum on Higher Education', evidence prepared for submission to the Committee on Higher Education under the Chairmanship of Lord Robbins, Dec. 1963, copy in Archives of Headmistresses' Association, Modern Records Centre, University of Warwick (MSS 188/3/12/2), pp. 7–8.
20 Ibid., p. 8.
21 E.M. Thomas, 'A problem of talent', *The Times*, 19 May 1966, p. 19.

22 Kathleen Ollerenshaw, *The Girls' Schools*, London: Faber and Faber, 1967, p. 67.

23 Robbins gives the percentage of women at Sussex as 67 per cent in 1961/2, see Report of Committee on Higher Education (London: HMSO, 1963) Appendix Two (A), Cmnd 2154–II, p. 25. The University of Reading had the next highest percentage (46 per cent). Reading had long enjoyed a near equal proportion of men and women in its student body largely because it taught few technological subjects and had no medical school. See, for instance, H.G.G. Herklots, *The New Universities: an external examination*, London: Ernest Benn, 1928, p. 98.

24 Michael Sanderson, *The History of the University of East Anglia, Norwich*, London: Hambledon, 2002, pp. 51, 120.

25 'The new University of East Anglia', in the *Eastern Daily Times*, press cutting, no date but c. Autumn 1963, in Press Cuttings Album, 3 July 1963–22 Feb. 1964, Archives, University of East Anglia.

26 Sanderson, *University of East Anglia*, p. 120.

27 Report of Committee on Higher Education (Robbins Report), 1963, Appendix Two (A), Cmnd 2154–II, London: HMSO, p. 24.

28 Ibid., p. 25.

29 Anthony Sampson, *Anatomy of Britain*, London: Hodder and Stoughton, 1962.

30 Anthony Sampson, *Anatomy of Britain Today*, London: Hodder and Stoughton, 1965, pp. 235, 236.

31 Anthony Sampson, *The New Anatomy of Britain*, London: Hodder and Stoughton, 1971, p. 165.

32 Anthony Sampson, *The Changing Anatomy of Britain*, London: Hodder and Stoughton, 1982, pp. 131, 142.

33 Ollerenshaw, *The Girls' Schools*, p. 67.

34 See, for instance, Carol Dyhouse, *No Distinction of Sex? Women in British universities 1870–1939*, London: UCL Press, 1995. Sara Delamont's now classic exploration of 'double conformity' in the education of middle- and upper-class women is still useful. See 'The contradictions in ladies' education' in Sara Delamont and Lorna Duffin (eds), *The Nineteenth Century Woman, her Cultural and Physical World*, London: Croom Helm, 1978.

35 D.W. Hughes, *Careers for our Daughters*, London: A. & C. Black, 1936, p. 293.

36 University of Oxford, papers relating to the education of women at Oxford University, 1910–79, Joint Society Permissions, 1944–9, in Bodleian Library (Dep.c.698).

37 Ibid., letter from Kingsley Amis dated 7 Feb. 1946. Amis, as President-Elect of the Rhythm Club, emphasized that Club members took a high moral tone, dissociating themselves from jive, jitterbugging and similar forms of rowdyism, which he held to be quite erroneously associated with true American jazz music. The responses of the individual woman principals make interesting reading. The Principals of St Hugh's and St Anne's were dubious, in spite of or (equally likely) because of the loftily tongue-in-cheek tone of the request, and wanted to consult the Proctors. Janet Vaughan, Principal of Somerville, confessed to feeling uncertain about the society, and thought that they should try to find out something more about the people running it.

38 Ibid. Note dated 1 Nov. 1947.

39 Sheila Rowbotham, *Promise of a Dream*, London: Allen Lane, The Penguin Press, 2000, p. 49.

40 A.S. Byatt, 'Soul searching', *The Guardian*, 14 Feb. 2004.

41 See, for instance, Principals' Minute Books, 17 Oct. 1960, Dep.d.762, Bodleian Library.

42 Author's conversation with Cynthia Floud, Summer 1999.

43 Penelope Lively, *A House Unlocked*, London: Penguin, 2001, p. 178.

44 Andrea Newman, *A Share of the World*, London: Bodley Head, 1964; Margaret Forster, *Dames' Delight*, London: Jonathan Cape, 1964 (Consul, 1966, Sphere, 1968); Margaret Drabble, *The Millstone*, London: Weidenfeld and Nicolson, 1965; Judith Grossman, *Her Own Terms*, London: Grafton, 1988; Hilary Mantel, *An Experiment in Love*, London: Penguin, 1995.

45 *Fuss* (Forum for University Staff and Students), University of Kent, Dec. 1968, vol. 1, no. 1, p. 12. The cartoon was reprinted (with permission) from the *Times Education Supplement*.

46 Anthony Ryle, *Student Casualties*, London: Allen Lane, The Penguin Press, 1969, p. 124.

47 Ibid., p. 120. Dr S.E. Finlay, Secretary of the British Student Health Association, was quoted as having estimated, in 1966, that between 2 per cent and 3 per cent of unmarried female students in British universities became pregnant every year. Of these, he suggested that around one-third of the pregnancies resulted in abortions. Finlay's (1966) lecture on 'Abortion in British universities' is referred to in *Student* (London: Connaught Publications), Summer 1968, vol. 1, no. 2, p. 38.

48 Ibid., pp. 20–1.

49 C. McCance and D.J. Hall, 'Sexual behaviour and contraceptive practice of unmarried female undergraduates at Aberdeen University', *British Medical Journal*, 17 June 1972, pp. 694–700. The quotation is from an editorial commentary, 'Sex and the single girl', which accompanied the article in the same issue of the *BMJ*, p. 671.

50 Ibid., p. 672.

51 Ibid., see also pp. 698–9.

52 M. Schofield, *The Sexual Behaviour of Young Adults*, London: Allen Lane, 1973, p. 168.

53 Ibid., pp. 138–40.

54 Hera Cook, *The Long Sexual Revolution: English women, sex and contraception 1800–1975*, Oxford: Oxford University Press, 2004, pp. 268–9.

55 *Student* (London: Connaught Publications), 1968, vol.1, no. 1, p. 1.

56 *Student*, 1968, vol. 1, no. 2, p. 38.

57 *Student*, 1969, vol. 2, no. 3 and regular reports on Student Advisory Centre in each issue.

58 Max Handley, 'Students and mothers', *Student*, 1969, vol. 2, no. 1, pp. 33–5.

59 Faith Spicer, 'Face to face', *Student*, 1969, vol. 2, no. 1, pp. 36–7.

60 Laura Swaffield, 'Unwanted pregnancies: has contraception a social stigma?', *Leeds Student*, 5 Feb. 1971, pp. 6–7. See also 'Prudence reports on the pill' in Essex University's student paper, *Wyvern*, 16 Jan. 1970, pp. 10–11.

61 Churchill College, Cambridge, 'Reports, correspondence and papers re admission of women, with Minutes of the Governing Body's discussions, 1961–1975,' Churchill College Archives, CCGB 190/1. See also CCGB 190/2; CGB 190/3.

62 Ibid., see Report of Senior Tutor (R.H. Tizard) to College Council on Admission of Women, 23 Oct. 1967 (CC/168/67).

63 Churchill College Archives, 'Correspondence with other Cambridge heads of colleges and others, including fellows of Churchill, on the decision to admit women to Cambridge colleges, 1969–1971', CC GB 190/6, see Recommendations of Tutorial and Decanal Subcommittee on Admission of Women, 27 Jan. 1969 (CC/26/69). On 'sexual disciplinary problems' more generally, the subcommittee

recommended that 'girls' be treated in the same way as 'men'. For instance, 'The college's present policy is that it disapproves of fornication, and offenders are sent to live in digs. Although this is not an entirely suitable punishment, it was thought to be as suitable for women as for men.' This was a rather more relaxed attitude than one might have expected to find in some of the women's colleges of the time.

64 Cook, *The Long Sexual Revolution*, pp. 14–16, 268–70. For more detail see Michael Murphy, 'The contraceptive pill and women's employment as factors in fertility change in Britain, 1963–1980: a challenge to the conventional view', *Population Studies*, July 1993, vol. 47, no. 2, 221–43.

65 See Chapter 9.

66 *The Long Sexual Revolution*, pp. 337, 338–40.

67 See, *inter alia*, W.B. Creighton, *Working Women and the Law*, London: Mansell, 1979, esp. pp. 90–8, 151–5 and *passim*; Elizabeth M. Meehan, *Women's Rights at Work: campaigns and policy in Britain and the United States*, Basingstoke: Macmillan, 1985.

68 Meehan, *Women's Rights at Work*, pp. 33ff.

69 Ibid., see also Margherita Rendel, 'The winning of the Sex Discrimination Act', in Madeleine Arnot (ed.), *Race and Gender: equal opportunities policies in education*, Oxford: Pergamon, 1985, pp. 81–95.

70 See Conservative Party Archives in Bodleian Library, CCO 20/36/4 for circumstances leading to the setting-up of the Cripps Committee, CCO 20/36/7, for typescript of full report (published by the Conservative Political Centre in March 1969). Anthony Cripps, confronted by a mass of evidence suggesting discrimination against women in many areas of social life, emphasized that his brief had been to concentrate on areas of discrimination in legal provision. The report was later redrafted to take a more inclusive view of the whole question of sex discrimination by Geoffrey Howe ('Cripps Committee on Women's Rights: redraft by Geoffrey Howe of Further Study (Title to be agreed)' (CRD 3/38/2)). A published version, authored by Beryl Cooper and Geoffrey Howe, *Opportunity for Women*, London: Conservative Political Centre, appeared in Sept. 1969.

71 Creighton, *Working Women and the Law*, pp. 47–55.

72 House of Lords, *Special Report from the Select Committee on the Anti-Discrimination Bill*, London: HMSO, 27 Mar. 1973; House of Lords, *Second Special Report from the Select Committee on the Anti-Discrimination Bill*, Session 1972–73, London: HMSO, 18 Apr. 1973; House of Commons, *Special Report from the Select Committee on the Anti-Discrimination (No. 2) Bill*, London: HMSO, 26 June 1973.

73 Rendel, 'Winning of Sex Discrimination Act', p. 87.

74 See Minutes of Evidence taken before Select Committee of House of Commons on Anti-Discrimination Bill (note 72 above), paras. 258–305, pp. 38–49.

75 There is comprehensive documentation in the National Archives, ED 188/322, ED 188/323, ED 188/324, ED 188/325. The files cover proposals for legislation and contain representations from individuals and groups in response to the government's (1973) consultative document ('Equal opportunities for men and women: government proposals for legislation'); there is also departmental briefing material. Representations from individuals and some twenty-nine women's organizations summarized by the DES (ED 188/323), reveal widespread dissatisfaction with the educational provisions outlined in the consultative document, which were not considered sufficiently comprehensive nor forceful enough. See also ED 207/53.

76 National Archives, ED 188/322. Communication from 'The Joint Four' (Joint Executive Committee of the Associations of Headmistresses, Headmasters, Assistant Masters and Assistant Mistresses), results of survey undertaken 1972/3 on medical school admissions, originally sent to (Merrison) Committee on Regulation of Medical Profession, subsequently circulated to DES, DHSS; brief for meeting with university representatives, 9 Nov. 1973; Communication from Sir Frederick Dainton, Chairman of University Grants Committee, to Sir William Pile at the DES, 5 Nov. 1973. See also notes of meeting of DES officials with representatives of UGC and CVCP on 9 Nov. 1973; correspondence between A.B. Gilmour (Secretary to the Board of Science and Education, British Medical Association) and W.K. Reid at DES, 13 Dec. 1973 (all in ED 188/322); letter from R. Cattran at DHSS to E.B. Granshaw at DES dated 6 June 1973, in ED 207/53.

77 Letter to DES from Royal College of Veterinary Surgeons dated 27 Feb. 1974 and J.H. Thompson's reply to Mr Porter, Secretary and Registrar of the RCVS, 5 Mar. 1974, in National Archives, ED 188/323.

78 House of Lords, *Second Special Report from the Select Committee on the Anti-Discrimination Bill*, paras. 16–21, pp. 6–8. The Committee confessed that it had 'found it difficult to establish the truth in this matter' (p. 6).

79 National Archives, ED 188/322.

80 Correspondence, Sir William Pile to Sir Kenneth Berrill (Chair of UGC) and Professor Hugh Robson (CVCP), 17 Sept. 1973; see also notes of meeting at Elizabeth House (9 Nov. 1973) between DES officials and representatives of the UGC and CVCP. In National Archives, ED 188/322.

81 Correspondence between J.H. Thompson at the DES and Mr Porter, Secretary and Registrar of the Royal College of Veterinary Surgeons, Feb. and Mar. 1974, in National Archives, ED 188/323.

82 Correspondence, Margaret Thatcher to Robert Carr, 5 July 1973, in National Archives, ED 188/322.

83 Correspondence and comments on consultative document, 'Equal opportunities for men and women; government proposals for legislation', in National Archives, ED 188/322, 323, 324.

84 Pauline Hunt (on behalf of the North Staffordshire WEA), letter to DES dated 15 Nov. 1973; Catherine Belsey, Fellow and Tutor at New Hall, Cambridge, letter to DES dated 10 Oct. 1973; both in National Archives, ED 188/322

85 Correspondence in National Archives, ED 188/323.

86 Ibid.

87 See, for instance, J.H. Thompson, letters to Registrar of Oxford University, Vice-Chancellor of Cambridge, 8 Jan. 1974, in National Archives, ED 188/324.

88 G.E. Dudman to W.K. Reid, 19 Dec. 1973, in ED 188/324.

89 G.E. Dudman, note, Feb. 1974, ED 188/324.

90 J.H. Thompson to Mrs Douglas, 14 May 1974, in National Archives, ED 188/325. See also Thompson's memorandum on the subject dated 20 May 1974 in the same file, where he notes that the section in the draft legislation applying to universities 'is phrased in quite a gentlemanly fashion'; indeed, in its concluding section it was 'even obscure'. He emphasized again that there were 'obvious inconsistencies' in requiring universities to provide equal facilities for men and women and at the same time preserving single-sex institutions, since 'the latter will make it impossible for Oxford and Cambridge to comply with the former'. There remained the problems of how to 'protect' single-sex fellowships against the equality provisions for employment, and the 'new' problem of safeguarding men's colleges which had

risked the 'experimental' admission of a few women from the legislation designed to make 'quotas' illegal.

91 G.J. Warnock, 'The co-residence question', *The American Oxonian*, Apr. 1976, vol. LXIII, no. 2, p. 173.
92 University Grants Committee, *Returns from Universities and University Colleges in receipt of Treasury Grant, Academic Year 1959/60*, Cmnd 1489, London: HMSO 1961.
93 University Grants Committee, *Returns from Universities and University Colleges in receipt of Treasury Grant for Academic Year 1965/6*, Cmnd 3586, London: HMSO, 1967; see also volume in same series for academic year 1966/7; University Grants Committee, Department of Education and Science Series, *Statistics of Education 1968*, vol. 6: Universities, London: HMSO, 1970, p. viii.
94 E. Rudd and S. Hatch, *Graduate Study and After*, London: Weidenfeld, 1968.
95 R. Keith Kelsall, Anne Poole and Annette Kuhn, *Six Years After: first report on a national follow-up survey of ten thousand graduates of British universities in 1960*, Sheffield: Higher Education Research Unit, Department of Sociological Studies, 1970; R.K. Kelsall, A. Poole and A. Kuhn (eds), *Graduates: the sociology of an elite*, London: Methuen, 1972.
96 Anne Poole, 'Captives by choice?', in Kelsall *et al.*, *Graduates*, p. 140 and *passim*; Judith Hubback, *Wives Who Went to College*, London: Heinemann, 1957; Constance E. Arregger, *Graduate Women at Work*, Newcastle upon Tyne: Oriel Press, 1966.
97 Kelsall, *Graduates*, p. 168.
98 Ibid., p. 164.
99 Ibid., p. 144.
100 Ibid.; see, for instance, pp. 158–62, 169.
101 Ibid., p. 162.
102 Ibid., p. 163.
103 Poole may have been right here. In their study of the life histories of graduates of Girton College, Cambridge, Pat Thane and her co-researchers, Kate Perry and Amy Erickson, found that the cohort of women from the 1960s were most likely to express frustration with their options in life, and more likely than their predecessors and those who followed them to identify with feminism. See P. Thane, 'Girton graduates: earning and learning, 1920s–1980s', *Women's History Review*, 2004, vol. 13, no. 3, 357.
104 On the concern with 'wastage' of women teachers see R.K. Kelsall's study, funded by the Nuffield Foundation and published by the Ministry of Education, *Women and Teaching*, London: HMSO, 1963; M. Collins (ed.), *Women Graduates and the Teaching Profession: report of a working party of the British Federation of University Women*, Manchester: Manchester University Press, 1964.
105 University Grants Committee, *First Employment of University Graduates, 1961/62*, London: HMSO, 1963, p. 3.
106 Ibid., p. 4.
107 Ibid., p. 5.
108 University Grants Committee, *First Employment of University Graduates, 1965/66*, London: HMSO, 1967, p. 6, fig. 2.
109 Sir Maurice Dean, 52nd Meeting of Cambridge Women's Appointment Board, 13 Nov. 1965, CWAB Archives in Cambridge University Library, APTB 5/73–75.
110 Maureen Woodhall, 'The economic returns to investment in women's education', *Higher Education*, 1973, no. 2, 275–300.

111 Ibid. The phrase 'psychic income' is used in the abstract of the article, on p. 275, and again on p. 295.

112 Ibid., p. 297. For detail on the constraints faced by female graduates of the University of Liverpool in the postwar years see S. Aiston, 'A good job for a girl? the career biographies of women graduates of the University of Liverpool post 1945', *Twentieth Century British History*, 2004, vol. 15, no. 4, 361–87. For careers of female graduates of the University of Glasgow see J. Wakeling, 'University Women: origins, experiences and destinations at Glasgow University 1939–1987', PhD thesis, University of Glasgow 1998.

113 Crompton and Sanderson, *Gendered Jobs and Social Change*, esp. pp. 54–64.

114 Ibid., p. 58.

115 Author's interview with Carolyn Morris, formerly Robb, 4 Dec. 2003. Sarah Aiston's paper, '"A woman's place . . .": male representations of university women in the student press of the University of Liverpool, 1944–1979', has useful material on gender differentiation in employers' advertisements in student newspapers during the 1960s. She suggests that women were offered 'jobs', men 'careers'. This paper is forthcoming in *Women's Historical Review*, 2005.

116 Ruth Miller, 'Equality: the law is not all that needs changing', *The Times*, 2 May 1975.

117 Central Services Unit for Careers and Appointments Services, *University Graduates 1976: some details of first destination and employment*, p. 3.

118 University Grants Committee, *Universities Statistical Review, vol. 2: first destinations of university graduates*, 1984/5, p. 7; 1985/6, p. 7.

119 Department of Education and Science, 'First known destinations of first degree graduates from institutions in Great Britain, 1983–1990', Government Statistical Service, *Statistical Bulletin*, Mar. 1992, 4/92, Charts 3 and 4.

120 UGC, *Universities Statistical Review, vol. 2, First Destinations of University Graduates*, 1992/3, p. 9.

121 Higher Education Statistics Agency (HESA), *First Destination of Students Leaving Higher Education Institutions, 1994/95*, p. 7.

122 HESA, *First Destination of Students . . . 2000/01*, p. 10.

123 In 1970 26 per cent of students entering medical schools in Great Britain were female; in 1989, 49 per cent. For a useful discussion of some of the implications of this 'feminization' for the profession, see Mary Ann Elston, 'Women doctors in a changing profession: the case of Britain', in E. Riska and K. Wegan (eds), *Gender, Work and Medicine*, London: Sage, 1993, pp. 27–61. Over the last decade the proportion of women winning places in medical schools has risen steadily: in 2004 they represented 61 per cent of the intake in the UK (*The Times*, 28 June 2004, p. 20).

124 'The gender pay gap must go', *New Statesman*, 1 Nov. 1999; Alice O'Keeffe, 'Equality at work: it's a tough call – but should she have to make it?' *The Observer*, 11 Jan. 2004, p. 20.

125 Kate Purcell, 'Exploring the gender pay gap: equal opportunities for unequal outcomes?', Women and Equality Unit, Gender Research Forum, 8 Nov. 2002.

126 National Union of Students, Equal pay campaign, http://nusonline.co.uk.

127 Thane, 'Girton graduates', esp. pp. 358–60.

6 Siege mentalities

1 A chapter on higher education in Ray Strachey's *The Cause*, London: Bell, 1928, for instance, was titled 'The siege of Cambridge'. See also E. Moberly Bell's history of women's struggle for medical education, *Storming the Citadel: the rise of the woman doctor*, London: Constable, 1953.

2 Mary Beard, 'Pull as archer, in lbs', *London Review of Books*, 5 Sept. 1996, pp. 23–4 (review of E. Shils and C. Blacker, *Cambridge Women: twelve portraits*, Cambridge: Cambridge University Press, 1996).

3 Beard, 'Pull as archer', p. 23.

4 W. Holtby, 'Should women go to Oxford?', *News Chronicle*, 2 Feb. 1934.

5 A. Tennyson, *The Princess: a medley*, 1847, edition used here, London: King, 1876; J. Killham, *Tennyson and 'The Princess': reflections of an age*, London: Athlone Press, 1958.

6 A performance of *The Princess* was staged in Girton College, Cambridge, in February 1891 (see *Girton Review*, April 1891, and photographs in Girton College Archives). Students at Royal Holloway College staged a performance in June 1898 (photographs in Archives, Royal Holloway and Bedford New College). For a history of the Girls' Day School Trust (formerly Girls' Public Day School Trust), see J. Kamm, *Indicative Past: 100 years of the Girls' Public Day School Trust*, London: Allen and Unwin, 1971.

7 P. Thomson, *The Victorian Heroine: a changing ideal, 1837–1873*, London: Oxford University Press, 1956, p. 60; K. Millett, *Sexual Politics*, first published in 1969, this edition, London: Virago, 1977, p. 79.

8 There is an interesting discussion of the poem by Carol Christ in 'Victorian masculinity and the Angel in the House', in M. Vicinus (ed.), *A Widening Sphere: changing roles of Victorian women*, Bloomington: Indiana University Press, 1977.

9 W.S. Gilbert, *Princess Ida, or Castle Adamant*, in *The Savoy Operas*, London: Macmillan, 1927.

10 Ibid., p. 278.

11 R. McWilliams-Tullberg, *Women at Cambridge*, first published in 1975, this edition, Cambridge: Cambridge University Press, 1998, pp. 116, 165, plate 7.

12 Ibid. A photograph of the damaged gates is reproduced in A. Phillips (ed.), *A Newnham Anthology*, Cambridge: Newnham College, 1979.

13 A.D. Godley, 'The 1713 against Newnham', in *Lyra Frivola*, London: Methuen, 1899.

14 See Harold Macmillan, quoted in J. Morris (ed.), *The Oxford Book of Oxford*, Oxford: Oxford University Press, 1978: 'There were no women. Ours was an entirely masculine, almost monastic, society. We knew of course that there were women's colleges with women students. But we were not conscious of either' (p. 361).

15 C. Dyhouse, *No Distinction of Sex? Women in British universities, 1870–1939*, London: UCL Press, 1995, pp. 239–40.

16 V. Brittain, *The Women at Oxford: a fragment of history*, London: Harrap, 1960, p. 171.

17 C. Hobhouse, *Oxford As It Was, and As It Is Today*, London: Batsford, 1939.

18 Ibid., p. 102.

19 V. Woolf, *A Room of One's Own*, first published in 1929, this edition, Oxford: Oxford University Press, 1998.

20 Ibid., pp. 21–2.

21 Hobhouse, *Oxford As It Was*, p. 102.

22 K. Briant, *Oxford Unlimited*, London: Michael Joseph, 1937.

23 Ibid., p. 126.

24 Ibid., p. 133.

25 K. Thomas, 'College life, 1945–1970', in B. Harrison (ed.), *The History of the University of Oxford, vol. VIII, the twentieth century*, Oxford: Clarendon Press, 1994, p. 201.

26 Tennyson, *The Princess*, pp. 7, 9.

27 Dyhouse, *No Distinction of Sex?*, p. 216.

28 Thomas, 'College life', p. 201.

29 H. Lind, 'In loco parentis?', *Cherwell*, 11 Nov. 1961, p. 8.

30 Ibid.

31 J. Howarth, 'Women', in Harrison (ed.), *History of the University of Oxford*, p. 362. See also Dilys Powell, 'What every woman thinks', *Isis*, 4 June 1924, p. 13.

32 A. Bavin, 'The second class sex', *New Statesman*, 28 Apr. 1961, p. 669.

33 K. McLeod, 'Women in Oxford', *Isis*, 30 May 1962, p. 9; quoted by Howarth, 'Women', p. 374.

34 'Cherwell demands . . . this Great Reform Bill', *Cherwell*, 2 Nov. 1963, p. 7.

35 *Cherwell*, 21 Oct. 1964, p. 1.

36 'Cherwell demands . . .'

37 M. Walker, 'Longer hours in bird cages', *Cherwell*, 4 Mar. 1964, p. 3.

38 R. Chesshyre, 'Roedean third formers', *Cherwell*, 16 Feb. 1963, p. 6.

39 B. Moore, 'The simplest solution', *Cherwell*, 28 Apr. 1962, pp. 6–7.

40 S. Sedgwick Jell, 'Storming the bastion of reaction: coeducation', *Isis*, 25 Oct. 1970, pp. 13–15.

41 By 1970 nineteen JCRs in Oxford were alleged to have declared in favour of coresidence. See 'Co-education is favoured by undergraduates', *Oxford Times*, 29 May 1970 (press cuttings in University Registry Files, UR6/W/12/1, Oxford University Archives).

42 Dyhouse, *No Distinction of Sex?*

43 For Queen Elizabeth College, see N. Marsh, *The History of Queen Elizabeth College*, London: King's College, 1986.

44 J. Sondheimer, *Castle Adamant in Hampstead: a history of Westfield College 1882–1982*, London: Westfield College, 1983.

45 *Times Education Supplement*, 30 Nov. 1962.

46 G.E.M. de Ste Croix, 'The admission of women to New College', *Oxford Magazine*, 15 Oct. 1964, pp. 4–7.

47 C. Dalton, 'The history of women at New College', in *Ten Years of Women at New College: a commemorative programme*, Oxford: New College, 1990.

48 University of Oxford, Verbatim Report of Debate on CoResidence in Congregation, 30 May 1972, Supplement 3 to no. 3510 of the *Oxford University Gazette*, 7 June 1972, pp. 1058–9.

49 I. Bradley, 'Women breach Oxford defences', *Times Higher Education Supplement*, 25 Oct. 1974.

50 Ibid.

51 J.R. Lucas of Merton College in a debate on coresidence, in Oxford's Congregation in 1977, *Oxford University Gazette*, 16 Mar. 1977, Supplement 2 to no. 3691, p. 592.

52 The 'rogue' college in Oxford was University College: for the defence of its position see A.D. Stokes' paper, 'Coresidence' (1977), copy in Somerville College Archives,

Coresidence File. In Cambridge, similar arguments were put forward by Alan Cottrell, Master of Jesus College, in a letter to Edward Miller, Master of Fitzwilliam College and Chairman of the Colleges' Standing Consultative Committee on Equal Opportunities for Men and Women, 20 May 1975. (Copies distributed to all Heads of Colleges, this copy by courtesy of Peter Glazebrook, Vice Master of Jesus College).

53 A. Sampson, *The Changing Anatomy of Britain*, London: Hodder and Stoughton, 1982, p. 145.

54 J. Hart, 'Women at Oxford since the advent of mixed colleges', *Oxford Review of Education*, 1989, vol. 15, no. 3, 217.

55 Opposition to the idea of a mixed student union had been strong in several universities before the 1960s. For Manchester, see I. Gregory, *In Memory of Burlington Street, an appreciation of the Manchester University Unions 1861–1957*, Manchester: Manchester University Union, 1958, especially chapter 8, 'Lock the doors and keep the women out'.

56 'Queen Margaret College', Special Number of *Pass It On* (the magazine of the Women's Educational Union), Nov. 1935, vol. XV, no. 1. In Glasgow University Archives, DC 233/2/21/13.

57 G. Warner, *Conquering by Degrees: Glasgow University Union, a centenary history 1885–1985*, Glasgow: Glasgow University Union, 1985, p. 192.

58 M. Moss, J. Munro Forbes and R. Trainor, *University, City and State: the University of Glasgow since 1870*, Edinburgh: Edinburgh University Press for the University of Glasgow, 2000, p. 289.

59 Glasgow University Archives, Papers of Dominic D'Angelo, DC 168 1/2. See also newspaper cuttings in DC 168 1/1.

60 Discipline Books and Correspondence in Woolton Hall, entry in Discipline Book dated 13 Feb. 1985.

61 S. Griffiths, 'Women set to tame the chaps', *Times Higher Education Supplement*, 23 Mar. 1990, see also various press cuttings in Woolton Hall Archive.

62 Ibid.

63 F. Hunt and C. Barker, *Women at Cambridge: a brief history*, Cambridge: Cambridge University Press, 1998, p. 30.

64 At the time of writing, Aberdare Hall in Cardiff admits only women students. Ashburne Hall in Manchester accepts only female undergraduates but has places for postgraduates of both sexes. St Mary's College, Durham opened its doors to male students for the first time in 2005.

65 Howarth, 'Women', p. 375.

66 P. Ady, 'Mixed education and the women's colleges', *Oxford Magazine*, 3 Dec. 1964, pp. 138–40; A. Pirie, 'Women for New College', *Oxford Magazine*, 6 May 1965, p. 321; Letter from women dons welcoming New College initiative in *The Observer*, 12 July 1964; J. Hart, 'Some observations on the Report of the Working Party on Coresidence', 8 May 1971, in LMH Archives, Coresidence File.

67 P. Adams, *Somerville for Women: an Oxford College 1879–1993*, Oxford: Oxford University Press, 1996, ch. 16.

68 E. Llewellyn Smith, 'Does Oxford want a women's college?', *Oxford Magazine*, Michaelmas 1993, no. 97; V. Grove, 'Somerville girls', *Life and Times*, 7 Feb. 1992; R. Miles, 'First class citizens?', *Telegraph Magazine*, 18 Nov. 1995, pp. 28–31; L. Purves, 'Quiet – women at work', *The Times*, 9 Nov. 1994; N. Taylor, 'Separate sphere', *Guardian Higher*, 22 Feb. 2000.

69 Adams, *Somerville for Women*, pp. 339–51. See also Coresidence File, Somerville College Archives.

70 For Cambridge, for instance, see Survey Committee of the Cambridge University Women's Action Group, *Forty Years On . . . Report on the Numbers and Status of Academic Women in the University of Cambridge*, Cambridge, 1988; A. Spurling, *Report of the Women in Higher Education Research Project, 1988–1990*, Cambridge: King's College, May 1990. For both Oxford and Cambridge see Report of the Hansard Society Commission, *Women at the Top*, Jan. 1990.

7 Women students and the London medical schools, 1914–1939: the anatomy of a masculine culture

1 E. Moberly Bell, *Storming the Citadel: the rise of the woman doctor*, London: Constable, 1973, p. 175.

2 See the arguments of M. Gilchrist in *Surgo* (March 1948), discussed in C. Dyhouse, *No Distinction of Sex? Women in British universities, 1870–1939*, London: UCL Press, 1995, p. 44.

3 University of London, *Report of Subcommittee of the Academic Council on Medical Education of Women in London*, Part I, 1916, p. 4.

4 Dyhouse, *No Distinction of Sex?*, p. 12 and *passim*.

5 University of London, *Report . . . on Medical Education of Women in London*, p. 5.

6 Ibid., p. 4.

7 Ibid., p. 5.

8 University of London, *Report . . . on Medical Education of Women in London*, Part II, 1917, p. 7.

9 Ibid., pp. 5–8.

10 Ibid., pp. 7–8.

11 University of London, *Conference on Medical Education of Women in London, 30 Jan. 1917, Report of Proceedings*, 1917 (a copy of this Report has been bound in with the Committee Minutes, 1914–17, of St George's Hospital Medical School) (Archives, St George's Hospital).

12 St George's Hospital Medical School, Committee Minutes, 1914–17 (see Minutes of Meeting held on 12 Apr. 1915).

13 St George's Hospital Medical School, Student Register, vols 9 (1902–28) and 10 (1919–36).

14 R.J. Minney, *The Two Pillars of Charing Cross: the story of a famous hospital*, London: Cassell, 1967, p. 153.

15 *Charing Cross Hospital Gazette*, March 1917, vol. XVIII, no. 1. See Dean's Report, p. 11.

16 J.P. Margoliouth, 'More opportunities of training for women', *Oxford Times*, 23 Sept. 1916. See also W.J. Fenton's foreword to Emily L.B. Forster, *How to Become a Woman Doctor*, London: Charles Griffin & Co., 1918.

17 Quoted in J.G. Humble and P. Hansell, *Westminster Hospital, 1716–1974*, London: Pitman Medical Publishing, 1966, p. 104.

18 James Garner, 'Sex and Sensibility: the admission of women to St Mary's Hospital Medical School', unpublished dissertation for Intercalated BSc Course, Wellcome Institute for the History of Medicine, 1994, pp. 46–57.

19 See typescript summary of numbers of women admitted to St Mary's Hospital Medical School, 1116–25, in St Mary's Hospital Archives (MS/AD48/1).

20 Westminster Medical School Student Register, 1890–1932, in Archives, Chelsea and Westminster Hospital.

21 London Hospital Medical College, House Committee Minutes, 1916–18, Report of meeting on 18 May 1918 (London Hospital Archives).

22 Ibid., Report of meeting on 10 June 1918.

23 Dorothy Russell's estimate supplied to Miss Rew of the Medical Women's Federation (28.4.1928), in MWF Co-education File, 1928–31, Contemporary Medical Archives Centre (CMAC) at the Wellcome Institute for the History of Medicine.

24 London Hospital Medical College, Minute Book, vol. 10, p. 212, reported on 27 May 1918 (Archives, the London Hospital).

25 University of London, *Report . . . on Medical Education of Women in London*, Part II, 1917, p. 6.

26 H. Willoughby Lyle, *King's and some King's Men: being a record of the Medical Department of King's College London from 1830–1909 and of King's College Hospital Medical School from 1909–1934*, London: Oxford University Press, 1935, p. 33.

27 W.R. Merrington, *University College Hospital and its Medical School: a history*, London: Heinemann, 1976, p. 237.

28 University of London, *Conference on Medical Education of Women in London*, 1917, p. 3.

29 Ibid., p. 2.

30 Ibid.

31 Merrington, *University College Hospital*, pp. 237–9.

32 Ibid.

33 London Hospital Medical College Minute Book, vol. 10, Report of meeting on 23 Mar. 1920.

34 London Hospital Medical School, House Committee Minute Book, Meeting on 31 Oct. 1921 (p. 280); the 'Report of the Committee Appointed to Collect Evidence as to the Effect which the Admission of Women Students has had on the Welfare of the College' is bound in with these Minutes (London Hospital Archives).

35 London Hospital Medical School, House Committee Minutes, Report of meeting 9 Jan. 1922. The letter of protest from Students and Residents, dated 2 Jan. 1922, is bound in with these Minutes. Gladys Wauchope's own account of these events is given in her autobiography, *The Story of A Woman Physician*, Bristol: John Wright and Sons, 1963, pp. 46–52.

36 London Hospital Medical College, House Committee Minutes, Report of Meeting on 12 Feb. 1923.

37 Ibid., entry dated 26 Feb. 1923.

38 London Hospital Medical College Minute Book, vol. 12, entry dated 16 June 1923.

39 Ibid., entry dated 22 June 1925.

40 Garner, 'Sex and Sensibility'.

41 Contemporary Medical Archives Centre (CMAC) (SA/MWF/C.16).

42 Garner, 'Sex and Sensibility', pp. 84–8. Sir Almroth Wright was the author of *The Unexpurgated Case Against Woman Suffrage*, London: Constable, 1913, and supposedly the model for George Bernard Shaw's Sir Colenso Ridgeon in *The Doctor's Dilemma* (1906).

43 The petition (dated 12 March 1924) is preserved in the Archives of St Mary's Hospital (MS/AD46).

44 A copy of this counter-petition is preserved in CMAC (SA/MWF/C.16).

45 Copies of this Memorandum, dated Apr. 1924, in CMAC (SA/MWF/C.16).

46 Kathleen Norton, interview with author, 18 Sept. 1996.

47 Minutes of Meeting of Women Students addressed by Dr C.M. Wilson in library of St Mary's Hospital, 22 May 1924 (CMAC, SA/MWF/C.16).

48 Ibid.

49 M. Herford to C.M. Wilson, 2 June 1924 (CMAC, SA/MWF/C.16).

50 C.M. Wilson to M. Herford, 13 June 1924 (CMAC, SA/MWF/C.16).

51 Joan Ross to Chairman of Council of MWF, 2 July 1924 (CMAC, SA/MWF/C.16).

52 King's College Hospital, Minutes of the Medical Board 1926–37, report of meeting on 29 Nov. 1927 (Archives, King's College, KH/MB/M9).

53 Ibid., Report of Special Meeting on 28 Feb. 1928.

54 University of London, *Report of Subcommittee appointed to Consider the Present Position of Facilities for the Medical Education of Women in London*, 1923 (Senate Minutes, 1922–3, ST 2/2/39, pp. 16–17).

55 Ibid.

56 University of London, *Report . . . on the Medical Education of Women Undergraduates*, 1929 (ST 2/2/45, pp. 58–63).

57 Ibid., p. 63.

58 King's College Hospital, Minutes of Medical Board, 19 Feb. 1929, 20 Dec. 1929, Minutes of Committee of Management, 1929–32 (KH/CM/M22), pp. 128, 171, 177, 184.

59 Dale Spender, *Time and Tide Wait for No Man*, London: Pandora Press, 1984, pp. 242–55.

60 Press Cuttings for 17 Oct. 1924, Medical Women, vol. 6, part II, 1924–6, Archives, Royal Free Hospital.

61 *The Times*, 30 Mar. 1928. See Medical Women Press Cuttings, vol. 7, part I (Archives, Royal Free Hospital), *passim*. There was voluminous press coverage of these issues.

62 Joint Committee on Women in the Service of Hospitals, Office of NUSEC, 'Memorandum urging equal opportunities for women with men in the medical services in London', 1928 (CMAC, SA/MWF).

63 See, for instance, letters to Dr Kelynack from M. Kettle (8 Oct. 1924) and E. Casson (21 Oct. 1924) in CMAC (SA/MWF/C.15).

64 M.N. Kettle to Louisa Martindale, n.d. (Oct. 1924?), CMAC (SA/MWF/C.15).

65 MWF, Minutes of Council and Annual General Meetings, 1924–30, Report of meeting 11–12 May 1928 (pp. 187–9), CMAC.

66 MWF Co-education Files, Minutes of (Provisional) Committee on Co-education, report of meeting on 10 July 1928 (CMAC, SA/MWF/A4/2).

67 Keren Parkes to V. Kelynack, 30 June 1928, MWF Coeducation Files (CMAC, SA/MWF/A4/2).

68 C. Chisholm to V. Kelynack, 3 July 1928 (CMAC, SA/MWF/A4/2).

69 Report of meeting on 10 July 1928 (CMAC, SA/MWF/A4/2).

70 Report of meeting on 7 Feb. 1928 (CMAC, SA/MWF/A4/2).

71 Prof. J. Ryle to V. Kelynack, 15 Apr. 1937 (MWF Coeducation File, 1928–38, CMAC, SA/MWF/A4/2).

72 MWF, Minutes of Council and Annual General Meetings, 1924–30, 11–12 May 1928, pp. 187–9 (CMAC).

73 The volumes of press cuttings relating to medical women housed in the Royal Free Hospital Archives are invaluable here. On the attitudes of the popular press to gender issues more generally, see A. Bingham, *Gender, Modernity and the Popular Press in Interwar Britain*, Oxford: Oxford University Press, 2004.

74 See (for instance) C. Patrick Thomson, 'Britain's new sex war in the medical world

– can the women push open the door?', *The Sphere*, 20 Aug. 1929; *The Sunday Graphic*, 25 Mar. 1928.

75 *Birmingham Post*, 7 Dec. 1928.

76 *Northern Telegraph*, 25 Oct. 1924.

77 University of London, *Report of Committee on Medical Education*, 1929, p. 63.

78 *Guy's Hospital Gazette*, 29 Nov. 1930, vol. XLIV, no. 1105, p. 437.

79 *Guy's Hospital Gazette*, 11 Feb. 1939, vol. LIII, no. 1319, p. 39.

80 M.R. Higonnet, J. Jenson, S. Michel and M. Collins Weitz (eds), *Behind The Lines: gender and the two world wars*, New Haven, CT: Yale University Press, 1987; S. Kingsley Kent, *Making Peace: the reconstruction of gender in interwar Britain*, Princeton NJ: Princeton University Press, 1993.

81 Adrian Bingham, in *Gender, Modernity and the Popular Press*, argues that attitudes to gender reflected in popular newspapers of the period were often much more liberal than some historians have assumed.

82 I. Mann, *The Chase*, 1972 (typescript autobiography in Archives of St Mary's Hospital, London), p. 154.

83 C. Heward, *Making a Man of Him: parents and their sons' education at an English public school, 1929–50*, London: Routledge, 1988. It is worth reading Warwick Deeping's novel, *Sorrell and Son*, London: Cassell, 1925, for insights into paternal solicitude for a son's medical career and the troubled nature of masculine professional identity in the interwar years.

84 Merrington, *University College Hospital*, pp. 238–9.

85 R.T. Hinde, 'Women medical students', *Guy's Hospital Gazette*, 11 Mar. 1939, vol. LIII, no. 1321, pp. 85–6.

86 *Guy's Hospital Gazette*, 29 Nov. 1930, vol. XLIV, no. 1105, p. 437.

87 M. Littlewood, 'Makers of men: the anti-feminist backlash of the National Association of Schoolmasters in the 1920s and 1930s', *Trouble and Strife*, Spring 1985, no. 5, p. 27.

88 Heward, *Making a Man of Him*.

89 There are numerous examples. See for instance 'Daddy' Rowlands, mentioned in Wauchope, *The Story of A Woman Physician*, p. 49, or 'Daddy' Craig, in I. Hutton, *Memories of a Doctor in War and Peace*, London: Heinemann, 1960, p. 30.

90 F.M. Kenyon (later Taylor), *Memories* (unpublished typescript), p. 164. My thanks to Frances Kenyon's granddaughter, Mary Clare Martin, for making these, and her scrapbook and photograph albums, available to me.

91 Dame Josephine Barnes, interview with author, January 1997.

92 Garner, 'Sex and Sensibility', p. 81.

93 A. Allport 'History of the Rugby Football Club', in L.G. Housden (ed.), *Guy's Hospital Gazette: commemoration of the bicentenary of the hospital and of the centenary of the medical school, 1725–1925*, London: Ash and Co., 1925.

94 Ibid., pp. 168, 171.

95 J. Bourke, *Dismembering the Male: men's bodies, Britain and the Great War*, London: Reaktion Books, 1996, p. 196.

96 *Daily Mirror*, 18 Mar. 1928.

97 Kenyon, *Memories*.

98 *The Broad Way* (Westminster Hospital Gazette), Spring 1927, p. 144.

99 D. Cameron, *Feminism and Linguistic Theory*, London: Macmillan, 1985, pp. 155–6.

100 Dyhouse, *No Distinction of Sex?*, pp. 205–6.

101 See Press Cuttings, Medical Women, vol. 5 (1915–20) in the Archives of the Royal

Free Hospital, for a useful collection of newspaper articles discussing rowing and the 'femininity' of 'oarswomen'. See also Dyhouse, *No Distinction of Sex?*, pp. 202–3.

102 M. Burton Nelson, *The Stronger Women Get, the More Men Love Football*, London: The Women's Press, 1996.

103 H. Becker, B. Geer, E. Hughes and A. Strauss, *Boys In White: student culture in Medical School*, Chicago: University of Chicago Press, 1961, p. 3.

104 Ibid., p. 324.

8 'Apostates' and 'Uncle Toms': challenges to separatism in the women's college

1 Bedford College, Transcript of discussion in Council, July 1962 (Archives, Royal Holloway and Bedford New College, BC AR/385/9/4).

2 C. Dyhouse, *No Distinction of Sex? women in British universities 1870–1939*, London: UCL Press, 1995.

3 *University Degrees for Women: report of a conference convened by the Governors of the Royal Holloway College and held at the House of the Society of Arts on Saturday, 4th December 1897*, London: Spottiswode and Co., 1898; G. Sutherland, 'The plainest principles of justice: the University of London and the higher education of women', in F.M.L. Thompson (ed.), *The University of London and the World of Learning, 1836–1986*, London: Hambledon Press, 1990.

4 Sutherland, 'The plainest principles', p. 45.

5 M.J. Tuke, *A History of Bedford College for Women, 1849–1937*, Oxford: Oxford University Press, 1939, pp. 99–113.

6 N.B. Harte, *The Admission of Women to University College, London: a centenary lecture*, London: University College London, 1979, p. 3.

7 C. Callis, 'Sexual apartheid lingers on', *Stop Press*, 4 Feb. 1972, p. 7.

8 For the origins of this phrase, see Chapter 6 above.

9 M. Tuke, *Autobiographical Notes*, typescript in Newnham College Archives, n.d., p. 97.

10 See C. Dyhouse, 'The British Federation of University Women and the status of women in universities, 1907–1939', *Women's History Review*, 1995, vol. 4, pp. 476–7.

11 Tuke, *History of Bedford College for Women*, pp. 201–8.

12 N. Marsh, *The History of Queen Elizabeth College*, London: King's College, 1986, pp. 41–78; Dyhouse, *No Distinction of Sex?*, pp. 45–6.

13 *Report of the Committee appointed by the Governors to consider the Post-War Policy of the Royal Holloway College* (Royal Holloway and Bedford New College Archives, 1944).

14 See 'Minutes of Post-War Policy Committee' (RHBNC Archives, GB/203).

15 *Report of Committee on Post-War Policy*, J.R. Bacon's 'Minute of Dissent on Co-education', pp. 13–16.

16 Ibid., pp. 5–7.

17 When Dr Marjorie Williamson took over from Dr Edith Batho as Principal in 1962 she confessed herself 'staggered at just how old fashioned [the college] had become'. See C. Bingham, *The History of Royal Holloway College, 1886–1986*, London: Constable, 1987, p. 218.

18 Report of Academic Board to Council, 6 Jan. 1959, in Minutes of Council, 20 Jan. 1959, RHBNC Archives. See also 'Paper on difficulties of science departments',

ibid., 12/B, p. 539, and 'Statement of the position with regard to admission of men undergraduates to the College', 12/C, p. 542.

19 Sir Douglas Logan, Principal of the University of London, agreed to promote a Private Bill to enable the College to admit male students in the Parliamentary Session 1961–2. The Royal Holloway College Act received Royal Assent in May 1962 (RHBNC Archives, GB/1014/2).

20 C. Bingham, *The History of Royal Holloway College, 1886–1986*, London: Constable, 1987, pp. 214, 219.

21 See remark made by Mr Claughton at a meeting of the Post-War Policy Committee, 20 June 1944 ('Minutes of Post-War Policy Committee Meeting', RHC/ GB/203/2, RHBNC Archive).

22 Westfield College, 'Minutes of Council', 24 Oct. 1956 (Archives, Queen Mary and Westfield College); Bedford College, 'Admission of men: secretary's correspondence with Academic Board and Council', 1956–62 (BC AR/385/9/4), entry for 28 May 1956 (RHBNC Archives).

23 'Admission of Male Undergraduates to Women's Colleges', National Archives, UGC 7/811 (see correspondence between D. Logan and Sir Keith Murray, 11 Mar. 1958, also notes of meeting between UGC and representatives of Court and Senate of University of London, 19 Apr. 1956, p. 6).

24 Westfield College, 'Minutes of Council', 28 Nov. 1956.

25 Correspondence between Sir Douglas Logan and Sir Keith Murray, 10 Feb. 1958, in PRO/UGC 7/811.

26 'Memorandum by the Chairman of Council concerning future developments at Westfield College', Westfield College, Council Minutes, 27 Feb. 1963 (Archives, Queen Mary Westfield College).

27 Ibid., p. 4.

28 J. Sondheimer, *Castle Adamant in Hampstead: a history of Westfield College, 1882–1982*, London: Westfield College, 1983, pp. 142–4, tells the general story, and more details can be gleaned from the archival sources mentioned above.

29 Bedford College, 'Admission of men: secretary's correspondence', Reports of meetings of Academic Board on 5 Dec. 1956, 15 Jan. 1957, 12 Feb. 1957, 'Letter from Joint Faculties', 11 Mar. 1957, 'Principal's memorandum for Academic Board', 15 Jan. 1957 (RHBNC Archives, BC AR/385/9/4).

30 Ibid., Correspondence between Sir Douglas Logan and Council of Bedford College, Dec. 1960–Jan. 1961.

31 Members of the Academic Board, 'Memorandum on the admission of men undergraduates to the College', 6 Mar. 1962 (RHBNC Archives, BC AR/385/9/4).

32 Ibid., p. 2. See also 'Proposal in favour of admitting men undergraduates to Bedford College', n.d. (1963?), signed by fifteen members of Academic Board, p. 5 (RHBNC Archives, BC/GB/173).

33 'Memorandum on the admission of men', p. 4.

34 'Memorandum on the admission of men', p. 5.

35 For individual views of Heads of Department see collection of replies to the principal on the question of whether the issue of admitting male undergraduates should be re-opened, Mar. to May 1962 (RHBNC Archives, BC/AR/385/9/4); see also Memorandum signed by ten members of staff, 'Proposed admission of men undergraduates: reasons for considering the change inimical to the purposes of the College', 12 Mar. 1963 (RHBNC Archives, BC/GB/173).

36 'Proposed admission of men undergraduates: reasons for considering the change inimical', pp. 9–11.

37 Ibid., pp. 8, 14.

38 Ibid., p. 16.

39 'Minutes of Discussion', Bedford College Council, July 1962; 'Memorandum of Bedford College Union Society submitted to Robbins Committee', paras. 34–36; B.C. King and O.R. McGregor, 'The admission of men undergraduates' (Memorandum commenting on discussion in Council), July 1962, pp. 1–3 (RHBNC Archives, BC/AR/385/9/4).

40 'Minutes of Discussion', Bedford College Council, July 1962. McGregor almost certainly compiled Appendix 1, 'The statistical data' attached to 'Proposal in favour of admitting men' (GB/BC/173).

41 L. Bentley, *Educating Women: a pictorial history of Bedford College, University of London, 1849–1985*, Surrey: Alma Publishers, 1991, p. 77. This account mentions the 'bitter skirmishes' around the college's decision to go mixed but gives no detail. Bentley's history was written following the (again, highly controversial) 'merger' of Bedford with Royal Holloway College and its 'relocation' to Egham in 1982–5.

42 Even so, a large group of governors appear to have challenged the decision to the end, taking their opposition to the admission of men to the Privy Council; see correspondence between Universities Branch of the Department of Education and Science and the UGC in 1965 in National Archives, UGC/7/811 (Admission of male undergraduates to women's colleges).

43 See tables giving proportion of women on academic staff of Bedford compared with numbers and proportion of women academic staff in other institutions, 'Proposed admission of men undergraduates: reasons for considering the change inimical', Appendices.

44 Ibid., p. 6: 'No one supposes that a lecturer who accepts a post here must be specially concerned for the cause of women's education. Nevertheless he comes freely, knowing it to be a women's college. He may regard his position as a stepping stone, or he may after being here some time find it uncongenial. His course is then clear: to seek another post and to give the college loyal service until he obtains it.'

45 'Minutes of Council Discussion', July 1962.

46 Ibid.

47 W. Holtby, 'Should women go to Oxford?', *News Chronicle*, 2 Feb. 1934.

48 Janet Howarth, 'Women', in B. Harrison (ed.), *The History of the University of Oxford, vol. VIII, the twentieth century*, Oxford: Clarendon Press, 1994, p. 351.

49 G.E.M. de Ste Croix, 'The admission of women to New College', *Oxford Magazine*, 15 Oct. 1964, p. 7.

50 R. McWilliams-Tullberg, *Women at Cambridge*, Cambridge: Cambridge University Press, revised edition, 1998, ch. 10, esp. p 171. The description of Cambridge as 'a men's university – though of a mixed type', used as a subtitle in the first edition (London: Gollancz, 1975) of Rita McWilliams-Tullberg's book, was taken from the Asquith Commission of 1922 (see note 51).

51 *Report of Royal Commission on Oxford and Cambridge Universities* (Asquith Commission), 1922, Cmd 1588, p. 173.

52 J. Howarth, 'Women', esp. pp. 350, 358; V. Brittain, *The Women at Oxford: a fragment of history*, London: Harrap, 1960, p. 172; C. Dyhouse, *No Distinction of Sex?* pp. 239–42.

53 Howarth, 'Women', p. 357; McWilliams-Tullberg, *Women at Cambridge*, p. 187.

54 See, for instance, the remark of J.R.M. Butler of Trinity College, Cambridge in 1920, 'the chimera of female control [of the university] is an absurdity as great as that of

women entering men's colleges', quoted in T.E.B. Howarth, *Cambridge Between Two Wars*, London: Collins, 1978, p. 40.

55 B. Walsh, 'Women at Oxford, now and then', *Oxford Magazine*, Michaelmas 1993, p. 9.

56 J. Vaizey, 'The Nobel Prize', *Oxford Magazine*, 5 Nov. 1964, p. 58.

57 D. Balsdon, *Oxford Life*, London: Eyre and Spottiswode, first published 1957, this edition 1962, pp. 188–94.

58 R. Murray, *New Hall, 1954–1972: the making of a college*, Cambridge: New Hall, 1980. See also 'Papers of University Committee on Women Students, 1949–71' (Cambridge University Library, UA R 1795/A-E).

59 Archives of Churchill College, Cambridge, see 'Trustees' correspondence re admission of women, 1958' (CCGB 210/2). See letters from Open Door Council, Soroptimist Clubs, British Federation of University Women, Women's Freedom League.

60 Letter from Jock Colville to Sir Winston Churchill, 16 June 1958, in Churchill Papers (CHUR 2/568B/167), Churchill College Archives.

61 M. and D. Davies, *Creating St Catherine's College*, Oxford: St Catherine's College, 1997, p. 135; author's conversations with J. Simopoulos and W. Knapp, 2000–1.

62 *Report of Committee on Higher Education*, 1961–3 (Robbins Report), Appendix Two (A), 'Students and their Education', London: HMSO, 1963, pp. 24–6.

63 Harrison (ed.), *History of the University of Oxford*, pp. 210, 356, 584.

64 'After St Catherine's controversy – Worcester first to be co-ed?', *Cherwell*, 25 May 1963, p. 1.

65 *Report of Committee on Higher Education* (Robbins Report), 1961–3, Appendix Two (A), pp. 24–6; University of Oxford, *Report of Commission of Inquiry* (Franks Commission), Oxford: Clarendon Press, 1966, vol. 1, p. 51, vol. 11 (Statistical Appendix), p. 15.

66 See, for instance, J.B. Broadbent, letter in the *Cambridge Review*, 21 Nov. 1964, pp. 144–5.

67 For the protracted and difficult negotiations in Cambridge leading to the acceptance of the need for 'a third foundation' for women students, see papers of 'University Committee on Women Students, 1949–71' in Cambridge University Library (UA R 1797/A-E).

68 Sir William Hayter, 'How it all began', in *Ten Years of Women at New College: a commemorative programme*, Oxford: New College, 1990, pp. 15–16.

69 Ibid., p. 15.

70 See 'The admission of women to New College' (1964), document announcing intentions of Governing Body, widely circulated at the time (copy in RHBNC Archives (BC/AR/385/9/4) for instance). See also de Ste Croix, 'The admission of women to New College'.

71 Ste Croix, pp. 4–7.

72 C. Dalton, 'The history of women at New College', in *Ten Years of Women at New College* (note 68, below).

73 In Oxford, the Hebdomadal Council attempted to act as 'broker' negotiating the process of change before 1977; in Cambridge, a Standing Subcommittee of the Colleges' Committee tried to secure 'an orderly process' of change.

74 This view has been echoed by recent historians; see, for instance, J.A. Soares, *The Decline of Privilege: the modernization of Oxford University*, Stanford CA: Stanford University Press, 1999, pp. 97–100, 142.

75 J. Vaizey, 'Mixed colleges', *Oxford Magazine*, 11 Mar. 1965, p. 1; A. Pirie, 'Women

for New College', *Oxford Magazine*, 6 May 1965, pp. 321–2; S. Hunt, 'Monasticism – or mixed colleges?', *Oxford Magazine*, 30 Jan. 1965, p. 13.

76 University of Oxford, *Report of Commission of Inquiry*, Part 4 (Evidence of Individuals), evidence given by Lady Ogilvie, pp 130–40, by Dame Janet Vaughan, pp. 172–5, and by Dr L.S. Sutherland, pp. 168–71; File (six folders) on Coresidence, Archives, Lady Margaret Hall; Coresidence File, Somerville College Archives; the Minute books recording meetings between the Oxford Women Principals, 1959–79 (Bodleian, Dep.d.762) are also a good source here.

77 Antoinette Pirie and Dorothy Hodgkin, for instance, were particularly uneasy about the way in which members of the women's colleges were being represented as generally hostile to the New College initiative. They and fourteen other women from various colleges penned a letter to the *Observer* on this theme (*The Observer*, 12 July 1964). See also Somerville College Coresidence File, notes by Barbara Craig on an informal Fellows' meeting on coeducation, 12 June 1969 (Somerville College Archives).

78 See evidence given to Franks Commission, above.

79 Ibid.

80 Lord Franks, letter to Warden of New College, 15 Mar. 1965 (University of Oxford, Registry Files (UR6/W/12, file 1) (the letter was widely circulated).

81 Soares, *The Decline of Privilege*, pp. 97–100; A.H. Halsey, 'The Franks Commission', in Harrison (ed.), *History of the University of Oxford*, p. 726.

82 Vaizey, cuttings in the University Archives (UR6/W/12 file 1), see (*inter alia*) *The Guardian*, 23 Feb. 1965, 22 Mar. 1965, 11 Oct. 1965; *The Times*, 19 May 1966.

83 E.M. Thomas, 'A problem of talent', *The Times*, 19 May 1966.

84 *The Guardian*, 22 Mar. 1965.

85 'College coeducation', *The Guardian*, 11 Oct. 1965.

86 P. Ady, 'Mixed education and the women's colleges', *Oxford Magazine*, 3 Dec. 1964, pp. 138–40.

87 A. Pirie, 'Women for New College', p. 321.

88 *The Observer*, 12 July 1964.

89 *The Oxford Magazine*, 23 May 1969. This was in response to an article by Jonathan Glover, 'The case for coresidence', published in the same magazine (28 Feb. 1969), where the women's colleges were accused of being the 'fiercest opponents' of the mixed college.

90 F. Filson, 'Students call for colleges to go co-ed.', *Oxford Mail*, 29 May 1970, and 'Co-education is favoured by undergraduates', *Oxford Times*, 29 May 1970, which claimed that nineteen JCRs had declared in favour of coeducation (cuttings in OUA UR6/W/12 file 1). A very full case was argued by John Gray in 'Towards coeducation: the case for Exeter College becoming coresidential', 1969 (copy in Exeter College Archives, widely circulated at the time).

91 Clearly documented in correspondence of 1964–70 in Lady Margaret Hall Coresidence Files, LMH Archives.

92 'Report of Working Party on Co-residence', 1971, in Oxford University Archives (UR6/W/12 file 1). See Marie Hicks, 'The Price of Excellence: coresidence and women's integration at Oxford and Harvard Universities, 1964–1977', senior undergraduate Honours thesis, Department of History, Harvard University, Mar. 2000, ch. 2.

93 Letter from L.S. Sutherland to Vice-Chancellor, 25 May 1971 (OUA UR6/W/12 file 1).

94 'Co-residence: verbatim report of debate in Congregation on 30 May 1972', published in the *Oxford University Gazette*, Supplement 3 to No. 3510, 7 June 1972.

95 Ibid., p. 1059.

96 M. Alexander, 'Oxford's October Revolution', *Daily Telegraph*, 3 Feb. 1974 (OUA, UR6/W/12 file 4). See also J.M. Roberts, 'Women's colleges do not represent women's interests', *Times Higher Education Supplement*, 30 June 1972, in which the author alleged that 'Putting the men's colleges concerned into a terrible fright by promising that no bread would be forthcoming if they declined the stale crust offered, the women's colleges did very well for themselves.' Again, there are voluminous press cuttings in the Registry files.

97 Hebdomadal Council, *Report of the Committee on Co-residence*, vol. 272, 21 Apr. 1972, pp. 9–18, see also Supplement no. 6 to the *Oxford University Gazette*, vol. CII, May 1972; 'Co-residence: verbatim report of debate in Congregation on 30 May 1972', published in the *Oxford University Gazette*, Supplement 3 to no. 3510, 7 June 1972.

98 The events and controversies are documented in a series of Registry Files in the University of Oxford Archives on 'The admission of women to men's colleges', running from c. 1964–86 (Oxford University Archives, Bodleian Library, UR6/W/12 files 1–6). This collection of six files contains a mass of press cuttings and contemporary commentary on the issue of coeducation/coresidence, as well as a record of the difficult political history of the move towards mixed colleges in the university. Intensive use of this rich historical source was made by Hicks, 'The Price of Excellence' (note 92, above). My thanks to Mr Simon Bailey, Keeper of the Oxford University Archives, for permission to consult these files.

99 The university took legal advice on the position as it was likely to be affected by the Sex Discrimination Act of 1975 (OUA UR6/W12 file 4). The government's attempts to find acceptable 'solutions' to the problem of single-sex colleges in Oxford and Cambridge in the context of proposals for legislation on sex discrimination can be explored in files in the National Archives (ED 188/323–5), which contain correspondence from Oxford and Cambridge Universities and colleges on various issues.

100 A plea for the University Council to act as 'honest broker' was made by Nancy Trenaman (Principal of St Anne's) in a letter to the Vice-Chancellor, 16 Nov. 1971; this letter, and similar representations from the Principals of St Hilda's and Lady Margaret Hall (11 and 18 Nov. 1971) are in UR6/W/12 file 1. For developments in the 'University' position, 1976–7, see OUA UR6/W/12 files 4–6. For 'Report of the Committee appointed to Review Co-Residence' see the *Oxford University Gazette*, no. 3686, Supplement 1, 3 Feb. 1977, and for 'Verbatim report of the debate on co-residence in Congregation, 8 March 1977' see the *Oxford University Gazette*, no. 3691, Supplement 2, 16 Mar. 1977.

101 Mr T.F.R.G. Braun, 'Verbatim report of the debate', 1977, p. 592.

102 McWilliams-Tullberg, *Women at Cambridge*, pp. 185–7. The university retained the right to limit the numbers of women students until 1987.

103 Transcript of recorded interview with Muriel Bradbrook on the subject of the admission of men to Girton College (interviewers Kate Perry and Charles Larkum, 22 Sept. 1992), pp. 1–3, Girton College Archives.

104 M. McKendrick, Girton College Roll Speech on Coresidence, 1980, p. 2, Girton College Archives (GCAS 2/5/5).

105 A.R. Murray, 'Memorandum on the admission of women', Feb. 1974, New Hall

College Archives (NHAR 1/1/16). Murray's papers on 'The admission of women to men's colleges, 1970–5' provide useful insights into the attitudes of New Hall and Newnham Colleges and to the workings of the Colleges' Subcommittee.

106 Letter from Alan Cottrell, Master of Jesus College, Cambridge, to Edward Miller, Master of Fitzwilliam and Chairman of the Colleges' Standing Consultative Committee on Equal Opportunities for Men and Women, 20 May 1975. The letter was copied to all Heads of Colleges. (My thanks to Peter Glazebrook, Vice-Master of Jesus College, for a copy of this letter.)

107 R. Miles, 'First class citizens?', *Telegraph Magazine*, 18 Nov. 1995, pp. 28–31.

108 See arguments of King and McGregor, note 39, above.

109 Alexander, 'Oxford's October Revolution'.

9 Troubled identities: gender, status and culture in the mixed college since 1945

1 For a recent exploration of the links between gender, status and identity in the context of debates over coeducation in an American secondary school setting, see Celeste M. Brody *et al.*, *Gender Consciousness and Privilege*, London and New York: Falmer Press, 2000.

2 Report of the Special Committee on the Medical Education of Women in London, accepted by Senate, Feb. 1944; see correspondence between Principal of University of London and Dean of the London (Royal Free Hospital) School of Medicine for Women, 12 July 1945, Archives of Royal Free Hospital.

3 Ministry of Health, *Report of Inter-Departmental Committee on Medical Schools* (Goodenough Committee), London: HMSO, 1944, pp. 99–100.

4 See correspondence, Principal of University of London to Dean of Royal Free Hospital School of Medicine for Women, 12 July 1945 (Archives, Royal Free Hospital).

5 E.M. Killick, 'Co-education', *Magazine of the Royal Free Hospital School of Medicine*, 1946, vol. VIII, no. 19, and 'Editorial' in the same journal, 1947, vol. IX, no. 22, p. 1.

6 Ibid.

7 'Editorial', *Royal Free Hospital Magazine*, June 1953, vol. XV, no. 39, p. 1.

8 Marsh, *History of Queen Elizabeth College*, p. 201.

9 'Minutes of Post-War Policy Committee Meeting held on June 20 1944' (Archives, RHBNC, RHC/GB203/2, p. 2).

10 RHBNC Archives, GB/203/1, Report of discussion with Margery Fry, July 1943, pp. 37–40. Compare Chapter 6 above.

11 Ibid., Report of Sir William Marris's interview with Lynda Grier, 19 July 1943, p. 82.

12 Ibid., Discussion with Margery Fry, 8 July 1943, p. 38.

13 'Memorandum by the Chairman of Council concerning future developments at Westfield College', Westfield College, Council Minutes, 27 Feb. 1963 (Archives, Queen Mary Westfield College), p. 2.

14 Ibid., p. 10; 'Proposal in favour of admitting men', p. 2. The authors of the 'Proposal' alleged that 'Over the last ten years, out of ten graduate students of one supervisor in medieval history seven have abandoned their work unfinished on account of marriage; of the three who presented theses and gained their degrees one has become a university lecturer and remains unmarried, one was a nun and

the third was a man. Public money as well as professional time is lost in this way' (p. 2).

15 'Proposal in favour of admitting men undergraduates to Bedford College', 1963, p. 2 (BC/GB/173, Archives, RHBNC). This particular 'manifesto' was signed by nine men and two women.

16 Ibid., pp. 1–2 and 4.

17 Simon Sedgwick Jell, 'Storming the bastion of reaction: co-education', *Isis*, 25 Oct. 1970, pp. 13–15.

18 Correspondence, Mary Bennett to Lucy Sutherland, 30 Nov. 1970 (Archives, Lady Margaret Hall).

19 'Co-residence: verbatim report of debate in Congregation on 30 May 1972', p. 1058.

20 P. Ady, 'Mixed education and the women's colleges', *Oxford Magazine*, 3 Dec. 1964, pp. 138–40; A. Pirie, 'Women for New College', *Oxford Magazine*, 6 May 1965, p. 321; *The Observer*, 12 July 1964; J. Hart, 'Some observations on the Report of the Working Party on Coresidence' (8 May 1971), in LMH Archives, Coresidence File.

21 M. McKendrick, Girton College Roll Speech, 1980 (GCAS 2/5/5, Girton College Archives).

22 Hebdomadal Council, *Report of the Committee on Co-residence*, p. 11.

23 'Co-residence: verbatim report of debate in Congregation on 30 May 1972', p. 1059.

24 Ibid., p. 1063.

25 P. Adams, *Somerville for Women: an Oxford college 1879–1993*, Oxford: Oxford University Press, 1993, ch. 16.

26 See, for instance, R. Chesshyre, 'Roedean third formers', *Cherwell*, 16 Feb. 1963, p. 6; M. Walker, 'Longer hours in bird cages', *Cherwell*, 4 Mar. 1964, p. 3.

27 H. Lind, 'In loco parentis?', *Cherwell*, 11 Nov. 1961, p. 8; K. Thomas, 'College life, 1945–70', in B. Harrison (ed.), *The History of the University of Oxford, vol. VIII, the twentieth century*, Oxford: Clarendon Press, 1994, p. 202 and *passim*.

28 Report of Senior Tutor (R.H. Tizard), on Admission of Women to Churchill College Council, 23 Oct. 1967 (CC 168/67, Churchill College Archives).

29 Ibid.; see also King's College, Cambridge, 'Report of the Committee on Admission of Women', May 1969 (copy in NHAR 1/1/16, Archives, New Hall).

30 See correspondence between R.H. Tizard and T.E. Lawrenson, 31 May 1966, including copy of letter from T.E. Lawrenson to Prof. A.G. Lehmann, 11 Feb. 1964 (Reports, Correspondence and Papers re Admission of Women, with MSS of Governing Body Discussions, CCGB 190/1, Churchill College Archives).

31 Ibid., letter from Julia Friend to R.H. Tizard, 13 June 1966.

32 The claim that nineteen JCRs in Oxford had declared in favour of coresidence was made in an article, 'Co-education is favoured by undergraduates', *Oxford Times*, 29 May 1970 (press cuttings in Oxford University Archives, UR6/W/12 file 1).

33 Jesus College, 'JCR Report on Coresidence', 1976, submitted to Vice-Chancellor (OUA UR6/W/12, file 5).

34 See, for instance, 'Women against the quota' leaflet (UR6/W/12 file 4).

35 Lucy Sutherland had concluded that 'the tide in favour' of coeducation was 'too strong to stem' in 1971; see her letter to the Vice-Chancellor, 25 May 1971 (OUA UR6/W/12 file 1).

36 Communication from Professor R. Floud, Summer 2000.

37 'Women's rights', *Stop Press with Varsity*, 11 May 1973, p. 4.

38 J. Twigg, *A History of Queens' College, Cambridge, 1448–1986*, Suffolk: Boydell, 1987, p. 441.

39 S. Harris, 'Seven down, seven to go', *Stop Press with Varsity*, 3 Nov. 1979.

40 N. Maitlis, 'Move over, darling', *The Guardian*, 3 Oct. 1987; Fionnuala McHugh, 'Equality in the quads', *Sunday Times*, 16 Oct. 1988.

41 Quoted in McHugh, 'Equality in the quads'.

42 'Editorial', *Magazine of The London (Royal Free Hospital) School of Medicine for Women*, 1947, vol. IX, no. 21, p. 2.

43 M. McKendrick, Roll Speech, 1980.

44 S. Harris, 'Seven down'.

45 Ibid.

46 S. Kenyon, 'Leap year at Girton', article from *The Old Haileyburian* (n.d., 9596/6, Girton College Archives).

47 See, for instance, E.M. Chilver and D.M. Stewart, 'Men at LMH', *Isis Newsletter*, March 1979, no. 2. In response to a critical article on coeducation by Mary Warnock, Chilver and Stewart drew attention to the strength of the forthcoming male presence at LMH, contrasting this with the position of female minorities in former male colleges.

48 'Aristides','Girls at Brasenose', *Times Education Supplement*, 18 Jan. 1974.

49 In July 2000, the website of Trinity College, Cambridge announced that 'Partly in response to trends in society at large and in universities generally, there has been considerable relaxation in the rules that were deemed appropriate to the College in the past, most recently of all, membership of the College has been opened to women. Nevertheless it may perhaps be claimed that in the essential character of the College little change has taken place.' Since a recent updating of the website this passage no longer appears.

50 Copy of letter from Lady Ogilvie to warden of New College, Oxford, 8 June 1964, in Coresidence file, Archives, LMH.

51 Marilyn Butler, quoted in R. Miles, 'First class citizens?', *Telegraph Magazine*, 18 Nov. 1995, p. 30.

52 Survey Committee of the Cambridge University Women's Action Group, *Forty Years On . . . Report on the Numbers and Status of Academic Women in the University of Cambridge*, Cambridge, 1988, p. 9.

53 Ibid.

54 A. Spurling, *Report of the Women in Higher Education Research Project, 1988–1990*, Cambridge: King's College, May 1990.

55 Ibid., pp. 54–68.

56 King's College, Cambridge, *For the Record: 'twenty years on', a celebration* (King's College Archives).

57 Ibid., 'In the belly of the beast: women in academia', report of speech by G. Greer.

58 There is an interesting account of this initiative, and the college's reaction, in the same source.

59 J. Norland, *Her Generation*, Final Report, King's College Research Centre, Aug. 1998.

60 Libby Purves, 'Quiet – women at work', *The Times*, 9 Nov. 1994.

61 I. Bradley, 'Women breach Oxford defences', *Times Higher Education Supplement*, 25 Oct. 1974.

62 Norland, *Her Generation*, pp. 3–4, comments of Lucy King on self-esteem, eating disorders etc., in *For The Record*. See also an account by Caroline Kay on the tensions of being female in a male college, 'Sweet girl graduates? the first year of women undergraduates in New College' in *Ten Years of Women at New College: a commemorative programme*, Oxford: New College, 1990.

63 J. Vaizey, Editorial Comment in the *Oxford Magazine*, 11 Mar. 1965. See also comment on 'Women at Oxford', *Times Education Supplement*, 5 May 1972; J.M. Roberts, 'Women's colleges do not represent women's interests', *Times Higher Education Supplement*, 30 June 1972.

64 See (*inter alia*) 'Notes on the admission of women to mixed colleges, 1973–5', signed by eight Fellows of St Hilda's College, 5 May 1976 (OUA UR 6/W/12 file 4).

65 See, for instance, J. Gilman, 'Co-ed colleges – a mixed blessing?', *The Oxford Mail*, 23 Mar. 1977; B. Craig, letter to Editor of the *Times*, protesting about an article by Diana Geddes which had claimed that the best women applicants were being creamed off by the mixed colleges, *The Times*, 21 Mar. 1977, p. 15.

66 Copy of letter from Mary Bennett to Dean of Christchurch, 24 Oct. 1977, in Coresidence File, Somerville College Archives.

67 See, for instance, E. Llewellyn Smith, 'Does Oxford want a women's college?', *Oxford Magazine*, 1993, no. 97, pp. 6–13.

68 F. Maddocks, 'Women only, and wanting to keep it that way', *The Independent*, 9 Mar. 1992.

69 Adams, *Somerville for Women*, p. 350.

70 J. Gray, 'Towards coeducation: the case for Exeter College becoming coresidential', 1969, copy in Exeter College Archives.

71 R. Jackson, 'The disintegration of Oxford's male monopoly', *Times Higher Education Supplement*, 9 June 1972.

72 Ibid.

10 The student rag

1 D. Bramwell (ed.), *The Cheeky Guide to Student Life*, Brighton: Cheekyguides Ltd, 2003, p 323.

2 See www.britishpathe.com. Examples of footage include: *Students' rag – Brighton*, 2076.10 (Brighton Technical College students and others, 1920–9); *Degree Day is joy day*, 362.04 (University College Dublin, rag parade on 'Degree Day', 1924); *Always merry and bright*, 330.05 (Glasgow student parade, 1924); *A joyous rag*, 438.09 (Brighton Technical College students' rag procession, 1925); *20,000 eggs, soot and flour*, 428.22 (Rectorial election rag, Glasgow, 1925); *The pram rag*, 308.08 (Cambridge, n.d., 1920s?); *The Rag of Rags*, 454.13 (Manchester students' Shrove Tuesday procession, 1926); *Here comes the fire brigade*, 672.08 (Manchester student rag, 1927); *Alas poor Sister Jane*, 668.24 (Liverpool medical students versus engineers in mock funeral procession following battle for rag-mascot, 1927); *Manchester students' Great Charity Rag*, 716.09 (1928); *A city held up*, 808.01 (Birmingham Hospital rag, 1929); *Each year better than last*, 776.06 (Glasgow, 1929); *Pan to day (Pantoday)*, 776.20 (Liverpool, 1929); *1500 students*, 820.10 (Manchester Shrove Tuesday Rag, 1930); *It was a wonderful rag . . . yes indeed*, 665.03 (Cardiff, 1932); *Kate Kennedy Day*, 665.10 (St Andrew's, 1932, celebration of 'patroness of student chivalry'); *A city held up (aka Glasgow students' rag)*, 641.13, (Glasgow 1932); *Merry goes the day when the heart is young*, 735.25 (Northampton Institute students' annual 'Battle for the Carrot Rag', London, 1933); *The battle for Sister Jane*, 693.33 (medics versus engineers in Liverpool, 1933); *Kate Kennedy Day*, 779.05 (St Andrew's, 1934); *The battle of flowers*, 663.34 (flowery floats in Nice and student rag parade in Manchester, 1932); *Students' rag*, 845.22 (rag festivities in University College London, 1935); *Liverpool*

students, 851.37 (1936); *London students' rag*, 2076.10 (1940s); *Cambridge rag-time*, 42.35 (Cambridge students, 1952); *Glamour at no. 10 (aka Reading University rag)* 62.03 (1953); *Rag parade*, 57.06 (1956, Newcastle/Durham); *University rag frolics*, 55.37 (1956, Newcastle/Durham); *Student rag*, 1714.17 (Exeter students, 1961); *Hospitals Cup rag*, 167 (medical students, London, 1962). This list is not exhaustive.

3 M.M. Bakhtin (tr. H. Iswolsky), *Rabelais and his World*, Cambridge, MA: MIT Press, 1968; P. Stallybrass and A. White, *The Politics and Poetics of Transgression*, London: Methuen, 1986.

4 See, for instance, www.britishpathe.com, *Degree Day rag*, 322.15 (Dublin); *All in the cause of charity*, 826.33 (Portsmouth, 1929). Klan costumes were very common in rag processions before 1939. In 1935/6 Birmingham University's Guild of Undergraduates decided to order a large quantity (12 gross) of enamelled carnival badges/brooches depicting a Ku Klux Klan figure in lieu of the 'Billy the Bob Boy' immunity badges of the previous year (Annual Report of University of Birmingham Guild of Undergraduates, 1935/6, p. 19, University of Birmingham Archives).

5 Keith Thomas, *Rule and Misrule in the Schools of Early Modern England*, Stenton Lecture, 1975, University of Reading, 1976. For a more recent exploration of misrule and manhood in the early modern period see Alexandra Shepard, *Meanings of Manhood in Early Modern England*, Oxford: Oxford University Press, 2003, esp. pp. 95–125.

6 See, for instance, Kathleen R. Farrar, 'The mechanics' saturnalia', in D.S.L. Cardwell (ed.), *Artisan to Graduate: essays to commemorate the foundation in 1824 of the Manchester Mechanics' Institution, now in 1974 the University of Manchester Institute of Science and Technology*, Manchester: Manchester University Press, 1974, pp. 99–119; P. Slack, *Rebellion, Popular Protest and the Social Order in Early Modern England*, Cambridge: Cambridge University Press, 1984.

7 For the longstanding rivalry between King's and University Colleges, London, and the 'rags' associated with this, see 'Mayhem in the metropolis', an online exhibition produced by archivists at King's College London, (http://www.kcl.ac.uk/depsta/iss/archives//rag/contents.html

8 See for instance W.O. Skeat, *King's College London Engineering Society, 1847–1957*, London: Printed for King's College London Engineers Association for private circulation, 1957, p. 45. Skeat describes the notorious 'Pussyfoot Rag', during the course of which an American temperance campaigner was mobbed by medical and engineering students and unfortunately lost the sight of one eye in the fracas. See also ibid., pp. 90–1.

9 'Bruce Truscot' (E. Allison Peers, Gilmour Professor of Spanish at Liverpool University, 1922–52), *Redbrick University*, London: Faber and Faber, 1943, p. 168.

10 Norman Longmate, *Oxford Triumphant*, London: Phoenix House, 1954, p. 82. Longmate's chapter on 'Rowdyism' (pp. 75–84) discusses Eights Week, Bonfire Night, Bump Suppers, lavatory humour and boat-burning, and is a rich source for those interested in masculine student identity in this period.

11 Liverpool University's 2001 'Charities Appeal' rag magazine shows a lack of historical awareness in this respect in attributing the origins of rag to students in Oxford and Cambridge at the beginning of the twentieth century who were held to have 'dressed up in rags to collect money for the local poor', *2001 Rag Magazine*, p. 32, Liverpool University Archives.

12 Adrian Allan, 'From panto to rag', *The Recorder* (Liverpool University Alumni Magazine), Mar. 2000, Issue 120, p. 11.

13 Ibid.

14 *Owen's College Union Magazine*, Mar. 1896, no. 23, vol. III, p. 82 (University of Manchester Archives).

15 'Shrove Tuesday', *Owen's College Union Magazine*, Mar. 1898, no. 42, vol. V, p. 69.

16 Ibid.

17 'Rags' need to be seen as one of a number of 'traditions' invented and presented or represented as 'ancient' in universities both before and after the First World War, such as 'Kate Kennedy Day' in the University of St Andrew's, or 'Jantaculum' in Reading. See E. Hobsbawm and T. Ranger, *The Invention of Tradition*, Cambridge: Cambridge University Press, 1983, p. 1. For the representation of Kate Kennedy Day as 'ancient', see www.britishpathe.com, *Kate Kennedy Day*, 665.10; for Jantaculum see J.C. Holt, *The University of Reading: the first fifty years*, Reading: Reading University Press, 1977, pp. 84–5; W. Lloyd-Davies, 'The Gild of the Red Rose, 1897–1933', *Tamesis*, 1933, vol. xxxi, pp. 113–17.

18 Allen, 'From panto to rag', p. 12.

19 *Owen's College Union Magazine*, March 1896, no. 23, vol. III, p. 82.

20 *Owen's College Union Magazine*, Mar. 1904, no. 92, vol. XI, pp. 140–1.

21 *Manchester University Magazine*, Feb. 1907, no. 20, vol. III, p. 128.

22 Ibid., p. 144 (letter from 'Gaudeamus').

23 *Manchester University Magazine*, 1910, no. 41 ,vol. VI, p. 108.

24 *Manchester University Magazine*, 'Shrove Tuesday Supplement', 10 Mar. 1914, no. 5, vol. X.

25 A class dimension of this was interestingly illustrated by a writer in the *Manchester University Magazine* in 1913, who contemptuously dismissed the efforts of 'technical school people' to join in the Shrove Tuesday event, noting that 'they all dressed as golliwogs', *MUM*, Feb. 1913, no. 5, vol. IX, p. 102.

26 *Manchester University Magazine*, 1912, no. 57, vol. VIII, pp. 129–30.

27 Liverpool University, Panto Committee Minutes, 1922 (Liverpool University Archives).

28 *Manchester University Magazine*, 1913, no. 5, vol. IX, p. 107.

29 Brighton introduced an annual civic carnival in 1922, for instance. See 'Brighton carnival scrapbook' (1923) in Brighton Local History Collection, Brighton and Hove Museums and Art Galleries.

30 Allan, 'From panto to rag', p. 12.

31 Stallybrass and White, *Politics and Poetics of Transgression*, p. 8.

32 'Hegnib', 'Shrove Tuesday', *The Serpent*, 5 Mar. 1920, no. 4, vol. IV, pp. 118–22, Manchester University Archives.

33 Ibid.

34 Allan, 'From panto to rag', p. 12.

35 Copy of 1925 'Panto number' of *Sphinx*, and runs of *Pantosfinx* in Archives of University of Liverpool.

36 Bound volume of *Rag Rag*, 1924–40, Manchester University Archives.

37 A role sometimes taken by theatre managers, etc. In 1924 Manchester students invested the manager of the Hippodrome with the title 'Chief Controller of Misconduct', *Rag Rag, March 1924* (bound volume of *Rag Rag*, 1924–40, Manchester University Archives).

38 M. Moss, J. Munro Forbes and R.H. Trainor, *University City and State: the University of Glasgow since 1870*, Edinburgh: Edinburgh University Press for the University of Glasgow, 2000, p. 160; C.A. Oakley, *Union Ygorra: the story of the*

Glasgow University student over the last sixty years, Glasgow: Committee of Management, Glasgow University Union, 1950, pp. 10–15.

39 *Ygorra* from 1925 (Glasgow University Archives, DC 198); 'College Pudding' File, 1925–65 (Glasgow University Archives, GUA 34934–47, 50139–50141).

40 See (for instance) 'Degree day at the University', *Birmingham Gazette*, 9 July 1923, 'Degree Day at University: lively proceedings by students', *Birmingham Gazette*, 6 July 1925. In 1925 the *Gazette* reported that the male students had decorated the stage on which degrees were to be conferred by suspending 'flimsy articles of feminine attire' along a wire across the platform, 'much to the amusement of the graduettes, many with bobbed or shingled hair, who, wearing their robes and mortar boards, occupied the front seats . . . A formidable "elephant" with particularly large tusks, and accompanied by a coloured student, was the recipient of a BA amid the plaudits of a large assembly.' When H.A.L. Fisher visited Birmingham in November 1922, he was escorted from New Street Station to the university in a carriage pulled by students in fancy dress amid much noise and merriment, see 'A boisterous welcome: how undergraduates received Mr Fisher', *Despatch*, 11 Nov. 1922, and many similar articles in *Birmingham University Press Cuttings Book*, 1914–23, Birmingham Central Library.

1 M. Cheesewright, *Mirror to a Mermaid: pictorial reminiscences of Mason College and the University of Birmingham, 1875–1975*, Birmingham: Suttons, 1975, p. 134.

42 *The Mermaid*, 1923–4, no. 2, vol. 20, p. 45.

43 University of Birmingham, *Carnival Magazine*, Oct. 1926, no. 1, Birmingham University Archives. Birmingham's *Carnival* magazines sported beautifully drawn colour illustrations through the interwar period.

44 *Carnival*, October 1928, no. 3, Birmingham University Archives.

45 See 'Mayhem in the metropolis', online exhibition produced by archivists at King's College London (http://www.kcl.ac.uk/depsta/iss/archives//rag/contents.html). There is an image of 'Phineas Maclino', originally a wooden tobacconist's sign lifted from the Tottenham Court Road, in N. Harte and J. North, *The World of UCL 1828–1990*, London: UCL, 1991, p. 130.

46 See, for instance, www.britishpathe.com, *Students' rag*, 845.22; *Hospital Cup rag*, 167.16; King's College Union Society Press Cuttings and Photographs, King's College Archives (K/PC 1/3).

47 Ibid. See also the dramatic photograph of a bonfire in UCL quad (originally published in the *News Chronicle*) reproduced in UCL student handbooks after the Second World War, e.g. *UCL Student Handbook*, 1950–1, p. 70, UCL Records Office.

48 Ibid.

49 T. Kelly, *For Advancement of Learning: the University of Liverpool 1881–1981*, Liverpool: Liverpool University Press, 1981, p. 269; Allan, 'From panto to rag', *Liverpool University Recorder*, Mar. 2000, Issue 120, p. 13 (see photograph of Frank Kerr, President of Guild of Undergraduates with 'Sister Jane' on Panto Day in Jan. 1933); www.britishpathe.com, *The battle for Sister Jane*, 693.33; *Alas poor Sister Jane*, 668.24.

50 Allan, 'From panto to rag', p. 13; see also eye-witness account in letter from James Brophy to Adrian Allan, 10 Apr. 1987, Liverpool University Archives (A.5/4, D.404)

51 'Carnival magazine ban prospect', *Birmingham Mail*, 27 Oct. 1933, in University of Birmingham Press Cuttings Book, 1931–4, Birmingham Central Library.

52 *Birmingham Post*, 13 June 1926, in Birmingham University Press Cuttings Book,

1925–8, Birmingham City Library. That year, Birmingham's Student Carnival raised £4000, as compared with Manchester's £6000, Glasgow's £7400.

53 Ibid.

54 C. Dyhouse, *No Distinction of Sex? Women in British universities, 1870–1939*, London: UCL Press, 1995, chapters 2, 3 and 5.

55 *The Serpent*, Mar. 1927, no. 4, vol. XI, p. 94; 'The police and the rag', *Manchester Guardian*, 20 Feb. 1930, Manchester University Press Cuttings Book, no. 8, 1923–33, University of Manchester Archives. The Constable's objection, on this occasion, was to 'coffee stalls manned by women students'. This may have been because stalls involved women working on the street, rather than inside a cafe?

56 *Carnival*, Oct. 1932, p. 12, University of Birmingham Archives.

57 Resolutions of informal meeting of Wardens of Women's Halls of Residence, held 28 Nov. 1930 at Ashburne Hall, in Vice-Chancellor's Discipline Files, University of Manchester Archives, VCA/7/280/1–5.

58 Letter from M.A. Clarke to Dr Moberly, 9 Feb. 1932, Vice-Chancellor's Discipline Files, Manchester University Archives, VCA/7/280 2/5.

59 Manchester University Women Students' Union Rag Subcommittee Minute Book, 1933–41, University Archives.

60 Minutes of Manchester University Women's Union Precis Volumes no. 2, 21 Feb. 1935, University Archives.

61 Ibid.

62 M. Tylecote, *The Education of Women at Manchester University, 1883–1933*, Manchester: Manchester University Press, 1941, p. 123; see also Ian G. Gregory, *In Memory of Burlington Street: an appreciation of the Manchester University Unions 1861–1957*, Manchester: Manchester University Union, 1958, chapter 4 and esp. pp. 51–2.

63 *The Serpent*, Feb. 1937, vol. XXI, pp. 64–5.

64 Manchester Women's Union Rag Subcommittee Minute Book, 1933–41, 21 Feb. 1938, University Archives.

65 Universities of Liverpool, *Rag Magazine*, 80th Anniversary issue, 2003, p. 14, Liverpool University Archives.

66 'Women and those "rags"', *The Star*, 9 Dec. 1929, cutting in King's College Union Society Press Cuttings Book, King's College Archives, K/PC 1/3.

67 'Kisses at 6d each: on sale by 20 girl students', press cutting in Glasgow University archives, GUA 30552; letter of complaint from Rev. G.W. Clarke to Principal, 14 Jan. 1930, op. cit.

68 See, for instance, Norman Longmate on male rowdyism in *Oxford Triumphant*: 'Women are peculiarly to blame. Nurses, students from the domestic science colleges, foreign maids learning English in Oxford – all those females who seem to be in some sense hangers-on of the University while not belonging to it – are always prominent in the crowd, urging the men to new demonstrations of male wit and valour. Many undergraduates who might, if left to themselves, behave sensibly, allow themselves to be incited by the shrill cries and ready laughter of such women to crude, pointless and often dangerous exploits', pp. 77–8.

69 Letter from Manchester and Salford Medical Charities Fund to Vice-Chancellor, in Vice-Chancellor's Discipline Files, Manchester University Archives, VCA/7/280/4/5.

70 See, for instance, Glasgow University's arrangements for Charities Day, 1937, together with maps of city collecting districts, Glasgow University archives, DC 157/6/21; Birmingham University Guild of Undergraduates Annual Reports on Carnival, University Archives.

71 'Carnival warning note: Carnival Frankenstein', *Birmingham Mail*, 3 Feb. 1927, Birmingham University Press Cuttings Book, 1925–8, Birmingham Central Library.

72 Ibid.

73 Press cutting from *Manchester Evening News*, 24 Feb. 1931, in Vice-Chancellor's Discipline Files, University of Manchester, VCA/7/280/1.

74 'Birmingham students' carnival', *Birmingham Post*, 29 Feb. 1927, University Press Cuttings Book, Birmingham Central Library.

75 Guild of Undergraduates Annual Reports, 1934–5, University Archives; Press Cuttings Book, Central Library.

76 *Evening Despatch*, 31 Oct. 1942, in University Press Cuttings Book, 1941–5, Birmingham Central Library; 'Report on Sheffield University rag', Mass Observation Archive, University of Sussex, TC 36/1/E.

77 'Bruce Truscot', *Redbrick University*, p. 169.

78 *Birmingham Gazette*, 4 Nov. 1946, *Birmingham Mail*, 2 Nov. 1946, cuttings in University Press Cuttings Book, 1949–51, Birmingham Central Library.

79 *Birmingham Post*, 4 Nov. 1946, op. cit.

80 *Birmingham Gazette*, 3 Nov. 1947, op. cit.; Birmingham University Guild of Undergraduates, Annual Report, 1951–2, Birmingham University Archives.

81 Birmingham University Guild of Undergraduates Annual Reports, 1950/1, 1955/6, Birmingham University Archives.

82 Ibid.

83 Ibid., 1957/8.

84 *Guild News*, 7 Nov. 1957, University of Birmingham Archives.

85 Guild of Undergraduates Annual Report 1960/1, Birmingham University Archives.

86 N. Harte, *The University of London, 1836–1986*, London: University of London Press, 1986, p. 246.

87 'Give these students a public spanking!', *Manchester Daily Dispatch*, 23 Feb. 1952, Manchester University Students' Press Cuttings Book, 1951–3, Manchester University Archives.

88 Miss Brockbank, 'Rag hooligans', *Evening Chronicle*, 26 Feb. 1952, Students' Press Cuttings Book, op. cit.

89 'Students, learn the right lessons', *Liverpool Evening Express*, 19 Feb. 1954.

90 'Rag students are warned', *Evening Chronicle*, 31 Jan. 1956, Manchester University Students' Cuttings Book, vol. 3, Manchester University Archives.

91 Universities of Liverpool, *Rag Magazine*, 80th annual issue, 2003, p. 14.

92 *Liverpool Daily Echo*, 16 Feb. 1961, in University of Liverpool Press Cuttings Book, 1960–1, Liverpool University Archives; Special meetings of Senate, 21 Feb. 1961, 17 May 1961, in Senate Minutes, vol. 47, University of Liverpool Archives.

93 Liverpool University, *Guild Gazette*, 6 Feb. 1961, p. 8, University Archives.

94 'Students plan new "rag" role', *Birmingham Post*, 26 Jan. 1968, 'Students rally – but in a good cause', *Birmingham Post*, 12 Feb. 1969, in University Press Cuttings Book, 1967–70, Birmingham Central Library.

95 A. Allan, 'From panto to rag', p. 13.

96 Dyhouse, *No Distinction of Sex?*, pp. 221–9.

97 See undated photograph of five awkward-looking female students, four of them sporting college scarves, the fifth dressed as a nurse (?) in Royal Holloway College Archives, RHC PH/260/1. It is worth comparing this photograph with the image on the cover of Glasgow's rag magazine, *Ygorra*, in Jan. 1927. The latter depicts a monster caveman, covered in hair and oozing testosterone, equipped with a giant

nailed club and collecting tin, looming over the tenements of Glasgow (Glasgow University Archives, DC1981216).

98 See C. Bingham, *The History of Royal Holloway College, 1886–1986*, London: Constable, 1987, p. 235; *Hollocaust*, 1970–5, in Royal Holloway College Archives, AS/203/1–4. The first issue of *Hollocaust* carried a message from Frank Muir to the effect that student rags went to great lengths to get 'virginity and money', and advising that 'when rape is inevitable, lie back and enjoy it'.

99 M. Sanderson, *The History of the University of East Anglia*, Norwich, London: Hambledon, 2002, p. 129.

100 F. Zweig, *The Student in the Age of Anxiety*, London: Heinemann 1963.

101 The introduction of mandatory grants followed the recommendations of the Anderson Committee, see Ministry of Education, *Grants to Students, 1959/60*, Cmd 1051, London: HMSO, 1960; *Report of the Committee on the Age of Majority* (Latey Committee), Cmnd 3342, London: HMSO 1967. See also discussions in Chapter 9.

102 See, for instance, A. Cockburn and R. Blackburn (eds), *Student Power: problems, diagnosis, action*, Harmondsworth: Penguin in association with *New Left Review*, 1969; S. Caine, *British Universities, purpose and prospects*, London: Bodley Head, 1969, esp. chapter 6, 'Student malaise', pp. 103–53.

103 J. Green, *All Dressed Up: the Sixties and the counter-culture*, London: Jonathan Cape, 1998, esp. chapter 20, 'Student power: seize the time'.

104 Thomas, *Rule and Misrule*, p. 35.

105 E. Ashby and M. Anderson, *The Rise of the Student Estate in Britain*, London: Macmillan, 1970, pp. 134–5.

106 See, for instance, www.britishpathe.com, 2225.16, *Isle of Wight pop festival*, 1969; 3314.07, *Soul in Hyde Park*, 1968; 3324.09, *Pop and hippie festival*, Paris and Belgium, 1969.

107 University of Loughborough, Vice-Chancellor's Speech at 2003 (10 July) Degree Ceremony. My thanks to Hannah Baldwin, Loughborough Press Office and the Loughborough Students' Union for relevant information. Loughborough is a university with a strong reputation for sports science, engineering and technology. Men still outnumber women in its student population. This may go some way towards explaining the unrivalled success of its rag efforts in recent years, as also does the fact that Loughborough Students' Union has a full-time rag organizer who is granted a year's sabbatical leave from study.

108 See, for instance, '*Ygorra* faces ban for sexist image', *Glasgow Herald*, 17 Feb. 1975; 'Students halt sexist cattle show', *Glasgow Herald*, 22 Jan. 1975, and many similar reports in Charities Week Press Cuttings, 1P6/9/3, Glasgow University Archives.

109 'Rag rage hits Glasgow', *The Scotsman*, 18 Jan. 1983, Cuttings File 1P6/9/3, Glasgow University Archives.

Conclusion

1 See for instance I. Zweiniger-Bargielowska (ed.), *Women in Twentieth-Century Britain*, Harlow: Pearson Education, 2001; S. Rowbotham, *A Century of Women: the history of women in Britain and the United States*, London: Viking, 1997.

2 Pauline Perry, 'Hope fulfilled or hope deferred?', in M.R. Masson and D. Simonton, (eds), *Women and Higher Education: past, present and future*, Aberdeen: Aberdeen University Press, 1996.

3   For a recent example of an attempt to reconsider the role of women in the 1950s see J. Giles, *The Parlour and the Suburb: domestic identities, class, femininity and modernity*, Oxford: Berg, 2004.

4   'The Nobel Prize', *Oxford Magazine*, 5 Nov. 1964.

5   R. Jackson, 'The disintegration of Oxford's male monopoly', *Times Higher Education Supplement*, 9 June 1972.

6   For qualifications of female school-leavers see M. Arnot, M. David and G. Weiner, *Closing the Gender Gap: postwar education and social change*, Cambridge: Polity Press, 1999. For 'moral panic' about boys' underachievement, see D. Epstein, J. Elwood, V. Hey and J. Maw (eds), *Failing Boys? Issues in gender and achievement*, Buckingham: Open University Press, 1998.

7   A paper by W. Arulampalam, R.A. Naylor and J. Smith, 'Doctor who? who gets admission offers in UK medical schools', Royal Economic Society Annual Conference, Nottingham 2005, argues that by 1996/7 males (along with mature students and non-whites) were being discriminated against in UK medical schools' intake.

8   J. Quinn, *Powerful Subjects: are women really taking over the university?*, Stoke-on-Trent: Trentham Books, 2003.

9   There is currently a 'Women's Union' with its own magazine, *Gender Agenda*, at the University of Cambridge. This was established in 1997, as part of (rather than separate from) the Cambridge University Students' Union: see http://www.cusu.cam.ac.uk/campaigns/womens/womens_union.htm.

10 An article on rag activities at Sidney Sussex College, Cambridge, which appeared in the *Cambridge Student*, 25 Nov. 2004, shows that gendered attitudes can still shape controversy around rag. Attempts to raise money by students earlier in the week involved stage acts 'from the nauseating to the smutty'; the evening was allegedly 'peppered with references to the complaints made by members of the Women's Union', especially in relation to a scheduled 'lady-pulling event'. However, the consensus among those at the bar ('not noticeably male-dominated'), was that controversy 'had merely fuelled interest in the event'. My thanks to Dr Alex Shepard for this reference.

11 Ibid. See, for instance, Angelique Chrisafis, 'Higher education: behaving rather badly', *The Guardian*, 6 Nov. 2001, Education Pages, p. 10; Glen Owen and Laura Peek, 'Stop drinking and put your clothes on', *The Times*, 3 Oct. 2001.

12 See, for instance, Mark Townsend, 'Women graduates face top-up fees crisis', *The Observer*, 14 Dec. 2003, p. 13.

Select bibliography: works used in text

Note: Full details of archival and other sources are given in the endnotes

Adams, P., *Somerville for Women: an Oxford College 1879–1993*, Oxford: Oxford University Press, 1996.

Aiston, S., 'A good job for a girl? the career biographies of women graduates of the University of Liverpool post 1945', *Twentieth Century British History*, 2004, vol. 15, no. 4, 361–87.

Anderson, K., *Women and the Universities, A Changing Pattern*, Fawcett Lecture, Bedford College, University of London: 1963.

Anderson, R.D., 'Universities and élites in modern Britain', *History of Universities*, 1991, vol. 10, 230–6.

Anderson, R.D., *Universities and Elites in Britain since 1800*, Basingstoke: Macmillan, 1992.

Armytage, W.H.G., 'Flexner to Truscot: the stocktaking phase of civic university development, 1930–1944', *Universities Review*, 1953, vol. 26, 4–11.

Arnot, M. (ed.), *Race and Gender: equal opportunities policies in education*, Oxford: Pergamon, 1985.

Arnot, M., David, M. and Weiner, G., *Closing the Gender Gap: postwar education and social change*, Cambridge: Polity Press, 1999.

Arregger, C.E. (ed.), *Graduate Women at Work: a study by a working party of the British Federation of University Women*, Newcastle-upon-Tyne: Oriel Press, 1966.

Ashby, E. and Anderson, M., *The Rise of the Student Estate in Britain*, London: Macmillan, 1970.

Bakewell, J., *The Centre of the Bed*, London: Hodder and Stoughton, 2003.

Bakhtin, M.M. (tr. H. Iswolsky), *Rabelais and his World*, Cambridge, MA: MIT Press, 1968.

Balsdon, D., *Oxford Life*, London: Eyre and Spottiswode, 1962 (first published 1957).

Becker, H., Geer, B., Hughes, E. and Strauss, A., *Boys In White: student culture in Medical School*, Chicago, IL: University of Chicago Press, 1961.

Becket, E.M., *The University College of Nottingham*, Nottingham: Henry Saxton, 1928.

Bentley, L., *Educating Women: a pictorial history of Bedford College, University of London, 1849–1985*, Surrey: Alma Publishers, 1991.

Bingham, A., *Gender, Modernity and the Popular Press in Inter-war Britain*, Oxford: Oxford University Press, 2004.

Bingham, C., *The History of Royal Holloway College, 1886–1986*, London: Constable, 1987.

Biscoe, V., *300 Careers for Women*, London: Lovat Dickson Ltd, 1932.

Blackburn, R.M. and Jarman, J., 'Changing inequalities in access to British universities', *Oxford Review of Education*, 1993, vol. 19(2), 197–215.

Blake, C., *The Charge of the Parasols: women's entry to the medical profession*, London: The Women's Press, 1990.

Bonner, T.N., *To the Ends of the Earth: women's search for education in medicine*, London and Cambridge MA: Harvard University Press, 1992.

Bourke, J., *Dismembering the Male: men's bodies, Britain and the Great War*, London: Reaktion Books, 1996.

Bramwell, D. (ed.), *The Cheeky Guide to Student Life*, Brighton: Cheekyguides Ltd, 2003.

Briant, K., *Oxford Unlimited*, London: Michael Joseph, 1937.

Brittain, V., *The Women at Oxford: a fragment of history*, London: George G. Harrap, 1960.

Brody, C.M. *et al.*, *Gender Consciousness and Privilege*, London and New York: Falmer Press, 2000.

Bryson, E., *Look Back in Wonder*, Dundee: David Winter and Son, 1966.

Burton Nelson, M., *The Stronger Women Get, the More Men Love Football*, London: The Women's Press, 1996.

Caine, S., *British Universities: purpose and prospects*, London: Bodley Head, 1969.

Cardwell, D.S.L. (ed.), *Artisan to Graduate: essays to commemorate the foundation in 1824 of the Manchester Mechanics' Institution, now in 1974 the University of Manchester Institute of Science and Technology*, Manchester: Manchester University Press, 1974.

Cheesewright, M., *Mirror to a Mermaid: pictorial reminiscences of Mason College and the University of Birmingham, 1875–1975*, Birmingham: Suttons, 1975.

Cockburn, A. and Blackburn, R. (eds), *Student Power: problems, diagnosis, action*, Harmondsworth: Penguin, in association with *New Left Review*, 1969.

Collins, M. (ed.), *Women Graduates and the Teaching Profession*, Manchester: Manchester University Press, 1964.

Cook, H., *The Long Sexual Revolution: English women, sex and contraception 1800–1975*, Oxford: Oxford University Press, 2004.

Cooke, J.M., 'Women and the Professions, 1890–1939', unpublished DPhil thesis, University of Sussex, 1997.

Corbett, M.J., *Representing Femininity: middle-class subjectivity in Victorian and Edwardian women's autobiographies*, New York and Oxford: Oxford University Press, 1992.

Creighton, W.B., *Working Women and the Law*, London: Mansell, 1979.

Crompton, R. and Sanderson, K., *Gendered Jobs and Social Change*, London: Unwin Hyman, 1990.

Davies, M. and D., *Creating St Catherine's College*, Oxford: St Catherine's College, 1997.

Day, L., *The Looker In*, London: Jonathan Cape, 1961.

de Beauvoir, S., *The Second Sex*, London: Cape, 1953.

Deslandes, P., *Oxbridge Men: British masculinity and the undergraduate experience, 1850–1920*, Bloomington, IN: Indiana University Press, 2005.

Digby, A., *Making a Medical Living: doctors and patients in the English market for medicine, 1720–1911*, Cambridge: Cambridge University Press, 1994.

Drabble, M., *The Millstone*, London: Weidenfeld and Nicolson, 1965.

Dyhouse, C., *Feminism and the Family in England 1880–1939*, Oxford: Blackwell, 1989.

Dyhouse, C., *No Distinction of Sex? Women in British universities 1870–1939*, London: UCL Press, 1995.

Dyhouse, C., 'The British Federation of University Women and the status of women in universities, 1907–1939', *Women's History Review*, 1995, vol. 4, 465–85.

Elston, M.A., 'Women doctors in the British health services: a sociological study of their careers and opportunities', unpublished PhD thesis, University of Leeds, 1986.

Epstein, D., Elwood, J., Hey, V. and Maw, J. (eds), *Failing Boys? Issues in gender and achievement*, Buckingham: Open University Press, 1998.

Forster, M., *Dames' Delight*, London: Jonathan Cape, 1964.

Friedan, B., *The Feminine Mystique*, London: Gollancz, 1963.

Garner, J.S., 'The great experiment: the admission of women students to St Mary's Hospital Medical School, 1916–1925', *Medical History*, 1998, vol. 42, 68–88.

Gaukroger, A. and Schwarz, L., 'A university and its region: student recruitment to Birmingham, 1945–1975', *Oxford Review of Education*, 1997, vol. 23(2), 185–202.

Giles, J., *The Parlour and the Suburb: domestic identities, class, femininity and modernity*, Oxford: Berg, 2004.

Glass, D.V. (ed.), *Social Mobility in Britain*, London: Routledge, 1954.

Glass, D.V. and Gray, J.L., 'Opportunity and the older universities', in L. Hogben (ed.), *Political Arithmetic: a Symposium of Population Studies*, London: Allen and Unwin, 1938.

Green, J., *All Dressed Up: the sixties and the counter-culture*, London: Jonathan Cape, 1998.

Gregory, I., *In Memory of Burlington Street, an appreciation of the Manchester University Unions 1861–1957*, Manchester: Manchester University Union, 1958.

Grossman, J., *Her Own Terms*, London: Grafton, 1988.

Hall, J. and Caradog Jones, D., 'The social grading of occupations', *British Journal of Sociology*, 1950, vol. 1, 33–40.

Halsey, A.H., *Change in British Society*, Oxford: Oxford University Press, fourth edition, 1995.

Halsey, A.H., Heath, A.F. and Ridge, J.M. (eds), *Origins and Destinations: family, class and education in modern Britain*, Oxford: Clarendon Press, 1980.

Hamer, E., *Britannia's Glory: a history of twentieth century lesbians*, London: Cassell, 1996.

Harrison, B., *Prudent Revolutionaries: portraits of British feminists between the wars*, Oxford: Oxford University Press, 1987.

Harrison, B. (ed.), *The History of the University of Oxford, vol. VIII: the twentieth century*, Oxford: Clarendon Press, 1994.

Harte, N.B., *The Admission of Women to University College, London: a centenary lecture*, UCL Press, 1979.

Harte, N., *The University of London, 1836–1986*, London: University of London Press, 1986.

Heath, A., *Social Mobility*, Glasgow: Fontana, 1981.

Heilbrun, C.G., *Writing A Woman's Life*, New York and London: The Women's Press, 1988.

Herklots, H.G.G., *The New Universities: an external examination*, London: Ernest Benn, 1928.

Heward, C., *Making a Man of Him: parents and their sons' education at an English public school 1929–50*, London: Routledge, 1988.

Higher Education Funding Council, *Young Participation in Higher Education*, Bristol: HEFCE, Jan. 2005.

Higonnet, M.R., Jenson, J., Michel, S. and Collins Weitz, M. (eds), *Behind the Lines: gender and the two world wars*, New Haven, CT and London: Yale University Press, 1987.

Hobhouse, C., *Oxford As It Was, and As It Is Today*, London: Batsford, 1939.

Hobsbawm, E. and Ranger, T., *The Invention of Tradition*, Cambridge: Cambridge University Press, 1983.

Hoggart, R., *A Local Habitation* (*Life and Times*, 1: 1918–1940), London: Chatto and Windus, 1988.

Hollis, P., *Jennie Lee: a life*, Oxford: Oxford University Press, 1997.

Holt, J.C., *The University of Reading: the first fifty years*, Reading: Reading University Press, 1977.

Howarth, J. and Curthoys, M., 'Gender, curriculum and career: a case study of women university students in England before 1914', in P. Summerfield (ed.), *Women, Education and the Professions*, Leicester: History of Education Society Occasional Publications, No. 8, 1987.

Howarth, J. and Curthoys, M., 'The political economy of women's higher education in late nineteenth and early twentieth century Britain', *Historical Research*, 1987, vol. 60(142), 208–31.

Howarth, T.E.B., *Cambridge Between Two Wars*, London: Collins, 1978.

Hubback, J., *Wives Who Went to College*, London: Heinemann, 1957.

Hughes, D.W., *Careers for Our Daughters*, London: A. & C. Black Ltd, 1936.

Humble, J.G. and Hansell, P., *Westminster Hospital, 1716–1974*, London: Pitman Medical Publishing, 1966.

Hunt, F. and Barker, C., *Women at Cambridge: a brief history*, Cambridge: Cambridge University Press, 1998.

Hutton, I., *Memories of a Doctor in War and Peace*, London: Heinemann, 1960.

Jarausch, K.H. (ed.), *The Transformation of Higher Learning, 1860–1930: expansion, diversification, social opening and professionalisation in England, Germany, Russia and the United States*, Chicago, IL: University of Chicago Press, 1983.

Jephcott, P. with Seear, N. and Smith, J.H., *Married Women Working*, London: Allen and Unwin, 1962.

Jones, J. and Castle, J., 'Women in UK universities, 1920–1980', *Studies in Higher Education*, 1986, vol. 11(3), 289–97.

Kamm, J., *Indicative Past: 100 years of the Girls' Public Day School Trust*, London: Allen and Unwin, 1971.

Kelly, T., *For Advancement of Learning: the University of Liverpool 1881–1981*, Liverpool: Liverpool University Press, 1981.

Kelsall, R.K., *Women and Teaching*, London: HMSO, 1963.

Kelsall, R.K., Poole, A. and Kuhn, A. (eds), *Graduates: the sociology of an elite*, London: Methuen, 1972.

Kelsall, R.K., Poole, A. and Kuhn, A., *Six Years After: first report on a national follow-up survey of ten thousand graduates of British universities in 1960*, Sheffield: Higher Education Research Unit, Department of Sociological Studies, 1970.

Killham, J., *Tennyson and 'The Princess': reflections of an age*, London: Athlone Press, 1958.

King's College, Newcastle upon Tyne (Education Department), *The Education of Girls*, Newcastle, 1952.

Kingsley Kent, S., *Making Peace: the reconstruction of gender in interwar Britain*, Princeton, NJ: Princeton University Press, 1993.

Kotschnig, W.A., *Unemployment in the Learned Professions: an international study of occupational and educational planning*, London: Oxford University Press, 1937.

Lawrence, C., 'Incommunicable knowledge: science, technology and the clinical art in Britain 1850–1914', *Journal of Contemporary History*, 1985, vol. 20, 503–20.

Layard, R., King, J. and Moser, C., *The Impact of Robbins*, Harmondsworth: Penguin, 1969.

Lehmann, R., *Dusty Answer*, London: Chatto and Windus, 1937.

Leneman, L., 'Medical women at war, 1914–1918', *Medical History*, 1994, vol. 38, 160–77.

Lindsay, K., *Social Progress and Educational Waste: being a study of the 'free place' and scholarship system*, London: Routledge, 1926.

Lively, P., *Spiderweb*, London: Viking, 1998.

Lively, P., *A House Unlocked*, London: Penguin, 2001.

Longmate, N., *Oxford Triumphant*, London: Phoenix House, 1954.

McCance, C. and Hall, D.J., 'Sexual behaviour and contraceptive practice of unmarried female undergraduates at Aberdeen University', *British Medical Journal*, 17 June 1972, 694–700.

McWilliams-Tullberg, M., *Women at Cambridge* (first published 1975), Cambridge: Cambridge University Press, 1998.

Malleson, H., *A Woman Doctor: Mary Murdoch of Hull*, London: Sidgwick and Jackson, 1919.

Mangan, J. and Walvin, J. (eds), *Manliness and Morality: middle class masculinity in Britain and America, 1800–1940*, Manchester: Manchester University Press, 1987.

Mantel, H., *An Experiment in Love*, London: Penguin, 1995.

Marsh, N., *The History of Queen Elizabeth College*, London: King's College, 1986.

Martindale, L., *The Woman Doctor and Her Future*, London: Mills and Boon, 1922.

Martindale, L., *A Woman Surgeon*, London: Gollancz, 1951.

Masson, M.R. and Simonton, D. (eds), *Women and Higher Education: past, present and future*, Aberdeen: Aberdeen University Press, 1996.

Meehan, E.M., *Women's Rights at Work: campaigns and policy in Britain and the United States*, Basingstoke: Macmillan, 1985.

Merrington, W.R., *University College Hospital and its Medical School*, London: Heinemann, 1976.

Miles, A., *Social Mobility in Nineteenth and Twentieth Century England*, Basingstoke and London: Macmillan, 1999.

Millett, K., *Sexual Politics* (first published 1969), London: Virago, 1977.

Moberly Bell, E., *Storming the Citadel: the rise of the woman doctor*, London: Constable, 1953.

Moss, M., Munro Forbes, J. and Trainor, R., *University, City and State: the University of Glasgow since 1870*, Edinburgh: Edinburgh University Press, for the University of Glasgow, 2000.

Mowat, C.L., *Britain between the Wars, 1918–1940*, London: Methuen, 1968.

Murray, F., *Women as Army Surgeons*, London: Hodder and Stoughton, 1920.

Murray, R., *New Hall, 1954–1972: the making of a college*, Cambridge: New Hall, 1980.

Myrdal, A. and Klein, V., *Women's Two Roles*, London: Routledge and Kegan Paul, 1956.

Newman, A., *A Share of the World*, London: Bodley Head, 1964.

Newsom, J., *The Education of Girls*, London: Faber, 1948.

Ollerenshaw, K., *Education for Girls*, London: Faber and Faber, 1961.

Ollerenshaw, K., *The Girls' Schools*, London: Faber and Faber, 1967.

Oram, A., *Women Teachers and Feminist Politics, 1900–39*, Manchester: Manchester University Press, 1996.

Payne, G. and Abbott, P. (eds), *The Social Mobility of Women: beyond male mobility models*, London: Falmer Press, 1990.

Perkin, H., *The Rise of Professional Society: England since 1800*, London: Routledge, 1989.

Peterson, J., 'Gentlemen and medical men: the problem of professional recruitment', *Bulletin of the History of Medicine*, 1984, vol. 58, 457–73.

Phelps Brown, H., *The Inequality of Pay*, Oxford: Oxford University Press, 1977.

Phillips, A. (ed.), *A Newnham Anthology*, Cambridge: Cambridge University Press, for Newnham College, 1979.

Propp, V., *Morphology of the Folktale* (ed. L.A. Wagner) Austin, TX: University of Texas Press, 1968.

Pugh, M., *Women and the Women's Movement in Britain 1914–1959*, Basingstoke and London: Macmillan, 1992.

Quinn, J., *Powerful Subjects: are women really taking over the university?*, Stoke-on-Trent: Trentham Books, 2003.

Riddell, Lord, *Dame Louisa Aldrich-Blake*, London: Hodder and Stoughton, n.d. (1926?).

Riska, E. and Wegan, K. (eds), *Gender, Work and Medicine*, London: Sage, 1993.

Roper, M. and Tosh, J. (eds), *Manful Assertions: masculinities in Britain since 1800*, London and New York: Routledge, 1991.

Rowbotham, S., *A Century of Women: the history of women in Britain and the United States*, London: Viking, 1997.

Rowbotham, S., *Promise of a Dream*, London: Allen Lane, The Penguin Press, 2000.

Rudd, E. and Hatch, S., *Graduate Study and After*, London: Weidenfeld, 1968.

Ryle, A., *Student Casualties*, London: Allen Lane, The Penguin Press, 1969.

St John, C., *Christine Murrell, M.D.: her life and her work*, London: Williams and Norgate, 1935.

Sampson, A., *Anatomy of Britain*, London: Hodder and Stoughton, 1962.

Sampson, A., *Anatomy of Britain Today*, London: Hodder and Stoughton, 1965.

Sampson, A., *The New Anatomy of Britain*, London: Hodder and Stoughton, 1971.

Sampson, A., *The Changing Anatomy of Britain*, London: Hodder and Stoughton, 1982.

Sanderson, M., *The Universities and British Industry, 1850–1970*, London: Routledge, 1972.

Sanderson, M., *The Universities in the Nineteenth Century*, London: Routledge, 1975.

Sanderson, M., *Educational Opportunity and Social Change in England*, London: Faber and Faber, 1987.

Sanderson, M., *The History of the University of East Anglia, Norwich*, London: Hambledon Press, 2002.

Schofield, M., *The Sexual Behaviour of Young Adults*, London: Allen Lane, 1973.

Schofield, M. (in collaboration with J. Bynner, P. Lewis and P. Massie), *The Sexual Behaviour of Young People*, London: Longmans, 1965.

Scott, J.W., 'The evidence of experience', *Critical Inquiry*, 1991, vol. 17, 773–97.

Shepard, A., *Meanings of Manhood in Early Modern England*, Oxford: Oxford University Press, 2003.

Shils, E. and Blacker, C., *Cambridge Women: twelve portraits*, Cambridge: Cambridge University Press, 1996.

Simon, B., *A Student's View of the Universities*, London: Longmans, Green and Co., 1943.

Skeat, W.O., *King's College London Engineering Society 1847–1957*, London: King's College Engineers Association, 1957.

Slack, P., *Rebellion, Popular Protest and the Social Order in Early Modern England*, Cambridge: Cambridge University Press, 1984.

Soares, J.A., *The Decline of Privilege: the modernization of Oxford University*, Stanford, CA: Stanford University Press, 1999.

Sondheimer, J., *Castle Adamant in Hampstead: a history of Westfield College 1882–1982*, London: Westfield College, 1983.

Spurling, A., *Report of the Women in Higher Education Research Project, 1988–1990*, Cambridge: King's College, May 1990.

Stallybrass. P. and White, A., *The Politics and Poetics of Transgression*, London: Methuen, 1986.

Strachey, R., *Careers and Openings for Women: a survey of women's employment and a guide for those seeking work*, London: Faber and Faber, 1935.

Sutherland, G., 'The plainest principles of justice: the University of London and the higher education of women', in F.M.L. Thompson (ed.), *The University of London and the World of Learning, 1836–1986*, London: Hambledon Press, 1990.

Thane, P., 'Girton graduates: earning and learning, 1920s–1980s', *Women's History Review*, 2004, vol. 13(3), 347–61.

Thomas, K., *Rule and Misrule in the Schools of Early Modern England*, Stenton Lecture 1975: University of Reading, 1976.

Thomson, P., *The Victorian Heroine: a changing ideal, 1837–1873*, London: Oxford University Press, 1956.

'Truscot, B.' (E. Allison Peers), *Redbrick University*, London: Faber and Faber, 1943.

Tuke, M.J., *A History of Bedford College for Women, 1849–1937*, Oxford: Oxford University Press, 1939.

Twigg, J., *A History of Queens' College, Cambridge, 1448–1986*, Suffolk: Boydell, 1987.

Tylecote, M., *The Education of Women at Manchester University, 1883–1933*, Manchester: Manchester University Press, 1941.

Vicinus, M. (ed.), *A Widening Sphere: changing roles of Victorian women*, Bloomington, IN: Indiana University Press, 1977.

Wakeling, J., 'University Women: Origins, Experiences and Destinations at Glasgow University 1939–1987', PhD thesis, University of Glasgow 1998.

Warner, G., *Conquering by Degrees: Glasgow University Union, a centenary history 1885–1985*, Glasgow: Glasgow University Union, 1985.

Wauchope, G.M., *The Story of a Woman Physician*, Bristol: John Wright and Sons, 1963.

Whiteley, L.D., *The Poor Student and the University: a report on the scholarship system, with particular reference to awards made by Local Educational Authorities*, London: George Allen and Unwin, 1933.

Wilberforce, O., *Octavia Wilberforce: the autobiography of a pioneer woman doctor* (ed. P. Jalland), London: Cassell, 1989.

Willoughby Lyle, H., *King's and some King's Men: being a record of the Medical Department of King's College London from 1830–1909 and of King's College Hospital Medical School from 1909–1934*, London: Oxford University Press, 1935.

Witz, A., *Professions and Patriarchy*, London: Routledge, 1992.

Women's Group on Public Welfare, *The Education and Training of Girls*, London: National Council of Social Service, 1962.

Woodhall, M., 'The economic returns to investment in women's education', *Higher Education*, 1973, no. 2, 275–99.

Zweig, F., *Women's Life and Labour*, London: Gollancz, 1952.

Zweiniger-Bargielowska, I. (ed.), *Women in Twentieth-Century Britain*, Harlow: Pearson Education, 2001.

Index

abortion 104–6
Abortion Law Reform Act 107
accommodation: at home 12, 28;
    mixed halls 107, 156, 208; rented
    45; in universities 12, 15; of women
    12, 23, 194
Adams, Pauline 183
Ady, Peter 167, 176
age of majority 103, 107, 178, 201
age of marriage *see* marriage
age participation ratio 4, 7
agriculture, study of 37–8, 43, 48
Aiston, S. 219, 231
Albemarle Report 92
Aldrich-Blake, Louisa 71, 76
Alexander, Marguerite 168
All Souls College (Oxford) 184, 207
Amis, Kingsley 103, 226
Anderson, Dame Kitty 82
Anderson, M. 201
Anderson, R.D. 4, 34–5
'apostates' 155–6, 159
Armytage, W.H.G. 23, 51
Arregger, Constance 91, 113
Ashby, (Lord) Eric 201
Asquith Commission 84
Astor, Nancy 146
Austin, Lord 196

Bacon, Janet 158
Bakewell, Joan 95–6
Bakhtin, M.M. 187, 190–1

Barnes, Dame Josephine 75, 152
Barnett, Lady 146
Basden, Margaret 140, 143
Bavin, Anne 127
Beard, Mary 121
Beatles, the 201
Beauvoir, Simone de 79
Becker, H. 154
Bedford College (London): advisers
    48; debates 155–6, 159–61, 170;
    history of 156–9; lectures 82; men
    129, 156, 158–61, 166, 170, 173,
    175; questionnaire 7, 9; study at 15,
    18, 20, 22, 28, 32, 42–4, 48
Bell, E. Moberley 61–2, 137, 149
Bell, Henry 130, 164
Belsey, Catherine 110
Bennett, Mary 165
Bentley, L. 241
betrayal 155, 157, 161, 171
Bingham, Adrian 237–8
Bingham, Caroline 158
Birmingham 192, 196–8, 200–1; *see
    also* University of Birmingham
Blackburn, Robert M. 97–8
Blacker, Carmen 121
Blackstone, Tessa 97
Blake, Sir Peter 201
'bluestockings' 56, 93, 100, 125
Board of Education: committees 12,
    16; grants and scholarships 6,
    15–16, 18, 22–7, 29, 40, 42–3, 89;

reports 49; teacher training 23, 51, 88; *see also* Ministry of Education; 'pledge' to teach; teacher training
Bone, Honor 70
Boot, Jesse 21
Bourke, Joanna 152
Bradbrook, Muriel 169, 183–4
Bradley, Ian 131, 182
Branson, Richard 106
Brasenose College (Oxford) 167–8, 180
Brazil, Angela 72
Briant, Keith 126
Brighton 250
British Federation of University Women 83, 91
British Medical Association 70, 109
Brody, Celeste M. 245
Bryson, Elizabeth 70–1, 76
Buss, Frances Mary 32, 42
Butler, Joyce 108
Butler, Prof Marilyn 169–71, 181
Butler Education Act 56
Byatt, A.S. 104

Cambridge colleges 169, 172; *see also colleges by name*; Oxbridge: colleges of; University of Cambridge
Cambridge Students' Union 110, 132
Cambridge University Women's Action Group (CUWAG) 181
Cambridge University Women's Appointments Board (CWAB) 88–91, 94–5, 101, 114–15
Cameron, Deborah 153
careers: advisers 48, 87, 90, 94, 103; aspirations for men 36–41, 52; aspirations for women 41–3, 60, 98; discrimination 73–4, 76, 90, 141–3; dual careers of women 94, 117; of men graduates 52–4; professional 35; 'two-phase' model for women 114, 117; of women graduates 48–52, 55, 57–8, 61, 87–9, 113–17, 137, 166
Carnegie Trust 3–4
carnival *see* student rags
Castle, Barbara 28, 108
Castle, Josephine 97
Caston, Geoffrey 111
Central Bureau for the Employment of Women 87–8

Charing Cross Hospital (London) 139–41, 144–5
charities *see* student rags
Cheatle, Sir Lenthal 145
Chester, Georgie 195
childcare 57–8, 94, 96, 113
Chilver, Elizabeth 166
Chisholm, Catherine 147
Christ, Carol 232
Churchill, Winston 163
Churchill College (Cambridge) 107, 163, 165, 169, 178–9, 227–8
civil service 52, 65, 100
Clare College (Cambridge) 165, 169, 179
class *see* social class
coeducation xii, 172; and academic standards 164, 166, 170; for academics 180; at London 156; in medicine 62, 73–4, 138, 145, 147; at Oxbridge 86, 127, 130, 133, 156–7, 162, 182; and pregnancies 107; reports favouring 85, 156; and sexual behaviour 159, 164, 178; and student preferences 160; *see also* coresidence
colleges: mascots 188, 192; mixed 123, 129, 134, 157, 165, 170, 172–85; single-sex xii, 86, 108, 110–13, 128–9, 156–7, 165, 172, 178, 183, 206–7; visitors to 107, 128, 163; women's xi, 86, 122–3, 155–71, 174, 176; *see also* Cambridge colleges; *colleges by name*; Oxbridge: colleges; Oxford colleges; universities
Colleges of Advanced Technology 99
Colville, Jock 163
Committee of Vice-Chancellors and Principals (CVCP) 109
contraception 92, 104–7, 205–6
Cook, Hera 107
Cooke, J.M. 221
Corbett, M.J. 216
Corbett-Ashby, Mrs 146
coresidence: Oxbridge 103, 111–12, 131, 163–71, 177, 207; and 'permissiveness' 107; rush to 157, 168–9; and status 176; and women's colleges 111, 123, 176
cost of university education 12–16, 46, 80, 87; *see also* finance of university education

Cottrell, Alan 169
Crichton-Browne, Sir James 153
Cripps, Anthony QC 108
Crombie Hall (Aberdeen) 178
Crompton, Rosemary 91, 115
Crowther Report 92
'cultural capital' 58
curriculum *see* subject choices
Curthoys, Mark 41
CUWAG (Cambridge University
    Women's Action Group) 181
CWAB *see* Cambridge University
    Women's Appointments Board
CVCP (Committee of Vice-Chancellors
    and Principals) 109

Davies, Emily 122, 183
Day, Lois 95
Dean, Sir Maurice 114
Deeping, Warwick 238
Delamont, Sara 226
Department of Education and Science
    109–13; *see also* Board of
    Education; Ministry of Education
Depression ix, 4, 7, 19, 30, 39, 47, 49,
    205
Deslandes, Paul xi–xii
Digby, Anne 215
discrimination *see* gender; Sex
    Discrimination Act; sex wars in
    medicine
dissecting room 63, 67–8, 72, 138
doctors, women 57, 60–78; *see also*
    medicine
domestic science, study of 36–7
Drabble, Margaret 105
driving 60–1, 75
Dudman, G.E. 110–11
Dyhouse, Carol xi–xiii

Economic and Social Research Council
    (ESRC) xii, 7
Edgerton, David 220
Edmonds, Dr Florence 75
education *see* cost of university
    education; finance of university
    education; schools; universities
Eisenmann, Linda 219
Ellis, G.S.M. 16, 19
Elston, Mary Ann 62, 215, 222, 231
engineering: and men 52, 58; and
    rowdyism 187; study of 36–9; and
    women 85

employers: opposition to women
    91–2, 94, 115
employment of women 35, 51, 56–7,
    90, 113–17, 149; and companies 52,
    91; *see also* careers; gender;
    marriage; war
equal opportunities x, 108, 112, 116,
    138, 160, 178, 180–1, 185, 207; *see
    also* careers: discrimination in
Equal Pay Act 108, 115
equality *see* gender
ESRC *see* Economic and Social
    Research Council
examinations: school 16, 18; university
    entrance 14, 67–8; for women 16
Exeter College (Oxford) 163, 171, 184

Fabian Society 20
Fairfield, Letitia 147
fairy-tales 64, 68, 76–7, 122
Family Reform Act 178
family support 32–3, 43–7, 55; *see also*
    fathers; mothers; parents
fathers: and daughters' education 43;
    and sons' careers 38, 47; support
    from 31–2
Fawcett Society 108
femininity: and ambition 64; escape
    from 41, 64–5, 70; and families 71;
    and lady doctors 63–4, 69–72, 75;
    and male ideals 179; and status 174
feminism: critiques by 46, 206, 208;
    and doctors 61, 69, 147; and
    education 205; and equality 108,
    110, 138, 146, 160; and femininity
    179; 'first wave' 205; and going to
    university x, 42, 57, 97, 205; and
    historians xi, 204; male 161; and
    marriage 93; and medicine 205;
    'nadir' of 205; 'second wave' 79, 97,
    108, 115, 205–7; and separatism
    155, 206; in universities 121–2,
    125; and women's liberation 114
Fenton, Dr 139–40
fertility 107, 205
finance of university education 13–33;
    debt ix; family 28–33; figures 17;
    investment 89, 114–15, 208; loans
    14, 27–8; mandatory grants 200,
    254; *see also* cost of university
    education
Fisher, H.A.L. 251
Floud, Jean 34

food in colleges 125
Forster, Emily 219
Forster, Margaret 95, 105
Franks, Lord 83, 166
Franks Commission 155, 165–6
freemasonry 74, 218
Friedan, Betty 79–80
Fry, Margery 174
Furneaux, W.D. 161

Gardner, Helen 104, 167
Garner, James 143, 152, 218
gate hours 107, 126–7, 128, 178
Gaukroger, Alison 85
gender: and colleges 177–8; and
    culture 177–80, 184–5; and
    earnings 117, 140, 208; and
    employment 35, 41, 52, 57–8, 91,
    94, 114–16; and intellect 16, 81, 86;
    and marriage 175; and medicine 62,
    73–4, 77, 108–9, 116–17, 141–3,
    150; and mothers 13, 79; politics of
    121, 138, 150–1, 184–5; and
    scholarships 18–24, 109; and
    schools 108, 150; and social change
    204; and social class 10, 36, 113;
    and sport 152; and status 172–85;
    and student rags 187, 190, 193–4,
    200, 208; and teaching 23; unease
    about 70–1; and university
    admissions 94, 153, 161, 173; and
    university education 100, 103, 108,
    112, 128, 130, 156, 204–9; and
    university heads 171; and university
    teachers x, 132, 181, 208–9
General Medical Council 70
Gibson, Miss 142
Gilbert, W.S. 123, 131
Giles, J. 255
Gilliat, Sir William 151
Gillie, Annis 147
Girls' Public Day School Trust 20, 122
Girton College (Cambridge) 86, 88,
    107, 129, 134, 169, 176–7, 179–80,
    183
Gissing, George 87
Glass, David 5, 34
Glyn-Jones, Miss 142
Godley, A.D. 124
Gonville and Caius College
    (Cambridge) 123
Goodenough Report 62, 85, 173
Goodyear, E. 195

Gould, Sir Alfred Pearce 141
graduates see student numbers
grants see Board of Education; finance
    of university education;
    scholarships
Gray, J.L. 5
Gray, John 184, 243
Greer, Germaine 181–2
Gregory, I. 234
Grier, Lynda 174
Grossman, Judith 105
Guy's Hospital (London) 139, 141,
    148, 150–2, 179

Haggard, Rider 70, 72
Haldane Commission 158
Hall, John 8
Halliday, Dr 145
halls of residence see accommodation;
    colleges
Halsey, A.H. x, 34
Hamilton, William 108
Hart, Jenifer 80–1, 131, 176
Hatch, S. 113
Hayes, B.C. 44
headmasters 54–5, 109
headmistresses 101, 109, 194
Heath, Edward 108
HEFCE (Higher Education Funding
    Council for England) x
Heilbrun, Carolyn 64, 216
Herford, M. 144
Heriot-Watt College 99
Herklots, H.G.G. 226
Hertford College (Oxford) 112, 168,
    182
HESA see Higher Education Statistics
    Agency
Heward, Christine 38, 45, 149, 150
Hicks, Marie 243–4
Higonnet, Margaret 149
Higonnet, Patrice 149
Higher Education Funding Council for
    England (HEFCE) x
Higher Education Statistics Agency
    (HESA) x, 116, 207
Hill, Bridget 167
Hilton, Irene 90
Hobhouse, Christopher 125–6
Hodgkin, Prof Dorothy 163, 167, 206,
    243
Hogben, Lancelot 5
Hoggart, Richard 5–6, 38

Hollis, Patricia 3
Hollond, Prof M.T. 86
Holloway, Sir Thomas 21
Holt, J.C. 103
Holtby, Winifred 122–3, 161
hospitals, London 61–2, 65–6, 77, 129;
    see also hospitals by name;
    medicine
House of Commons 108
House of Lords 108–9
Howarth, Janet 41, 86, 133
Howarth, T.E.B. 242
Howat, Rosaline 67
Howe, Geoffrey 228
Hubback, Judith 56, 79–80, 113, 219
Hughes, D.W. 103
Hunt, Pauline 110
Hutton, Isabel 60–1, 66, 68–9, 71, 77

identities, troubled 172, 181–4; see
    also sexual identity; student culture
Imperial College (London) 16
incomes 15, 19, 30, 46, 55;
    discrimination in 90; means test 19;
Institute of Education (London) 114,
    164
Ireland 186

Jacks, M.L. 81
Jackson, B. 46
Jackson, Robert 184, 207
Jarman, Jennifer 97–8
Jell, Simon Sedgwick 128
Jesus College (Cambridge) 169
Jesus College (Oxford) 168
John, Augustus 199
Jones, D. Caradog 8
Jones, Jennifer 97
Jules, Frank 74

Kansas, University of 154
Kay, Caroline 247
Kelsall, R. Keith 113–14, 160
Kelynack, Violet 147
Kenealy, Arabella 63–4
Kent, Susan Kingsley 149
Kenyon, Frances Margaret 65, 67–8,
    73, 151–3
Kenyon, Kathleen 165, 167–8, 176–7
Kettle, Marguerite 146
King, Prof B.C. 160–1, 175
King's College (Cambridge) 165, 169,
    178–9, 181–2

King's College (London): domestic
    science 129; engineering 85;
    medicine 84, 139–40, 144–5, 147–8,
    151–3; questionnaire 8–11; rivalry
    with UCL 192–3, 195; sport 153,
    192, 195; study at 30, 32, 45–6, 68,
    77, 158; teacher training 22;
    women 156, 158
Knutsford, Lord 72–3, 142, 151
Kuhn, Annette 113

Lady Margaret Hall (Oxford) 84, 128,
    134, 174, 176–7, 247
Latey Committee 107, 201
law: careers in 52, 116; study of 36–7
Lawrence, C. 215
Lawrenson, T.E. 178
Lawson, Marie 70
Lee, Jennie 3, 33
Lehmann, Rosamund 95
lesbianism 70
Lind, Harold 126
Linnett, Prof 111
Littlewood, Margaret 150
Lively, Penelope 95, 104
Liverpool 188, 190–1, 199–200;
    see also University of Liverpool
Logan, Sir Douglas 159
London 39, 49, 67, 192, 195, 201;
    see also colleges by name; hospitals
    by name; University of London;
London Hospital 72, 74, 140–3, 145–6,
    150–1, 153
London School of Medicine for
    Women 62–3, 66–7, 138, 140, 143,
    146, 152–3, 173; see also Royal Free
    Hospital
Longmate, Norman 188, 249, 252
Lucy Cavendish College (Cambridge)
    129, 172

Macadam, Elizabeth 146
McGregor, Oliver R. 155, 160–1, 175
Mackinnon, A. 219
Macmillan, Harold 232
McWilliams-Tullberg, Rita 241
Magdalene College (Cambridge) 177,
    179
Major, Kathleen 165
Malleson, Hope 69, 71, 75
Man, Isle of 26
Manchester 27, 188–91, 194, 196, 200;
    see also University of Manchester

Mann, Prof Ida 64–6, 68–70, 72–5, 143, 149
Mantel, Hilary 105
Margoliouth, J.P. 140
marriage: age of 83, 90, 92–4, 175, 205–6; and doctors 148; 'marriage risk' 90, 94; rejection of 70; of students 104, 109; and universities 56, 80, 95; and women's careers 48, 51, 55, 57, 62, 64, 68, 77, 91, 95, 113
Marsden, D. 46
Martindale, Louisa 75, 146
masculinity xi–xii, 47, 74, 77, 126, 131, 137–54, 162, 171, 177, 180, 184, 187, 202, 207; and camaraderie 173, 178, 187; competitive 192–6; and emasculation 150
Mass Observation Archive 197
Medical Register 61
medical schools see hospitals by name, medicine
Medical Women's Federation 63, 75, 84, 137, 144, 146–7
medicine: careers in 137, 141–3, 151; and coeducation 138, 145, 153–4; cost 41; and fathers 38, 41, 60; general practice 77; and inequality x, 61–2, 76–7, 84, 90, 116–17; and men 52; mission for 63–4, 66, 69, 73; and rowdiness 72, 187; salaries 61, 74; study of 13, 31, 36–7, 58, 60–1, 65, 73, 139, 148; and women 41, 73, 206; see also dissecting room
Melville, Frances 83
Merrington, W.R. 141
Merry, Dr Edith 89
Merton College (Oxford) 168
Middlesex Hospital (London) 139
Miller, Nancy 64
Miller, R.L. 44
Millett, Kate 122
Milne, Jane Johnston 101
Ministry of Education 51
Minney, R.J. 139
missionaries 76
Mitchison, Lois 81
Mitchison, Naomi 81
Morley, Prof Edith 20, 25
Morris, Carolyn 115
Morris, Miss 194
Moser, C.A. 160

mothers: duties of 13–14, 30, 45; as graduates 79; and sons' careers 45–6; support of 30–1, 44
motor cars 75–6
Mowat, C.L. 12
Murdoch, Dr Mary 63, 65–7, 69, 71, 75
Murphy, Michael 228
Murray, Sir Keith 159
Murray, Dame Rosemary 169, 244–5
Murrell, Christine 70, 72, 147

Naish, Charlotte 75
National Association of Schoolmasters 150
National Council for Civil Liberties 108
National Health Service 77, 198
national service 54, 127, 177, 199
National Union of Societies for Equal Citizenship 146
National Union of Students 25
National Union of Teachers 18
National Union of Women Teachers 92
Nelson, Mariah Burton 153
New College (Oxford) 130, 155, 162, 164–7
New Hall (Cambridge) 86, 129, 163–4, 169, 172
New Zealand 76
Newman, Andrea 95, 105
Newnham College (Cambridge) 83, 86, 88, 107, 123–5, 129, 169, 172
Newsom, John 81
Nightingale, Florence 69
Norland, Joanna 182
Norton, Kathleen 67, 73–4, 144

occupations: of fathers 8; of mothers 8, 31–3, 45; see also employment
Ogilvie, Lady Mary 94, 165–6, 171, 181
Ollerenshaw, Kathleen 92, 94, 100–2
Open University 3
Oram, A. 212
Oriel College (Oxford) 177
Owen's College (Manchester) 189
Oxbridge: and coeducation 130–2, 141–2; colleges 110, 126, 129, 166; cost 12; fellows 110, 125–32, 170, 182, 184, 207; numbers attending 4, 9; numbers of women 9, 41, 84–5, 102, 175; rags 187–8; regulations of 103, 177–8; scholarships for 18; segregation at x, 161–71, 206; social class 5, 11,

34, 102; women as members of
121, 124, 132; *see also* University of
Cambridge; University of Oxford
Oxford colleges 110, 172; men's 127,
162, 167, 182; mixed 131, 176, 183;
principals of 80, 103–4, 130, 162,
165–8, 170, 176, 183; women's 80,
95, 125, 127, 166–7, 175, 177, 183;
see also colleges by name
Oxford Union 125, 132
Oxford Women's Suffrage Society 140

parents: duties of 3; investment in
daughters' education 88; reluctance
of 31–2, 43–4; sacrifices 3, 30, 149;
support of 44, 59; *see also* fathers;
mothers
Parkes, Keren 147
paternalism 151, 177, 199
Pathé News 186, 188, 195–6, 201,
248–9
Paul, A.S. 195
Paul, Margaret 176–7
Pembroke College (Oxford) 128
Perkin, Harold xiii, 34
Peterson, M. Jeanne 215–6
Phelps Brown, Sir Henry 58
Pickford, Prof Mary 75
Pirie, Antoinette 167, 176, 243
'pledge' to teach 18, 24–5, 34, 40, 43,
50, 60, 89
Political and Economic Planning 56, 80
polytechnics 97, 99, 115
Poole, Anne 113, 115
postgraduates 160
Powell, Dilys 127
pregnancy 92, 104–6, 107
Priestley, Sir Raymond 85
Pring, Charles 73
professions 35, 39, 62–3, 113, 116
professors 13, 38, 54
Pugh, Martin 35

Queen Elizabeth College (London)
129, 157, 173
Queen Margaret College (Glasgow) 83
Queen's College (Oxford) 167
Queens' College (Cambridge) 179
Quinn, Jocey 208
quotas: and medicine 62, 85, 109, 206;
at Oxbridge 86, 112, 129, 167–8

'rag' *see* student rags

regulations of colleges 107, 126–8
Reid, Elizabeth Jesser 156, 160, 170
Reid, W.K. 110
Rendel, Margherita 108
Revis, W.H. 21
Rhondda, Lady 146
Riddell, Lord 69–71
Robbins Report x, 82–3, 94, 98, 101–2,
160, 164–6, 184, 201
Roberts, J.M. 244
Robertson, Grant 196
Robins, Elizabeth 68, 70
Ross, Joan 144
Rowbotham, Sheila 103–4
Royal College of Veterinary Surgeons
109
Royal Free Hospital 63, 72, 85, 112,
137–8, 145, 173, 179
Royal Holloway College:
accommodation 12; architecture
126, 131, 158; as college 156–7;
committees 158; funds158; and
marriage 56; men 129, 158, 173–5;
questionnaire 7, 9; rags 200, 253–4;
scholarships 21; study at 19, 27, 32,
42, 44, 48, 50, 52, 57; trust for 159
Royal Infirmary (Manchester) 196
Royal Society 54
Rudd, E. 113
Ryle, Anthony 105
Ryle, Prof John 147

St Anne's College (Oxford) 94, 127,
134, 167, 176–7, 181
St Bartholomew's Hospital (London)
139, 141, 153
St Catharine's College (Cambridge)
179
St Catherine's College (Oxford) 163,
168
St George's Hospital (London) 84,
139, 141
St Hilda's College (Oxford) 103–4,
128–9, 162, 165, 169, 172, 176, 183
St Hugh's College (Oxford) 28, 134,
165, 167, 176–7
St John, Christopher 70, 72
St Mary's Hospital (London) 72–4,
139–40, 143–6, 149–53
St Thomas's Hospital (London) 139
Ste Croix, Geoffrey de 162, 164, 166
Sampson, Anthony 102, 131
Sanderson, Kay 91, 115

Sanderson, Michael 34, 48, 101–2, 200, 215

Scharlieb, Mary 69–70

Schofield, Michael 92, 105–6

scholarships: charities 20; figures 17; Kitchener 20, 24; local authority 14–16, 19–20, 39–40; piecing together 13–16; school 20–2; state 18; university 14, 20–2; for women 144

schools, as backgrounds 6; elementary 5, 23, 49–51, 88, 199; girls' 194; public 38, 141, 150; secondary 23, 25–6, 41, 49–50, 55

Schwartz, Leonard 85

science: and careers 48, 51–2, 58, 89, 114–15; study of 36–8, 41, 46, 67, 83, 87, 159, 175, 209

Scotland 3–4, 7, 32–4, 82, 98–9, 102, 178, 187, 206

Scott, J.W. 216

Seear, (Baroness) Nancy 108, 223

'selling the pass' (poem) xiii, 129–30, 135–6

servicemen 141, 149–50, 193, 205

Sex Discrimination Act 112, 115, 129, 132, 168, 176

sex wars in medicine 62, 138, 148–9; see also gender

sexual behaviour of women 92, 94, 103, 105–6, 159, 178, 196, 205

sexual identity 70–1, 105, 122

'sexual revolution' 103–7, 206

Sheavyn, Phoebe 83

Shils, Edward 121

Sidney Sussex College (Cambridge) 255

'siege mentalities' 121, 123, 127, 130, 133–4

Simon, Brian xiii, 25, 36

Sir Richard Stapley Educational Trust 16–17

'sit-in' 201

Six Point Group 108

Skeat, W.O. 249

Smithers, Prof Alan 98

Soares, J.A. 242

social class: definition 8; and fathers 38, 47; of female graduates 55–6; and gender x; of male graduates 55; and marriage 57, 92; origin vs. destination 54–5; and scholarships 24, 28–9; in Scotland 4, 7; of

students 5–11, 31, 97; and teaching 51, 58; and town-gown relations 198–9

social mobility 34–59; through education 45; inter-generational 58–9; through marriage 57

Somerville College (Oxford) 123, 127–9, 134, 166–7, 174, 176–7, 183

Sondheimer, Janet 129, 240

Spencer Foundation xii, 7

Spicer, Dr Faith 106

sport: facilities for 176, 179; halls of residence 133; medical schools 74, 139, 143, 148, 151–3, 173, 179, 207; mixed colleges 180; motor sports 75; and rivalry 192, 195; schools 71

Spurling, Andrea 181

Stallybrass, Peter 187, 190

Status of Women Committee 108

Steedman, Carolyn 214

Steele, Tommy 199

Stewart, Alice 167

Stewart, W.A.C. 26

Strachey, Ray 88–9

student culture 186, 202; counter-culture 201; and engineers 187; and gender 181, 195, 204, 206, 208; image 204; and medics 187; and misogyny 123–4, 131, 193; raiding parties 126, 187, 192, 199; rowdiness 72, 123, 133, 177, 182, 187, 189, 191, 193–4, 198; see also masculinity

Student Health Service 105–6, 227

student numbers ix, 4; mature students 202, 204; in medicine 78, 207; men's 'underperformance' xi, 98, 207–8; rise after 1970 ix–x, 35, 98; stagnation in 35, 82–7, 97–8, 205; in teaching 91; women's share of ix–x, 35, 79, 82–7, 94, 97–117, 205

student press 106, 126, 128, 164, 179–80, 189–90

student protest 200–1

student rags xii, 72, 186–203; and carnival 186, 190–4, 196–8, 200–2; and charities 186, 191–3, 196, 198, 202; definitions 186; and gender 187, 190, 192–6, 200, 208; magazines 189, 191–4, 196–7, 199–200, 202, 249; offensive nature

of 186–7, 189–91, 194, 196, 199, 202, 208, 249–50, 255; origins 187; at Oxbridge 187–8; and pantomime 186, 188, 190–1, 193, 195–6, 198–9; *see also universities by name*
student unions 110, 132, 160, 178, 188, 191, 194–5, 202, 208, 254–5
subject choices 36-7, 52-3, 83, 98, 100–1, 206–8
Sullivan, Sir Arthur 123, 131
Supple, Barry 100
Sutherland, Dr Lucy 165–7, 171, 246

Taylor, G.F. 153
teaching as career 48, 50–1, 53, 55–6, 60, 87, 113, 115–16, 166; commitment to 20, 26–7, 40, 42–3; salaries 28
teacher training 20, 22–3, 25–6; colleges 51, 83, 87, 97, 114, 205–6; cost 87; cuts in 49, 88, 97, 115, 206; day training departments 22, 24; numbers in 87, 114; women numbers in 87
Tennyson, Alfred Lord 122–3, 126, 134, 174
Thane, Pat 219, 224, 230
Thatcher, Margaret 108, 110
theology: careers in 52; study of 36–7
Thomas, E.M. 82–3, 101, 166
Thomas, Keith 80, 126, 187, 201
Thompson, J.H. 109–12, 229–30
Trinity College (Cambridge) 247
'Truscot, Bruce' (E. Allison Peers) 6, 187–8, 197
Tuke, Margaret 156–7

UGC *see* University Grants Committee
'Uncle Toms' 155–6, 165–6, 170
unemployment 30; and class 40; of doctors 61, 73, 205; escape from 40; of fathers 16, 33, 47, 54; of graduates 4–5; of teachers 25–6, 49, 53, 205; of women 49
universities: civic 9, 23, 82, 102, 112, 129, 156; 'new' 97, 99, 100–3, 166, 200, 202, 206; numbers of ix; post-1992 97, 99, 202; redbrick 6, 8; Scottish 3–4; and town-gown relations 189, 197–8; women's 156
University College London 158; medicine 74, 84, 139–41, 144–5, 150; questionnaire 7–11; rivalry with King's 192–3, 195; study at 13, 25, 42, 50, 54–5, 89, 152; women 156
University College of Aberystwyth 23
University College of Bangor 22
University College of Cardiff 22
University College of Hull 29
University College of Nottingham: questionnaire 8–11; scholarships 21; study at 14, 47; teacher training 22
University Grants Committee (UGC) 11–12, 77, 82, 84, 86, 102, 109, 114, 158–60
University House (Birmingham) 178
University of Aberdeen 105, 178
University of Birmingham: rags191–4, 196–8, 249, 251; teacher training 22; women 85, 101, 178
University of Bristol: coeducation 157; questionnaire 7–11; study at 13, 15, 24–5, 31, 33, 38, 41, 43–4, 59, 77; teacher training 23–4
University of Cambridge: committees 168–9; degrees for women x, 83, 123, 156, 162, 169, 172; as men's university 84, 111, 124, 134, 161–2, 169, 181, 206–7; scholarships for 19; and sex discrimination 110; study at 15, 79, 95; teacher training 22; Vice-Chancellors 111, 169; women numbers 82, 84, 86, 102, 125, 162, 164, 169
University of East Anglia: rags 200; women 100–2
University of Edinburgh 3–4, 84, 138–9, 172
University of Essex 113
University of Glasgow 4, 83, 132, 138, 191, 193, 195–6, 202, 253–4
University of Keele 101–2
University of Kent 105
University of Lancaster 100
University of Leeds: medicine 138; pregnancy 106; questionnaire 8–11; social class 5–6, 38; study at 33, 38, 41, 45–6; teacher training 22
University of Liverpool: medicine 77; professors 98; questionnaire 8–11; rags 188–91, 193–6, 198; study at 40, 45; teacher training 22
University of London 11, 82, 84, 129, 185; colleges 157, 174–5; degrees

for women 138, 156; medical schools 137–54, 172–5; questionnaire 7–8; Senate 85, 138, 140, 145, 148, 173, 198
University of Loughborough 202, 254
University of Manchester: accommodation 12; halls of residence 133; questionnaire 7–11; rags188–99, 250, 252; scholarships 21–2; student attitudes 200; study at 13, 22, 26–7, 29–31, 33, 39, 42, 45–6, 49–50, 67, 77; teacher training 22, 24; women 83
University of Newcastle-upon-Tyne 22, 81
University of Oxford: account of 125; committees 168, 176, 184; coresidence 112, 156, 184; degrees for women x, 83, 156, 162, 172; male bias 111, 122, 124, 134, 161, 183, 206–7; officers 111, 124, 167; professors 66; student attitudes 200; study at 32, 73, 77, 80, 144, 152; teacher training 23, 81; women numbers 82, 84, 86, 102, 124–5, 130, 162, 164; see also Oxbridge; Oxford colleges
University of Reading: questionnaire 7–11; rags 250; study at 24, 38, 42–3, 45–6, 50; teacher training 23; women 226
University of St Andrew's 250
University of Sheffield 22, 113, 197–8
University of Southampton 23
University of Sussex: curriculum 101; handbook 100; social class 102; student health 105; women 100–2, 115, 226
University of Warwick 100

vacations, university 30
Vaizey, John 155, 163–6
Vaughan, Janet 67–8, 75, 165–6, 171, 226
veterinary studies 85, 109
Victoria and Albert Museum 69
vocational goals see careers
Voltaire 184

Wadham College (Oxford) 84, 167–8
Wakeling, J. 231
Wales 82, 98, 102
war: changes during 26, 50, 54; and medicine 61–2, 73, 76–7, 84–5, 89, 149, 173; and student rags 190, 197; and women's education 83, 98; and women's employment 88–9
Warnock, G.J. 112
Warnock, Mary 167, 247
waste: through marriage 80, 90, 109, 114; of talent (class) 5; of talent (gender) 91; of women's education 56, 62, 79–81, 87–92, 94–6, 109, 113–15, 155
Wauchope, Dr Gladys 61–5, 72–3, 75, 142, 236
WEF see Women's Employment Federation
Wellcome Institute 143
Wellcome Trust xii
Wells, Joseph 84
Westfield College (London): as 'Castle Adamant' 129; as college 157, 159; study at 20; men 129, 158–9, 173, 175; women 156
Westminster Hospital (London) 140, 144–5, 153
White, Allon 187, 190
Whiteley, L. Doreen 5, 11–12, 17–20, 28–9, 31
widows 30–1, 45, 55–7
Wigram, Rosamond 71
Wilberforce, Octavia 65, 67–8, 70, 73, 76
Wilby, Peter 210
Williamson, Dr Marjorie 239
Wilson, Dr Charles McMoran (Lord Moran) 144, 151–2
Witz, Ann 62
'woman question' 122
Women in Media 108–9
Women's Employment Federation (WEF) 88, 90, 222
Women's Group on Public Welfare 81
women's studies 207
Woodhall, Maureen 114–15
Woolf, Virginia 125
Woolton Hall (Manchester) 133
Worcester College (Oxford) 128, 155, 164
Wright, Sir Almroth 74, 143, 236

Yorkshire 6, 19, 28, 75

Zweig, Ferdynand 200